Returning Foreign Fighters: Responses, Legal Challenges and Ways Forward

Francesca Capone · Christophe Paulussen ·
Rebecca Mignot-Mahdavi
Editors

Returning Foreign Fighters: Responses, Legal Challenges and Ways Forward

ASSER PRESS

Springer

Editors
Francesca Capone
Istituto DIRPOLIS
Scuola Superiore Sant'Anna
Pisa, Italy

Christophe Paulussen
Research Department
T.M.C. Asser Instituut
The Hague, The Netherlands

Rebecca Mignot-Mahdavi
School of Law, Manchester International
Law Centre
The University of Manchester
Manchester, UK

ISBN 978-94-6265-570-6 ISBN 978-94-6265-571-3 (eBook)
https://doi.org/10.1007/978-94-6265-571-3

Published by T.M.C. ASSER PRESS, The Hague, The Netherlands www.asserpress.nl
Produced and distributed for T.M.C. ASSER PRESS by Springer-Verlag Berlin Heidelberg

This T.M.C. ASSER PRESS imprint is published by the registered company Springer-Verlag GmbH, DE, part of Springer Nature.
The registered company address is: Heidelberger Platz 3, 14197 Berlin, Germany

Foreword

The world of counter-terrorism is full of quick turns and surprises, and it forms a fascinating subject for academic research in law, social science and history. Time and again people and governments are confronted with dreadful acts of terrorism that demonstrate how the phenomenon of terrorism is real and constitutes a real threat to the lives of ordinary people, as well as to international peace and security. Hence, serious study of terrorism and the fight against it is not detached from reality so that it would be conducted in some academic ivory tower. Scholars in various disciplines do their best to use their knowledge and skills to deliver research that would help in building a safer world, free from, or at least protected against, terrorism. In particular from the perspective of legal research, one of the main outcomes of that continuous undertaking is that combating terrorism with the wrong means, for instance through policies and practices that violate human rights, will be counterproductive. Human rights violations in the name of countering terrorism easily become a reason for subsequent acts of terrorism, both as a structural cause within societies suffering of terrorism, conflict, poverty and exclusion and as a triggering cause for individuals that are susceptible for being recruited into terrorism.

International, European and national counter-terrorism law itself reflects these dilemmas. Many of its central features and instruments have been crafted in panic, as a hasty political response to a high-profile terrorist attack or other unexpected negative development. Sadly, such ill-advised responses to a threat that in itself is real tend to perpetuate themselves. As a result, important dimensions of the available framework of counter-terrorism law are not only problematic as to their compatibility with human rights but also ineffective in respect of the actual threat.

The rapid adoption of international, European and national instruments against the flow of persons from European or other countries to Syria, Iraq or other conflict zones where they might engage in acts of terrorism or other forms of physical violence has become yet another example of these troubling tendencies. UN Security Council Resolution 2178 (2014), the Additional Protocol to the Council of Europe Convention on the Prevention of Terrorism (2015) and the EU Directive on Combating Terrorism (2017) all suffer from conceptual and legal flaws that greatly reduce their effectiveness in addressing the problem, while at the same time putting human rights at risk. To mention only one example, the three instruments create mutually incompatible legal obligations for states in respect of acts of violence committed by 'foreign fighters' during an armed conflict abroad.

This excellent collection of eleven expert studies on the phenomenon of foreign (terrorist) fighters allows the interested reader to gain a thorough understanding of the phenomenon and the policies and measures undertaken by the international community and individual states to combat it. Historical, political, jurisdictional, evidentiary, judicial, punitive, administrative, humanitarian and many other aspects of the matter are carefully examined by the skilful authors. The individual chapters have been expertly edited by a strong editorial team and thereby integrated into a book that will prove a rewarding reading experience. The collection does not fail to address the fate of family members of perpetrators of violence, or the threat posed to European or other nations by conflict-hardened returnees who would be in need of care and rehabilitation but who might also constitute a genuine security threat to others. The seemingly easy but actually quite thorny solution of citizenship-stripping also has its own chapter in the volume. Aptly, the final chapter in the book looks into the consequences for freedom of expression of measures to combat the foreign fighter phenomenon, demonstrating how even the most well-established and unquestioned human rights may be at risk when the toolbox of counter-terrorism instruments is opened.

Oxford, UK
January 2022

Martin Scheinin
British Academy Global Professor
University of Oxford
Former UN Special Rapporteur on
Human Rights and Counterterrorism

Prof. Martin Scheinin is British Academy Global Professor at the University of Oxford. With the status of part-time professor he remains at the European University Institute which he joined as Professor of International Law and Human Rights in 2008 after 15 years as professor in Finland. In 1993–1998 he was Professor of Constitutional Law at the University of Helsinki where he also attained his doctorate in 1991. In 1998–2008 he was Professor of Constitutional and International Law and Director of the Institute for Human Rights at Åbo Akademi University in Turku, Finland. From 1997–2004 he was a member of the United Nations Human Rights Committee, the treaty body acting under the International Covenant on Civil and Political Rights. In 2005 he was appointed as the first United Nations Special Rapporteur on human rights and counter-terrorism, a position of trust he held until July 2011. He served as the EUI Dean of Graduate Studies from January 2016 to January 2019. Currently he also serves as member of the Scientific Committee of the EU Fundamental Rights Agency.

Contents

Editors and Contributors

About the Editors

Dr. Francesca Capone is Associate Professor of International Law at the Sant'Anna School of Advanced Studies—Pisa. Prior to be being appointed as Associate Professor, she served as Assistant Professor (tenure track), Senior Research Fellow and Coordinator of the Master in Human Rights and Conflict Management at the same academic institution (2014–2021). In 2012–2013, she worked as Research Fellow in public international law at the British Institute of International and Comparative Law in London, UK. She has been Visiting Fellow and Guest Lecturer at several academic institutions across Europe, including Leiden University and the Max Planck Institute for Comparative Public Law and International Law. She has undertaken research on a wide range of topics, in particular she has written extensively on international law and counter-terrorism. She co-edited, together with Dr. Christophe Paulussen and Prof. Andrea de Guttry, the volume *Foreign Fighters under International Law and Beyond* (T.M.C. Asser Press/Springer 2016). The volume has been well received and widely cited, becoming one of the most relevant academic contributions in the field. Her book *Reparations for Child Victims of Armed Conflict: State of the Field and Current Challenges* (Intersentia 2017) won the 2018 Ciardi Prize for the best book in the field of international humanitarian law.

Dr. Christophe Paulussen, LL.M. M.Phil. is Senior Researcher at the T.M.C. Asser Instituut and Coordinator of its research strand 'In the Public Interest: Accountability of the State and the Prosecution of Crimes', Coordinator of the inter-faculty research platform 'International Humanitarian and Criminal Law Platform' and Research Fellow at the International Centre for Counter-Terrorism—The Hague. He is also Editor-in-Chief of the journal *Security and Human Rights*, Member of the Executive Board of the Royal Netherlands Society of International Law, Member of the Editorial Board of the *Journal of Human Trafficking, Enslavement and Conflict-Related Sexual Violence* and Member of the Board of Advisors to the Editorial Board of the *Yearbook of International Humanitarian Law*. His areas of interest are international humanitarian law, international criminal law, in particular the law of the international criminal(ised) tribunals and counter-terrorism and human rights, in particular the issue of foreign fighters. On the latter topic, he has advised several national delegations, as well as the EU, the Council of Europe and the UN. He has written extensively in all the above-mentioned areas. He is also co-editor of the books *Fundamental Rights in International and European Law: Public and Private Law Perspectives* (2015), *Foreign Fighters under International Law and Beyond* (2016), *Legal Responses to Transnational and International Crimes. Towards an Integrative Approach* (2017) and *Human Dignity and Human Security in Times of Terrorism* (2019).

Dr. Rebecca Mignot-Mahdavi is Lecturer in International Law at the University of Manchester, where she is Director of the LLM Programmes in Public International Law and International Law and Security. She is Managing Editor of the Yearbook of International Humanitarian Law, Associate Fellow at the T.M.C. Asser Institute, Coordinator of the ESIL Interest Group on International Law and Technology, Research Fellow at the International Centre for Counter-Terrorism and Member of the Board of Directors of the International Society for Military Law and the Law of War. She holds a Ph.D. in Law from the European University Institute and the French School of Advanced Studies in the Social Sciences. Her book *Drones and International Law: A Techno-Legal Machinery* is forthcoming with Cambridge University Press. Her work reflects on counter-terrorism and, more precisely, on our evolving legal and policy capacity to deal with security threats, where new forms of non-state transnational risk, counter-risk strategy and technology are in play. Her research interests and expertise are in public international law, legal theory, international humanitarian law, human rights law and criminal law, which altogether allow her to explore counter-terrorism policies in a comprehensive manner.

Contributors

Anne Brekoo B.A. M.Sc. is Ph.D. Candidate within the European Doctorate in Law and Economics (EDLE) at the Erasmus University Rotterdam, in cooperation with the University of Bologna and the University of Hamburg. Prior to joining the Ph.D. programme, she completed a B.A. in Liberal Arts and Sciences: Law in an International Context from University College Tilburg. She then obtained an Advanced M.Sc. in International Relations and Diplomacy from the University of Leiden in cooperation with the Clingendael Institute and is currently pursuing an M.A. in Military Strategic Studies at the Dutch Defence Academy. Her Ph.D. research focuses on individual criminal deterrence in the context of international crimes such as those committed in the conflict in the former Yugoslavia. She specifically investigates whether and how jurisdictional pluralism—the existence of multiple actors that may initiate criminal prosecution—influences criminal decision-making processes. Her broader research interests include nationality deprivation and statelessness, on which she has previously published, as well as international negotiation and mediation processes.

Dr. Hanne Cuyckens is Assistant Professor of international law at Leiden University College. She obtained her Ph.D. in October 2015 from the University of Leuven, Belgium. Her Ph.D. assessed to what extent the law of occupation was still suited to deal with contemporary situations of occupation and has led to a monograph entitled *Revisiting the Law of Occupation* published by Brill Nijhoff in 2017. Her main areas of specialisation are international human rights law, international humanitarian law and international criminal law. Her current research focuses on foreign fighters and more particularly on the interaction between international humanitarian law and counter-terrorism legislation in their prosecution. At Leiden University College, she among others teaches courses on sovereignty and statehood, international humanitarian law and global security.

Prof. Helen Duffy is Professor of International Human Rights and Humanitarian Law at the University of Leiden and runs 'Human Rights *in* Practice,' a legal practice specialising in strategic human rights litigation and international legal advice. She has brought groundbreaking cases in the European, African, Interamerican and UN systems and intervened in national cases in multiple jurisdictions. Before setting up her practice, she worked for leading NGOs (Legal Director/INTERIGHTS; Counsel/Human Rights Watch; Legal Director/*Centro para Accion Legal en Derechos Humanos* Guatemala), the Prosecutor's Office of the International Criminal Tribunal for the former Yugoslavia, Lord Justice Scott's Iraq Inquiry and the UK Govt. legal service in the UK. She has a PhD (Leiden University), LLM (University College London) and LLB Hons (Glasgow University). She is Honorary/Visiting Professor at Glasgow, Melbourne and American universities and is on the board of several NGOs. Her books include *The 'War on Terror' and the Framework of International law* (CUP, 2nd ed. 2015), *Strategic Human Rights Litigation: Understanding and Maximising Impact* (Hart, 2018) and *Law Applicable to Armed Conflict* (with Bohrer and Dill, CUP 2020).

Jason E. Fritz, Ph.D. is Researcher and Consultant on peacebuilding, foreign fighters, fragile and conflict states, the intersection of security and development, the politics of policing and political violence. Prior to his current consulting at Valens Global, Jason was Security Development SME at the World Bank and Senior Research Associate at the Brookings Institution's Foreign Policy programme. Before that, he was Applied Researcher and Consultant on a wide array of defence and foreign policy issues. Jason received his Ph.D. in Justice, Law and Criminology and M.S. in Terrorism and Homeland Security Policy from American University's School of Public Affairs. He received his B.S. in Mathematical Sciences from the United States Military Academy at West Point. He is Lecturer at Johns Hopkins University's Center for Advanced Governmental Studies, where he teaches military strategy, and is Contributing Editor at *War on the Rocks*.

Dr. David Malet is Associate Professor of Public Affairs at American University. Previously, he served as Director of the Security Policy Studies Programme at the George Washington University Elliott School of International Affairs. He also taught at the University of Melbourne, Australia, and at Colorado State University, where he was Director of the Center for the Study of Homeland Security. From 2000–2003, he served as Research Assistant on national security issues to US Senate Majority Leader Tom Daschle. Professor Malet has been researching foreign fighters since 2005 and is Author of *Foreign Fighters: Transnational Identity in Civil Conflicts* (Oxford University Press, 2013 1st edition, 2017 2nd edition) and Co-editor of *Transnational Actors in War and Peace: Militants, Activists, and Corporations in World Politics* (Georgetown University Press, 2017). He regularly consults on foreign fighter policy challenges for government, international and civil society organisations. He recently led a study for PERIL studying counter-narratives and anti-government extremism in the USA. His second manuscript, *Biotechnology and International Security* (Rowman and Littlefield, 2016), examines the militarisation of human enhancement and other new forms of asymmetric warfare. His interest in military applications of biotech stems from his experience working in the congressional office that was the target of the 2001 anthrax attacks, and he led a study of public risk communications following bioterrorism funded by the US Environmental Protection Agency. His work has been published in outlets including *Foreign Affairs, TIME* and *The Washington Post*, and he provides analysis to media including NPR, CNN, CBC, *The Guardian, Al Jazeera* and *Xinhua.* In the P/CVE sector, he currently serves on the Research Advisory Council of the RESOLVE Network and the Independent Review Panel of GCERF.

Tanya Mehra LL.M. is Senior Research Fellow and Programme Lead (Rule of Law Responses to Terrorism) at the International Centre for Counter-Terrorism—The Hague. With a background in international law, she is involved in conducting research, providing evidence-based policy advice and advising governments on a rule of a law approach in countering terrorism. Her main areas of interest are international (criminal) law and rule of law approaches in countering terrorism, with a special focus on accountability of terrorism-related crimes and human rights implications of countering terrorism approaches. Other topics of interests include the repatriation of foreign terrorist fighters, battlefield evidence and the use of administrative measures in the counter-terrorism context. She works closely with policy makers, judges, prosecutors and other actors of the criminal justice sector as well as international organisations such as UN CTED, the EU, NATO and the GCTF. She worked as Senior Consultant to UN CTED on developing global guidelines to facilitate the collection of information and evidence by the military within a rule of law framework and was responsible, under the auspices of GCTF Criminal Justice and Rule of Law (CJ-ROL) Working Group Co-chairs Nigeria and Switzerland, for developing the Abuja Recommendations on the Collection, Use and Sharing of Evidence for Purposes of Criminal Prosecution of Terrorist Suspects, the Glion Recommendations on a Rule of Law-based Use of Administrative Measures in a CT context and more recently the Accountability Memorandum focusing on the criminal justice linkages between terrorism and core international crimes, human trafficking, migrant smuggling, SGBV crimes including sexual slavery and crimes against children (all three documents are available at www.thegctf.org).

Dr. Thomas Renard is Director of the International Centre for Counter-Terrorism (ICCT), a think tank based in The Hague. His research focuses on (counter-) terrorism and (counter-)radicalisation in Europe. His recent work covered the evolution of counter-terrorism policy in liberal democracies since 2001, (returning) foreign fighters, radicalisation in prison and terrorist recidivism. His latest book is *The Evolution of Counter-Terrorism since 9/11* (Routledge, September 2021). His research has been published in many journals and think tanks, including *International Affairs, Perspectives on Terrorism, CTC Sentinel, Cambridge Review of International Affairs, ICCT* or *RUSI*. He is also Senior Associate Fellow at the Egmont Institute, Member of the expert pool of the EU's Radicalisation Awareness Network (RAN), Associate Researcher at the UNESCO-PREV Chair at the University of Sherbrooke and sits on a number of scientific committees.

Dr. Rumyana van Ark is Researcher in (Counter-)Terrorism and Human Rights at the Asser Institute of the University of Amsterdam. She is Senior Member of the Implementing Partner Team of the USA and Norway led GCTF Initiative to develop a Toolkit addressing racially and ethnically motivated violent extremism. In 2021, she was part of the consortium team of experts within the European Commission funded Radicalisation Awareness Network (RAN) as well as part of the team evaluating the operation of EU Directive 2017/541 on Combatting Terrorism. She is currently Member of the Advisory Board of the PREPARE Project (https://prepare-project.eu/). She is also Senior Coordinator and Research Fellow at the International Centre for Counter-Terrorism (ICCT). Her research focuses on the evolving relationship between the individual (terror suspect) and the state following acts of terrorism. Her academic and professional experience on this topic spans over 7 years. Her first peer-reviewed works were published in 2013. Since then, her work has been published in various academic and professional journals, as part of edited book collections and within governmental reports. Her latest published work is the chapter on '*Individual Terrorist Suspects as the New Folk Devil: New Labour, Rights Tokenism and Security Compulsions?*' in the edited collection examining 'The New Labour Constitution: 20 Years On'. She is currently co-authoring a book on '*Children's Rights, 'Foreign Fighters' and 'Counter-Terrorism: The Children of Nowhere*' to be published within the Elgar Studies in Human Rights collection in 2023.

Dr. Bibi van Ginkel LL.M. is Owner and Founder of *The Glocal Connection—Platform for Shared Security*, a newly founded consultancy firm dedicated to facilitating multi-stakeholder engagement on highly sensitive security issues with a special focus on rule of law and prevention solutions. Van Ginkel's expertise spans the wide variety of focus areas of CT and C/PVE, from rule of law issues to trends and threat developments, counter-terrorism, CVE responses and prevention strategies in combination with development-aid initiatives. Prior to founding her own organisation, she worked as Research Fellow at ICCT and as Senior Research Fellow at the Security Unit of the Research Department of the Netherlands Institute for International Relations 'Clingendael'. She has also worked as Senior Consultant to the United Nations Counter-Terrorism Executive Directorate (UNCTED) on a project developing global guidelines to facilitate the collection of information and evidence by military and other relevant criminal law actors within a rule of law framework. Finally, she has served as Member of the Peace and Security Committee of the Dutch Advisory Council on International Affairs for 12 years. She is Member of the Advisory Council to the Royal Netherlands Marechaussee and the Netherlands Advisory Committee on Public International Law (CAVV).

Dr. Marloes van Noorloos is Associate Professor of criminal law at Tilburg University in the Netherlands. In 2011, she defended her Ph.D. thesis *Hate speech revisited. A comparative and historical perspective on hate speech law in the Netherlands and England & Wales* at Utrecht University (Intersentia, 2011). She is International Expert on the criminalisation of speech (e.g. hate speech, terrorist speech, blasphemy, defamation). She has conducted research on a wide range of topics in criminal justice and beyond, including terrorist offences; transitional justice, truth and memory laws; migration and criminal law and the right to privacy and criminal procedure. Her work deals with comparative, Dutch and European/international law, particularly the relationship between criminal law and fundamental rights.

Thomas Van Poecke LL.M. is Ph.D. Fellow at the Research Foundation—Flanders (FWO) for the period 2019–2023. He is affiliated to the KU Leuven Law and Criminology Faculty's Institute for International Law and the Leuven Centre for Global Governance Studies (GGS), where he works as Junior Researcher and Teaching Assistant since 2017. Thomas' research focuses on the relationship between criminal law instruments on terrorism and international humanitarian law. Thomas holds an LL.M. from the Geneva Academy of International Humanitarian Law and Human Rights (2016–17) and a Master of Law (Double Degree) from KU Leuven and the University of Zurich (2014–16).

Dr. Laura van Waas is Founder and Co-director of the Institute on Statelessness and Inclusion, the first and the only human rights NGO dedicated to promoting the right to a nationality and the rights of stateless people globally. She is also Assistant Professor at Tilburg Law School and Editor-in-Chief (with Prof. Michelle Foster) of the Statelessness and Citizenship Review. Since starting to work on statelessness in 2004, Laura has carried out a wide array of research and teaching projects. Her Ph.D. manuscript, 'Nationality Matters' (Intersentia, 2008), is widely used as a reference for understanding international statelessness law by researchers and practitioners all over the world, as is the edited collection 'Nationality and Statelessness under International Law' which she edited together with Alice Edwards (Cambridge University Press, 2014). She has worked as Consultant for UNHCR's headquarters in Geneva as well as the regional offices for the Middle East and North Africa in Beirut and for Asia and the Pacific in Bangkok. She has also undertaken consultancy work for, among others, UNHCR, UNICEF, OHCHR, Plan International, Open Society Foundations, the Women's Refugee Commission, the United States Department of State, the European Parliament and the Norwegian Refugee Council.

Abbreviations

AANES	Autonomous Authority for North East Syria
ACHPR	African Charter on Human and Peoples' Rights
ACHR	American Convention on Human Rights
ACommHPR	African Commission on Human and Peoples' Rights
AIVD	Dutch General Intelligence and Security Service
API	Advance Passenger Information
CA3	Common Article 3
CC	Criminal Code
CCPR	International Covenant on Civil and Political Rights
CESCR	UN Committee on Economic, Social and Cultural Rights
CETS	Council of Europe Treaty Series
CGLPL	*Contrôleur Général des Lieux de Privation de Liberté*
CIA	Central Intelligence Agency
CoE	Council of Europe
COI	Commission of Inquiry
CONTEST	United Kingdom's Strategy for Countering Terrorism
CRC	Convention on the Rights of the Child/Committee on the Rights of the Child
CSO(s)	Civil Society Organisation(s)
CT	Counter-Terrorism
CTC	UN Security Council Counter-Terrorism Committee
CTED	UN Security Council Counter-Terrorism Committee Executive Directorate
CTG	Counter-Terrorism Group
CTIVD	Dutch Review Committee on the Intelligence and Security Services
CUTA	Coordination Unit for the Threat Analysis
DDP	Home Office's Desistance and Disengagement Programme
DWR	De Ware Religie/Die Wahre Religion (the true religion)
ECHR	European Convention on Human Rights
ECtHR	European Court of Human Rights
ESCRs	Economic, Social and Cultural Rights

EU	European Union
EWCA	England and Wales Court of Appeal
EWHC	England and Wales High Court
FCO	Foreign and Commonwealth Office
FF(s)	Foreign Fighter(s)
FIJAIT	*Fichier judiciaire automatisé des auteurs d'infractions terroristes*
FNLA	National Front for the Liberation of Angola
FTF(s)	Foreign Terrorist Fighter(s)
GCTF	Global Counterterrorism Forum
IACHR	Inter-American Commission on Human Rights
IAC(s)	International armed conflict(s)
IACtHR	Inter-American Court of Human Rights
IB	International Brigades
ICC	International Criminal Court
ICCPR	International Covenant on Civil and Political Rights
ICCT	International Centre for Counter-Terrorism—The Hague
ICESCR	International Covenant on Economic, Social and Cultural Rights
ICJ	International Court of Justice
IED(s)	Improvised Explosive Device(s)
IHL	International Humanitarian Law
IHRL	International Human Rights Law
IIIM	International, Impartial and Independent Mechanism to Assist in the Investigation and Prosecution of Persons Responsible for the Most Serious Crimes under International Law Committed in the Syrian Arab Republic
IO(s)	International Organisation(s)
IS	Islamic State
ISIL	Islamic State of Iraq and the Levant
ISIS	Islamic State in/of Iraq and Syria
KLA	Kosovo Liberation Army
LTTE	Liberation Tigers of Tamil Eelam
NATO	North Atlantic Treaty Organization
NCTV	Dutch National Coordinator for Security and Counter-Terrorism
NES	North East Syria
NGO(s)	Non-Governmental Organisation(s)
NIAC(s)	Non-International Armed Conflict(s)
NSAG(s)	Non-State Armed Group(s)
OCHA	UN Office for the Coordination of Humanitarian Affairs
OHCHR	Office of the High Commissioner for Human Rights
OM	Dutch Public Prosecution Service
OSCE	Organization for Security and Co-operation in Europe
PKK	Kurdistan Workers' Party
PNR	Passenger Names Record
PTSD	Post-traumatic Stress Disorder
QPR	*Quartier de Prise en charge de la Radicalisation*

SCM	Syrian Center for Media and Freedom of Expression
SDF	Syrian Democratic Forces
TFEU	Treaty on the Functioning of the European Union
TIS	Category of Individuals Sentenced for Terrorist Offences
TPIM(s)	Terrorism Prevention and Investigation Measure(s)
UK	United Kingdom
UKSC	United Kingdom Supreme Court
UN	United Nations
UNCESCR	United Nations Committee on Economic, Social and Cultural Rights
UNCRC	United Nations Convention on the Rights of the Child/United Nations Committee on the Rights of the Child
UNGA	United Nations General Assembly
UNHCR	Office of the United Nations High Commissioner for Refugees
UNHRC	United Nations Human Rights Committee
UNICEF	United Nations International Children's Emergency Fund
UNITAD	United Nations Investigative Team to Promote Accountability for Crimes Committed by Da'esh/ISIL
UNODC	United Nations Office on Drugs and Crime
UNSC	United Nations Security Council
UNTS	United Nations Treaty Series
US	United States
VSSE	Belgian intelligence service
WOM	Wet Openbare Manifestaties (Dutch Public Manifestation Act)

Chapter 1
Introduction

Francesca Capone, Christophe Paulussen and Rebecca Mignot-Mahdavi

Content

Abstract In this introductory chapter, the editors contextualise the topic of returning foreign fighters and provide a general overview of the book's structure and contents, presenting its different parts and chapters.

Keywords Foreign fighters · ISIS · Foreign terrorist fighters · Returnees · Family members · Criminal law · Administrative measures

The notion of returning foreign fighters epistemologically reflects the framework of the nation State, somehow even more strongly than the notion of foreign fighters.[1] The term designates people who go fight abroad other peoples' wars and cross States' boundaries again to go back home once the fight is over. This term, by affirming the framework of the nation State, simultaneously denies the universalist proposition of jihadist movements. While the authors of this volume have not coined the term returning foreign fighters themselves, and might even criticise its theoretical assumptions in some occasions, they seize it as an object of study and take its epistemological underpinnings seriously by asking how States themselves actually take care or do not take care of 'their' foreign fighters.

[1] Li 2020.

F. Capone (✉)
Scuola Superiore Sant'Anna, Pisa, Italy
e-mail: f.capone@santannapisa.it

C. Paulussen
T.M.C. Asser Instituut, The Hague, The Netherlands
e-mail: c.paulussen@asser.nl

R. Mignot-Mahdavi
School of Law, Manchester International Law Centre, University of Manchester, Manchester, United Kingdom
e-mail: rebecca.mignot-mahdavi@manchester.ac.uk

F. Capone et al. (eds.), *Returning Foreign Fighters: Responses, Legal Challenges and Ways Forward*, https://doi.org/10.1007/978-94-6265-571-3_1

Although the foreign fighters phenomenon is not a uniform movement but includes a broad range of actors, motivations and ideologies, and encompasses movements from and to many parts of the world, this book mainly focuses on the return of individuals from Syria and Iraq to European countries. This means that more research will be required on the topic and we are perfectly aware of the fact that this volume does not (and also cannot) represent the final effort to discuss and analyse the foreign fighters (FFs) phenomenon.[2]

Like many other complex and ever-evolving issues, the rise and changing fortunes of FFs, in particular those who joined ISIS and are commonly addressed as foreign terrorist fighters (FTFs),[3] would deserve to be monitored closely for a long time. Yet, we felt the need to capture the current moment, despite the fact that States and International Organisations (IOs) are still striving to deal with the terrible toll of an unprecedented global pandemic and other major current crises, including the climate crisis and the armed conflict in Ukraine.

Indeed, also as regards returning FFs, a term that we define broadly as encompassing prospective returnees as well as actual ones, States, as well as IOs, are facing an increasing number of challenges. This, in a nutshell, is 'just' a further facet of a phenomenon that triggers legal, moral and security concerns at the horizontal level (i.e. the relationship between States) and at the vertical level (i.e. the relationship between States and individuals). The lack of a uniform approach makes it extremely complex to provide durable and fruitful solutions. For example, the scant uniformity across the domestic approaches to the prosecution, as well as to the rehabilitation and reintegration of returning FFs, can have significant security ramifications in the context of what to do with returned, convicted and released FFs.

As States and IOs are still 'learning by doing', the role of the academic community is to help steer the process by bridging the divide between international standards and their implementation at the national level and between security concerns and human rights law. In addition to doctrinal research, some of the chapters in this book take a socio-legal viewpoint, and such scholarly work can also contribute to formulating diagnoses that other actors or disciplines can use to shape sound and well-informed policies. Furthermore, the academic community can and should assist in identifying ways forward that are both effective, sustainable and international law-compliant. Those are, ultimately, the goals that the present volume seeks to pursue by collecting contributions that tackle different, although interrelated aspects connected to the

---

[2] de Guttry et al. 2016, p. 2. In the previous volume, we defined as foreign fighters "individuals, driven mainly by ideology, religion and/or kinship, who leave their country of origin or their country of habitual residence to join a party engaged in an armed conflict". Although several years have passed since the volume has seen the light we still endorse this definition, which, in our view, is broad enough to cover the multifaceted aspects of this phenomenon.

[3] UNSC 2014, preambular para 8, famously defines FTFs as "individuals who travel to a State other than their States of residence or nationality for the purpose of the perpetration, planning, or preparation of, or participation in, terrorist acts or the providing or receiving of terrorist training, including in connection with armed conflict". This definition, as we highlighted also in the previous volume, is quite controversial and it triggers a number of important issues. See, inter alia, Krähenmann 2014; Krähenmann 2016, pp. 234–241; Capone 2016, pp. 232–237.

return of FFs and their family members. In particular, with regard to the status of FFs' family members some additional caveats are needed. In fact, a cursory look at the current international legal framework and especially at the United Nations Security Council (UNSC)'s relevant resolutions will show that UN Member States are not only required to criminalise and punish certain conduct, but also to implement reintegration and rehabilitation strategies, with an emphasis on the importance to develop measures tailored to the specific needs of women and children. More in detail, UNSC Resolution 2396 (2017) underscores the dual status of FFs' family members, who "may have served in many different roles, including as supporters, facilitators, or perpetrators of terrorist acts", but may also be victims of terrorism.[4] This ambiguity is not just a matter of labels, but represents a complex problem in itself, which calls for a holistic and forward-looking approach.

In response to this wide array of issues and questions, the present volume's scope is to provide the reader, i.e. academics, policy makers, practitioners and the public at large, with a thorough and analytical overview of some key aspects, selected by the editors on the basis of the outstanding expertise of the authors who agreed to contribute to this collective endeavour. In fact, whereas the previous volume on FFs that two of the current editors published a few years ago, aimed at offering a broad overview of the phenomenon, representing a manifestly multidisciplinary collection of 25 essays authored by experts with different backgrounds, the present one has a much narrower focus as it expressly zooms in on the responses that the international community and individual States are implementing in response to returning FFs and their families. Furthermore, when discussing national responses, the geographical scope of the present volume is, as explained earlier, focused on European countries.

In more detail, this book consists of 12 chapters, divided into three parts. Part I of the volume sets the scene and it starts, after this introduction by the editors (this chapter), with a chapter authored by Thomas Renard that tackles the main issues that Europe is facing to deal with the return of FFs and their families (Chap. 2). It is followed by a contribution from David Malet and Jason E. Fritz that provides a historic overview of the phenomenon and discusses patterns of returnee behaviour and State responses to returnees, comparing the current situation to past scenarios prior to the twenty-first century (Chap. 3). The last chapter of this part, authored by Francesca Capone, will question the victims/perpetrators dichotomy, reflecting on the status and role of FFs' family members (Chap. 4).

Part II of the volume explores the international dimension. The first contribution, by Bibi van Ginkel, discusses the extent to which the current international legal framework provides useful guidance in this domain and whether the actors involved on the international plane, in particular the UN and the Global Counterterrorism Forum (GCTF), are playing a sufficiently effective and impactful role (Chap. 5). The second contribution, authored by Helen Duffy, focuses on the reach of human rights obligations and the jurisdictional challenges that the presence of FFs and their family members in Syrian camps is posing to their States of origin (Chap. 6).

---

[4] UNSC 2017, para 31.

Finally, Part III of the volume delves into the national dimension and offers a critical overview of the key and most problematic aspects that need to be addressed in this context. This part starts with a contribution by Christophe Paulussen and Tanya Mehra on the prosecution of FFs at the national level and the evidentiary and charging matters that arise before domestic courts (Chap. 7). The chapters after that discuss, respectively, the qualification of the activities of (returned) FFs under national criminal law (Chap. 8, authored by Thomas Van Poecke and Hanne Cuyckens) and the lack of individualisation of sentences and their enforcement at the expense of reintegration, with a focus on France as a case study (Chap. 9, authored by Rebecca Mignot-Mahdavi). Next, in Chap. 10, Laura van Waas and Anne Brekoo examine the approaches that States of origin of FFs are enacting in order to treat as 'foreign' their own citizens and focus on two specific and highly controversial strategies, i.e. deprivation of nationality and denial of readmission. The following chapter, by Rumyana van Ark, discusses the role of family courts as part of States' counter-terrorism toolkit and it questions the degree to which this represents a welcome development to enhance the protection of the children of FFs (Chap. 11). The last chapter is authored by Marloes van Noorloos, who, using the Netherlands as a case study, analyses the boundaries of freedom of expression in relation to terrorist speech, reflecting on the potential ramifications for the right to freedom of expression of the measures adopted at the domestic level that affect FFs at large and in particular returnees (Chap. 12).

The idea for this book project originated in February 2019. The idea back then was to organise a conference on the topic of returning foreign fighters and to develop the conference papers into chapters that would feature in a follow-up publication to our 2016 book *Foreign Fighters under International Law and Beyond*. Although the conference did not materialise in the end, the idea of the edited volume was born and did not leave our minds since. When the project, after a relatively slow start, finally got up to speed, the world was confronted with the COVID-19 pandemic, putting a few things quickly into perspective. Although the crisis, which has affected both editors and authors, slowed down the book project, the latter was never abandoned. We have to admit that we are quite proud of the fact we have continued with this edited volume despite everything that happened since, and we are immensely grateful for the patience, professionalism and flexibility of the authors and of Frank Bakker and Kiki van Gurp from T.M.C. Asser Press. We are also extremely thankful and honoured that Prof. Martin Scheinin, the very first UN Special Rapporteur on the promotion and protection of human rights and fundamental freedoms while countering terrorism, was willing to write the foreword to our book. Finally, we would like to thank Nashab Parvez, intern at the T.M.C. Asser Instituut, for his meticulous work on making sure the drafts were put in the required format and to Agori Michopoulou, Farouk Souriti, Kaya van der Horst and Lily Zanjani, all interns at the T.M.C. Asser Instituut as well, for their assistance with the index and list of abbreviations.

As indicated, the FFs topic will not go away. In August 2021, the Taliban seized power in Afghanistan after the United States (US) and the Taliban had agreed for the US to withdraw from the country where it had fought its longest war ever. These events led to fears of Afghanistan becoming "a new base for international terrorist groups like al-Qaeda and a home for foreign fighters to train and plot".[5] Conflict zones and fragile States may indeed attract new FFs or welcome FFs relocating from other conflict areas, but most of the attention in the last few years has been on how to respond to FFs (and their families) who wish to return or are already returning to their country of origin or habitual residence. Also the tragic armed conflict in Ukraine, currently unfolding in front of our eyes, has led to discussions whether the foreign volunteers joining the Ukrainian armed forces could be viewed as FFs in the first place (according to our definition, which is not limited to people joining non-state armed groups, they could), whether travelling to Ukraine to fight would be unlawful and what the risks are of those fighters' involvement in the conflict, as well as their return. Although these situations are not discussed in the present book, we hope that the observations, recommendations and calls for caution that can be found in the chapters of the current volume will be useful to any future debates on (returning) FFs, both in the academic world and in the world of policy makers and practitioners, as well as to the public at large.

References

Byman D (2021) Counterterrorism Successes Against Foreign Fighters. Lawfare. https://www.lawfareblog.com/counterterrorism-successes-against-foreign-fighters. Accessed 2 June 2022

Capone F (2016) Countering "Foreign Terrorist Fighters": A Critical Appraisal of the Framework Established By the UN Security Council Resolutions. ItYIL 25(1):227–250

de Guttry A, Capone F, Paulussen C (2016) Introduction. In: de Guttry A, Capone F, Paulussen C (eds) Foreign Fighters Under International Law and Beyond. T.M.C. Asser Press, The Hague, pp 1–4

Krähenmann S (2014) Foreign Fighters Under International Law. Geneva Academy Briefing No. 7

Krähenmann S (2016) The Obligations Under International Law of the Foreign Fighter's State of Nationality or Habitual Residence, State of Transit and State of Destination. In: de Guttry A, Capone F, Paulussen C (eds) Foreign Fighters Under International Law and Beyond. T.M.C. Asser Press, The Hague, pp 229–258

Li D (2020) The Universal Enemy: Jihad, Empire, and the Challenge of Solidarity. Stanford, Stanford University Press

UN Security Council (2014) Resolution 2178 (2014), UN Doc. S/RES/2178

UN Security Council (2017) Resolution 2396 (2017), UN Doc. S/RES/2396

[5] Byman 2021.

Part I
Setting the Scene

Chapter 2
Europe and Its Returning Foreign Fighters: Overview of the Policy Response

Thomas Renard

Contents

Abstract A number of European foreign fighters returning from Syria and Iraq have been involved in terrorist activities in Europe, such as terrorist attacks or recruitment activities. The attack on the Brussels Jewish Museum in May 2014, particularly, triggered a whole new counter-terrorism response to this challenge in Europe, compared with the policy response to the previous generations of returnees. This chapter looks into the evolution of the European policy response to returnees from Syria and Iraq since 2012, focusing on the key stages of this approach, namely: detection, prosecution, prison management, and rehabilitation. Throughout this chapter, a number of important challenges and dilemmas are highlighted.

Keywords Returnees · Counter-terrorism · Prison · Radicalisation · Prosecution · Rehabilitation

This chapter was finalised mid-2021. Newer developments have not been taken into account.

T. Renard (✉)
International Centre for Counter-Terrorism (ICCT), The Hague, The Netherlands
e-mail: t.renard@icct.nl

F. Capone et al. (eds.), *Returning Foreign Fighters: Responses, Legal Challenges and Ways Forward*, https://doi.org/10.1007/978-94-6265-571-3_2

2.1 Introduction

Before the mobilisation of jihadi volunteers for Syria and Iraq, Europe had been confronted with (returning) foreign fighters. However, the threat and the counter-terrorism challenges were never as high as during the past decade. This chapter describes the evolution of the policy response to (returning) foreign fighters in Europe since 2012. It focuses on the various dimensions of the response, as well as its various levels, and notably the European and national levels.

The mobilisation of European volunteers for the jihad in Syria was unprecedented. Europeans had travelled to fight jihad abroad before, in Afghanistan, in Bosnia, in Iraq, or in Somalia, among other places.[1] But never in such numbers. Since 2012, more than 5000 men and women have travelled from Europe to the Levant in order to join a jihadi group (mainly Jabhat al-Nusra and the Islamic State, ISIS). This is twice as many as all those who had travelled to Afghanistan (since the 1980s), Bosnia (1990s), Somalia (since the 1990s), Iraq (2000s) and Yemen (since 2010s) combined.[2] For some countries, like Belgium, there were seven times more of these so-called foreign fighters travelling to Iraq and Syria after 2012 than to all other jihadi theatres in the past.[3]

Another major difference with previous mobilisations was the greater presence of women among European departees, representing around 20 percent of the total contingent, whereas female foreign fighters were a much rarer occurrence previously.[4] Together with these women, the jihad in Iraq and Syria also became more 'family-friendly': an unprecedented number of children, around 1600, either travelled with their parents or were born in the region.[5]

Progressively, the mobilisation of foreign fighters came to be seen as a global challenge, discussed at the UN level notably, as well as a European challenge addressed by the EU institutions. However, within Europe, the phenomenon was mostly limited to a cluster of Western European countries. More than 80 percent of all European fighters originated from only five countries: France, Germany, UK, Belgium and the Netherlands.[6] Other countries impacted by this phenomenon include Denmark, Sweden, Finland, Austria, Spain, Italy, Portugal or Ireland.

The unprecedented number of European departees inevitably resulted in an equally unprecedented number of returnees in Europe. In 2019, it was estimated that around 1600 of the European foreign fighters had returned, or at least had left the conflict zone in Syria and Iraq.[7] The vast majority had returned before the fall of 2015. This represents around 30 percent of the initial contingent of foreign terrorist fighters (FTFs). It is indeed generally considered that about a third of the contingent was

---

[1] Malet 2018.

[2] Ibid.

[3] Renard and Coolsaet 2018b.

[4] Entenmann and Van Ginkel 2016.

[5] Cook and Vale 2019; Renard and Coolsaet 2018c.

[6] Barrett 2017; Entenmann and Van Ginkel 2016.

[7] King 2019, p. 44.

killed during the conflict, and the other third remains in the area, whether in detention or at large. Interestingly, the rate of returns oscillates quite significantly across countries in Europe. For instance, about half of the foreign fighters from Denmark (70/159) and the UK (450/900) have returned, whereas only 20 percent of those from France (290/1300) and the Netherlands (60/300) returned. In Germany (350/1050) and Belgium (135/430), the rate of return is at 30 percent. No study has yet looked into these different ratios across countries, but one possible explanation could be that the very national dynamics of recruitment also worked the other way around. As it is known that many foreign fighters lived in relatively homogenous national or linguistic groups,[8] it could be hypothesized, for instance, that friendship and kinship ties had an impact on the dynamics of defection and return. The geographic localisation of these contingents may have facilitated some returns (if stationed near the Turkish border, e.g.), or perhaps it was yet another combination of factors that explain this discrepancy in the national rates of return. In any case, there is room for more research in this specific aspect.

Intelligence services know from previous conflicts that veteran jihadis can constitute a serious security threat, and this challenge was already discussed at national and EU levels since 2013, notably under the leadership of the EU Counter-terrorism Coordinator, Gilles de Kerchove.[9] However, this did not result in concrete legal or administrative measures to prevent or manage returning fighters before 2014. As a result, a number of volunteers returned to Europe in 2012–14, either unnoticed or without systematic monitoring.

The terrorist attack committed by Mehdi Nemmouche in Brussels in May 2014 was a turning point in this regard. Nemmouche, a French citizen, allegedly radicalised in prison, had left for Syria in late 2012, only days after his release from prison. After spending over a year in the conflict zone, he returned to Europe via Malaysia and Singapore with the intention of plotting an attack. On 24 May 2014, he killed four people in the Jewish Museum of Brussels. This was the first successful attack by a returning fighter from Syria in Europe, following at least one failed attempt in France in February 2014.[10]

Nemmouche's attack crystallised the threat of returnees. At that point, it became clear that at least some returning fighters could be a direct security threat to Europe, requiring not only a national response but also a European and international one given the transnational nature of the threat. The Brussels Jewish Museum attack was followed by a number of meetings at the European and international levels in order to consider policy options to deal with foreign fighters and returnees. For instance, an informal meeting of EU Ministers of Interior (among the "most concerned countries") took place in Milan in July 2014, which led to an "action plan" regarding (returning) foreign fighters.[11] Discussions at the international level led eventually to the adoption of UN Security Council (UNSC) Resolution 2178 in September 2014 regarding

[8] CSIS 2016, p. 64.

[9] Quatremer 2014.

[10] Callimachi 2016.

[11] Nielsen 2014.

foreign terrorist fighters.[12] The urgency of taking measures against returnees was further reinforced following the terror attack on *Charlie Hebdo* in January 2015 involving a returnee from Yemen (Chérif Kouachi). A week later, the Belgian police dismantled a terrorist cell in Verviers, which was constituted by returnees from Syria, allegedly plotting a coordinated attack. National responses to returning foreign fighters have evolved since 2014, as will be further detailed in this chapter, but 2014 was clearly the turning point in deciding that returnees from Syria and Iraq could not be handled in the same way as previous waves of returnees: a stronger legal and security response was needed.

2.2 Returnees: One Label, Many Realities

The two-stream flow of foreign fighters, back and forth between Europe and Syria-Iraq, remained relatively uninterrupted from 2012 until 2015. Nonetheless, several 'waves' or 'generations' of returning foreign fighters can be distinguished. According to the RAN manual on returnees, the first generation of returnees consisted mostly of disillusioned volunteers who had allegedly travelled to Syria for humanitarian reasons, or to fight the Assad regime, whereas the second generation consisted more of battle-hardened fighters, possibly still radicalised or with violent intentions.[13] Renard and Coolsaet speak instead of two main waves of return, reflecting the key evolutions of the situation in Syria rather than different profiles (as the RAN manual recognises itself that there are large overlaps of profiles between the alleged 'generations').[14]

The first wave of returns, in fact the majority of returns—occurred in 2012–14, prior to the establishment of the so-called caliphate, whereas a second wave took place in 2014–16, following the beginning of the US-led Global Coalition against Daesh strikes and the progressive loss of territory by ISIS. From late 2016 onwards, very few returns occurred, in spite of expectations that the number of returnees would spike,[15] as ISIS had lost control of most territories bordering Turkey, thus complicating cross-border smuggling, and border security had been significantly strengthened across Europe. While there was no 'third wave' following the fall of the caliphate, but only a trickle of returnees, there were still more than 400 adult European foreign fighters detained in Syria and Iraq in 2021, and more still at large (or unaccounted).[16] The issue of repatriation is not addressed in this chapter,[17] but this significant contingent constitutes another potential 'wave' of returnees in the future (although a very uncertain one).

---

[12] UNSC 2014.

[13] RAN 2017, p. 20.

[14] Renard and Coolsaet 2018a, p. 4.

[15] Europol 2017, p. 7.

[16] Renard and Coolsaet 2020.

[17] See Chap. 6 by Duffy in this volume.

Beyond 'waves' we can also distinguish between the main 'ways' of return, of which we identify mainly three: the "Turkish highway",[18] that is basically returning through Turkey, the same way that was used to travel into Syria; the clandestine route, that is basically returning through illegal routes, notably mingling among migrants' flows as the attackers in Paris (November 2015) and Brussels (March 2016) did; and repatriation or expulsion (what media often qualified as 'repatriation' was is in fact more a form of organized expulsion of foreign fighters detained in Turkey). A few European citizens were repatriated from Syria and Iraq, although almost exclusively unaccompanied children.[19] The repatriation of adult fighters detained in Syria and Iraq remains highly contentious and hypothetical at the time of writing these lines, in 2021.

Regarding the profile and motivation of these returnees, it is almost impossible to make any type of generalisation. There is no "homogenous profile".[20] The RAN manual distinguished, for instance, between four main profiles: the disillusioned /remorseful; the opportunistic (still driven by ideology but seeking better life conditions); the soldier (sent back to Europe to conduct an attack or with a specific mission); and the unwilling returnee (captured and repatriated).[21] Of course, these profiles are ideal-types that do not reflect the real-life complexity of the cases. Furthermore, it should be emphasised that these profiles are not linked to any specific 'wave' or 'way' of return described above. In other words, these various profiles could be found among early as well as late returnees. For instance, the first wave of returnees included a number of individuals traumatised by war (i.e. presenting PTSD symptoms), disappointed by life in Syria, or individuals disillusioned by jihad, particularly following the war between jihadi groups (mainly between ISIS and Jabhat al-Nusra) in 2013, which resulted in a number of foreign fighters, including friends and former 'brothers in arms', fighting and killing one another.[22] But, it also included individuals who travelled back and forth to recruit friends, collect their social benefits, get hospitalised or give birth before returning to Syria. It also included the first individuals sent back to Europe in order to perpetrate an attack, such as Mehdi Nemmouche. Similarly, the second 'wave' included a number of traumatised and disillusioned foreign fighters, but also the members of the Abdelhamid Abaaoud-network, responsible for the attacks in Paris in November 2015 and Brussels in March 2016,[23] and other die-hard jihadis. Upon return, the experience of returnees also varies extensively. Some are incarcerated, others not. Some go back to their previous lives, while others struggle to re-socialise. Some are traumatised by their experience, while others miss the exhilaration of war.[24] Such heterogeneous profiles highlight the complexity of

[18] Yayla 2019.

[19] Renard and Coolsaet 2020.

[20] French Senate 2018, p. 51.

[21] RAN 2017, p. 7.

[22] Doornbos and Moussa 2016.

[23] Suc 2018.

[24] Greenwood 2019; Crettiez and Ainine 2017.

developing a single policy response to returnees, which has led European authorities to develop a tailored, flexible approach, as described in the next section.

Furthermore, discussions on returnees often lose sight of the fact that not all foreign fighters were…fighters. While the vast majority joined a terrorist organisation and supported the group's ideology and use of violence, not all of them participated directly in violent actions. Indeed, some had a more supportive role, such as working in the administration, among many possible non-fighting tasks.[25] In terms of risk-assessment, this implies that individuals that did not participate directly in violent actions in Syria and Iraq may have a different profile than those who fought, murdered civilians or raped women. This fact partially undermines the distinction that was traditionally made, including among intelligence services,[26] between male FTFs (allegedly fighters) and female FTFs (allegedly 'jihadi brides' or 'breeding mothers'). However, a key challenge with regard to risk-assessment and prosecution is precisely to determine what each individual concretely did (and did not do) during the conflict. A large number of returnees or currently detained fighters in Syria and Iraq claim—often abusively—that they never participated in violent acts or that they were only cooks or drivers—some even claim they arrived in Syria 'by accident'.[27]

European intelligence services are well aware of this variety of profiles and motivations. In 2015, for instance, the head of the Belgian intelligence service (VSSE) already specified that:

> not all returnees are dangerous. Of course not. Some are tormented by what they saw there [in Syria], they have seen atrocities and don't want to hear about it anymore. There are also adventurers who didn't find what they were looking for. But there is also a small minority, completely radicalised, coming back with a plan, with a mission. They deserve our utmost attention.[28]

Similarly, the EU Counter-terrorism Coordinator Gilles de Kerchove said in November 2014 that "we don't know how many [fighters] will return…and among those who will return, we don't know how many will engage in violent activities". De Kerchove then speculated that it would possibly be only a fraction of all returnees, but it is still a threat that is "important enough to prevent the heads of [European] intelligence services from sleeping at night."[29] A similar assessment still applies to the women currently detained in Syria, some of which are considered to have distanced themselves from the jihadi ideology, whereas others are deemed to remain clearly committed.[30] Overall, only a small number of returnees from Syria and Iraq have been involved in plots or attacks in Europe. Hegghammer and Nesser identified 11 European returnees from Syria-Iraq plotting an attack between 2012 and June 2015

[25] De Bont et al. 2017.

[26] See for instance the distinction made by the French intelligence services: French Senate 2018, p. 51.

[27] French Senate 2018, p. 51. See also: Independent 2019.

[28] Lamfalussy and Laruelle 2015.

[29] Quatremer 2014.

[30] VSSE 2019, pp. 14–15.

(thus before the attacks in Paris and Brussels).[31] In a 2017 study, Vidino, Marone and Entenmann identified 12 returnees from Syria-Iraq involved in terrorist attacks in Europe between June 2014 and June 2017.[32] While a number of (foiled) plots involving returnees may have been missed by these authors, it still remains a tiny portion of all 1600 returnees that have engaged in violent terrorism-related acts after their homecoming; and the involvement of foreign fighters in terrorist plots seems to have decreased since 2014 (relatively to plots that do not involve FTFs)[33]—probably at least partly as a result of the arrest and incarceration of most returnees since then.

Furthermore, it should be emphasised that most attacks by returnees were in fact perpetrated by commandos, that is: foreign fighters trained in a special unit of ISIS (called 'Emni') and sent back to Europe with the specific mission to conduct an attack.[34] In contrast, there are only a few plots that are linked to returnees that were not part of that special unit of ISIS. In fact, there is substantive evidence that many foreign fighters were willing to wage jihad in Syria (or elsewhere before) but unwilling to conduct terrorist attacks in Europe.[35]

The threat from returning fighters is, of course, not limited to the risk of attacks. It also includes individuals that may engage in recruitment, training, logistical or propaganda activities, taking advantage of their charismatic position.[36] Some of these veteran fighters could then become the hubs of the next jihadi mobilisation, as it has occurred before (the so-called 'veteran effect').[37] It is also possible to consider that some disillusioned or even genuinely disengaged returnees could fall back into violent extremism in the future. Depending on the type of threat considered and the time horizon, the number of returnees evaluated 'at risk' can then vary greatly.

2.3 Dealing with Returnees: The Evolution of the Policy Response in Europe

Returnees present a multifaceted challenge (with social and security dimensions notably) as well as various dilemmas (ethical and legal notably). This section reviews some of these key challenges and dilemmas raised by returnees, as well as the main efforts undertaken in Europe to manage returnees, from detection efforts to prosecution, detention and post-release policies. It also highlights how a more systematic and comprehensive approach emerged progressively between 2012 and 2020.

---

[31] Hegghammer and Nesser 2015.

[32] Vidino et al. 2017.

[33] Nesser 2021, p. 154.

[34] Suc 2018.

[35] Greenwood 2019. See also Byman 2019; Hegghammer 2013.

[36] Milton 2020; Bakker and de Roy van Zuijdewijn 2018; Byman 2019.

[37] Byman 2019.

2.3.1 Detection and Risk-Assessment

Dealing with returnees implies that authorities are able to detect the return of foreign fighters and evaluate the risk they pose. Detection was particularly difficult in the first phase of the Syrian conflict. As said above, many European foreign fighters were travelling back and forth to Syria in 2012–15, largely unhindered. This was due to a number of reasons, including but not limited to: European countries were not always able to identify all their foreign fighters (departees) in the first place; there was a lack of information-sharing between European countries, as well as a lack of use of European and international databases; and of course, the fact that many foreign fighters were coming back through indirect or even clandestine routes, making their detection all the more complicated. In the words of the head of the Belgian VSSE in 2015: "it is not simple to know who has returned, and when".[38]

As mentioned above, the policy response to returnees really started to take shape following the attack by Mehdi Nemmouche in 2014 and was further consolidated in the aftermath of subsequent plots and attacks. Discussions on foreign fighters were already taking place at the EU level since 2013, notably under the leadership of the EU Counter-terrorism Coordinator,[39] but with only limited policy impact. In October 2014, however, the EU Ministers of Justice and Home Affairs discussed a number of concrete measures aimed at addressing specifically the threat from returnees, including the adoption of the EU Passenger Names Record (PNR) Directive; the strengthening of checks at the external borders of the Schengen area; or the improving of information-exchange between member states, notably through Europol and Eurojust.[40] It was also in late 2014 that the Global Counterterrorism Forum (GCTF) agreed on 'The Hague—Marrakech Memorandum on Good Practices for a More Effective Response to the FTF Phenomenon', which included a series of recommendations, including on the detection of returnees.[41]

The results of this policy shift were evident, although not immediate. The EU PNR Directive, under discussion since 2011, was adopted in 2016. It allows comparing travellers' data with various databases, including those on foreign fighters. A regulation amending the Schengen borders code was adopted in March 2017 to reinforce checks against relevant databases at external borders (including for EU citizens, which were previously subject to minimum checks only at external borders[42]), together with a Handbook for border guards (the 'Schengen Handbook') amended in 2016, to include risk indicators to better identify returnees.[43] The exchange of information on FTFs through Europol and Eurojust databases increased significantly after 2015, particularly in the aftermath of the November 2015 Paris attacks.[44] Previously,

---

[38] Lamfalussy and Laruelle 2015.

[39] EPRS 2015.

[40] Council of the EU 2014.

[41] GCTF 2014. See Chap. 5 by van Ginkel in this volume.

[42] EPRS 2018, p. 10.

[43] Ibid.

[44] Council of the EU undated.

EU member states were only insufficiently using these databases, as highlighted by the EU Counter-terrorism Coordinator,[45] hence limiting the capacity of European law enforcement agencies to detect suspected foreign fighters. Furthermore, since 2015, the EU has sought to increase the interoperability of its various databases in relation to the FTF-threat, leading to the adoption of two regulations in this regard in May 2019,[46] seeking to avoid that individuals registered in some databases but not others, or under different aliases, could pass unnoticed.

Frontex, the EU borders agency, also received a stronger mandate in the fight against terrorism. In February 2018, it launched Operation Themis (following the Triton Programme), patrolling the Mediterranean Sea, notably with the aim of collecting "intelligence and other steps aimed at detecting foreign fighters and other terrorist threats at the external border",[47] information which is then passed onto Europol and EU member states. Two other major operations in the Mediterranean were coordinated by Interpol (Neptune I in 2018, and Neptune II in 2019), leading to the identification of respectively "four" and "a dozen" suspected foreign fighters in the area.[48]

All these international initiatives are, of course, designed to support member states, which are at the forefront of the efforts to detect returning foreign fighters. Intelligence services and law enforcement agencies are particularly central to these efforts, notably by collecting more information on prospective travellers and on foreign fighters still abroad, via a monitoring of social media accounts or through surveillance of communications with foreign fighters' friends and families notably. This has allowed intelligence services to anticipate the return of some fighters, not least when they announced or alluded to their intention to return in their communications. Cooperation among European intelligence services has also increased significantly in the face of the threat of (returning) foreign fighters. In addition to the strengthening of bilateral exchanges, this cooperation has notably taken place in the context of the so-called 'Counter Terrorism Group' (CTG), an informal club gathering representatives of intelligence services from EU member states plus Norway and Switzerland.[49] Relevant intelligence also comes from the US-led intelligence operation Gallant Phoenix, which collects intelligence on foreign fighters in Syria and Iraq.[50]

Complementing the work of intelligence services, a number of administrative measures can be taken to complicate the travelling of returning fighters and facilitate their arrest. Many of these measures appeared in the context of the foreign fighters' threat or were systematically implemented as a result of it. They vary from one country to another, but they generally include: the revocation of travel documents (passports and/or ID) and the freezing of financial assets, which together significantly

[45] Council of the EU 2016.

[46] Council of the EU undated.

[47] Frontex 2018.

[48] Interpol 2018, 2019.

[49] Renard 2016.

[50] Martin 2018.

complicate the travel and crossing of borders, whereas European Arrest Warrants facilitate the arrest and extradition of returnees.

Finally, some European countries have negotiated an agreement with Turkey in order to ensure early notification among relevant services when a foreign fighter is arrested by Turkish authorities and to ensure coordination if and when Turkish authorities decide to deport the foreign fighter (as there is no extradition agreement between Turkey and EU countries). This is notably the case of France (the so-called 'protocole Cazeneuve'), Belgium ('procédure hotspot'), and Germany. The need for such agreement resulted from the significant number of foreign fighters arrested en route to Syria or on their way back, but also following specific incidents linked to miscommunicated deportations: in 2014, Turkish authorities deported three French foreign fighters on a flight to Marseille, whereas French authorities were told the plane would land in Paris, resulting in the disappearing of the returnees until their arrest the next day.[51] In 2015, Belgian foreign fighter Ibrahim el-Bakraoui, one of the later suicide bombers in the attack in Brussels in March 2016, was arrested in Turkey and put on a plane to Amsterdam without properly warning Belgian authorities. As a result, el-Bakraoui disappeared until the attacks.[52]

The combination of all these measures, together with the erosion of the flow of foreign fighters, has contributed to a much better capacity to detect (potential) returnees. However, the system is not infallible. For instance, one of the most wanted British foreign fighters was arrested in Spain in April 2020, although it is not clear how he managed to reach Spain.[53] Following the Turkish offensive in northern Syria in October 2019, there have also been several escapes from Kurdish detention facilities, resulting in a number of European foreign fighters crossing into Turkey. While many of these individuals (mainly women and children) were then arrested or surrendered to Turkish authorities, it cannot be excluded that some foreign fighters manage to return undetected. It is also possible that some FTFs have managed to travel to other countries undetected (e.g. Turkey, Egypt, Yemen, Libya or Afghanistan), and that they could seek to return to Europe only months or years later.

2.3.2 Prosecution

There is a relatively large consensus that returnees should be prosecuted, certainly when there is evidence of a criminal offence. This was one of the recommendations of the GCTF's 'The Hague-Marrakech Memorandum' and the UNSC.[54] In line with this recommendation and with the UNSC Resolution 2178 calling for the criminalisation of the travel for terrorist purposes (attacks or training), or the financing of such travel

[51] French Senate 2018, pp. 150–151.

[52] RTL 2016.

[53] Chulov and Sabbagh 2020.

[54] GCTF 2014; UNSC 2014.

(translated into an EU Directive in 2017[55]), there has been a strengthening of the criminal code in most European countries, with the addition of a number of new terrorist offences.[56] Further to the broadening of the terrorist offence, a number of additional laws were also adopted in EU member states to facilitate proceedings in terrorism investigations, for instance, extending prosecutorial powers, provisional detention or house searches.[57]

Returnees from the first 'wave' were not always prosecuted, however, either for lack of evidence against them, or because they were not considered a security threat. This included notably those that had travelled to Syria for humanitarian purposes or were clearly disillusioned individuals. Nevertheless, with the jihadi nature of the conflict becoming clearer and the threat from returnees becoming more salient, particularly following the first attacks on European soil, the prosecution of returnees has become progressively more systematic. In fact, since 2014–15, all returning fighters have been systematically under judiciary investigation in a number of countries, including France, Belgium and the Netherlands.[58] In Germany, a criminal investigation is opened in every case, but not necessarily leading to prosecution.[59] In other countries, judiciary investigations are less systematic or more complicated for legal reasons. For instance, the UK government has said repeatedly that it would prosecute anyone who has travelled abroad to engage in terrorism, and yet at the same time, only 40 British returnees, out of about 450, have been "successfully prosecuted" so far.[60] Sweden has convicted almost none of its 150 returnees, as it had not criminalised the participation in a terrorist organisation until January 2020.[61] As a result, the rate of prosecution of returnees varies across European countries. It is estimated that 76 percent[62] of the French returnees were "judiciarised" and about 70 percent of the Belgian returnees were prosecuted,[63] whereas only 10 percent of the UK returnees were prosecuted, and this figure is closer to zero percent in Sweden.

It should be noted that the systematisation of prosecution concerned only male returnees at first. For some time, women were considered mainly as victims, or at least of no particular concern, and therefore they were not prosecuted in most cases. This gender discrepancy seems to have come to an end in several European countries, notably in Belgium, Netherlands and France.[64] In Germany as well, the prosecution of women seems to have become more the norm, although still not systematic.[65] Illustrating the change of risk-assessment on female foreign fighters,

---

[55] EU 2017.

[56] Eurojust 2016.

[57] Eurojust 2016.

[58] Renard and Coolsaet 2018b; French Senate 2018, p. 52.

[59] Heinke and Raudszus 2018, pp. 49–50.

[60] Dearden 2019; Dawson 2019.

[61] Grönvik 2019; The Local 2019a.

[62] CAT and CEP 2019.

[63] Based on the author's own data collection (see Renard 2020).

[64] Renard and Coolsaet 2018b; French Senate 2018, p. 52.

[65] Heinke and Raudszus 2018.

the Dutch justice minister argued in 2019 that the return of Dutch women from Syria could be a "direct risk to the national security of the Netherlands".[66]

The systematisation of the prosecution of returnees was possible in some countries because prosecutors made the specific tactical decision to go after a minimal offence. Indeed, most returnees have been convicted for their participation in a terrorist organisation, whereas only a small minority of returnees have been convicted for more serious terrorist offences (such as kidnapping, beheading or participation in a terrorist attack), whether committed in Syria or in Europe (such as Mehdi Nemmouche, for instance, sentenced in 2019 to life in prison). As a result, most sentences pronounced are relatively short, in the range of 3–5 years. The average sentence for returnees is around six years and a half in Belgium and France[67] and around four years and a half in Germany.[68] Strikingly, the laws criminalising foreign fighting activities, resulting from UNSC Resolution 2178, do not seem to have been used by national prosecutors, who prefer relying on well-established and pre-existing offences (mainly participation in a terrorist organisation), hence raising questions about the necessity of such new laws, at least in Europe.

This prosecutorial tactic aiming at the minimal offence has proven effective, albeit debatable from an ethical point of view. First, the generalisation of relatively short sentences for returnees may be misunderstood in large segments of the population as a form of impunity. Second, the absence of prosecution for the crimes committed in Syria and Iraq, which were serious and on a large-scale, raises questions about the ability of European courts to render justice, notably in the eyes of the many victims of terrorism, whether in Europe or the Levant. In this regard, it is notable that Eurojust called, in 2020, for EU member states to prosecute returnees also for core international crimes committed in the Levant, which it considered "essential to ensure criminal responsibility of perpetrators and to deliver justice to victims".[69] So far, only a few cases of cumulative prosecution for terrorism and international crimes have been conducted in Europe.[70] In this regard, it is worth mentioning the creation of a common register within Eurojust in 2019 to share information among all EU member states on ongoing terrorism investigations and prosecutions, to improve cross-border coordination and identify potential cross-links between investigations.[71] This tool seems apt in light of the transnational nature of returnees' networks but also to facilitate investigations that aim to identify the more serious crimes committed in Syria.

Another prosecutorial tactic that has become more common over the years is the prosecution *in absentia* of foreign fighters, even when presumed dead.[72] France, Belgium and the Netherlands have notably started such trials in a systematic manner,

---

66 Van Wilgenburg 2019.

67 CAT and CEP 2019; see also author's own calculation (Renard 2020).

68 Raudszus 2020.

69 Eurojust 2020, p. 4.

70 See Chap. 8 by Van Poecke and Cuyckens in this volume.

71 Guarascio 2019.

72 AFP 2020.

which means that when these foreign fighters return (if they do), they will be arrested and jailed immediately. In contrast, trials *in absentia* are not permitted by law in Germany, although this does not prevent ongoing investigations against FTFs detained in Syria.[73] Regarding the type of evidence that is being used to prosecute returnees, it consists essentially of internet evidence (notably social media pictures or messages); 'battlefield evidence', which is essentially evidence collected in former ISIS territories (such as administrative registers, financial documents, etc.); and intelligence.[74] Each of these sources of evidence presents its own challenge and difficulties, with different ramifications in every country. For instance, German courts have restrictions on data obtained from social media accounts or via intelligence-gathering means. The UK also prohibits the use of intercept evidence in court.[75]

Finally, it should be mentioned that returnees who are not prosecuted or convicted are not necessarily left unchecked. At the very least, returnees continue to be monitored by security services. They can also be subject to specific administrative measures, such as the 'Terrorism Prevention and Investigation Measures' (TPIMs) in the UK, which can include overnight residence requirements, electronic tagging or restrictions of communication.[76] Alternatively, returnees can be directed towards rehabilitation programmes (i.e. deradicalisation or disengagement).

2.3.3 Prison Management

The unprecedented number of returnees in Europe, and the high rates of prosecution and conviction in some countries, has resulted in an equally unprecedented number of returnees in prison. Although unprecedented, the number of returnees in jail at any point in time has remained manageable since not all returnees were convicted and those convicted were not all jailed at the same time, with the result that some returnees entered prison when others were already coming out. However, the real challenge resulted from the fact that these returnees came in addition to an increasing number of terrorist convicts and radicalised inmates from 2014 onwards. In 2020, there were more than 1400 individuals in custody for terrorism-related offences in Europe, and more than 3000 when adding individuals 'radicalised' or 'at risk of radicalisation', the vast majority of whom are linked to jihadi terrorism.[77] While unprecedented in scope, and a very serious concern, this phenomenon remains marginal overall, representing less than 1 percent of the entire prison population in Europe.[78] Furthermore,

[73] EPRS 2018, p. 44; Roithmaier 2019.

[74] See Chap. 7 by Paulussen and Mehra in this volume.

[75] EPRS 2018, pp. 44–45; Dworkin 2019, p. 9.

[76] Dawson 2019.

[77] Basra and Neumann 2020, p. 9.

[78] In 2018, there were 495,000 prisoners in the EU.

it is possible that this population peaked around 2018, although this remains to be confirmed.[79]

While constituting only a small fraction of all terrorist convicts, returnees have been of particular concern given their profile and experience. They have essentially raised two main types of security concerns. First, it was feared that returnees could use prisons to strengthen their networks with other jihadis or criminals and even plot attacks from their cells. There were, for instance, anecdotal accounts from returning fighters seeking to recreate networks among returnees in French prisons.[80] There are also a few cases of returnees attempting to engage in violent plots from prison, although these cases remain highly exceptional. At least two plots involving returnees in prison have been identified, both in France. In 2019, Mohammed Taha El Hannouni, sentenced to seven years for joining ISIS in Syria, attacked two prison officers in Le Havre.[81] A few months later, in 2019, a terrorist plot was foiled, possibly also targeting prison officers, involving Zakaria Chedili, who had been sentenced to six years in prison for having joined ISIS in Syria.[82]

Second, the incarceration of returnees, together with other terrorist convicts, also led to a growing concern about radicalisation in prison. Radicalisation in prison traditionally refers to the fear that 'ordinary inmates' could be radicalised by terrorist convicts, although it can also be understood as the 'over- or re-radicalisation' of terrorist convicts (as reflected by the common assessment that "rarely do people come out of prison better than when they went in … they can come out even more motivated than before"[83]). Radicalisation in prison is certainly not a new phenomenon, but it became more prominent—or at least more monitored—in the context of the threat from ISIS. There are even historical precedents of returnees from previous jihadi conflicts that had been relatively influential in 'radicalising' other inmates. This was notably the case with Djamel Beghal (who had travelled to Afghanistan in 2000 and was arrested in 2001) or Lionel Dumont (a returnee from the jihad in Bosnia) in France, both of whom have been known to have a particular influence on other inmates.[84] Beghal is considered, for instance, to have been the mentor of Chérif Kouachi and Amedy Coulibaly, both perpetrators of the 2015 attacks against *Charlie Hebdo* and the *HyperCasher* supermarket.

The multiplication of terrorist attacks committed by individuals suspected of having been radicalised in prison, such as Chérif Kouachi or Mehdi Nemmouche as well as Mohamed Merah before them, pushed the issue of prison radicalisation higher on the policy agenda. In addition to terrorist attacks, policy-makers were concerned by the combination of a growing number of terrorist convicts (including returnees) with the increasingly attractive narrative of ISIS in 2014–15. This led European countries to consider the management of extremist offenders in prison as a

[79] Basra and Neumann 2020, p. 10.

[80] Thomson 2018.

[81] FranceInfo 2019.

[82] AFP 2019.

[83] AFP 2018a.

[84] AFP 2018b; Laruelle 2017.

key priority, leading countries like Belgium to adopt a specific strategy to deal with radicalisation in prison in 2015.[85] The Council of the European Union raised, on several occasions, the importance of addressing radicalisation in prison, notably in its Conclusions of 2015 and 2019.[86]

Regarding the management of returnees in prison, it is not different from that of other extremist offenders. Almost every European country has opted for a mixed-model of detention regime, involving the concentration or isolation of the most dangerous inmates and the dispersal of the others among the regular prison population.[87] To implement these strategies, European penitentiary administrations have created specialised units within the prison system to deal with these individuals suspected of recruiting or radicalising others, including the so-called 'D-Rad:Ex unit', established in Belgium in 2016, the 'Separation Centres', established in the UK in 2017, or the 'Radicalisation Support Unit' (Quartier de Prise en charge de la Radicalisation, QPR) established in France in 2018. While some returnees have been placed in these units, this was far from systematic, and there is not enough evidence to assess whether returnees were more likely to be placed in these units compared with other terrorist offenders.[88] The Netherlands is perhaps the only country in Europe having followed an alternative pathway, concentrating all its extremist offenders in two terrorist wards. The limited number of terrorist offenders in custody in the Netherlands (36 in 2020) might explain why this approach is possible in that country and not in others.

Beyond security regimes, most European countries have worked on improving their capacity to detect problematic behaviours and take appropriate measures in response. This was done notably by training the penitentiary staff, as well as setting up new specialised units within the penitentiary administration tasked with the centralisation and evaluation of information on radicalised inmates. In addition to information from penitentiary staff and intelligence services, prison authorities rely on risk-assessment tools (such as the VERA-2R or the ERG22+) to evaluate returnees and other terrorist offenders.[89]

Various rehabilitation programmes have also been developed across Europe over the years. The content or conditions of these programmes vary widely from one country to another, although it appears that such programmes are often closer to a form of psycho-social support and help to reinsertion than to an attempt at so-called 'deradicalisation'. Not all returnees (or terrorist offenders more broadly) have been able to participate in these programmes, however, either because they refused to take part or because they came out of prison before they were on offer. Furthermore, these programmes raise some important ethical questions. First, their effectiveness is nearly impossible to evaluate. Is it, therefore, money well spent? Second, there are issues with inmates taking advantage of these programmes to benefit from early

[85] Service Public Fédéral 2015.

[86] Council of the EU 2015, 2019.

[87] Basra and Neumann 2020.

[88] In Belgium, this does not seem to be the case.

[89] Basra and Neumann 2020.

release, without guarantees on their 'sincerity', as suggested by some cases of terrorist offenders who 'tricked' such programmes before re-offending. This was notably the case of Usman Khan in the UK, who stabbed several people to death while participating in one of these rehabilitation programmes. Finally, it appears that most 'ordinary inmates' are not offered any form of similar support in prisons across Europe. This implies that extremist offenders receive in some regards a more 'favourable' regime of detention compared to other inmates.[90] In addition to generating potential tensions among inmates, this discriminating regime begs a fundamental question: are European countries doing too much for extremist offenders or too little for 'ordinary inmates'?

2.3.4 *Post-release*

Similarly to the penitentiary approach, there is no distinction between returnees and other terrorist offenders in the post-penitentiary approach. Most European countries favour a release under probation, which permits to impose a series of conditions on the former inmate and keep a form of control during a period of time. These probation measures can include participation in a rehabilitation programme, exclusion from travel abroad or going to certain areas on the national territory, exclusion from accessing the internet, obligation to meet a probation officer and/or police officer on a regular basis, etc. In addition to such probation measures, former extremist inmates will continue to be monitored at the very least by intelligence services, but also usually through multi-agency platforms that vary from one country to another. In Germany, special coordinators for returnees have been appointed to facilitate this multi-agency approach.

In spite of existing mechanisms for post-penitentiary monitoring, European policy-makers fear recidivism among released terrorist offenders. It has become one of the main policy priorities in the area of counter-terrorism in light of the expected release of most returnees and extremist offenders in the period leading to 2025. As a result, some countries have decided to strengthen the post-penitentiary approach. In the UK, for instance, a new law was adopted in 2020 to avoid the automatic early release of terrorist convicts, and therefore ensure that they remain in jail for their whole sentence. As a result, probation measures are no longer possible, but the new law also strengthens security measures that can be decided outside the judiciary framework, such as TPIMs (see above).[91] Similarly, in France, a new law was adopted in 2020 to extend judiciary controls over released terrorist offenders, even

[90] To be clear, most extremist offenders in prison are under tight monitoring and security regimes, which is hardly conceived as a form of "favour". However, in the context of rehabilitation programmes, some of them are also offered with more opportunities to meet psychologists or participate in reinsertion activities, compared with other inmates. Overall there are more resources spent on them, proportionally, than on ordinary inmates.

[91] Grierson 2020.

after the end of their licensing period.[92] Furthermore, several European countries are increasingly stripping binational terrorist convicts or suspects of their nationality, which eventually results in the expulsion of the offender at the end of the sentence, thus transferring the burden of the post-release monitoring to a third country (although in practice, nothing prevents intelligence services from maintaining a form of monitoring on some of these individuals once abroad, directly or indirectly).

The common assumption behind these new laws and measures is that terrorist offenders present a high risk of recidivism. However, recent research suggests on the contrary that terrorist offenders would have a much lower risk of recidivism than ‘ordinary criminals’.[93] While this research does not necessarily distinguish returnees from other terrorist offenders, there are good indications that a majority of returnees will not re-offend, based on evidence from the past.[94] A note from the Belgian counter-terrorism fusion centre, the Coordination Unit for the Threat Analysis (CUTA), concluded that 84% of the male returnees from Syria (37/44) and 95% of women returnees (19/20) had been showing signs of disengagement, excluding returnees still in prison (whose rate of disengagement was around 50 percent).[95]

In spite of low rates of recidivism, released returnees and terrorist offenders remain a serious threat. Terrorism is by nature a rare occurrence in Europe; hence a low rate of recidivism among hundreds of returnees is still a threat to be closely monitored by security services. However, the necessity of security measures should be weighed against their negative impact on the chances of rehabilitation and reintegration of released offenders. For instance, tight security measures (such as frozen assets, e.g.) may prevent a released offender from getting a new job or returning to a normal life, whereas measures that infringe on human rights may stir up the individual’s grievances and undermine the broader counter-terrorism approach. In other words, policy-makers should ensure that the measures they take to decrease recidivism do not actually increase that risk. Such evaluations, however, seem absent from the decision-making process behind these recent measures.

2.4 Conclusion

Returning foreign fighters from Syria and Iraq are undoubtedly one of the most serious security challenges faced by European countries over the past decade. While not a new phenomenon, the scope of the mobilisation for Syria and the attacks perpetrated on European soil have triggered an important policy response that has largely redefined the contours of counter-terrorism policies in Europe. An entire arsenal of tools and measures was developed to manage returnees, ranging from

[92] Chapuis and Auffret 2020. See Chap. 9 by Mignot-Mahdavi in this volume.

[93] Renard 2020; Silke and Morrison 2020.

[94] Byman 2019.

[95] Interview with a CUTA official, Brussels, November 2019.

the ability to detect them to their prosecution, management in prison and after their release.

While European countries are now certainly much better equipped to deal with this challenge than they were in 2012, and while some good practices have emerged across Europe, there are still some major gaps. In terms of prosecution, for instance, the inability of some countries to prosecute returnees is just as troubling as the inability of most countries to prosecute them for the more serious crimes committed in Syria and Iraq. The management of returnees in prison has raised real concerns that should not be discarded, even though the number of serious incidents remains limited. The long-term impact of this incarceration period, however, remains to be assessed, notably to evaluate the extent to which returnees may have used their time in detention to establish new networks or radicalise other inmates. Furthermore, the main fear is that a number of returnees could re-offend after their release from prison. While some studies are pointing to low rates of recidivism, as mentioned above, this remains a key concern for security services.

Three key challenges loom ahead. First, the monitoring of returnees over the long term. Indeed, returnees could genuinely disengage for several years or simply keep a low profile, and then re-radicalise or reconnect with jihadism at the next opportunity. This requires long-term monitoring but also maintaining enough resources and expertise on this topic, which could be challenging in the post-COVID-19 era.

Second, the international dimension of returnees' networks will further complicate the work of the European judiciary and security services. Returnees from different nationalities could remain in contact for years or decades, forcing European services to continue exchanging information on a regular basis. The citizenship-stripping and deportation of more returnees could further strengthen the international aspects of this challenge, as these former European citizens could possibly remain in contact with friends and family in Europe. Adding to this, returnees to non-European countries could remain in contact with European returnees in the future, notably returnees in North Africa, requiring a good degree of cooperation between European and North African security services.[96]

Third, an assessment of the proportionality and effectiveness of all measures developed over the past years to cope with (returning) foreign fighters are still lacking. It is unclear, for instance, how longer prison sentences for returnees or terrorist offenders will make Europe safer. It is equally unclear how such measures will not actually increase the existing challenge of prison radicalisation. Similarly, one can legitimately ask whether stripping foreign fighters of their nationality and expelling them abroad, at the risk of losing control over them, will effectively keep the threat offshore. Some measures adopted against returnees and terrorist offenders seem driven by fear more than evidence, as well as by an elusive quest for complete security. Meanwhile, the costs and possibly counter-productive effects of these measures remains largely unassessed.

To conclude, it is perhaps worth remembering that in spite of the significant strengthening of the policy response to returnees, European governments remain

[96] Renard 2019.

extremely fearful of the challenge of returnees, to the point that they oppose firmly the idea of repatriating foreign fighters still detained abroad. In fact, European ministers have regularly commented publicly that they would largely prefer to see these fighters dead rather than back.[97] If this should be an assessment of the public trust in the policy response to returnees, it is not an encouraging one.

References

AFP (2018a) Jailbird jihadists, a security threat for Europe. https://www.france24.com/en/20180319-jailbird-jihadists-security-threat-europe. Accessed 29 September 2021

AFP (2018b) L'Algérie va rejuger l'islamiste Djamel Beghal, condamné à vingt ans de prison par contumace en 2003. https://www.lemonde.fr/societe/article/2018/07/16/incertitude-sur-le-sort-de-l-islamiste-djamel-beghal-qui-sort-de-prison-lundi_5332053_3224.html. Accessed 29 September 2021

AFP (2019) Projet d'attentat déjoué: des armes et une allégeance à l'EI trouvées. https://www.lepoint.fr/justice/projet-d-attentat-en-france-des-armes-et-une-allegeance-a-l-ei-trouvees-01-08-2019-2327935_2386.php. Accessed 29 September 2021

AFP (2020) Ouverture aux assises de Paris du procès de jihadistes morts ou recherchés. https://www.lepoint.fr/societe/ouverture-aux-assises-de-paris-du-proces-de-jihadistes-morts-ou-recherches-06-01-2020-2356309_23.php. Accessed 29 September 2021

Bakker E, de Roy van Zuijdewijn J (2018) Yes: Returning foreign fighters are future terrorists. In: Jackson R, Pisoiu D (eds) Contemporary debates on terrorism. Routledge, London, pp. 131–137

Barrett R (2017) Beyond the Caliphate: Foreign fighters and the threat of returnees. Soufan Center. https://thesoufancenter.org/wp-content/uploads/2017/11/Beyond-the-Caliphate-Foreign-Fighters-and-the-Threat-of-Returnees-TSC-Report-October-2017-v3.pdf. Accessed 27 September 2021

Basra R, Neumann P (2020) Prisons and Terrorism: Extremist Offender Management in 10 European Countries. International Centre for the Study of Radicalisation. https://icsr.info/wp-content/uploads/2020/07/ICSR-Report-Prisons-and-Terrorism-Extremist-Offender-Management-in-10-European-Countries_V2.pdf. Accessed 27 September 2021

Byman D (2019) Road warriors: Foreign fighters in the armies of jihad. Oxford University Press, Oxford

Callimachi R (2016) How ISIS built the machinery of terror under Europe's gaze. https://www.nytimes.com/2016/03/29/world/europe/isis-attacks-paris-brussels.html. Accessed 29 September 2021

CAT, CEP (2019) Quelles menaces et quels enjeux après la chute du califat? Compte-rendu de la conférence internationale sur le terrorisme. http://cat-int.org/wp-content/uploads/2020/01/Compte-rendu-FR.pdf. Accessed 27 September 2021

Chapuis N, Auffret S (2020) La majorité veut renforcer le contrôle des détenus pour terrorisme à leur sortie de prison. https://www.lemonde.fr/societe/article/2020/03/12/la-majorite-veut-renforcer-le-controle-des-detenus-pour-terrorisme-a-leur-sortie-de-prison_6032771_3224.html. Accessed 29 September 2021

Chulov M, Sabbagh D (2020) Spanish police arrest former British rapper turned Isis extremist. https://www.theguardian.com/world/2020/apr/21/spanish-police-arrest-former-british-isis-extremist. Accessed 29 September 2021

Cook J, Vale G (2019) From Daesh to 'Diaspora' II: The challenges posed by women and minors after the fall of the caliphate. CTC Sentinel 12(6):30–45

[97] The Local 2019b; DN 2015.

Council of the EU (2014) Press release. 3336th Council meeting, Justice and Home Affairs, 9–10 October. https://www.consilium.europa.eu/media/25127/145033.pdf. Accessed 27 September 2021
Council of the EU (2015) Conclusions of the Council of the European Union and of the Member States meeting within the Council on enhancing the criminal justice response to radicalization leading to terrorism and violent extremism. Press Release. https://www.consilium.europa.eu/en/press/press-releases/2015/11/20/conclusions-radicalisation/. Accessed 27 September 2021
Council of the EU (2016) State of play on implementation of the statement of the members of the European Council of 12 February 2015, the JHA Council Conclusions of 20 November 2015, and the Conclusions of the European Council of 18 December 2015. Note from the EU Counter-Terrorism Coordinator. 6450/16. https://www.statewatch.org/media/documents/news/2016/mar/eu-council-c-t-coordinator-report-6450-16.pdf. Accessed 27 September 2021
Council of the EU (2019) Council conclusions on preventing and combating radicalization in prisons and on dealing with terrorist and violent extremist offenders after release. https://data.consilium.europa.eu/doc/document/ST-9727-2019-INIT/en/pdf. Accessed 27 September 2021
Council of the EU (undated) Response to the terrorist threat and recent terrorist attacks in Europe. https://www.consilium.europa.eu/en/policies/fight-against-terrorism/foreign-fighters/. Accessed 27 September 2021
Crettiez X, Ainine B (2017) "Soldats de Dieu": Paroles de djihadistes incarcérés. L'Aube, Paris
CSIS (2016) The foreign fighters phenomenon and related security trends in the Middle East. https://www.canada.ca/en/security-intelligence-service/corporate/publications/the-foreign-fighters-phenomenon-and-related-security-trends-in-the-middle-east.html. Accessed 27 September 2021
Dawson J (2019) Shamima Begum: What powers exist to deal with returning foreign fighters? House of Commons Library. https://commonslibrary.parliament.uk/shamima-begum-what-powers-exist-to-deal-with-returning-foreign-fighters/. Accessed 27 September 2021
Dearden L (2019) Only one in 10 jihadis returning from Syria prosecuted, figures reveal. https://www.independent.co.uk/news/uk/home-news/shamima-begum-isis-return-uk-syria-jihadis-terror-threat-prosecute-nationality-a8790991.html. Accessed 29 September 2021
De Bont R et al. (2017) Life at ISIS: The roles of Western men, women and children. In: Kowalski M (ed) Special Issue: Jihadists in Syria and Iraq: Recalibrating Concepts, Threat Radar, and Reintegration Policies. Security and Global Affairs. https://www.universiteitleiden.nl/binaries/content/assets/governance-and-global-affairs/isga/isga-journal_special_issue-4.pdf. Accessed 27 September 2021
DN (2015) Prime minister defends 'better dead' jihadi comments. https://www.dutchnews.nl/news/2015/03/prime-minister-defends-better-dead-jihadi-comments/ Accessed 27 September 2021
Doornbos H, Moussa J (2016) The Greatest Divorce in the Jihadi World. Foreign Policy. https://foreignpolicy.com/2016/08/18/the-greatest-divorce-in-the-jihadi-world/. Accessed 27 September 2021
Dworkin A (2019) Beyond good and evil: Why Europe should bring ISIS foreign fighters home. European Council on Foreign Relations (ECFR). https://ecfr.eu/publication/beyond_good_and_evil_why_europe_should_bring_isis_foreign_fighters_home/. Accessed 27 September 2021
Entenmann E, van Ginkel B (2016) The Foreign Fighters Phenomenon in the European Union. Profiles, Threats & Policies. The International Centre for Counter-Terrorism (ICCT) Research Paper. https://icct.nl/app/uploads/2016/03/ICCT-Report_Foreign-Fighters-Phenomenon-in-the-EU_1-April-2016_including-AnnexesLinks.pdf. Accessed 27 September 2021
EU (2017) Directive 2017/541 of the European Parliament and of the Council of 15 March 2017 on combating terrorism and replacing Council Framework Decision 2002/475/JHA and amending Council Decision 2005/671/JHA
Eurojust (2016) Foreign Terrorist Fighters: Eurojust's Views on the Phenomenon and the Criminal Justice Response: Fourth Eurojust Report. https://www.statewatch.org/media/documents/news/2017/jun/eu-eurojust-ff-finding.pdf. Accessed 27 September 2021

Eurojust (2020) Cumulative prosecution of foreign terrorist fighters for core international crimes and terrorism-related offences. https://www.eurojust.europa.eu/sites/default/files/Partners/Genocide/2020-05_Report-on-cumulative-prosecution-of-FTFs_EN.PDF. Accessed 27 September 2021

European Parliamentary Research Service (EPRS) (2015) 'Foreign fighters': Member States' responses and EU action in an international context. Briefing. https://www.europarl.europa.eu/EPRS/EPRS-Briefing-548980-Foreign-fighters-FINAL.pdf. Accessed 27 September 2021

European Parliamentary Research Service (EPRS) (2018) The return of foreign fighters to EU soil: Ex-post evaluation. https://www.europarl.europa.eu/RegData/etudes/STUD/2018/621811/EPRS_STU(2018)621811_EN.pdf. Accessed 27 September 2021

Europol (2017) European Union Terrorism Situation & Trend Report (Te-Sat) 2017. Publications Office of the European Union. https://www.europol.europa.eu/tesat/2017/. Accessed 28 September 2021

FranceInfo (2019) Surveillants de prison agressés au Havre: le détenu mis en examen pour "tentative d' assassinats" à caractère terroriste. https://www.francetvinfo.fr/societe/prisons/surveillants-de-prison-agresses-au-havre-le-detenu-mis-en-examen-pour-tentative-d-assassinats-a-caractere-terroriste_3505205.html. Accessed 29 September 2021

French Senate (2018) Rapport fait au nom de la commission d'enquête sur l'organisation et les moyens des services de l'État pour faire face à l'évolution de la menace terroriste après la chute de l'État islamique. French Senate, Paris, 4 July

Frontex (2018) Frontex launching new operation in Central Med. Press release. https://reliefweb.int/report/italy/frontex-launching-new-operation-central-med. Accessed 29 September 2021

GCTF (2014) The Hague—Marrakech Memorandum on Good Practices for a More Effective Response to the FTF Phenomenon. https://www.thegctf.org/documents/10162/140201/14Sept19_The+Hague-Marrakech+FTF+Memorandum.pdf. Accessed 29 September 2021

Greenwood M (2019) When foreign fighters come home: the story of six Danish returnees. Perspectives on Terrorism 13(4):27–38

Grierson J (2020) Unconvicted terrorism suspects face indefinite controls under UK bill. https://www.theguardian.com/politics/2020/may/20/unconvicted-terrorism-suspects-face-indefinite-controls-under-uk-bill. Accessed 29 September 2021

Grönvik J (2019) How Sweden Deals with Returning ISIS Fighters. https://www.vice.com/en/article/3k9j8b/how-sweden-deals-with-returning-isis-fighters. Accessed 29 September 2021

Guarascio F (2019) EU sets up tool for easier conviction of jihadist fighters as hundreds may return. https://www.reuters.com/article/uk-eu-terrorism-idUKKCN1VQ1YN. Accessed 29 September 2021

Hegghammer T (2013) Should I Stay or Should I Go? Explaining Variation in Western Jihadists' Choice between Domestic and Foreign Fighting. American Political Science Review 107(1):1–15

Hegghammer T, Nesser P (2015) Assessing the Islamic State's commitment to attacking the West. Perspectives on Terrorism 9(4):14–30

Heinke D, Raudszus J (2018) Germany's returning foreign fighters and what to do about them. In: Renard T, Coolsaet R (eds) Returnees: who are they, why are they (not) coming back and how should we deal with them? Egmont Paper 101. https://www.egmontinstitute.be/content/uploads/2018/02/egmont.papers.101_online_v1-3.pdf?type=pdf. Accessed 29 September 2021

Independent (2019) 'I got cheated. All of us got cheated': Captured German Isis member says he regrets joining terror group. https://www.independent.co.uk/news/world/middle-east/isis-syria-fighter-germany-lucas-glass-islamic-state-assad-islam-a8769911.html. Accessed 29 September 2021

Interpol (2018) INTERPOL-led Mediterranean operation closes ranks on foreign terrorist fighters. Press release. https://www.interpol.int/ar/1/1/2018/INTERPOL-led-Mediterranean-operation-closes-ranks-on-foreign-terrorist-fighters. Accessed 29 September 2021

Interpol (2019) Foreign terrorist fighters detected during INTERPOL maritime border operation. Press Release. https://www.interpol.int/en/News-and-Events/News/2019/Foreign-terrorist-fighters-detected-during-INTERPOL-maritime-border-operation. Accessed 29 September 2021

King J (2019) Discours de clotûre de Sir Julian King, Commissaire européen à la sécurité de l'Union. In: Quelles menaces et quels enjeux après la chute du califat? Compte-rendu de la conférence internationale sur le terrorisme. CAT and CEP. https://f.hypotheses.org/wp-content/blogs.dir/2725/files/2020/01/CAT_conf7nov2019.pdf. Accessed 29 September 2021

Lamfalussy C, Laruelle J (2015) Jaak Raes (Sûreté de l'Etat): Savoir qui est rentré de Syrie, ce n'est pas si simple. https://www.lalibre.be/belgique/2015/02/07/jaak-raes-surete-de-letat-savoir-qui-est-rentre-de-syrie-ce-nest-pas-si-simple-2ZH6OSHTYFBCHFFICEL2QABG2M/. Accessed 29 September 2021

Laruelle J (2017) L'ombre du "gang de Roubaix" autour des frères Saouti. https://www.dhnet.be/actu/faits/l-ombre-du-gang-de-roubaix-autour-des-freres-saouti-59673121cd706e263ec7dcd8. Accessed 29 September 2021

Malet D (2018) The European experience with foreign fighters and returnees. In: Renard T, Coolsaet R (eds) Returnees: who are they, why are they (not) coming back and how should we deal with them? Egmont Paper 101. https://www.egmontinstitute.be/content/uploads/2018/02/egmont.papers.101_online_v1-3.pdf?type=pdf. Accessed 29 September 2021

Martin D (2018) German intelligence part of secret anti-terror unit targeting returning IS fighters—report. https://www.dw.com/en/german-intelligence-part-of-secret-anti-terror-unit-targeting-returning-is-fighters-report/a-42441378. Accessed 29 September 2021

Milton D (2020) Lessons from September 11 about the post-conflict threat posed by foreign terrorist fighters. Journal of Policing, Intelligence and Counter Terrorism 15(2):136–153

Nesser P (2021) Foiled Versus Launched Terror Plots: Some Lessons Learned. In: Key determinants of transnational terrorism in the era of Covid-19 and beyond. Trajectory, disruption and the way forward. Research Paper. Volume II. European Institute for Counter Terrorism and Conflict Prevention. https://www.eictp.eu/wp-content/uploads/2021/03/EICTP-Katalog-Langfassung-Terrorism-Vol-2-002.pdf. Accessed 29 September 2021

Nielsen N (2014) EU states adopt new counter-terrorism plan. EUObserver, 9 July. https://www.denederlandsegrondwet.nl/id/vjlbccvrllzj/nieuws/eu_states_adopt_new_counter_terrorism?ctx=vhcogs0sygx4&start_tab0=160. Accessed 29 September 2021

Quatremer J (2014) Djihadistes européens: "le danger est assez important pour empêcher les services de renseignements de dormir". https://www.liberation.fr/debats/2014/11/23/djihadistes-europeens-le-danger-est-assez-important-pour-empecher-les-services-de-renseignements-de-_1812980/. Accessed 29 September 2021

RAN (2017) RAN Manual: Responses to returnees: Foreign terrorist fighters and their families. Radicalisation Awareness Network (RAN). https://ec.europa.eu/home-affairs/system/files_en?file=2020-09/ran_br_a4_m10_en.pdf. Accessed 29 September 2021

Raudszus J (2020) The Strategy of Germany for Handling Foreign Fighters. Italian Institute For International Political Studies. https://www.ispionline.it/en/pubblicazione/strategy-germany-handling-foreign-fighters-24761. Accessed 29 September 2021

Renard T (2016) Bilateral, European and global: the 3 external layers of Belgium's counter- terrorism policy. In: Renard T (ed) Counterterrorism in Belgium: key challenges and policy options. Egmont Paper 89. http://www.thomasrenard.eu/uploads/6/3/5/8/6358199/egmont_paper_89_official_final.pdf. Accessed 29 September 2021

Renard T (2019) Returnees in the Maghreb: A European perspective. Security Policy Brief. Egmont Institute. http://www.thomasrenard.eu/uploads/6/3/5/8/6358199/spb120_-_returnees_maghreb.pdf. Accessed 29 September 2021

Renard T (2020) Overblown: Exploring the Gap Between the Fear of Terrorist Recidivism and the Evidence. CTC Sentinel 13(4):19–29

Renard T, Coolsaet R (2018a) Returnees: who are they, why are they (not) coming back and how should we deal with them? Egmont Paper 101, Egmont Institute, Brussels. https://www.egmontinstitute.be/content/uploads/2018a/02/egmont.papers.101_online_v1-3.pdf?type=pdf. Accessed 29 September 2021

Renard T, Coolsaet R (2018b) From the Kingdom to the caliphate and back: Returnees in Belgium. In: Renard T, Coolsaet R (eds) Returnees: who are they, why are they (not) coming back and how

should we deal with them? Egmont Paper 101. https://www.egmontinstitute.be/content/uploads/2018b/02/egmont.papers.101_online_v1-3.pdf?type=pdf. Accessed 29 September 2021
Renard T, Coolsaet R (2018c) Children in the Levant: Insights from Belgium on the dilemmas of repatriation and the challenges of reintegration. Security Policy Brief. https://www.egmontinstitute.be/children-in-the-levant-insights-from-belgium-on-the-dilemmas-of-repatriation-and-the-challenges-of-reintegration/. Accessed 29 September 2021
Renard T, Coolsaet R (2020) From bad to worse: The fate of European foreign fighters and families detained in Syria, one year after the Turkish offensive. Security Policy Brief. https://www.egmontinstitute.be/from-bad-to-worse-the-fate-of-european-foreign-fighters-and-families-detained-in-syria/. Accessed 29 September 2021
Roithmaier K (2019) Germany and its returning foreign terrorist fighters: New loss of citizenship law and the broader German repatriation landscape. ICCT Publications. https://icct.nl/publication/germany-and-its-returning-foreign-terrorist-fighters-new-loss-of-citizenship-law-and-the-broader-german-repatriation-landscape/. Accessed 29 September 2021
RTL (2016) Selon Erdogan, Ibrahim El Bakraoui a été extradé vers la Belgique qui l'a relâché: le parquet dément. https://www.rtl.be/info/belgique/faits-divers/selon-erdogan-ibrahim-el-bakraoui-a-ete-extrade-vers-la-belgique-qui-l-a-relache-le-parquet-dement-804612.aspx. Accessed 29 September 2021
Service Public Fédéral (2015) Plan d'action contre la radicalisation dans les prisons. Belgian Federal Ministry of Justice. https://justice.belgium.be/sites/default/files/downloads/Plland%27actionradicalisation-prison-FR.pdf. Accessed 27 September 2021
Silke A, Morrison J (2020) Re-offending by released terrorist prisoners: Separating hype from reality. ICCT Publications. https://icct.nl/publication/re-offending-by-released-terrorist-prisoners-separating-hype-from-reality/. Accessed 29 September 2021
Suc M (2018) Les espions de la terreur. HarperCollins, Paris
The Local (2019a) Sweden debates fate of returned foreign fighters. https://www.thelocal.se/20190224/sweden-debates-fate-of-returned-foreign-fighters/. Accessed 29 September 2021
The Local (2019b) 'It would be better if they had died in battle': Danish justice minister on returning Syria fighters. https://www.thelocal.dk/20190327/it-would-be-better-if-they-had-died-in-battle-danish-justice-minister-on-returning-syria-fighters/ Accessed 27 September 2021
Thomson D (2018) The returned. Polity Press, Cambridge
UN Security Council (2014) Resolution 2178 (2014), UN Doc. S/RES/2178
Van Wilgenburg W (2019) Dutch minister refuses US offer to help repatriate ISIS women and their children in Syria. https://www.kurdistan24.net/en/story/20692-Dutch-minister-refuses-US-offer-to-help-repatriate-ISIS-women-and-their-children-in-Syria. Accessed 29 September 2021
Vidino L et al (2017) Fear thy neighbor: Radicalization and jihadist attacks in the West. Italian Institute of For International Political Studies. https://www.ispionline.it/en/pubblicazione/fear-thy-neighbor-radicalization-and-jihadist-attacks-west-16784. Accessed 29 September 2021
VSSE (2019) Rapport annuel 2019. https://www.vsse.be/sites/default/files/paragraphs/1-ra2020-fr-version10-single-light.pdf. Accessed 29 September 2021
Yayla A (2019) Turkish ISIS and AQ Foreign Fighters: Reconciling the Numbers and Perception of the Terrorism Threat. Studies in Conflict & Terrorism. https://doi.org/10.1080/1057610X.2019.1628613

Chapter 3
Historical Responses to Foreign Fighters and Returnees

David Malet and Jason E. Fritz

Contents

Abstract This chapter examines the historical emergence of national policies and international instruments for addressing foreign fighters and returnees beginning in the eighteenth century and how the political considerations that guided them continue to shape contemporary state responses. We begin with an overview of recent scholarship about foreign fighting and how research indicates that various groups may be analysed comparatively. It proceeds with an examination of national and international policy responses, explaining the wide discrepancies as a function of the degree of political support or opposition of different regimes to foreign fighting in particular circumstances. We explain how past approaches differ from current national laws and international approaches. We find that supranational attempts to organise legal impediments to foreign fighting are group-specific that create barriers to stemming future foreign fighter mobilisation in support of future threats by requiring broad consensus. We conclude by identifying understudied and emerging areas of policies toward foreign fighters and returnees for future research.

D. Malet (✉)
School of Public Affairs, American University, Washington, DC, United States
e-mail: malet@american.edu

J. E. Fritz
Center for Advanced Governmental Studies, Johns Hopkins University, Washington, DC, United States
e-mail: jfritz16@jhu.edu

F. Capone et al. (eds.), *Returning Foreign Fighters: Responses, Legal Challenges and Ways Forward*, https://doi.org/10.1007/978-94-6265-571-3_3

Keywords Foreign Fighters · Returnees · Terrorism · United Nations Security Council Resolutions · Jihadis · Foreign Volunteers

3.1 Introduction: Learning from the Past

This chapter examines the historical emergence of national policies and international instruments for addressing foreign fighters and returnees beginning in the eighteenth century and how the political considerations that guided them continue to shape contemporary state responses. The potential for returning Islamic State (IS) foreign fighters to engage in extremist violence inspired the first binding international instruments obliging all states to prevent their citizens from becoming foreign fighters for certain organisations, repatriate them, and prosecute them. However, prior to the adoption of United Nations Security Council Resolutions 2178 (2014) and 2396 (2017) addressing "foreign terrorist fighters (FTF)", there had been two centuries of national laws and international enforcement efforts intended to constrain foreign fighters. The legacy is a patchwork of widely varying national responses and precedents that remain in effect, guiding policies toward FTF returnees as well as approaches to other foreign fighters who do not qualify as FTF under the terms of the Resolutions. It is, therefore, necessary to examine approaches to foreign fighters through history prior to Resolution 2178 to understand how countries respond to returnees today.

Identifying patterns of returnee behaviour and state responses to returnees prior to the twenty-first century, when law enforcement and intelligence agencies began to systematically track foreign fighters for jihadi groups, is difficult due to the lack of data available. Additionally, scholarly research on foreign fighters as a category of actors also only began to appear in the 2000s, and few are comparative beyond jihadis.[1] This chapter begins with an overview of recent scholarship about foreign fighting and how research indicates that various groups may be analysed comparatively. It proceeds with an examination of national and international policy responses, explaining the wide discrepancies as a function of the degree of political support or opposition of different regimes to foreign fighting in particular circumstances. We explain how past approaches differ from current national laws and international approaches. Finally, we identify understudied and emerging areas of policies toward foreign fighters and returnees for future research.

[1] Moore 2015, p. 396.

3.2 Who Counts as Foreign Fighters?

Foreign fighters are non-citizens of conflict states who join insurgencies during civil conflicts.[2] They have been commonplace in modern international history and are identifiable in more than one-quarter of insurgencies fighting for a variety of causes over the past two hundred years. Foreign mercenaries have served rulers throughout history, and many historical laws concerning foreign fighting have had mercenaries in mind. But records throughout the modern era reveal that foreign fighters often work for little money, or even spend personal fortunes to volunteer, and they include both combatants and those providing logistical and political support to rebels.[3] The common denominator is that the volunteers identify with rebels because of some shared socio-political identity interests that transcend national boundaries and which they have been persuaded to defend.[4]

Scholarship on foreign fighters as a distinct category of actors did not emerge until the 2000s in the wake of al Qaeda and IS actions against international forces occupying Afghanistan and Iraq. Comparative analyses of different foreign fighter groups, including historical ethnic and ideological movements and contemporary jihadis, have demonstrated functional similarities and consistent behaviour patterns across different foreign fighter groups. Just as 'terrorist' is considered a category of actor based on activity and legal distinction rather than an adherent to a particular cause, so can 'foreign fighters' and responses to them be examined across cases.[5]

Similarly, despite the existence of dozens of foreign fighter cohorts and hundreds of thousands of individuals, the first binding international instrument addressing foreign fighters as a distinct category and mandating member states to intervene against them came only in 2014 with Resolution 2178. And this measure did not include all foreign fighters, but only individuals affiliated with IS or al Qaeda were designated as FTF. The timing of the resolution coincided with the declaration of the IS caliphate in Syria and Iraq and its attraction of an estimated 40,000 fighters, volunteers, and family members.

Marrero Rocha notes that roughly twenty percent of foreign volunteers in IS were European Union nationals or residents, and that the magnitude of this cohort produced the impetus to require member states to address a threat that could span internal European borders.[6] The Council of Europe updated its 2005 Convention for

---

[2] Malet 2013, p. 9.

[3] For a detailed discussion of the similarities and differences between the characteristics of mercenaries and foreign fighters, and how they might be regarded differently in particular circumstances, see de Guttry et al. 2016, p. 156. Sommario notes that neither mercenaries nor foreign fighters who fight as insurgents against states have rights as prisoners of war under Additional Protocol I of the Geneva Convention (1977). However, because mercenaries are defined as motivated by private gain or material compensation, it is often difficult to charge foreign fighters with being mercenaries.

[4] Malet 2013, pp. 45–48.

[5] See Acciai 2021; Arielli 2018; de Guttry et al. 2016; Malet 2013; Koch 2021.

[6] Marrero Rocha et al. 2019, p. 46.

the Suppression of Terrorism, which criminalised participation in terrorist organisations, to require member states to enact criminal statutes that would bring them into compliance with Resolution 2178.[7]

However, it is worth noting that there had been larger cohorts of foreign fighters than IS in the previous century: Communists aligned with the Soviet Union who fought in the Russian and Spanish Civil Wars, who had posed potentially even graver threats to European security. Additionally, it had then been a quarter-century since the founding of al Qaeda by jihadi foreign fighters in Afghanistan, so the threat was not novel. What had changed was that 'foreign fighters' were now a recognised and studied category, and research argued that some returnees posed an elevated terrorism risk. The large numbers of IS volunteers raised the probability of an attack, and several returnees to Belgium and France conducted high profile, high casualty attacks during this timeframe.[8]

Prior national and international efforts to address foreign fighters also came in response to large cohorts appearing at different points since the late eighteenth century, and many of them remain in place. Given the limited scope of Resolutions 2178 and 2396 to designated FTF, these other measures serve as the basis for international actions—or inactions—against other contemporary foreign fighters. These include hundreds of volunteers fighting IS on behalf of Kurdish and other minority groups, thousands in the Ukraine Civil War, and others in less-heralded conflicts in countries including Myanmar and the Central African Republic.

Resolutions 2178 and 2396 do not mandate specific criminal charges for individuals serving as foreign fighters, or even as FTF, but all states are obligated to repatriate their citizens and prosecute suspects charged with related activities such as recruitment and facilitation. The specified crimes and the punishments remain domestic affairs in individual countries, although Resolution 2396 urges for the harmonisation of laws. Also, at the international level, the International Criminal Court only has authority over nationals of states that are party to the Rome Statute and jurisdiction in non-member states in particular circumstances of international agreement.[9] Therefore, without a primary source of authority or common statutes on FTF, let alone foreign fighters for other causes, it is worth studying the evolution of responses to fighters and returnees because international law remains a patchwork of initiatives that must be understood in the context of their historical precedents.

There has been little systematic analysis of the post-conflict militant activities of returned foreign fighters other than jihadis to date. Individual jihadis such as the founding generation of al Qaeda persisted in the field long beyond the wars for which they enlisted ended, in part because of the policies of Arab states that did not permit them to return. However, the communist foreign fighter movement persisted

[7] Marrero Rocha et al. 2019, p. 47.

[8] Hegghammer 2013; Byman and Shapiro 2015; Malet and Hayes 2020.

[9] Thomson 1994, p. 55; Heinsch 2016, pp. 165, 179; Dubey 2021. The Rome Statute gives the Court jurisdiction when non-members states agree or under referral by the United Nations Security Council. Dubey notes the Court jurisdiction has recently claimed full jurisdiction in cases where one alleged crime takes place in a member state. This would apply to FTF who transited member states en route to Syria, recruited in member states, etc.

for decades longer and had tens of thousands more members than the jihadis to date, and yet returnees were apparently reintegrated with few incidents. In other cases, such as ethnic diaspora involvement in homeland wars, the foreign fighters exhibited similar patterns in which a notable few continued militant activity at home or abroad, but most returnees left no subsequent records of note. These findings indicate that only exceptional returned foreign fighters pose security threats and that state policies toward returnees likely plays a deciding factor in whether or not they remain engaged in violent extremism.[10]

3.3 Foreign Fighter Returnees from the 'New World'

Modern national laws restricting foreign fighters began in the newly formed United States at the end of the eighteenth century, despite the lauded role of the foreign volunteers who had been instrumental in winning the American Revolution (1775–1783). As with subsequent cases of foreign fighting, the exact number of them is unknown due to the lack of available records and debates over who should count as foreign or as true volunteers as opposed to military volunteers who may have been conscripted to fight in America. The latter category includes several hundred Black Haitian French colonial subjects who fought as a militia against the British in Georgia, some of whom would later be instrumental in the success of Haiti's Revolution in 1804, including the future king, Henri Christophe.[11]

The approximately 500 European private volunteers in the American Revolution crossed the ocean to fight for various causes, ranging from philosophical beliefs in liberty to a desire to strike a blow against the British Empire.[12] But some evidently had more pragmatic nationalist and anti-imperial aspirations. One famous case was Tadeusz Kosciszuko of Poland, who honed his engineering skills for the Continental Army, designing fortifications at West Point and besieging the British in the Carolinas, before returning home to lead nationalist uprisings against the Russian Empire. Presaging the weaving of the al Qaeda network in the Afghan wars two hundred years later, he maintained contacts and strategised with other American Revolution returnees, such as John Paul Jones of Scotland, father of the United States Navy, who had been in the service of Russia after being denounced as a pirate in Britain.[13]

Not only were there no international standards for addressing returnees, but national policies were erratic, perhaps because they were autocratic. For example, the Marquis de Lafayette in 1777 disobeyed a royal decree by Louis XVI that French officers should stay out of the American Revolution, but was nonetheless welcomed back by the monarch two years later after his military successes and permitted to

---

[10] Arielli 2018, pp. 149–150; Malet 2015, pp. 455, 467; Malet 2020.

[11] Bhatia 2015.

[12] Malet 2018, p. 9.

[13] Storozynski 2011, pp. 189–191.

return with more war materiel. Although caught up as a returnee in the tumult of the subsequent decades of French politics, Lafayette would retain a sufficient reputation from his foreign fighter exploits that he was known as "the Hero of the Two Worlds".[14]

Later in the nineteenth century, Italian nationalist Giuseppe Garibaldi would also enjoy the same title. Initially exiled because of his radical politics, he gained combat experience and built a paramilitary force fighting in Brazil and Uruguay, members of which accompanied his return to fighting in the International Legion for the Risorgimento. As a returnee, Garibaldi became a national hero and an international icon of liberation. However, he also became a potential liability for the fledging Italian government when he, and his sons, after his death, encouraged their "Red Shirt" followers to become foreign fighters in other conflicts such as the Franco-Prussian War and uprisings against the Ottoman Empire in the Balkans.[15]

Although Garibaldi is the most famous European foreign fighter who participated in nineteenth-century uprisings in South America, the nexus between local activists and European recruits began in wars of national liberation far earlier. In 1806, Francisco de Miranda enlisted hundreds of fighters during a tour of Europe in his unsuccessful bid to wrest Venezuela from the Spanish Empire. Miranda's efforts, launched from the United States but funded by Great Britain for strategic reasons, were aided by political philosophers Tom Paine and Jeremy Bentham, who also provided intellectual and logistical transnational support to the anti-colonial insurgencies in America and Greece, respectively. The success of the American Revolution had transformed the nominal pursuit of liberty into a legitimate political cause, triggering liberal and nationalist revolutions in Europe and Latin America. And while Miranda failed in his efforts to launch successful revolutions with external support in Venezuela, Argentina, and Uruguay, he was only a forerunner to more famous names.[16]

Simon Bolivar organised approximately 7000 volunteers from the British Isles, mostly unemployed soldiers from the recently concluded Napoleonic Wars. Beginning in 1819, two British Legions and an Irish Legion under John Devereux fought victoriously, and still more were recruited from Italy and elsewhere in continental Europe.[17] Records indicate that nearly half of these fighters deserted or resigned, suggesting that monetary reward may not have been the primary motivation for the foreign fighters despite the usual descriptions of them as mercenaries. Flores argues that "it seems the great majority of volunteers…joined the armed conflicts for idealistic or psychological reasons, not for monetary reward." Instead, their motivations were "ideological" (pro-liberty) and "practical" (dealing a strategic defeat to Spain, Britain's enemy at the time).[18] Moreover, British writers such as Jeremy Bentham recruited volunteers for the cause. He would continue facilitating foreign fighter

[14] Leepson 2012, pp. 11–13.
[15] Arielli 2018, pp. 214–215.
[16] Flores 2016, pp. 32, 35.
[17] Thomson 1994, p. 88.
[18] Flores 2016, p. 35.

recruitment in the Greek War of Independence, fundraising to send Philhellenes to fight alongside British volunteer Lord Byron.[19] Philhellene supporters would also subsequently travel to Mexico as separatists in the 1835–36 Texas Revolution.[20]

The networks of foreign fighters for national liberation from European empires in the eighteenth and nineteenth centuries had similarities to modern jihadis fighting against the Western international order, and so did the returnees. Some of the prominent European foreign fighters in the Americas, including Garibaldi, Casimir Pulaski in the American Revolution, and Herman Ehrenberg in Texas, had already been active in militant nationalist movements at home and were fleeing persecution by the authorities. Unknown numbers used their war experience to build connections and skills which they planned to bring to bear for their causes after their return. Political scientist Sidney Tarrow describes this type of militant expatriate as "birds of passage" who are simply using countries of refuge as foreign staging grounds for their cause.[21] Today this use of foreign fighting as training for domestic attacks, a phenomenon known as 'blowback', is the principal concern about returning jihadis.

However, as with the jihadis, the names of most other foreign fighters are lost to history because they made no notable impact as returnees. There have been handfuls of individuals among every cohort of foreign fighters who returned and engaged in terrorism or other activity supporting militant groups. There are others who become "career foreign fighters", moving between different groups and frequently into leadership positions despite their lack of ties to local rebels because of their international reputations and connections.[22] Some of them, including Garibaldi and al Qaeda progenitor Abdullah Azzam, also envisioned standing forces of foreign fighters that could be deployed to trouble spots as needed.[23] It has 'bled out' to other conflicts perhaps more than 'blow back' from returnees that have shaped international responses to foreign fighting.

3.4 Responses to Foreign Fighters and Returnees

During the nineteenth century, a number of countries adopted laws that would remove political rights, ranging from the loss of citizenship to foreign military service.[24] While the growth of nationalism and national armies undoubtedly delegitimated mercenary service to other sovereigns, the motives for banning foreign service—and foreign fighting—were due to pragmatic foreign policy calculations about avoiding national liability for the actions of individual citizens. With penalties against foreign fighting enacted, by definition, returnees would necessarily be criminals subject to

[19] Malet 2018, p. 7.
[20] Malet 2013, pp. 67–69, 73.
[21] Tarrow 2005, p. 51.
[22] Daymon et al. 2020.
[23] Hegghammer 2020.
[24] Thomson 1994, p. 88.

prosecution. Yet despite the threat, as with Resolution 2178, tens of thousands of individuals remained undeterred from fighting for various causes. One reason for this may be that penalties, and whether states even sought them, remained wholly inconsistent both between national governments and by different states depending on the political affiliations of different foreign fighter groups.

3.4.1 Legal Statutes

In 1794, the United States passed the Neutrality Act, which Thomson describes as "the first domestic law in the world" that prevented citizens from joining foreign military forces. The Act prohibited citizens or inhabitants of the United States from accepting commissions or enlisting in the service of foreign states. It was further amended in 1817 to include fighting for foreign "colonies, districts, or people".[25] The statute, which remains in effect, also established criminal offenses for being involved in a war against a friendly nation, and for foreign military recruitment or enlistment within the United States. It remained legal, however, to travel to elsewhere to join foreign forces that do not otherwise fall afoul of the law.[26]

On the surface, it would seem puzzling that the United States would initiate such a ban after it had recently won independence in large part because of foreign fighter assistance and at a time when its norms of national identity would have been particularly weak. But the fact that the newly independent states of Latin America also quickly banned their citizens from participating in revolutions in neighbouring countries is telling. The new states of the New World were in weak positions during their post-colonial periods, and they sought to pursue neutrality policies to avoid 'foreign entanglements' that might risk their diplomatic positions. The Neutrality Act stemmed from the presence of Americans on French ships fighting against the British Navy, and the response of the United States was to indict returnees from foreign conflicts because they threatened national security.[27]

Penalising returnees for violating neutrality and national interests, rather than violating sovereignty and norms of citizenship, became the organising principle for addressing returning foreign fighters in the two centuries before Resolution 2178. The diplomatic balancing of the Concert of Europe and emerging norms of sovereignty precipitated these changes among the Great Powers of the time. In 1814, Great Britain signed a treaty with Spain in which it agreed to prevent its subjects from fighting for governments in Latin America and threatened to suspend the pay of any military veterans who did so. Although the regime was expanded in 1819 with the Foreign Enlistment Act to prevent subjects from fighting on behalf of any entity "assuming to exercise the powers of government in any foreign country", none of the measures

[25] Thomson 1994, p. 78.

[26] See Footnote 25.

[27] Thomson 1994, pp. 82, 87, 88.

were effective.[28] By 1870, enough Britons had volunteered in the American Civil War that the looming Franco-Prussian War that Parliament was compelled to update the Act to apply to all subjects of the Empire. Although the last prosecution under the law in Britain occurred in 1896, it remained in effect until 1937 in Canada until it was superseded by a new law criminalising participation on either side of the Spanish Civil War.[29]

3.4.2 *Politics and Prosecutions*

By the time of the Spanish Civil War, approximately two-thirds of the countries in the world had passed regulations prohibiting their citizens from serving abroad. Certain individuals might be lauded upon their returns by their governments for serving as foreign volunteers or mercenaries when their activities aligned with the national interest. After Nigeria outlawed volunteer pilots and medics aiding the rebels in the Biafra War (1967–1970), France not only did not prosecute, but it lionised its citizens who ignored the edict and founded Médecins sans Frontières (Doctors without Borders) to continue their work.[30] In 1975, the United Kingdom granted an exemption to criminal penalties under the Foreign Enlistment Act to permit recruitment of British professional mercenaries by the anti-Communist National Front for the Liberation of Angola (FNLA).[31]

Responses to different foreign fighters in the Yugoslav Wars of the 1990s demonstrate that assessments of threat, strategic interest, and political support determine whether foreign fighter returnees are regarded as threats or heroes. The roughly 5000 Muslim foreign fighters who volunteered to be mujahidin for Bosnia, some of whom had bled-out from Afghanistan and other conflicts, were tolerated by the West while they were useful for fighting the Yugoslavian Federal forces and Serb extremist militias. But once the war had ended, and the United States demanded their removal as a security threat, most were dispersed. However, none faced prosecutions for their actions in either Western or Arab states. At the same time, British and American mercenaries, adventurers, and both left and right-wing extremists who volunteered for Croatian rebel forces were permitted to come and go for multiple tours with no follow-up.[32] And the several hundred diaspora Albanians, mostly from Germany and the United States, who joined the Kosovo Liberation Army (KLA) as the Atlantic Brigade faced no sanctions for displaying the flags of their countries of residence while fighting the sovereign Yugoslav Federal Army. The American contingent was honoured by members of Congress.[33]

---

[28] Thomson 1994, p. 57.

[29] Thomson 1994, p. 81; Howard and Reynolds 1986, p. 13.

[30] Thomson 1994, pp. 82, 89, 93.

[31] Kinsey 2006, p. 49.

[32] Arielli 2018, p. 183.

[33] Hockenos 2003, pp. 238–261.

However, when they were deemed to be threats to national interests, foreign fighters in the nineteenth and twentieth centuries faced the same consequences of extra-legal detention or refusal to permit repatriation that IS volunteers faced in the twenty-first century. The strategy of forestalling blowback by invalidating the citizenship of foreign fighters and attempting to detain them overseas has a precedent more than a century older than the IS caliphate. More than two thousand European nationals of various nationalities became foreign fighters on the rebel Boer side in the South African War (Second Boer War) during 1899–1902. British authorities asserted that detained foreign fighters had lost their rights to consular support by violating their countries' neutrality agreements, and kept them in offshore prison camps, with repatriation in some cases taking years beyond the end of the war. Foreign fighters who deserted and made their way to South African cities were deported as likely security threats.[34]

These wide variations in approach presaged the twenty-first century debates over the repatriation of IS volunteers and their families, and different standards of treatment for returned foreign fighters for various causes. International instruments, prior to and including Resolution 2178 and 2396, concerning non-state foreign participants in armed conflicts require repatriation and prosecution by countries of origin. For example, the International Convention Against the Recruitment, Use, Financing and Training of Mercenaries, introduced in 1989 and ratified in 2001 partly in response to foreign fighter cases like Angola, requires that detained suspect's home countries be notified immediately to make arrangements to repatriate them for prosecution.[35] But this approach, as with the agreements on FTF, assumes that states will facilitate the return of their citizens rather than removing their citizenship and transferring the burden to the state where the suspect is detained. Returned mercenaries might facilitate recruitment into their organisation just as some returned foreign fighters do, but the latter is perceived to be a greater security risk because of concerns of domestic terrorism, and during the IS era, many states have attempted to avoid repatriation.

Although the precedent has not been held for IS foreign fighters and supporters, in the largest recorded cases of foreign fighters, the international community worked to repatriate the combatants even though they were also deemed to be high-risk for domestic plots and radicalisation. The International Brigades (IB) in the Spanish Civil War worked directly under the leadership of the Communist International, which reported directly to the Soviet Union. As with IS, foreign fighters in the IB included men and women as medical volunteers or propagandists, and other individuals who claimed that they had gone to perform civilian services for the Spanish public.[36] Nonetheless, all were suspected of being Communists or sympathisers at a time when most Western governments viewed Bolshevism and Marxist subversion as

[34] Kennedy and Holdridge 2020, pp. 112, 121.

[35] International Convention Against the Recruitment, Use, Financing and Training of Mercenaries, United Nations Treaty Collection 2001, pp. 4–5.

[36] Malet 2013, pp. 112, 121.

bigger national security threats than the fascist powers the volunteers had gone to fight.[37]

There was, in fact, blowback and bleed out from the IB, although the impact was negligible in the West. Roughly one hundred Chinese Communists joined the IB in Spain. Some returned to fight with Mao Zedong's forces in the Chinese Civil War. Enough IB veterans of different nationalities joined the estimated 40,000 foreign volunteers among Mao's troops that foreign physicians were known as "Spanish Doctors" regardless of their nationalities.[38]

In addition to domestic security threats from returning battle-tested and networked would-be revolutionaries, the lessons of the First World War and the fraying peace of the 1930s provided most countries with reasons to maintain an official distance from the proxy war in Spain. All of the great European powers of the 1930s participated in a Non-Intervention Committee established by the League of Nations to control entry into Spain, discourage volunteers, and facilitate the withdrawal of those who had already deployed.[39] In September 1938, the League of Nations finally brokered a withdrawal of foreign forces from Spain, not only coordinating the repatriation of 10,000 IB fighters to their home countries but even providing each of them with small amounts of financial support so that they could reintegrate effectively.[40]

Various countries, including the United States and Canada, passed domestic neutrality laws criminalising participation in the war or providing material support, although it appears that law enforcement used these principally as deterrents and to stop volunteers from traveling rather than to prosecute returned fighters.[41] As with IS foreign fighters, the burden of evidence was one obstacle. The United Kingdom Director of Public Prosecutions did not prosecute British returnees because it believed that it would be too difficult to gather evidence from Spain for criminal trials.[42]

There do not appear to have been efforts to penalise IB returnees in most instances. United States consular officials in Spain aided Americans deserting the IB with repatriation.[43] However, American returnees were not permitted to serve in combat units during most of the Second World War despite being among the only Americans with combat experience, and some IB returnees and domestic supporters were kept on watch lists for decades.[44] And some did remain engaged in militant politics, with no further legal repercussions, including providing materiel and financial support for pro-Communist foreign volunteers in the Nicaraguan Civil War during the 1980s.[45]

[37] Gerassi 1986, p. 14.

[38] Jones 2016.

[39] Howard and Reynolds 1986, pp. 13–14.

[40] Richardson 1982, p. 73.

[41] Rosenstone 1996, p. 90.

[42] Kinsey 2006, p. 135.

[43] Carroll 1994, p. 148.

[44] Carroll et al. 2006, pp. 45–46.

[45] Nelson and Hendricks 1996, p. 355; Malet 2020, p. 45.

3.4.3 Responses to Jihadis Prior to Resolution 2178

Much like the Spanish Civil War, the Soviet invasion of Afghanistan in 1979 initiated the mobilisation of foreign fighters, in this case, jihadis, that led and recruited a generation or more of fellow travellers. Responding to calls to defend Afghan Muslims against the Soviet occupation, tens of thousands of fighters trained and deployed to engage in an array of activities, including actual fighting, logistics support to rebels, or humanitarian works.[46] Caught up in the politics of the late Cold War, these fighters enjoyed state support. The United States directly trained and equipped them and permitted leaders to recruit from within the United States.[47] Pakistan and Saudi Arabia played essential roles in hosting and financing these fighters.[48] Training camps were established in Pakistan, Iran, Egypt, and China.[49]

Many states condemned the Soviet invasion and refused to take action to prevent foreign fighter mobilisation from supporting the rebellion. As the war wound down, Western states did not appear to see these fighters as a threat. There was no known jihadi animus against Western states, and the forerunners to modern terrorist groups did not appear to view the Western world as anything more than a source of funds and recruits.[50] Their operational focus was, until the 1990s, myopic on the Middle East, North Africa, and South Asia. These fighters were generally not viewed as threats, and no new major legal actions were taken against them.[51] Many returned home, while others migrated to new jihadi battlegrounds in Somalia, Bosnia, and Chechnya.

Much like in Afghanistan, foreign fighters came to Bosnia with the purpose of defending the Muslim population there from Western atrocities. During the course of the war, it is estimated that between a few hundred and a few thousand fighters mobilised, primarily from the Arab world.[52] Increasingly radicalized, many of these fighters were expelled after the war. Many returned home, but the legal climate was changing as states dealt with a global rise in terrorist attacks and some returnees were arrested, such as in Saudi Arabia.[53] These arrests were typically in the interest of the origin state's security interests rather than a broader interest in stemming foreign fighters.

Bosnia was not the only Balkan state targeted by foreign fighters. Nearly 500 individuals fought in Croatian armed groups in Croatia and Bosnia.[54] There is no record of any of these fighters facing prosecution upon return to the states of origin

---

[46] Malet 2013, pp. 174–178.

[47] Byman 2019, pp. 27–28.

[48] Byman 2019, pp. 30–31.

[49] Malet 2013, p. 163.

[50] Nesser 2015, p. 32.

[51] Govier and Boutland 2020, p. 94.

[52] Byman 2019, p. 45.

[53] Byman 2019, p. 53.

[54] Arielli 2012, p. 2.

for the act of having been foreign fighters.[55] The war in Chechnya also attracted a number of foreign fighters. Approximately 160 fighters joined the first war from 1994 to 1996, including some Afghan-Arabs.[56] Another few hundred engaged in the second Chechen war from 1999 to 2009.[57] Many of these fighters transitioned to other conflicts, such as Iraq and later Syria, as Russian oppression squashed the Chechen insurgency.

The terrorist attacks of 11 September 2001 resulted in the United Nations passing a Security Council Resolution (UNSCR 1373/2001) that encouraged Member States to pass legislation to make terrorist activity and travelling to commit terrorist activity illegal. The resolution targeted terrorism specifically, not foreign fighters, and without establishing definitions. The spate of new anti-terrorism legislation that followed appears to have had little effect on stemming the flow of foreign fighters to conflict zones. As the American war in Iraq continued after 2003, at least a few thousand foreign fighters mobilised to combat the occupation.[58] Yet, little was done to stem this flow. Foreigners caught in Iraq were tried in Iraqi courts, while the United States applied diplomatic pressure on the states providing fighters or transit for the fighters.[59] The legal repercussions were limited to terrorist activity itself and states had few tools to prevent mobilisation. Many of the foreign fighters in Iraq during this time period helped create the organisation that eventually became IS.

Despite major mobilisations in Afghanistan in the 1980s, in the Balkans and the Caucasus in the 1990s, and in Iraq in the 2000s, states produced few tools to prevent or punish foreign fighters. In the case of the Soviet-Afghan War, foreign fighters received material support from states that would now consider their activities illegal and near-term politics trumped the growing threat. The only major change to legal instruments between the Spanish Civil War and the rise of IS was in the aftermath of the 9/11 attacks, but those changes were focused specifically on terrorism and were not uniformly enforced while focusing mostly on internal security and only when necessary, diplomatic relations.

3.5 Conclusion: Looking to the Future

Foreign fighters have been a facet of conflict for centuries, but the international community did not conceive of them as such until the 2000s and the Iraq War. Because of this, few supranational measures were taken to prevent their mobilisation prior to 2014 to address the mass of fighters joining IS. After 2001 and the 9/11 attacks, major steps were taken to prevent terrorism and travelling to commit terrorism, but not foreign fighting. Even the 2014 resolution specifically targets fighters joining al

[55] Arielli 2012, pp. 13–15.

[56] Moore and Tumelty 2008, p. 418.

[57] Bakke 2014, p. 166.

[58] Hewitt and Kelley-Moore 2009, p. 211.

[59] Oppell 2007.

Qaeda and IS and not foreign fighters universally. The historical record suggests that returning foreign fighters were often left to themselves, unless considered a threat to the state to which they returned. However, the record is not clear on why states do not outlaw foreign fighting outright, but it is reasonable to expect that states in an anarchic system would wish to reserve the right to support these activities when it suits them. The implication is that supranational measures will continue to target specific organisations and will require all major powers to agree on each specific organisation. This was successful against IS, but that does not guarantee success against the next major threat to regional or global stability.

While foreign fighters for various causes have recorded being disillusioned by their former comrades or beliefs, there is one subset that has not been analysed: foreign fighters who were kicked out of their groups in the middle of the conflict. There are records of individuals who were 'expelled' or 'asked to leave' from groups ranging from foreign fighter units in the Texas Revolution to Al-Muhajiroun to IS. Whether for ideological disloyalty or unacceptable crimes, there is untapped information about expelled foreign fighters that may prove useful.[60]

Another understudied factor of returnees is their connections to facilitators and supply networks of materiel. Mandel notes that in the twenty-first century, for the first time since the emergence of the nation-state, more weapons are in the hands of private parties than governments.[61] This includes foreign fighter groups and their roles in transporting weapons between insurgencies and terrorist networks. Small arms proliferation is an under-examined facet of the growing prevalence of foreign fighters since the late twentieth century.

One other area for future research is the role of foreign fighters on state foreign policy. The history of foreign fighting is replete with states using groups of fighters as proxies, or to pacify domestic political audiences. Many of the United States' conflicts in the War on Terror have been waged against fighters from ostensible allies, such as Saudi Arabia, Tunisia, Kuwait. Foreign fighters surely created difficulties in diplomacy between states, but the extent and effect are understudied. The study of foreign fighters focuses heavily on the supply and demand of fighters, but not nearly enough on the politics around the phenomenon. Politics that, as seen in this chapter, typically result in few foreign fighters having been prosecuted for their actions prior to the rise of IS.

---

[60] Brown 1999, pp. 294, 305; Dodwell et al. 2016, pp. 35–36.

[61] Mandel 2002, p. 7.

References

Books, Chapters in Books, (Online) Articles

Acciai E (2021) Garibaldi's Radical Legacy: Traditions of War Volunteering in Southern Europe (1861–1945). Routledge, London

Arielli N (2012) In Search of Meaning: Foreign Volunteers in the Croatian Armed Forces, 1991–95. Contemporary European History 21:1–17

Arielli N (2018) From Byron to Bin Laden: A History of Foreign War Volunteers. Harvard University Press, Cambridge, Massachusetts

Bakke K (2014) Help Wanted? The Mixed Record of Foreign Fighters in Domestic Insurgencies. International Security 38:150–187

Bhatia P (2015) How Haitians Helped Win the American Revolution. https://www.ozy.com/true-and-stories/how-haitians-helped-win-the-american-revolution/61439/. Accessed 20 September 2021

Brown G (1999) The New Orleans Greys. Republic of Texas Press, United States

Byman D (2019) Road Warriors: Foreign Fighters in the Armies of Jihad. Oxford University Press, New York

Byman D, Shapiro J (2015) Be Afraid. Be a Little Afraid. The Threat of Terrorism from Western Foreign Fighters in Iraq and Syria. Policy Paper 34, The Brookings Institution, Washington DC

Carroll P (1994) The Odyssey of the Abraham Lincoln Brigade: Americans in the Spanish Civil War. Stanford University Press, Palo Alto, California

Carroll P, Nash M, Small M (eds) (2006) The Good Fight Continues: World War II Letters from the Abraham Lincoln Brigade. New York University Press, New York

Daymon C, de Roy van Zuijdewijn J, Malet D (2020) Career Foreign Fighters: Expertise Transmission across Insurgencies. RESOLVE Research Paper, United States Institute of Peace, Washington DC

de Guttry A, Capone F, Paulussen C (eds) (2016) Foreign Fighters under International Law and Beyond. T.M.C. Asser Press, The Hague

Dodwell B, Milton D, Rassler D (2016) The Caliphate's Global Workforce: An Inside Look at the Islamic State's Foreign Fighter Paper Trail. United States Military Combatting Terrorism Center, United States Military Academy, West Point, New York

Dubey U (2021) Jurisdiction of the International Criminal Court Over Non-party States: Legitimate or Ultra Vires? https://www.jurist.org/commentary/2021/05/utkarsh-dubey-icc-jurisdiction-over-nonparty-states/. Accessed 21 September 2021

Flores M (2016) Foreign Fighters Involvement in National and International Wars: A Historical Survey. In: de Guttry A et al. (eds) Foreign Fighters under International Law and Beyond. T.M.C. Asser Press, The Hague, pp 27–47

Gerassi J (1986) The Premature Anti-Fascists. Praeger, New York

Govier T, Boutland D (2020) Dilemmas Regarding Returning ISIS Fighters. Ethics & Global Politics 13:93–107

Hegghammer T (2013) Should I Stay or Should I Go? Explaining Variation in Western Jihadists' Choice Between Domestic and Foreign Fighting. American Political Science Review 107:1–13

Hegghammer T (2020) The Caravan: Abdallah Azzam and the Rise of Global Jihad. Cambridge University Press, Cambridge

Heinsch R (2016) Foreign Fighters and International Criminal Law. In: de Guttry A et al. (eds) Foreign Fighters under International Law and Beyond. T.M.C. Asser Press, The Hague, pp 161–185

Hewitt C, Kelley-Moore J (2009) Foreign Fighters in Iraq: A Cross-National Analysis of Jihadism. Terrorism and Political Violence 21:211–220

Hockenos P (2003) Homeland Calling: Exile, Patriotism, and the Balkan Wars. Cornell University Press, Ithaca, New York

Howard V, Reynolds M (1986) The MacKenzie-Papineau Battalion: The Canadian Contingent in the Spanish Civil War. Carleton University Press, Ottawa
Jones G (2016) The Chinese Volunteers Who Fought in the Spanish Civil War – Their Amazing Courage and Obscure Fates. https://www.scmp.com/magazines/post-magazine/long-reads/article/1989792/chinese-volunteers-who-fought-spanish-civil-war. Accessed 24 September 2021
Kennedy WM, Holdridge C (2020) The Recognized Adjunct of Modern Armies: Foreign Volunteerism and the South African War. European Review of History: Revue européenne d'histoire 27:111–133
Kinsey C (2006) Corporate Soldiers and International Security: The Rise of Private Military Companies. Oxon, England
Koch A (2021) The Non-Jihadi Foreign Fighters: Western Right-Wing and Left-Wing Extremists in Syria. Terrorism and Political Violence 33:669–696
Leepson M (2012) An Adopted Hero, An Adopted Son. GW Magazine 22:11–13
Malet D (2013) Foreign Fighters: Transnational Identity in Civil Conflicts. Oxford University Press, New York
Malet D (2015) Foreign Fighter Mobilization and Persistence in a Global Context. Terrorism and Political Violence 27:454–473
Malet D (2018) The European Experience with Foreign Fighters and Returnees. In: Renard T, Coolsaet R (eds) Returnees: Who Are They, Why Are They (Not) Coming Back and How Should We Deal with Them? Egmont Institute, Brussels, pp 6–18
Malet D (2020) Workers of the World, Unite! Communist Foreign Fighters 1917–91. European Review of History: Revue européenne d'histoire 27:33–53
Malet D, Hayes R (2020) Foreign Fighter Returnees: An Indefinite Threat? Terrorism and Political Violence, 32:1617–1635
Mandel R (2002) Armies Without States and the Privatization of Security. Lynne Reinner, Boulder, Colorado
Marrero Rocha I, Humberto M, Mendoza T (eds) (2019) Jihadism, Foreign Fighters and Radicalization in the EU: Legal, Functional and Psychosocial Responses. Routledge, London
Moore C (2015) Foreign Bodies: Transnational Activism, the Insurgency in the North Caucasus and 'Beyond'. Terrorism and Political Violence 27:395–415
Moore C, Tumelty P (2008) Foreign Fighters and the Case of Chechnya: A Critical Assessment. Studies in Conflict & Terrorism 31:412–433
Nelson C, Hendricks J (eds) (1996) Madrid 1937: Letters of the Abraham Lincoln Battalion from the Spanish Civil War. Routledge, New York
Nesser P (2015) Islamist Terrorism in Europe: A History. Hurst & Company, London
Oppell R (2007) Foreign Fighters in Iraq are Tied to Allies of U.S.: Saudi Arabia and Libya. https://www.nytimes.com/2007/11/22/world/middleeast/22fighters.html. Accessed 20 September 2021
Richardson D (1982) The Comintern Army. University Press of Kentucky, Lexington
Rosenstone R (1996) Crusade of the Left: The Lincoln Battalion in the Spanish Civil War. Pegasus, New York
Storozynski A (2011) Kosciuszko Ksiaze chlopow. W.A.B., Warsaw, Poland
Tarrow S (2005) The New Transnational Activism. Cambridge University Press, New York
Thomson J (1994) Mercenaries, Pirates, and Sovereigns: State-Building and Extraterritorial Violence in Modern Europe. Princeton University Press, Princeton

Other Documents

International Convention Against the Recruitment, Use, Financing and Training of Mercenaries, opened for signature 4 December 1989, 2163 UNTS 75 (entered into force 20 October 2001)

Chapter 4
The Status of Foreign Fighters' Family Members Under Counter-Terrorism Law and International Humanitarian Law: Overcoming the Victims/Perpetrators Dichotomy?

Francesca Capone

Contents

Abstract Following the military defeat of the Islamic State of Iraq and Syria (ISIS), the States of nationality of the individuals who flocked to the Middle East to join the group have been urged to develop a proactive approach to deal with the situation. At present, family members of ISIS fighters are detained in improvised prisons in Iraq as well as in overcrowded refugee camps in Syria, under the authority of the Syrian Democratic Forces (SDF). As States of origin, including European ones, remain mainly concerned about their national security and in most instances oppose a blanket refusal to any request for repatriation submitted by their nationals, one of the main issues to address is whether the wives and children of foreign fighters (FFs) should be regarded as 'victims' of terrorism or 'perpetrators/terrorists'. Although such a complex question would clearly deserve to be analysed adopting a multidisciplinary approach, the scope of the present chapter is to determine if and how international law can contribute to shedding light on the matter. More in detail, after a brief analysis of the roles played by foreign women and children affiliated with ISIS, this chapter will

F. Capone (✉)
Scuola Superiore Sant'Anna, Piazza Martiri della Libertà 33, 56127 Pisa, Italy
e-mail: f.capone@santannapisa.it

F. Capone et al. (eds.), *Returning Foreign Fighters: Responses, Legal Challenges and Ways Forward*, https://doi.org/10.1007/978-94-6265-571-3_4

reflect on how they fit within the current international legal framework, looking in particular at international counter-terrorism (CT) law and international humanitarian law (IHL) and discussing if and how the latter can help to overcome some of the shortcomings of the former.

Keywords Foreign Fighters · Women · Children · Victims · Terrorists/perpetrators · Counter-terrorism law · International humanitarian law

4.1 Introduction

After the military defeat of the Islamic State of Iraq and Syria (ISIS), Ms Shamima Begum—a UK citizen who joined the Islamic State group aged 15—became the living example of how foreign fighters' (FFs)[1] States of nationality are struggling to deal with women and children allegedly affiliated with this terrorist group and to which degree the debate concerning their status (as 'victims' or 'perpetrators') and role within the group is polarised.[2] As is well known, the FFs phenomenon represents one of the most challenging aspects of the current global fight against terrorism.[3] Even though the participation of foreigners in armed conflicts fought abroad cannot be described as a new problem, the rise and subsequent defeat of ISIS have posed unprecedented challenges to individual States and the international community at large.[4] Despite the lack of more accurate data, it is possible to affirm that in Syria the Syrian Democratic Forces (SDF) hold about 14,000 foreigners suspected of ISIS affiliation. The number encompasses 2000 men and boys from almost 60 different countries who are detained in overcrowded prisons and 12,000 foreign women and

[1] FFs have been defined as "individuals, driven mainly by ideology, religion and/or kinship, who leave their country of origin or their country of habitual residence to join a party engaged in an armed conflict", thus placing the accent on the individuals' departure from their State of origin in order to support one of the actors, an armed group or a State's armed forces, engaged in an armed conflict. De Guttry et al. 2016, p. 2. The term FTFs, which will be used in the present contribution when speaking of the UN Security Council Resolutions, are "individuals who travel to a State other than their States of residence or nationality for the purpose of the perpetration, planning, or preparation of, or participation in, terrorist acts or the providing or receiving of terrorist training, including in connection with armed conflict". See UN Security Council (2014) Resolution 2178 (2014) UN Doc. S/RES/2178 (2014), Capone 2016a, pp. 232–237.

[2] Ms Begum left the UK in 2015 to join ISIS. In 2019, while she was pregnant and held in al-Hawl refugee camp in north-east Syria, she asked to be repatriated to her State of origin and raise her child there (as the first two children had died of malnutrition). The request was denied by the UK Government, which also stripped her of citizenship. In the meantime, she was moved to another camp and gave birth to a son who died of pneumonia. She challenged the Home Secretary's decision and in July 2020 the Court of Appeal held that she had been denied a fair hearing because she could not make her case from the Syrian camp and thus she should be allowed to return to the UK to fight the decision to remove her British citizenship. Court of Appeal (United Kingdom) (Civil Division), Case No: T2/2020/0644,T3/2020/0645 and T3/2020/0708, Judgement, 16 July 2020, paras 121–122.

[3] De Guttry et al. 2016.

[4] Krähenmann 2014; Bílková 2018.

children who are family members of ISIS suspects—some of them perhaps ISIS members themselves—in squalid camps.[5] In Iraq, the scenario is equally grim as 17,000 foreigners charged with terrorism offences are held in prison. While most are ISIS fighters, the tally also includes their wives and children.[6] Since January 2020, Iraq has conducted at least 794 criminal trials against those suspected of association with ISIS and affiliated groups under its anti-terrorism legal framework. In at least 44 cases, the defendants were children at the time of their purported criminal activity.[7] The complexity of the situation, certainly worsened by the current global pandemic, has further exacerbated the divide between the actors involved in countering the FFs phenomenon.

On the one hand, there are the actors dealing with FFs in the countries of destination. The SDF, i.e. a non-State actor (opposed to the current Syrian Government) which is exercising governmental functions on parts of Syrian territory with the support (if not under the control) of the USA, has declared on various occasions that it is neither willing nor able to prosecute FFs and is equally not capable of managing the camps where FFs' family members are held.[8] Instead, the Iraqi Government is relying on its sovereign right to prosecute adult FFs,[9] both men and women, but is asking States of origin to repatriate children, many of whom are detained on national security-related charges for their alleged association with ISIS.[10] Notably, whereas the SDF in Syria seeks to draw a distinction between fighters, who are detained, and family members who are held in displacement camps, Iraqi authorities are more inclined to regard all foreigners with some affiliation with ISIS as terrorist fighters, with the possible exception of children, should their countries of origin claim them back.[11]

On the other hand, there are the States of origin of FFs, which in an effort to protect first and foremost their national security, have so far adopted different approaches, mainly opposing the return of adults and allowing in some circumstances the repatriation of children. Thus, a uniform response to the issue, one that facilitates the identification of the measures to apply to victims and perpetrators, is still lacking. The European States particularly affected by the FFs phenomenon, like the Netherlands, UK, France, Belgium and Germany, have also failed to implement a common strategy despite the existence of a more detailed and advanced regional legal framework and dedicated policies.[12] Without delving into the obligations incumbent upon

---

[5] Tayler 2020a, p. 1.

[6] Loveluck and Salim 2020.

[7] Human Rights Watch 2020; The Bulan Institute for Peace Innovations 2020, p. 4.

[8] Aljazeera 2019.

[9] Agnès Callamard (Special Rapporteur on Extrajudicial, Summary, or Arbitrary Executions) (2018) Report of the Special Rapporteur on Extrajudicial, Summary or Arbitrary Executions on Her Mission to Iraq, U.N. Doc. A/HRC/38/44/Add.1; Council of Europe 2020a, pp. 3–4.

[10] Wille 2018.

[11] Van Esveld 2017.

[12] Capone 2017; Council of Europe 2020b; European Parliament resolution of 26 November 2019 on children's rights on the occasion of the 30th anniversary of the UN Convention on the Rights of the Child (2019/2876(RSP)). See Chap. 2 by Renard in this volume.

States of origin of FFs and their family members, which have been already analysed and discussed by the present author elsewhere,[13] this chapter is concerned with the status of women and children as their alleged affiliation with ISIS and the realities of life under the group oftentimes blur the lines between the category of 'victims' of terrorism and that of 'terrorists/perpetrators'.

This work rests on two main assumptions: first, that the distinction between victims and perpetrators does not necessarily reflect the complexity of the situation; and second, that States should always assess the status of each individual on a case-by-case basis. However, the distinction is useful to frame and discuss the question of how to deal with FFs' family members through the lenses of international law. More in detail, after a brief analysis of the roles played by foreign women and children affiliated with ISIS, this chapter will reflect on how they fit within the current international legal framework. Although it does not represent the only viable option to carry out the present analysis, this work will be focussing on international counter-terrorism (CT) law and international humanitarian law (IHL). The latter, in fact, can contribute to overcoming the strict dichotomy between victims and perpetrators that is particularly evident in criminal prosecutions against FFs' family members. This is especially true at the national level, where real or alleged security threats trigger an ever-growing body of criminal laws, mainly enacted in response to the obligations stemming from the international legal framework to criminalise certain conducts and acts.

The choice to focus on CT law and IHL is motivated by a number of factors. With regard to counter-terrorism law, the relevance of this set of norms is self-explanatory, especially since the international community has placed particular emphasis on the necessity to deal with the FFs phenomenon and its long-term consequences in a concerted way. In relation to IHL, it is worth underscoring that the participation of FFs in the wars fought in Iraq and Syria makes the rules applicable to armed conflicts particularly pertinent. In fact, as already argued by some authors,[14] IHL is undoubtedly relevant in the framework of the prosecution of FFs and, in spite of its complex relationship with counter-terrorism law,[15] may also be able to provide some additional insight into how to deal with FFs' family members.

4.2 The Role of Women and Children Affiliated with ISIS[16]

Prior to discussing the roles that FFs' family members have played in the ranks of ISIS and the consequences connected to their presence in the group, it is important to stress that the author is fully aware of the risks stemming from defining and categorising

[13] Capone 2019.

[14] Cuyckens and Paulussen 2019.

[15] Ibid., p. 544; McKeever 2020, p. 43. See also Chap. 8 by Van Poecke and Cuyckens in this volume.

[16] An earlier version of this section is also included in Capone 2019, pp. 74–77.

women and children by virtue of their association with particular men or groups of men.[17] It must also be borne in mind that one female individual could 'bridge' different categories, potentially being a minor, an orphan, a wife or widow, a mother, a former combatant, and several or all of these at the same time.[18] Obviously, the only way to avoid dangerous generalisations would be to analyse each case on an individual basis, and this is, indeed, what States (of origin and destination alike) should do. However, a simplified and nonspecific approach is needed to provide answers to broader questions, such as, to which extent the current international legal framework identifies accompanying family members of FFs as victims or perpetrators.

With regard to women, it should be underscored that after the first two waves of returnees, respectively in 2013–2014 and early 2015,[19] States of origin adopted a lenient approach towards female FFs, moving from the assumption that they only played ancillary roles and therefore could not pose any significant threat to national security.[20] Nowadays, the evolving understanding of female FFs evidences that the depiction of women as 'jihadi brides' or *Muhajirat*, i.e. female migrants, is not adequate to grasp the complexity of women's contribution to ISIS and, more generally, their role as active participants in Islamist insurgencies.[21] A similar discourse concerns children recruited by ISIS as the sophisticated brainwashing and indoctrination techniques have challenged the 'hard-fought for' victim-oriented approach towards child soldiers in other settings.[22] The following sections will shed further light on those issues, paving the way for a reflection on the status of FFs' family members under counter-terrorism law and international humanitarian law.

4.2.1 Women

As anticipated above, a more repressive approach has been recently adopted towards women affiliated with ISIS.[23] In relation to FFs in the course of the first waves of returns, women were perceived as overall harmless 'victims', capable of playing only a limited logistical role. Recent studies, instead, present a different and more complex picture that challenges the narrow-minded narrative of females as hopeless and passive individuals lured to the Middle East and forced to join ISIS against their will.[24] The proactive role of women and girls has been attributed to a shift in ISIS' position on the status of women in combat roles, which occurred between 2015 and 2018. In fact, it was the group itself—weakened by the armed attacks and increasing

[17] On this point see Ní Aoláin 2019, p. 2.

[18] Diakonia Lebanon 2019, p. 9.

[19] European Parliamentary Research Service (EPRS) 2018.

[20] Ibid., p. 36.

[21] Loken and Zelenz 2018, p. 51.

[22] Capone 2017, p. 161.

[23] EPRS 2018, p. 36.

[24] Loken and Zelenz 2018, pp. 52–53.

military defeats—that allowed women to perform more active roles, including most recently stating that "it is obligatory for women to take up arms".[25]

As a result of this new approach, it has been ascertained that women in the ranks of ISIS have often received sniper training, carried Kalashnikovs and worn suicide vests; they became members of the Al-Khansaa brigade and have been actively involved in propaganda and recruitment, grooming other women and girls online.[26] Girls recruited into ISIS have also been trained to best support their husbands to whom they may have been married from the age of nine. While they may not have engaged in combat roles, girls have generally been referred to as 'sisters of the Islamic State' alongside adult females. Accordingly, they may also have been involved in activities such as recruitment and dissemination of propaganda when they were considered to be mature enough.[27]

The recent insights into women's increasing involvement in recruitment and other activities have resulted in changing practices in several different countries of origin, also across Europe. A study by the Egmont Institute—featuring analyses of policies for returnees in Belgium, Germany, and the Netherlands by several prominent scholars of counter-terrorism—confirmed that in these three EU Member States, "[u]ntil recently, women were treated with more clemency, but this has now come to an end".[28] For example, in Germany, for several years, male FFs were automatically subject to criminal investigation upon arrival, whereas evidentiary thresholds were much higher in order for women to be investigated upon return. However, starting from December 2017, Germany's federal judicial authorities announced a tougher stance on female returnees to remove gender discrepancies in investigation and prosecution practices.[29] This entails that female FFs are likely to face criminal investigation and administrative measures upon their return or following their repatriation (if these procedures were not already initiated *in absentia*). The increasing perception of foreign women in the ranks of ISIS as a major security threat and the fact that they are likely to switch from the role of victims/facilitators to perpetrators explain, but perhaps does not justify, the fact that they are currently depicted as security threats.[30]

---

[25] Cook and Vale 2018, p. 28.

[26] Gielen 2018, pp. 455–456.

[27] EPRS 2018, p. 37.

[28] Renard and Coolsaet 2018b, p. 4.

[29] EPRS 2018, p. 46.

[30] Russia represents a notable exception as since 2017 it has implemented a repatriation scheme for Russian women and especially children located in Syria and Iraq. In particular, Kadyrov, the strongman ruler of Chechnya, has lobbied Vladimir Putin for the return of Russian-speakers from ISIL organizing nearly a dozen evacuation flights from Syria to Grozny. See Roth 2019. Whereas the scheme at the beginning included also women, after the defeat of the Islamic State the focus has been placed exclusively on children, as Russia has no agreement in place with Syria or Iraq that allows the transfer of women jailed for ISIL membership to serve their sentences at home. Another exception to the widespread apathy of the interested States is represented by Kazakhstan, which at the beginning of May 2019 repatriated from Syria 231 nationals, mostly children.

4.2.2 Children

Generally speaking, children associated with armed groups enter this environment in one of three ways: they are abducted or conscripted through force or serious threats; they present themselves and become enlisted/enrolled; or they are born into armed forces or groups.[31] Research on ISIS shows that the children in its ranks belong to various categories, i.e. they are the sons and daughters of foreigners who joined the fight, the children of local fighters, abandoned children found in ISIS-controlled orphanages, children coercively taken from parents, and runaway children/adolescents, in some instances foreigners, who volunteered for service to ISIS.[32] Therefore, during the short life of the self-proclaimed Caliphate, there were at least three main categories of foreigners under the age of 18 years affiliated with ISIS. First, the teenagers motivated by a desire to belong somewhere, who travelled to Syria by themselves, were often lured by a precursor who facilitated the trip. Second, the foreign jihadists were leaving in family groups, i.e. those who participated in a 'family jihad', whose ambition was to live in a 'true Islamic society' and escape from what they perceived as discrimination and harassment in Western countries where they were residing. The third category is made up of children born in Syria and Iraq by one foreign parent or both. In a terrorist group like ISIS, family units tended to remain intact, as many adults who moved to the Caliphate took their families along with them or started a family there.[33]

Within these networks, fighters were encouraged to train their children to become the next generation of jihadists, 'lion cubs' (or *ashbal*),[34] allowing ISIS to forge and groom its more loyal members.[35] There is compelling evidence that in the ranks of ISIS, children as early as six have been exposed to jihadi indoctrination and as early as nine have received military training.[36] Even though the declared approach followed by the affected States of origin towards children still stranded in Syria and Iraq is to consider them as 'victims' rather than perpetrators, the decisions taken so far display a completely different story. Belgium, for example, has openly declared its willingness to readmit to its territory all children under the age of ten without actively pursuing their repatriation, but by simply allowing relatives to bring them back, and to treat the older ones on a case-by-case basis.[37] Similarly, France is struggling with the lack of clear commitment towards its nationals still detained or located in Syria and Iraq. The French Government so far has repatriated from Syria only 17 children of French jihadists,[38] and French media have shared the news that the grandparents of two French children held with their jihadist mother in Syria have brought a case

---

[31] Drumbl 2012, p. 132.

[32] Capone 2017, pp. 175–176.

[33] See Bloom and Horgan 2015.

[34] Benotman and Malik 2016, p. 25.

[35] Capone 2016b, pp. 199–201.

[36] Almohammad 2018, pp. 19–22.

[37] Renard and Coolsaet 2018a, pp. 4–5.

[38] Broches 2020.

before the European Court of Human Rights (ECtHR).[39] The claimants contend that France is allowing the children to be exposed to inhumane and degrading treatment in a camp beset by illness and malnutrition in violation of Article 3 of the European Convention of Human Rights (ECHR)[40] and Article 3(1) of its Protocol No. 4,[41] according to which no one shall be deprived of the right to enter the territory of the State of which he is a national.

In Germany, domestic courts have started to order the Government to repatriate German children as well as their mothers/guardians. On 6 November 2019, the Higher Administrative Court of Berlin-Brandenburg (OVG Berlin-Brandenburg) confirmed the decision of the lower court and held that the German Government must repatriate a German citizen who in 2014 travelled from Germany to the territory held by ISIS in Syria, together with her three minor children.[42] More precisely, the Court found that the situation in the SDF-camp constituted a danger to the life of the children, and therefore the State had to comply with its duty to protect its nationals abroad. The mother was allowed to travel back to Germany with her children, firstly because it was considered to be in their best interests and secondly because the Government had failed to prove that she constituted a threat to public safety. In particular, the Government did not provide evidence on her exact role under ISIS and how she would pose a concrete danger to citizens living in Germany. According to the Court, claiming that a general danger can result from the return of ISIS fighters is insufficient to outweigh the fundamental protection of family ties, as enshrined in the German Constitution.[43]

4.3 'Victims' or 'Terrorists/Perpetrators' Under the Current International Legal Framework

The inclusion of FFs' family members in one of the two categories, i.e. victims or terrorists/perpetrators, is often not an easy task, as legally sound definitions of both categories are lacking. Under international law, the term 'victim' is not defined by any specific binding treaty or norm.[44] However, there are different instruments dealing

[39] Daou 2019.

[40] European Convention for the Protection of Human Rights and Fundamental Freedoms, as amended by Protocols Nos. 11 and 14, opened for signature 4 November 1950, ETS 5 (entered into force 3 September 1953).

[41] Protocol 4 to the European Convention for the Protection of Human Rights and Fundamental Freedoms, securing certain Rights and Freedoms other than those already included in the Convention and in the First Protocol thereto, opened for signature 16 September 1963, ETS 46 (entered into force 1 November 1998).

[42] Oberverwaltungsgericht Berlin-Brandenburg 10. Senat, OVG 10 S 43.19 (6 November 2019).

[43] Ibid., paras 33–41. Basic Law for the Federal Republic of Germany in the revised version published in the Federal Law Gazette Part III, classification number 100-1, as last amended by Article 1 of the Act of 28 March 2019 (Federal Law Gazette I p. 404), Article 6.

[44] Bassiouni 2006, p. 207; de Casadevante Romani 2010, pp. 220–223.

with particular categories of victims, such as, *inter alia*, victims of abuse of power, victims of enforced disappearance, victims of international crimes and victims of gross violations of international human rights law and serious violations of IHL.[45] The latter category, for instance, is defined by the Basic Principles and Guidelines on the Right to a Remedy and Reparation for Victims of Gross Violations of International Human Rights Law and Serious Violations of International Humanitarian Law (Basic Principles and Guidelines) as

> […] persons who individually or collectively suffered harm, including physical or mental injury, emotional suffering, economic loss or substantial impairment of their fundamental rights, through acts or omissions that constitute gross violations of international human rights law, or serious violations of international humanitarian law.[46]

Furthermore, according to the Basic Principles and Guidelines, "where appropriate, and in accordance with domestic law, the term 'victim' also includes the immediate family or dependants of the direct victim and persons who have suffered harm in intervening to assist victims in distress or to prevent victimisation".[47] Clearly, the conditions of victims exist regardless of whether the perpetrator of the violation is identified, apprehended, prosecuted, or convicted and regardless of the family relationship between the perpetrator and the victim.[48] This last point is, of course, particularly relevant and should be taken into due account when dealing with the wives and children of ISIS fighters.

Notably, in relation to the categories of victims listed above, all the relevant crimes (abuse of power, enforced disappearance, breaches of international criminal law, gross violations of international human rights law and serious violations of IHL) are duly defined under international law or at least can rely on the existence of well-developed legal frameworks. Yet, in the case of victims of terrorism, a number of factors—from the lack of a universally agreed definition of terrorism, to the fact that terrorism is an international crime that seriously violates human rights (and thus its victims tend to be subsumed under other categories)—have delayed the adoption of an international norm on victims of terrorism and their rights. Nonetheless, it must be conceded that some efforts have been undertaken at the regional level by the European Union (EU), through the adoption of Directive 2017/541 on combating terrorism,[49] and by the Council of Europe (CoE) through the Convention on the Prevention of Terrorism and the Guidelines on the Protection of Victims of Terrorist Acts adopted by the Committee of Ministers on 2 March 2005 and revised in 2017.[50]

---

[45] Ibid., pp. 238–244.

[46] UN General Assembly (2005) Basic Principles and Guidelines on the Right to a Remedy and Reparation for Victims of Gross Violations of International Human Rights Law and Serious Violations of International Humanitarian Law UNBPG 2005, UN Doc. A/RES/60/147.

[47] Ibid., para 8.

[48] de Casadevante Romani 2010, p. 241.

[49] The Council Directive (EU) 2017/541 of 15 March 2017 on combating terrorism and replacing Council Framework Decision 2002/475/JHA and amending Council Decision 2005/671/JHA [2017] OJ L88/6 (EU Directive on combating terrorism).

[50] CoE Convention on the Prevention of Terrorism, opened for signature 16 May 2005, CETS No. 196 (entered into force 1 June 2007); Council of Europe (Committee of Ministers) 2017.

The EU Directive on combating terrorism explicitly refers to the definition of victims enshrined in Directive 2012/29/EU of the European Parliament and of the Council of 25 October 2012 establishing minimum standards on the rights, support and protection of victims of crime,[51] and hence it establishes that

> [A victim of terrorism] is a natural person who has suffered harm, including physical, mental or emotional harm or economic loss, insofar as that was directly caused by a terrorist offence, or a family member of a person whose death was directly caused by a terrorist offence and who has suffered harm as a result of that person's death. Family members of surviving victims of terrorism, as defined in that Article, have access to victim support services and protection measures in accordance with that Directive.[52]

The Directive exhaustively lists a number of serious crimes, e.g. attacks against a person's life, as intentional acts that can amount to terrorist offences when, and insofar as, committed with a specific terrorist aim, namely to seriously intimidate a population, to unduly compelling a government or an international organisation to perform or abstain from performing any act, or to seriously destabilise or destroy the fundamental political, constitutional, economic or social structures of a country or an international organisation.[53] The Directive, in line with the FTFs Resolutions,[54] includes amongst the offences the receiving of terrorist training and travelling to a country other than that Member State for the purpose of committing, or contributing to the commission of, a terrorist offence. Notably, this approach replicates the shortcomings of the Security Council's Resolutions with respect to foreign fighters' accompanying family members, which will be discussed more at length in the coming sub-sections. The Directive, however, specifies that when recruitment and training for terrorism are directed towards a child, Member States should ensure that judges can take this circumstance into account when sentencing offenders, although there is no obligation on judges to increase the sentence. Unfortunately, by placing emphasis only on the judges' discretion, the Directive fails to shed light on children's victimhood. The text is equally silent on the status of women.

At the CoE level, similar weaknesses can be identified. More in detail, according to Article 13 of the Convention on the Prevention of Terrorism

> Each Party shall adopt such measures as may be necessary to protect and support the victims of terrorism that has been committed within its own territory. These measures may include, through the appropriate national schemes and subject to domestic legislation, inter alia, financial assistance and compensation for victims of terrorism and their close family members.

However, the Convention does not include any definition of victims, which is instead contained in the Guidelines on the Protection of Victims of Terrorist Acts.

---

[51] Directive 2012/29/EU of the European Parliament and of the Council of 25 October 2012 establishing minimum standards on the rights, support and protection of victims of crime, and replacing Council Framework Decision 2001/220/JHA OJ L 315, 14 November 2012.

[52] EU Directive on combating terrorism, operative part, para 27.

[53] Ibid., para 8.

[54] Mainly, UN Security Council (2014) Resolution 2178 (2014), UN Doc. S/RES/2178 (2014); UN Security Council (2017) Resolution 2396 (2017), UN Doc. S/RES/2396 (2017).

As stated in the Guidelines, the term victims of terrorist offences refer to "any person who has suffered direct physical or psychological harm as a result of a terrorist act, and, in appropriate circumstances, of their close family". In order to circumscribe the potentially endless list of terrorist offences, the Convention makes reference to the sectoral treaties on terrorism listed in its Appendix.[55] Furthermore, the 2017 Additional Protocol to the Council of Europe Convention on the Prevention of Terrorism includes all the offences, including preparatory acts and passive conducts, that are regarded as key to counter the FTFs phenomenon.

With regard to the status of terrorists/perpetrators, it is worth stressing that the inclusion of FFs' family members in this category is usually loosely based on (a) their relationship with FFs in the ranks of ISIS and/or (b) their own membership in the organisation/participation in the group's activities. The former option is conceptually and legally wrong as individual criminal responsibility is personal and cannot stem from kinship, whereas the latter would require an assessment of the actual involvement of each individual in the group's activities. Despite an exponential increase in prosecutions related to the armed conflict in Iraq or Syria over the past few years,[56] domestic courts seem primarily capable of prosecuting merely for membership of a terrorist organisation rather than for actual terrorist conduct.[57] However, being a member of a terrorist organisation is a concept that is often prone to different (and sometimes questionable) interpretations at the domestic level and for which no definition is provided at the international or regional level.[58] In fact, a broad interpretation of membership has in a number of cases allowed domestic courts to convict women for simply being family members of alleged ISIS fighters or performing basic services and tasks such as household chores. In many of these cases, no account was taken of the degree to which a woman's association with the group was voluntary or coerced.[59]

Therefore, it does not come as a surprise that prosecution for membership is seen as a drawback by all parties involved, i.e. by those who were forced to join ISIS or played only limited roles in the organisation, and by FFs' States of origin as this approach would infer that any returnee, including those who have committed the

---

[55] Notably, the numerous counter-terrorism treaties that have been adopted so far have been described as 'sectoral' as they require States parties to criminalise particular methods of transnational violence commonly used by terrorists, establish extensive jurisdiction over specific offences, and investigate, apprehend and 'prosecute or extradite' individual perpetrators. See Saul 2015.

[56] Mehra 2018, p. 3; Van Schaack 2019.

[57] Paulussen et al. 2019. On the role of family courts in relation to the repatriation of children, see Chap. 11 by van Ark in this volume.

[58] Capone 2019, p. 73. For example, the EU Directive on combating terrorism at Article 2(3) states that "'terrorist group' means a structured group of more than two persons, established for a period of time and acting in concert to commit terrorist offences; 'structured group' means a group that is not randomly formed for the immediate commission of an offence and that *does not need to have formally defined roles for its members, continuity of its membership or a developed structure*" (emphasis added). The definition of terrorist group enshrined in the Directive does not clarify what exactly constitutes membership in said group.

[59] UNAMI and OHCHR 2020, p. 10.

most serious crimes, could walk away with a lighter sentence.[60] In 2016, Germany's top federal prosecutor Peter Frank presented the issue as follows:

> What proof can we get from a war zone where all state structures have collapsed? Cooperation in terms of legal help doesn't work either in Syria or Iraq. If we are able to determine they are returnees from the ranks of the 'Islamic State' or other groups, then mostly we can only prove their membership in a terrorist organization. But we often get the impression that *these people weren't just put on guard duty or received weapons training in Syria, but were involved in bodily harm, killings and bombing attacks.*[61]

In other words, States of nationality oftentimes fear that allowing the return (or proactively seeking the repatriation) of FFs as well as their wives and children can not only jeopardise their national security but also result in criminal and administrative measures that do not reflect the gravity of the crimes committed in Syria and Iraq.[62] Thus, insisting on their alleged faults and crimes rather than engaging in a more comprehensive discourse that also addresses their potential victimisation remains the most obvious and less challenging choice, at least in the short term.

In light of these considerations, it seems trivial to observe that the concepts of victims and perpetrators continue to be difficult to delineate, especially since counter-terrorism law at the domestic level is overshadowing the implementation of other branches of law that could assist in better framing the position of those who have been forced to join ISIS and/or carried out only ancillary activities. Furthermore, the application of national counter-terrorism legislation does not always mirror the efforts made at the international level to strike a better balance between different needs and values. As the next sections are going to show, both international counter-terrorism law and international humanitarian law are relevant to shed light on how to determine the status of those who lived under ISIS, with the latter perhaps able to sort out some of the deficiencies of the former.

4.3.1 International Counter-Terrorism Law

As is well known, a plethora of international norms, institutions, and procedures specifically designed to deal with terrorism has emerged over the past 50 years.[63] To use Saul's categorisation, international counter-terrorism law comprises disparate norms stemming from different sources, mainly counter-terrorism treaties and UN

---

[60] Cuyckens and Paulussen 2019, p. 538. As noted by the authors: "All persons who have joined IS will receive more or less the same sentence (in Western Europe usually around five to six years), no matter whether they were forced to join IS and served the Caliphate not by fighting but by preparing meals (in which case this standard sentence may be on the high side) or whether they were leading the group and responsible for international crimes such as war crimes, crimes against humanity and genocide (in which case this standard sentence would be very low)." Capone 2019, p. 83.

[61] Deutsche Welle (DW) 2016.

[62] Cuyckens and Paulussen 2019, p. 539.

[63] Capone 2019, p. 83; van den Herik and Schrijver 2013, pp. 20–25; Saul 2012, p. 67.

Security Council Resolutions.[64] Notably, all sectoral CT treaties are silent on the issue of victims of terrorism, and so is the UN Draft Comprehensive Convention against International Terrorism, a document that was never finalised.[65] At the domestic level, counter-terrorism law is mainly made of the criminal norms that are adopted and implemented to respond to the international stimulus and criminalise certain conducts and acts.[66]

Paradoxically, the need to envisage a more comprehensive and nuanced approach to the impact that terrorism might have on different segments of the population has been triggered by the phenomenon of FFs. More in detail, in the Resolutions dealing with FTFs, the UN Security Council has expressly recognised and underscored the peculiarities attached to the status of women and children. To this end, Resolution 2396 (2017) calls upon Member States to assess and investigate individuals whom they have reasonable grounds to believe are terrorists or FTFs, and also "distinguish them from other individuals, including their accompanying family members *who may not have been engaged in foreign terrorist fighter-related offenses*".[67] Furthermore, the Resolution underlines that

> [...] women and children associated with foreign terrorist fighters returning or relocating to and from conflict may have served in many different roles, including as supporters, facilitators, or perpetrators of terrorist acts, and require special focus when developing tailored prosecution, rehabilitation and reintegration strategies, and *stresses the importance of assisting women and children associated with foreign terrorist fighters who may be victims of terrorism*, and to do so taking into account gender and age sensitivities.[68]

Unfortunately, the terminology used in the Resolution is very vague; for instance, it refers to "victims of terrorism" without defining them, which reflects many of the shortcomings already highlighted in relation to the counter-terrorism framework in general as well as to the first FTFs Resolution adopted in 2014.[69]

In fact, the words "foreign terrorist fighter-related offenses" encompass a wide range of activities, including preparatory acts that are criminalised "based on the belief that they could lead to a terrorist offence".[70] It also includes passive conducts, such as receiving a terrorist training, which raises significant issues in relation to women and children who might have been forced to take part in training activities.[71] As a result, States affected by the phenomenon have been able to implement domestic

---

[64] Ibid.; see also Capone 2016a, pp. 237–242.

[65] Hmoud 2006, p. 1031; Cassese 2006, pp. 945–947.

[66] Capone 2021, pp. 732–733.

[67] UN Security Council (2017) Resolution 2396 (2017), UN Doc. S/RES/2396 (2017), para 4 (emphasis added).

[68] Ibid., para 31 (emphasis added).

[69] UN Security Council (2014) Resolution 2178 (2014), UN Doc. S/RES/2178 (2014). On the often problematic implementation of the Resolution at the domestic level, see Ip 2020, p. 103; Ragazzi and Walmsley 2018; Capone 2016a; Krähenmann 2014.

[70] Van der Heide and Geenen 2015, p. 170.

[71] Cuyckens and Paulussen 2019, pp. 549–551.

legislation that thrives on the Resolutions' vagueness and allow them to get around "inconvenient rule of law-compliant accountability".[72]

The recognition of FTFs' family members as 'potential victims' represents, on the one hand, a blatant understatement, for example, in the case of children recruited by ISIS, due to its departure from the assumption that all child soldiers are first and foremost victims.[73] On the other hand, it can still be hailed as an important advancement, if not in substance, at least in form. In fact, Resolution 2396 (2017) mitigates a lacuna found in most States of nationality. Stuck in their struggle to prosecute people who have ties with ISIS—even those who have actually committed crimes in Iraq and Syria—States do not differentiate between FTFs and their family members. On the contrary, the Resolution asks them to operate such distinction and underscore that family members of FTFs, including women, "may be victims of terrorism".

Notably, this language was not included at all in the draft Resolution on the prosecution, rehabilitation, and re-integration of foreign terrorist fighters and their families, which was negotiated in 2020, and in the end, was not adopted due to a US veto.[74] Furthermore, the draft Resolution failed once again to duly address the situation of children, despite the fact that in the words of the UN Special Rapporteur on the Promotion and Protection of Human Rights and Fundamental Freedoms while Countering Terrorism, they "should only exceptionally be subject to criminal sanction (and in those cases in line with juvenile justice standards)".[75]

At the regional level, the current counter-terrorism legal instruments rest more or less on the same shortcomings of the international set of norms. As discussed above, in Europe, both the EU and the CoE have legislated on the matter, encompassing instruments and norms that tackle FTFs and victims of terrorism. In spite of those efforts, however, the vast range of conducts that fall within the umbrella term 'terrorist offences', coupled with the lack of a straightforward approach to the issue of membership in a terrorist organisation, make it very difficult to single out those who were forced to participate in ISIS' activities and/or were not involved in any terrorist-related tasks. Therefore, the existing counter-terrorism legal framework provides insufficient answers to the questions of how to draw a line between victims and terrorists/perpetrators, and this inevitably triggers the need to look for additional insight elsewhere and complement or possibly improve the current approach.

4.3.2 International Humanitarian Law

IHL and counter-terrorism law are traditionally seen as two very different legal regimes; amongst the many points of distinction, there is the fact that, as Pejic

[72] Ní Aoláin 2020.
[73] Capone 2017; UNICEF 2007.
[74] Tayler 2020b, p. 3.
[75] Ní Aoláin 2020.

notes, the former regulates both lawful and unlawful violence, whereas any act of violence designated as terrorist is unlawful under the latter legal regime.[76] Of course, this is also reflected in the way the two regimes deal with the victims vs terrorists/perpetrators dichotomy. Hence, it can be helpful to discuss the status of FFs' accompanying family members through the lenses of IHL,[77] in light of the fact that they are currently held or detained in Iraq and Syria for security reasons and in connection to the non-international armed conflicts (NIACs) fought on the territories of those two States.

A preliminary caveat is, however, necessary as under IHL, the definition of 'victims' refers primarily to all those who suffer because they are affected by an armed conflict; i.e. they are classified as "war victims".[78] Since the key objective of IHL is to protect war victims, this definition potentially covers an entire population that has been caught up in an armed conflict and therefore, it is not viable nor relevant for the purpose of the present work. Thus, the IHL regime leaves open the question of actions required when protection fails and who falls under the category of victims of breaches of IHL. Luckily, this gap has been filled by the Basic Principles and Guidelines mentioned above,[79] as they contain a definition of victims that apply to both violations of human rights law and violations of IHL. Considering that FFs' accompanying family members were under the ISIS ranks, their classification as victims of IHL would depend on whether it is possible for this regime to deal with intra-party violence, i.e. violations of *jus in bello* committed by the group against its own members.[80]

The issue has been examined at length by the International Criminal Court (ICC) in relation to sexual violence committed by a non-State Armed Group (NSAG) against child soldiers under its authority in the famous *Ntaganda* case.[81] Without lingering on the various matters addressed by the ICC and the many commentators of this ground-breaking decision,[82] what is worth underscoring here is that in NIACs, the beneficiaries of Common Article 3 (CA3),[83] which sets the minimum standard of protection, also include members of the same party, as long as the person concerned is taking no direct part in the hostilities, has laid down the arms or is *hors de combat*. The most blatant example of a violation committed by ISIS towards its own members

[76] Pejic 2012, p. 172.

[77] See Chap. 8 by Van Poecke and Cuyckens in this volume.

[78] Zegveld 2003, p. 501.

[79] See Sect. 4.3. See also Evans 2012, pp. 17–43.

[80] The traditional doctrinal view on the scope of application of IHL holds that this branch of law is primarily, although not exclusively, concerned with the relations among members of opposing parties to an armed conflict and not with those occurring within the same armed force or group. See Poltronieri Rossetti 2019, pp. 51–52.

[81] ICC, *Prosecutor v Ntaganda*, Judgment on the appeal of Mr. Ntaganda against the "Second decision on the Defence's challenge to the jurisdiction of the Court in respect of Counts 6 and 9", 15 June 2017, Situation in the Democratic Republic of the Congo, ICC-01/04-02/06-1962 (*Ntaganda Appeal Jurisdictional Decision* 2017).

[82] Rodenhäuser 2016; Longobardo 2019; Kenny and McDermott 2019.

[83] Pictet 1960; Schindler 1979, p. 147; Moir 2002, p. 35; Cullen 2010; Pejic 2011.

is perhaps the recruitment and use of children under the age of 15 years,[84] which is prohibited in both international armed conflicts (IACs) and non-international armed conflicts (NIACs) and is, by its very nature, a violation committed against individuals belonging to the same armed group.[85] Other violations of IHL covered by CA3 and suffered by women and children in the ranks of ISIS encompass well documented and widespread sex and gender-based violence, including *inter alia* rape, sexual slavery and forced marriage,[86] as well as torture and arbitrary killings. Therefore, FFs' wives and children that were members of ISIS could *also be victims of the same group* if they did belong to the category of protected persons according to CA3.[87]

The question remains how to determine whether, in light of their functions and status within the group, women and children can be included in this category. In relation to the latter, labelling an NSAG as 'terrorist' is irrelevant and carries zero consequences: children in the ranks of ISIS should be treated exactly like all children affiliated with armed forces or groups, i.e. first and foremost as victims.[88] With regard to the former, some additional considerations are needed. Whereas under CT law a 'terrorist' will always be condemned for his/her behaviour, under IHL a combatant or someone taking direct part in hostilities without enjoying the combatant status will not necessarily act in violation of the relevant set of rules. Due to the fact that, for the purpose of this work, the FFs who participated in the NIACs fought in Iraq and Syria, joined a NSAG, i.e. ISIS, they did not enjoy the combatant status that is attached to "[m]embers of the armed forces of a Party to a conflict (other than medical personnel and chaplains)"[89] involved in IACs. Nonetheless, the principle of distinction, being one of the pillars of IHL and a rule of customary law applicable to both IACs and NIACs,[90] still allows to differentiate between unprivileged combatants (who do not enjoy the formal combatant status reserved to IACs) and civilians, i.e. who clearly do not qualify as combatants and lose their protection status only in case of direct participation in hostilities.[91] Also, it is important to note that civilian direct participation may be prosecuted under domestic law but does not constitute a violation of IHL and is not a war crime *per se* under treaty or customary IHL.[92]

A clear-cut interpretation of the principle of distinction is definitely valid when assessing the use of military force and the purpose of targeting. However, in other

---

[84] Jørgensen 2019, pp. 18–22.

[85] Kenny and McDermott 2019, p. 963; Rodenhäuser 2016, p. 171.

[86] Jørgensen 2019, p. 16; Report of the Secretary-General (2018) Children and Armed Conflict in the Syrian Arab Republic, UN Doc. S/2018/969, para 17.

[87] Notably, the protection offered by Additional Protocol II to the Geneva Conventions extends also to members of the same group, but Iraq and Syria are not parties to it. See Kenny and McDermott 2019, p. 964.

[88] Capone 2016b; Capone 2017; Nyamutata 2020.

[89] Protocol Additional to the Geneva Conventions of 12 August 1949, and relating to the Protection of Victims of International Armed Conflicts (Protocol I), opened for signature 8 June 1977, 1125 UNTS 3 (entered into force 7 December 1978) Article 43(2).

[90] Henckaerts and Doswald-Beck 2005; see also Chap. 5 by van Ginkel in this volume.

[91] Cuyckens and Paulussen 2019, p. 243.

[92] Pejic 2011, p. 33.

instances, for example, when discussing the lawfulness of detaining civilians who pose a threat to security,[93] an important development in modern IHL is the acceptance of the further distinction "between direct participation in hostilities and participation in the war effort. […]".[94] To this end, authors like Goodman propose to further differentiate amongst civilians who cannot be lawfully targeted, and thus equated to unprivileged combatants, by singling out two subsets, i.e. civilians who are indirect participants in hostilities; and civilians who are non-participants in hostilities.[95] Therefore, these two subsets of civilians include individuals who contribute to the war effort, as well as those who make no tangible contribution. But what does 'contributing to the war effort' mean concretely?

In primis, it does not imply a direct causal relationship or geographic proximity between the individual's activity and damage inflicted on the enemy, inferring that the activity need not occur on a battlefield.[96] According to the rules that govern IACs, indirect participation includes "subversive activity carried on inside the territory of a Party to the conflict or actions which are of direct assistance to an enemy Power."[97] Focussing more precisely on NIACs, as a leading treaty puts it, "civilians who support the armed forces (or armed groups) by supplying labour, transporting supplies, serving as messengers or disseminating propaganda are not direct participants, *but they remain amenable to domestic legislation against giving aid and comfort to domestic enemies*".[98] By the same token, FFs' family members who performed acts that meet this 'degree of support' provided to ISIS could be prosecuted for their actions under municipal law.

With regard to a lower threshold for indirect participation, it is useful to distinguish the category from non-participation. Having political sympathy or affiliation with the enemy power, as long as the attitude is not translated into action, is wholly insufficient to amount to indirect participation and it will leave the individual within the group of non-participants in hostilities.[99] Therefore, there are strong reasons to conclude that mere membership will not qualify as indirect participation unless it involves actions that are of direct assistance to the group. In a famous passage of the case *Anonymous v. The State of Israel*—examining the scope of application of a detention law—the Supreme Court of Israel concluded that "[I]t is insufficient to show any tenuous connection with a terrorist organisation";[100] instead, the detaining power must rely on the individual's particular "connection and contribution to the organisation […] that are sufficient to include him in the cycle of hostilities in its

---

93 Capone 2019, pp. 80–81.

94 ICRC 1987, Article 51(3), p. 619.

95 Goodman 2009, p. 51.

96 Ibid., p. 54.

97 ICRC 1958, Article 42, p. 258.

98 Bothe 2013, p. 672 (emphasis added).

99 ICRC 1958, Article 5, p. 56.

100 Supreme Court (Israel), *Anonymous v. The State of Israel*, Judgement, 11 June 2008, 47 ILM 768 (2008).

broad sense."[101] Furthermore, according to the Court, in order to assess a contribution precisely and exhaustively, the matter needs always to be examined on a case-by-case basis according to the circumstances.[102]

On the basis of these considerations, it is thus argued that IHL could, and should, come into play, to complement and enhance the criminal law approaches implemented at the domestic level, not only to prosecute FFs,[103] but also to address in a more pragmatic and result-oriented way the situation of their accompanying family members, for example by developing policies and tools aimed at better tackling the different connotations attached to each individual. In fact, whilst CT law's requirements to determine whether someone is a 'terrorist /perpetrator' are worryingly easy to meet, under IHL it is possible to differentiate between various sub-categories of combatants and protected persons and question what role each man, woman and child has played and which contribution he/she has brought to the military effort.

4.4 Concluding Remarks

As explained at the beginning of this chapter, it is very difficult, and perhaps not even possible, to use the categories of 'victims' and 'terrorists/perpetrators' in a straightforward way when we talk about FFs and their accompanying family members. Clearly, the problems and challenges at stake require more than a yes or no answer to the question of whether we should consider everyone who has been in Iraq and Syria to support ISIS as a terrorist. Nonetheless, given the growing number of information collected after ISIS' military defeat on the roles and status of different segments of the Caliphate's population, it is possible to reconstruct a scenario where ISIS affiliates have also been victims of the group.

Such a dynamic, which is very easy to imagine in other contexts, e.g. when it comes to children affiliated with NSAGs not labelled as 'terrorist', is incompatible with the current CT framework, according to which the membership in a terrorist organisation, whatever this term entails concretely, is considered a sufficient condition to dismiss any discussion on potential victimhood. Although counter-terrorism law has been overshadowing the application of any other relevant field of law,[104] the formulation of CT norms at the international level and their implementation at the municipal level remains challenging and, in most instances, defective. Reflecting more broadly, and through an IHL perspective, on the potential victims' status of FFs' family members as well as on the concrete actions that they have undertaken whilst in the group's ranks is very important also to identify the most effective responses to implement.[105] Adopting a blanket approach, i.e. prosecuting everyone and relying on whatever

[101] Ibid., para 21.

[102] Ibid.; see also Goodman 2009, p. 55.

[103] Cuyckens and Paulussen 2019, p. 563.

[104] Paulussen et al. 2019, p. 4.

[105] See Chap. 9 by Mignot-Mahdavi in this volume.

tenuous affiliation with ISIS under CT law, can perhaps satisfy the short-term security needs of the States of destination and origin of FFs, but in the long-term it will probably result in even more complex and articulated challenges.

References

Aljazeera (2019) SDF Calls for International Tribunal for ISIL Detainees. https://www.aljazeera.com/news/2019/03/sdf-calls-international-tribunal-isil-detainees-190325140845893.html. Accessed 24 January 2022

Almohammad A (2018) ISIS Child Soldiers in Syria: The Structural and Predatory Recruitment, Enlistment, Pre-training Indoctrination, Training, and Deployment. https://icct.nl/wp-content/uploads/2018/02/ICCT-Almohammad-ISIS-Child-Soldiers-In-Syria-Feb2018.pdf. Accessed 9 November 2021

Bassiouni MC (2006) International Recognition of Victims' Rights. Human Rights Law Review 6(2):203–279

Benotman N, Malik N (2016) The Children of Islamic State. Roméo Dallaire Child Soldiers Initiative. https://www.quilliaminternational.com/quilliam-releases-report-on-children-in-the-caliphate/. Accessed 9 November 2021

Bílková V (2018) Foreign Terrorist Fighters and International Law. Groningen Journal of International Law 6(1):1–23

Bloom M, Horgan J (2015) The Rise of the Child Terrorist. Foreign Affairs. https://www.foreignaffairs.com/articles/middle-east/2015-02-09/rise-child-terrorist. Accessed 9 November 2021

Bothe M (ed) (2013) New Rules for Victims of Armed Conflicts: Commentary on the Two 1977 Protocols Additional to the Geneva Conventions of 1949. Brill | Nijhoff, The Hague

Broches E (2020) What Is Happening with the Foreign Women and Children in SDF Custody in Syria? Lawfareblog. https://www.lawfareblog.com/what-happening-foreign-women-and-children-sdf-custody-syria. Accessed 9 November 2021

Capone F (2016a) Countering "Foreign Terrorist Fighters": A Critical Appraisal of the Framework Established By the UN Security Council Resolutions. ItYIL 25(1):227–250

Capone F (2016b) Child Soldiers: The Expanding Practice of Minors Recruited to Become Foreign Fighters. In: de Guttry A, Capone F, Paulussen C (eds) Foreign Fighters Under International Law and Beyond. T.M.C. Asser Press, The Hague, pp 187–204

Capone F (2017) "Worse" than Child Soldiers? A Critical Analysis of Foreign Children in the Ranks of ISIL. ICLA 17(1):161–185

Capone F (2019) The Children (and Wives) of Foreign ISIS Fighters: Which Obligations upon the States of Nationality? QIL, Zoom-in 60:69–97

Capone F (2021) Criminalising Terrorist Offences and the Phenomenon of Foreign Terrorist Fighters at the Municipal Level Without Defining Terrorism in International Law: Does the Trick Really Work? ICLA 21(4): 731–747

Cassese A (2006) The Multifaceted Criminal Notion of Terrorism in International Law. JICJ 4(5):933–958

Cook J, Vale G (2018) From Daesh to 'Diaspora': Tracing the Women and Minors of Islamic State. https://icsr.info/wp-content/uploads/2018/07/ICSR-Report-From-Daesh-to-'Diaspora'-Tracing-the-Women-and-Minors-of-Islamic-State.pdf. Accessed 10 November 2021

Council of Europe (2017) Revised Guidelines of the Committee of Ministers of the Council of Europe on the Protection of Victims of Terrorist Acts. https://rm.coe.int/protection-of-victims-of-terrorist-acts/168078ab54. Accessed 24 January 2022

Council of Europe (2020a) Committee on Legal Affairs and Human Rights Addressing the Issue of Daesh Foreign Fighters and Their Families Returning from Syria and Other Countries to the Member States of the Council of Europe. Introductory Memorandum. AS/Jur

(2020) 03. http://www.assembly.coe.int/LifeRay/JUR/Pdf/DocsAndDecs/2020/AS-JUR-2020-03-EN.pdf. Accessed 24 January 2022
Council of Europe (2020b) Committee on Social Affairs, Health and Sustainable Development. International Obligations Concerning the Repatriation of Children from War and Conflict Zones. Resolution 2321. http://assembly.coe.int/nw/xml/XRef/Xref-XML2HTML-en.asp?fileid=28581&lang=en. Accessed 24 January 2022
Cullen A (2010) The Concept of Non-international Armed Conflict in International Humanitarian Law. Cambridge University Press, Cambridge
Cuyckens H, Paulussen C (2019) The Prosecution of Foreign Fighters in Western Europe: The Difficult Relationship Between Counter-Terrorism and International Humanitarian Law. Journal of Conflict & Security Law 24(3):1–29
Daou M (2019) France Taken to Court for Refusing to Repatriate the Children of Jihadists. Available at https://www.france24.com/en/20190507-france-taken-court-over-repatriating-children-jihadists. Accessed 24 January 2022
de Casadevante Romani CF (2010) International Law of Victims. Max Planck Yearbook of United Nations Law 14:219–272
de Guttry A, Capone F, Paulussen C (2016) Introduction. In: de Guttry A, Capone F, Paulussen C (eds) Foreign Fighters under International Law and Beyond. T.M.C. Asser Press, The Hague, pp 1–4
Deutsche Welle (DW) (2016) German Prosecutor: Hard to Convict 'Islamic State' Returnees. https://www.dw.com/en/german-prosecutor-hard-to-convict-islamic-state-returnees/a-19148842. Accessed 24 January 2022
Diakonia Lebanon (2019) The Legal Status of ISIS: Affiliated Foreign Nationals Held in Detention in North-East Syria (The International Humanitarian Law Resource Desk). https://www.diakonia.se/contentassets/710fe542e0e141d38baa1620c429161a/legal-brief-on-foreign-nationals-held-in-detention-in-syria.pdf. Accessed 24 January 2022
Drumbl M A (2012) Reimagining Child Soldiers in International Law and Policy. Oxford University Press, Oxford
European Parliamentary Research Service (EPRS) (2018) The Return of Foreign Fighters to EU Soil Ex-post Evaluation. PE 621.811. https://www.europarl.europa.eu/RegData/etudes/STUD/2018/621811/EPRS_STU(2018)621811_EN.pdf. Accessed 24 January 2022
Evans C (2012) The Right to Reparation in International Law for Victims of Armed Conflict. Cambridge University Press, Cambridge
Gielen AJ (2018) Exit Programmes for Female Jihadists: A Proposal for Conducting a Realistic Evaluation of the Dutch Approach. International Sociology 33(4):454–472
Goodman R (2009) The Detention of Civilians in Armed Conflict, AJIL 103(1):48–74
Henckaerts JM, Doswald-Beck L (eds) (2005) Customary International Humanitarian Law. International Committee of the Red Cross and Cambridge University Press, Geneva/Cambridge
Hmoud M (2006) Negotiating the Draft Comprehensive Convention on International Terrorism: Major Bones of Contention. JICJ 4(5):1031–1043
Human Rights Watch (2020) Submission by Human Rights Watch to the UN Human Rights Committee in Advance of Its Review of Iraq. https://www.hrw.org/news/2020/08/07/submission-human-rights-watch-un-human-rights-committee-advance-its-review-iraq. Accessed 24 January 2022
ICRC (1958) Commentary on the Geneva Conventions of 12 August 1949, Volume IV. Geneva
ICRC (1987) Commentary on the Additional Protocols of 8 June 1977 to the Geneva Conventions of 12 August 1949. Martinus Nijhoff Publishers, Geneva
Ip J (2020) Reconceptualising the Legal Response to Foreign Fighters. ICLQ 69(1):103–134
Jørgensen NHB (2019) Children Associated with Terrorist Groups in the Context of the Legal Framework for Child Soldiers. QIL, Zoom-in 60:5–23
Kenny C, McDermott Y (2019), The Expanding Protection of Members of a Party's Own Armed Forces Under International Criminal Law. ICLQ 68(4):943–976
Krähenmann S (2014) Foreign Fighters Under International Law. Geneva Academy Briefing No. 7

Loken M, Zelenz A (2018) Explaining Extremism: Western Women in Daesh. European Journal of International Studies 3(1):45–68
Longobardo M (2019) The Criminalisation of Intra-Party Offences in Light of Some Recent ICC Decisions on Children in Armed Conflict. ICLA 19(4):600–634
Loveluck L, Salim M (2020) Iraq wants thousands displaced by the ISIS war to go home. They may be killed if they do. https://www.washingtonpost.com/world/middle_east/iraq-refugees-displaced-camps/2020/12/21/9a2b6188-3af6-11eb-aad9-8959227280c4_story.html. Accessed 20 February 2022
McKeever D (2020) International Humanitarian Law and Counter-Terrorism: Fundamental Values, Conflicting Obligations. ICLQ 69(1):43–78
Mehra T (2018) Bringing (Foreign) Terrorist Fighters to Justice in a Post-ISIS Landscape Part II: Prosecution by Foreign National Courts. https://icct.nl/publication/bringing-foreign-terrorist-fighters-to-justice-in-a-post-isis-landscape-part-ii-prosecution-by-foreign-national-courts/. Accessed 24 January 2022
Moir L (2002) The Law of Internal Armed Conflict. Cambridge University Press, Cambridge
Ní Aoláin F (2019) The Limits of Equality and Gender Discourses in Counter Terrorism: The Case of Women and Children in Syria and Iraq. Keynote Lecture, University of Minnesota Law MJIL Law Conference
Ní Aoláin F (2020) The Challenges of a New UN Security Council Resolution on Foreign Fighters. Just Security. https://www.justsecurity.org/72052/the-challenges-of-a-new-un-security-council-resolution-on-foreign-fighters/. Accessed 24 January 2022
Nyamutata C (2020) Young Terrorists or Child Soldiers? ISIS Children, International Law and Victimhood. Journal of Conflict & Security Law 25(2):237–261
Paulussen C, Cuyckens H, Fortin K (2019) The Prosecution of Foreign Fighters Under International Humanitarian Law: Misconceptions and Opportunities. https://icct.nl/publication/the-prosecution-of-foreign-fighters-under-international-humanitarian-law-misconceptions-and-opportunities/. Accessed 24 January 2022
Pejic J (2011) The Protective Scope of Common Article 3: More than Meets the Eye. IRRC 93(881):1–37
Pejic J (2012) Armed Conflict and Terrorism: There Is a (Big) Difference. In: Salinas de Frías AM, Samuel K, White ND (eds) Counter-Terrorism: International Law and Practice. Oxford University Press, Oxford, pp 171–204
Pictet J (ed) (1960) Commentary to the Third Geneva Convention relative to the Treatment of Prisoners of War. ICRC, Geneva
Poltronieri Rossetti L (2019) Intra-party Sexual Crimes Against Child Soldiers as War Crimes in Ntaganda. 'Tadić Moment' or Unwarranted Exercise of Judicial Activism? QIL, Zoom-in 60:49–68
Ragazzi F, Walmsley J (2018) The return of foreign fighters to EU soil: Ex-post evaluation. https://www.europarl.europa.eu/thinktank/de/document/EPRS_STU(2018)621811. Accessed 30 January 2022
Renard T, Coolsaet R (2018a) Children in the Levant: Insights from Belgium on the Dilemmas of Repatriation and the Challenges of Reintegration. Security Policy Brief No. 98. http://www.egmontinstitute.be/content/uploads/2018/07/SPB98-Renard-Coolsaet_v2.pdf?type=pdf. Accessed 24 January 2022
Renard T, Coolsaet R (eds) (2018b) Returnees: Who Are They, Why Are They (Not) Coming Back and How Should We Deal with Them? Assessing Policies on Returning Foreign Terrorist Fighters in Belgium, Germany and the Netherlands. Egmont Paper 101. http://www.egmontinstitute.be/content/uploads/2018/02/egmont.papers.101_online_v1-3.pdf?type=pdf. Accessed 24 January 2022
Rodenhäuser T (2016) Squaring the Circle? Prosecuting Sexual Violence Against Child Soldiers by Their 'Own Forces'. JICJ 14(1):171–193
Roth (2019) "We Aren't Dangerous": Why Chechnya Has Welcomed Women Who Joined ISIS. https://www.theguardian.com/world/2019/mar/02/we-arent-dangerous-why-chechnya-has-welcomed-women-who-joined-isis. Accessed 24 January 2022

Saul B (2012) The Emerging International Law of Terrorism. In: Saul B (ed) Terrorism: Documents in International Law. Hart, Oxford, pp 67–87
Saul B (2015) Terrorism and International Humanitarian Law. In: Saul B (ed) Research Handbook on International Law and Terrorism. Edward Elgar, Cheltenham, pp 208–231
Schindler D (1979) The Different Types of Armed Conflicts According to the Geneva Conventions and Protocol. Recueil des cours, Martinus Nijhoff/Brill, The Hague
Tayler L (2020a) "Bring Me Back to Canada" - Plight of Canadians Held in Northeast Syria for Alleged ISIS Links. Human Rights Watch, New York. https://www.hrw.org/sites/default/files/media_2020a/06/canada0620_web_1.pdf. Accessed 25 January 2022
Tayler L (2020b) Despite US Veto, Desperate ISIS Suspects and Families Remain at Risk. Just Security. https://www.justsecurity.org/72300/despite-us-veto-desperate-isis-suspects-and-families-remain-at-risk/. Accessed 24 January 2022
The Bulan Institute for Peace Innovations (2020) Detention and Prosecution of Former ISIS Fighters in Iraq: Lessons Learned and an Assessment of the Deficits of the Judicial System. Policy Paper August 2020. https://bulaninstitute.org/wp-content/uploads/2020/08/Policy-Paper-on-Iraq-pdf.pdf. Accessed 24 January 2022
UNAMI, OHCHR (2020) Human Rights in the Administration of Justice in Iraq: Trials Under the anti-Terrorism Laws and Implications for Justice, Accountability and Social Cohesion in the aftermath of ISIL. https://reliefweb.int/sites/reliefweb.int/files/resources/Iraq_-_ISIL_trials_under_the_anti-terrorism_laws_and_the_implications_for_justice_28012020.pdf. Accessed 24 January 2022
UNICEF (2007) The Paris Principles: 'Principles and Guidelines on Children Associated with Armed Forces or Armed Groups'. https://www.unicef.org/mali/media/1561/file/ParisPrinciples.pdf. Accessed 24 January 2022
Van den Herik L, Schrijver N (2013) The Fragmented International Legal Response to Terrorism. In: van den Herik L, Schrijver N (eds) Counter-Terrorism Strategies in a Fragmented International Legal Order: Meeting the Challenges. Cambridge University Press, Cambridge, pp 1–26
Van der Heide L, Geenen J (2015) Preventing Terrorism in the Courtroom – The Criminalization of Preparatory Acts of Terrorism in the Netherlands. Security and Human Rights 26(1):162–192
Van Esveld (2017) Iraq/KRG: 1400 Women, Children from ISIS Areas Detained. https://www.hrw.org/news/2017/09/20/iraq/krg-1400-women-children-isis-areas-detained. Accessed 24 January 2022
Van Schaack B (2019) National Courts Step Up: Syrian Cases Proceeding in Domestic Courts, Available at: https://papers.ssrn.com/sol3/papers.cfm?abstract_id=3327676
Wille B (2018) Unfair ISIS Trial in Iraq Hands Women Harshest Sentences. https://www.hrw.org/news/2018/02/21/unfair-isis-trial-iraq-hands-women-harshest-sentences. Accessed 24 January 2022
Zegveld L (2003) Remedies for Victims of Violations of International Humanitarian Law. IRRC 85(851):497–526

Part II
Responses to the (Returning) Foreign Fighters Phenomenon: The International Dimension

Chapter 5
The International Legal and Policy Framework on Returning Foreign Fighters: Focus on the United Nations and the Global Counterterrorism Forum

Bibi T. van Ginkel

Contents

Abstract This chapter provides an overview of the international policy developments regarding the problem of returnees, particularly stemming from the United Nations (UN) and the Global Counterterrorism Forum (GCTF). These developments include both the adoption of binding legal obligations, and non-binding recommendations and policy developments. It reflects on the role the GCTF has acquired within the international counter-terrorism architecture and the way it influences policy-making in other fora. Particularly, the way the GCTF contributes to the international attempts to curb the threat posed by returnees and relocators by paving the way for the UN to turn non-binding recommendations and good practices into binding obligations or detailed instructions for Member States to report on their obligations. In this chapter, attention is paid to the lack of a definition of the term returnees. Furthermore, the various focus areas of the multidisciplinary response to the threat posed by returnees are elaborated upon. These entail measures targeting travel movements, criminal

---

B. T. van Ginkel (✉)
The Glocal Connection—Platform for Shared Security, International Centre for Counter-Terrorism (ICCT), The Hague, The Netherlands
e-mail: bvanginkel@glocalconnection.eu

F. Capone et al. (eds.), *Returning Foreign Fighters: Responses, Legal Challenges and Ways Forward*, https://doi.org/10.1007/978-94-6265-571-3_5

justice approaches, rehabilitation and reintegration, and the special focus on families and children.

Keywords Foreign fighters · Foreign terrorist fighters · Returnees · United Nations · The Global Counterterrorism Forum · Human rights · Counter-terrorism · Terrorism · Legal framework

5.1 Introduction

Since the end of 2011 and the beginning of 2012, the international community has been faced with a rise in the number of foreign fighters (FFs).[1] Most travelled to Syria and Iraq to eventually join violent extremist organisations or terrorist organisations, and are therefore in many documents referred to as 'foreign terrorist fighters' (FTFs).[2] According to the data gathered by the Soufan Center, an estimated 40,000 people, originating from more than 110 countries, travelled to Syria and Iraq to join the so-called terrorist organisation 'Islamic State' (IS).[3] States considered this development to pose a threat to both international and national security. In the first place, because the violent extremist organisations destabilised the region and created great insecurity in the region, particularly with the establishment of the Caliphate by IS in June 2014. And secondly, because recruitment was taking place in many different countries, sometimes leading to travel to join the violent extremist organisations, and at times leading to the establishment of violent extremist networks or organisations within their own countries.

The steep rise in these numbers has led to the development of international and national policies to curb the threat by taking measures such as preventing travel by, for instance, revoking travel documents and criminalising acts such as recruitment, assistance to travel, and travel itself. At the international level, the Global Counter-terrorism Forum (GCTF)—which will be explained in greater detail below—drafted a non-binding good practices document on the issue of FTFs in 2014, called "The Hague-Marrakech Memorandum on Good Practices for a More Effective Response to the FTF Phenomenon".[4] The GCTF FTF memorandum paved the way for the

---

[1] Bakker et al. 2014, p. 1.

[2] Some international organisations only refer to FFs, others only to FTFs, and some refer to both terms in their documents. The United Nations refers to FTFs; the European Union (EU) refers to both the term FFs and FTFs; the Global Counterterrorism Forum (GCTF) refers to FTFs; the Organization for Security and Co-operation in Europe (OSCE) refers to FTFs; the Council of Europe (CoE) refers to both FFs and FTFs; and the North Atlantic Treaty Organization (NATO) refers to both FFs and FTFs.

[3] Barrett 2017, p. 7.

[4] See the GCTF website for the document: <https://www.thegctf.org/Portals/1/Documents/Framework%20Documents/2016%20and%20before/GCTF-The-Hague-Marrakech-Memorandum-ENG.pdf?ver=2016-09-01-150615-977> (last visited on 25 August 2020); GCTF 2014.

unanimous adoption of the United Nations (UN) Security Council (SC) Resolution 2178 (2014).[5] According to this resolution, Member States shall prevent and suppress recruiting, organising, transporting or equipping; prevent and suppress financing; and prevent travel of FTFs.

While at first, the international measures adopted concentrated on preventing the travel of FTFs, soon after, states began to worry about the return of these FTFs as well. In November 2017, a study based on the figures of 79 countries estimated that almost 7000 FTFs likely had been killed on the battlefield, while almost 15,000 had left the conflict zones, of which only 36% were imprisoned, and 46% was estimated to have travelled home without having entered the criminal justice system.[6] Although this study does not specify where these FTFs were imprisoned, nor where the remaining 20% of FTFs have gone, it nevertheless explains the concerns of the international community. Particularly since security threat reports of various organisations and states[7] warned that returning FTFs, also referred to as 'returnees', have potentially developed knowledge and experience on the use of weapons and explosives, and have become battle-hardened. An immediate concern was related to the possible direct instructions or the intention to plot to commit terrorist attacks in the countries of return. They could also try to form new cells, recruit new members or link up with existing (home-grown) terrorist cells. Through their earlier travel and membership of the violent extremist organisations in Syria and Iraq, they have acquired an extensive international network with potential contacts that might facilitate the trafficking of people, finances and goods. Moreover, due to their experiences in Syria and Iraq, they might come back either frustrated (particularly after the dismantling of the Caliphate) or traumatised and unstable, making them volatile and unpredictable in their behaviour. In a UN CTED (Counterterrorism Executive Directorate) Trends Report, it was also concluded that the returnees are likely to remain a significant long-term challenge.[8] Furthermore, terrorist attacks in various countries in 2014–2017 with links to returnees or IS showed the urgency of the matter.[9] This was also confirmed in a report by Europol in 2015.[10] Although these reports often refer to returnees and relocators as part of the same threat phenomenon, the details on relocators are very scarce. The earlier mentioned UN CTED Trends Report points out that there are only few accurate figures on the number of FTFs that travelled on to third countries. The limited information available mostly indicates East and North Africa, and South, South-East and Central Asia as main destinations.[11]

---

[5] UN Security Council 2014.

[6] Cragin 2017.

[7] UN Security Council 2017b; Barrett 2017, p. 7; Netherlands General Intelligence and Security Service 2017.

[8] UN CTED 2018, p. 1.

[9] Attacks occurred in Brussels at the Jewish Museum in 2014 and at a metro station and an airport in 2016, in Beirut in 2015, in Paris at a concert hall and football stadium in 2015, on the boulevard in Nice in 2016, in Manchester during a concert in 2017, and in Istanbul in 2017.

[10] Europol 2015.

[11] UN CTED 2018, p. 9; UN Security Council 2017b, paras 53, 63, 71–72.

Finally, as far as states have already developed rehabilitation and reintegration programmes to deal with the returnees, most programmes have not yet been evaluated and proven to be fully successful. For these reasons, governments have been very worried about the rising threat posed by returnees, which led to the development of national and international policies to deal with this issue. It must be stated from the offset that these policies do not deal with active repatriation of citizens from the conflict area but merely with setting up programmes to detect their travel, prosecute suspects and provide for effective rehabilitation and reintegration. In fact, so far, the international community is highly divided with regard to the question of repatriation followed by prosecution and rehabilitation and reintegration. While states like the United States (US), Russia, Kosovo, and Kazakhstan are promoting repatriation and have already repatriated large numbers of citizens,[12] European countries are mostly reluctant to do the same and rather promote prosecution in the region. This political disagreement recently amounted to a US veto to a draft resolution of the UN SC tabled by Indonesia with a focus on prosecution, rehabilitation and reintegration of terrorists, including FTFs and their accompanying families, in August 2020.[13]

This chapter provides an overview of the international legal and policy developments regarding the problem of returnees and relocators, particularly stemming from the UN and the GCTF. These developments hence include both the adoption of binding legal obligations and non-binding recommendations and policy developments. The rationale behind the focus on the UN and GCTF will be elaborated on in the next section. After that, the scope of the term returnees will be assessed. This section is followed by a section focusing on the main themes that are addressed by the UN and GCTF, namely measures targeting travel movements, criminal justice approaches, rehabilitation and reintegration, and the special focus on families and children. In the final section, several concluding remarks will be made.

5.2 Leading the International Policy Agenda

This chapter focuses on the role of the UN and the GCTF in the development of policies and legal obligations regarding returning FTFs (RFTFs). The fact that the focus is limited to these two international actors demands an explanation, although the fact that the UN features in this chapter makes sense, as the UN, after all, has fulfilled a leading role in policy development on issues of counter-terrorism for quite some time, especially given the number of binding UN SC resolutions that have been adopted on the topic.[14] The focus on the GCTF, however, might seem less logical, as the GCTF is not an international organisation established based on a convention, with

[12] Ní Aoláin 2019; The Moscow Times 2020; France 24 2019.

[13] See UN Security Council 2020.

[14] Building on the existing acquis of UN SC resolutions on counter-terrorism, the resolution adopted that specifically targets the challenges related to RFTFs is UN SC Resolution 2396 (2017).

organs, a charter and legal personality, and it does not adopt binding international policy documents.

The forum was established in 2011 with 30 members.[15] Its main goal is to bring together experts and practitioners from around the world to share experiences and expertise and to develop strategies and tools on how to counter the evolving terrorist threat. It, therefore, meets in apolitical and technical settings and has over the years produced a significant set of mainly non-binding good practices documents that are the result of consultations between diplomats, practitioners and experts, and are adopted with the consensus of all members, including the five permanent Member States of the UN SC. These features have opened the opportunity to use the GCTF as a laboratory for difficult international policy discussions on counter-terrorism, and this has resulted in documents that, in time, paved the way for the UN and other organisations to follow their example. A clear and already mentioned example is UN SC Resolution 2178 that was adopted right after the GCTF The Hague-Marrakech Memorandum on Good Practices for a More Effective Response to the FTF Phenomenon was endorsed in September 2014.[16]

In almost a decade, the GCTF has thus positioned itself as one of the most important players in the field of counter-terrorism. Since its establishment in 2011, 40 framework documents have been adopted on topics such as criminal justice and the rule of law, countering violent extremism, FTFs, detention and rehabilitation, and travel and border control. This is remarkable given the fact that GCTF framework documents are always non-binding. In many situations, however, they set a benchmark for states and international and regional organisations to follow. This is either a direct relation, such as is the case with the earlier mentioned UN SC Resolution 2178, as well as with the Council of Europe's 'Additional Protocol to the Convention on the Prevention of Terrorism' that also focuses on criminal law responses regarding the FTF phenomenon, and which turns the GCTF recommendations into binding obligations. Or more indirectly, in situations where the GCTF framework documents inform, for instance, the guiding documents of UN CTED, which form the basis of UN CTED's dialogue with UN Member States regarding their implementation obligations of UN SC Resolutions. Beyond the UN, an example can be found in the 'Guidelines on the Links between Terrorism and Transnational Organised Crime' developed by the Council of Europe, which follow the example of the GCTF 'Addendum to The Hague Good Practices on the Nexus between Transnational Organized Crime and Terrorism: Focus on Criminal Justice'.[17]

---

[15] See the website of the GCTF at <https://www.thegctf.org>. The membership consists of 29 states and the European Union.

[16] UN Security Council 2014; interviews (on file with the author) with relevant stakeholders show that the adoption of the SC resolution was made possible due to the extensive deliberations that had taken place within the context of the GCTF.

[17] Council of Europe Committee on Counter-Terrorism (Working Group of Experts on Terrorism and Transnational Organised Crime) 2020.

This authoritative position comes with a responsibility to ensure that these recommendations and good practices establish standards that are in full compliance with the rule of law, international law and human rights law. This point, in particular, is not without criticism. Most notably, the UN Special Rapporteur on the promotion and protection of human rights and fundamental freedoms while countering terrorism, professor Fionnuala Ní Aoláin, in her report to the UN General Assembly in 2019, addresses the role of soft law and new institutions in the creation, enforcement, oversight and regulation of counter-terrorism measures.[18] Although admitting that the term 'soft law' is often viewed as controversial,[19] the UN Special Rapporteur notes that

> the most uncontroversial definition is that 'soft law' constitutes those international norms, principles and procedures that are outside the formal sources of Article 38 (1) of the Statute of the International Court of Justice and lack the requisite degree of normative content to create enforceable rights and obligations but are still able to produce certain legal effects.[20]

She argues that the benefit of using soft law mechanisms is related to the speed of development, the informality and less onerous procedural limitations, and the fact that on many occasions, the formulation of the soft law norms is mostly done by like-minded states.[21] Yet, often soft law norms transpose into formal and binding legal frameworks,[22] either in a straightforward process by addressing the technical aspects of counter-terrorism as mentioned in a guidance document, or formulated in a principle or recommendation, in, for instance, a UN SC resolution with or without a reference to the original source, or by adding it to the reporting requirements by states under, for instance, UN SC Resolution 1373 (2001).[23] The UN Special Rapporteur furthermore concludes that, in particular, 'hard' security soft law regulations are easily transposed into formal and binding norms, whereas detailed human rights recommendations that outline the 'how to implement', do not benefit from the fast-track formalisation processes.[24] This sets the wrong example for states and other organisations that can easily refer to these informal processes and results to legitimise their own policies resulting in a trend that is imbalanced regarding checks and balances and losing legitimacy even beyond its development within a forum like the GCTF.

Given these developments, the influence of the platform and the severe criticism on the way it operates, it is merited to focus our attention on the way the GCTF has influenced the agenda regarding RFTFs.

---

[18] UN General Assembly 2019.

[19] Ibid., para 12.

[20] Ibid., para 8.

[21] Ibid., para 10.

[22] See for a more in-depth discussion on the role of soft law in law development for instance Abbott and Snidal 2000.

[23] UN General Assembly 2019, para 25.

[24] Ibid., paras 26 and 54.

5.3 Regulating Without Defining: Who Are Considered to Be Returnees?

Having explained the important role played by the GCTF in the development of international counter-terrorism laws and policies, and in particular its influence on the developments within the UN, we can now turn to the problem of countering RFTFs. The first question, when studying the various international documents adopted on returnees, relates to the identity of the targeted group. Who are these returnees? Is one only targeting former fighters who return to their country of nationality or citizenship? And should the fighting have been in the service of an international listed terrorist organisation? Or do returning fighters who joined the armed opposition, who in times with the support of Western states have fought the Assad regime in Syria, belong to this category as well? And are family members and children included?

The most prominent GCTF framework document on the issue of returnees is the GCTF 'Addendum to The Hague-Marrakech Memorandum on Good Practices for a More Effective Response to the FTF Phenomenon, with a focus on Returning FTFs' (hereafter GCTF Addendum on Returnees).[25] This document comprises a set of non-binding good practices, endorsed by the GCTF members in September 2016, and has a focus—as the title of the document suggests—on returning foreign terrorist fighters. The chapeau text of the GCTF Addendum on Returnees merely states, as a matter of defining the scope, that the document is concerned with FTFs that return home or travel to a third state. But already in the chapeau text, the document warns that it is hard to make a distinction between the category of 'home-grown' terrorists and 'foreign terrorist fighters', and that the radicalisation life cycle of RFTFs often starts at home.

Since the Addendum builds on the GCTF The Hague-Marrakech Memorandum of 2014 with a focus on FTFs, the description of the term FTF of that framework document might therefore be useful to elaborate here: FTFs are understood to be "individuals who travel abroad to a State other than their States of residence or nationality to engage in, undertake, plan, prepare, carry out or otherwise support terrorist activity or to provide or receive training to do so (often labelled as "terrorist training")". It must be stressed though that the Memorandum explicitly includes a disclaimer in a footnote, making clear that the Memorandum does not intend to say anything on the legal status of an FTF under international law, in particular international humanitarian, international human rights, or refugee law.

[25] GCTF 2016.

The GCTF Addendum on Returnees also makes a reference to the law enforcement tools detailed in UN SC Resolution 2178 (2014) to curb the threat of RFTFs. In this resolution, RFTFs as such are not defined, but a definition of the term FTF is included, namely "individuals who travel to a State other than their States of residence or nationality for the purpose of the perpetration, planning, or preparation of, or participation in, terrorist acts or the providing or receiving of terrorist training, including in connection with armed conflict".[26] However, the reference to UN SC Resolution 2178 (2014) does not provide absolute clarity on the exact scope of the term. As is the case with references on terrorism in all other UN SC resolutions, except Resolution 1566 (2004),[27] a definition of what terrorism entails is missing. The key issue, particularly in relation to the phenomenon of FTFs, is whether terrorist offences committed within the context of an armed conflict are included in the scope of this definition, in contrast to the limited scope of the many universal issue-specific conventions on terrorist crimes, which exclude acts committed during armed conflict.[28]

Notwithstanding the lack of a clear definition, it does appear that the GCTF framework document and the UN SC Resolution mostly target returning foreign *terrorist* fighters, and avoids making statements or recommendations on returning foreign fighters more generally.

5.4 The Multidisciplinary and Multi-stakeholder Response to the Threat Posed by Returnees

Given the complexity of the problem, an effective policy needs to be comprehensive, addressing various aspects of the problem, different phases of government intervention, and the involvement of multiple government agencies and non-state actors, all in good coordination and cooperation. The policy aspects that are mostly targeted by the GCTF and UN documents on RFTFs thus focus on travel movements, the criminal justice approach, and rehabilitation and reintegration processes.

The GCTF Addendum on Returnees focuses *inter alia* on detection and information sharing regarding RFTFs, the use of individual risk assessment tools, the need to work with multiple partners, including local government, civil society and private sector, and the importance of integrating rehabilitative measures in the criminal justice response.

[26] UN Security Council 2014.

[27] UN Security Council 2004.

[28] See for an elaborate discussion on the delimitation of terrorism crimes and war crimes or crimes against humanity committed during armed conflict Cuyckens and Paulussen 2019. See also Chap. 8 by Van Poecke and Cuyckens in this volume.

The most prominent document adopted by the UN SC on RFTFs is resolution 2396 (2017).[29] The resolution urges Member States to strengthen their efforts to stem the threat posed by FTFs by implementing measures on border control, criminal justice, information-sharing, and counter-extremism. The UN SC also refers to the emerging threat of returning foreign fighters who participated in some terrorist attacks in their countries of origin or nationality. The resolution furthermore calls on Member States to take appropriate action regarding suspected terrorists and their family members who entered their territories, including by considering appropriate prosecution, rehabilitation, and reintegration measures in compliance with domestic and international law. With regard to border control, the UN SC also pointed to the need to prevent counterfeiting, forgery or fraudulent use of identity documents. The UN SC, therefore, decided that Member States shall implement systems to collect biometric data and to develop and share information related to watchlists or databases of known and suspected terrorists, including FTFs.

5.4.1 Managing Travel, Detection and Identification

With regard to the threat posed by returnees, government responses, first of all, focus on managing the travel movements through detection, identification, and interception. The challenges that states are facing in this respect are related to travel via porous borders, the use of false or stolen documentation, the diversification of travel routes in order to avoid specific checkpoints, use of encrypted communication technology to conceal travel plans, and attempts to emerge in refugee flows. Policies, therefore, focus on ensuring identity and travel papers are not forged, by improving the control mechanisms at borders and by adopting measures for preventing the counterfeiting, forgery or fraudulent use of identity papers and travel documents. There is also a focus on strengthening border control, for instance, through the use of biometric data to verify a traveller's identity, registration and exchange of data collected through the use of Advance Passenger Information (API) systems and Passenger Name Records (PNR) systems, and the development of watchlists or databases of known and suspected terrorists for law enforcement and border security.[30] It is particularly interesting to note that the paragraphs in the UN SC Resolution 2396 regarding the use of API, PNR, watchlists and biometric data use binding language, making them obligations under Chapter VII of the UN Charter.

In addition to the GCTF Addendum on Returnees, the GCTF developed two relevant good practice documents particularly related to border control and travel: the GCTF Good Practices in the Area of Border Security and Management in the Context of Counterterrorism and Stemming the Flow of "Foreign Terrorist Fighters",

---

[29] UN Security Council 2017a.

[30] See ibid., paras 2, 11, 12, 13, and 15. These recommendations and obligations have been further elaborated in the 2018 Addendum to the 2015 Madrid Guiding Principles, see UN Security Council 2018. See also GCTF 2016, Recommendation 1.

and the GCTF New York Memorandum on Good Practices for Interdicting Terrorist Travel.[31] Particularly the latter document referred to UN SC Resolution 2396 and the requirement upon Member States to develop and implement systems to collect biometric data and to develop watchlists or databases of known and suspected terrorists. It also refers to the obligation upon Member States to collect and analyse API and PNR data in border screening. Recognising the challenges states might face, as installing and operating these systems is complex, resource-intensive and expensive, GCTF, with this Memorandum, developed guidelines for improving terrorist screening mechanisms and capabilities to interdict terrorist travel. It is important to note that whereas the Memorandum elaborates on the technical requirements and the methods to improve cooperation, it does mention the need to ensure that there is no arbitrary or unlawful interference with privacy and other human rights obligations, and that oversight on the storing and handling of the data is guaranteed.[32] It even includes a dedicated section on 'privacy, rights and redress'.[33] Following the argumentation of the UN Special Rapporteur mentioned before, and her criticism on the detailed technical instruction on hard security regulations, it is likely that the references to privacy, oversight and redress are still not considered enough of a reassurance that states fully comprehend the necessity of following the human rights requirements when implementing regulations on watchlisting and collection of API, PNR and biometric data. The Office of the High Commissioner for Human Rights (OHCHR) instead developed a set of guidelines that clarify the standard that needs to be fulfilled in this respect.[34] These ten guidelines link the various procedural steps that relate to the regulation of watchlisting to the specific human rights obligations, providing very tangible guidance in this regard, instead of merely referring to the need to abide by human rights obligations in a very general and abstract form.

5.4.2 Criminal Justice Approach

As reflected in the numbers of RFTFs that have likely returned home but have not entered into a criminal justice procedure, this is a major concern for states. This has partly to do with the lack of timely detection but also with the difficulty of securing relevant evidence from the battlefield regarding their involvement in crimes, regardless of whether these are international core crimes or terrorist crimes.[35] The UN SC, therefore, reiterates the obligation upon Member States to ensure that persons who participated in the financing, planning, preparation or perpetration of terrorist acts or in support of terrorist acts are brought to justice pursuant to UN SC Resolution 1373

[31] GCTF 2016, 2019.

[32] GCTF 2019, Good Practices 2 and 4.

[33] Ibid., Good Practices 14–16.

[34] OHCHR 2020.

[35] Eurojust 2020; van Ginkel 2016; UN CTED 2019. See also Chap. 7 by Paulussen and Mehra in this volume.

(2001).[36] The Council furthermore urges states to develop appropriate investigative and prosecutorial strategies.[37] There is particular reference to the need to support capacity building, to share best practices and technical expertise for the purpose of improving the collection, handling, preservation and sharing of relevant information and evidence, including information obtained from the internet or the conflict zone.[38] These issues are subsequently picked up in the GCTF Abuja Recommendations on the Collection, Use and Sharing of Evidence for Purposes of Criminal Prosecution of Terrorist Suspects.[39] The Abuja Recommendations furthermore focused on the issues related to international, regional and bilateral judicial cooperation, for instance, through strengthening mechanisms for mutual legal assistance, which are also referenced in UN SC Resolution 2396.[40]

5.4.3 Rehabilitation and Reintegration

Another important aspect of the criminal justice approach is related to strengthening strategies related to prosecution, rehabilitation and reintegration (PRR). UN SC Resolution 2396 "calls on Member States to assess and investigate suspected individuals whom they have reasonable grounds to believe are terrorists, including suspected foreign terrorist fighters and their accompanying family members, including spouses and children."[41] The Council stresses the importance of developing and implementing comprehensive risk assessments regarding these individuals. This issue is further elaborated upon in the GCTF Addendum on Returnees in various good practices that underline the importance of using these risk assessments to design tailor-made interventions and applying a case-by-case approach addressing specific categories of returnees.[42] The GCTF further specifies that developing individually tailored responses should also include addressing the underlying causes of the individual's radicalisation process, ensuring the environment an individual eventually returns to is safe and the individual's (mental) health is addressed. All this should translate into tailored and effective rehabilitation and reintegration interventions as part of a comprehensive strategy to screen, prosecute, rehabilitate and reintegrate, the so-called SPRR strategy.[43] The resolution also refers to the importance of developing rehabilitation programmes in consultation with local communities, mental health and

[36] UN Security Council 2017a, para 17, and see also UN Security Council 2001.

[37] UN Security Council 2017a, para 18.

[38] Ibid., para 20.

[39] GCTF 2018a. See also Chap. 7 by Paulussen and Mehra in this volume.

[40] UN Security Council 2017a, paras 22–25.

[41] Ibid., para 29.

[42] GCTF 2016, Recommendations 2 and 3.

[43] GCTF 2016, Recommendations 3, 4, 5 and 6. But see also GCTF 2012.

education practitioners and other relevant civil society organisations and stresses the overall importance to practice a whole of government approach and recognising the role civil society organisations can play.[44] These issues are once again further elaborated in the GCTF Addendum on Returnees with the recommendations that focus on the need to invest and develop a close partnership with local government and local communities, and on the need to engage and build sustainable partnerships with multidisciplinary actors in the private sector and civil society organisations.[45]

5.4.4 Families and Children[46]

Let us now turn to the role of families and children. The UN SC emphasises that women and children associated with RFTFs may have served in many different roles, including as supporters, facilitators, or perpetrators of terrorist acts. This may have implications for the tailored PRR strategies, particularly taking into account the possibility that they are victims of terrorism.[47] The Council furthermore points out that providing a whole of government approach to reintegration and rehabilitation of children is of particular importance to contribute to the well-being of children and to sustainable peace and security.[48] The principles that should guide these programmes have furthermore been elaborated in the 2018 Addendum to the 2015 Madrid Guiding Principles, developed under the auspices of the UN Counterterrorism Committee (UNCTC).[49] In 2019, the UN Secretary-General, furthermore, issued 'Key Principles for the Protection, Reparation, Prosecution, Rehabilitation and Reintegration of Women and Children with Links to United Nations Listed Terrorist Groups'.[50]

Within the context of the GCTF, a special framework document was developed to focus on returning families of FTFs.[51] In addition to the different roles already identified in the UN SC Resolution, the GCTF Good Practices also point out that family members might have travelled both voluntarily or involuntarily with FTFs. This could even be the result of human trafficking. Another problem occurs due to the lack of identification or citizenship documents. This could be the result of a conscious choice of the returning family members. However, it could also result from documents being taken away from them when they lived in the Caliphate or because children born there were never provided with citizenship papers. The GCTF Good Practices document deals with the issues of detection, identification and intake of returning families;[52]

[44] UN Security Council 2017a, paras 30, 32, and 35.

[45] GCTF 2016, Recommendations 4 and 5.

[46] See Chap. 4 by Capone in this volume.

[47] UN Security Council 2017a, para 31.

[48] Ibid., para 36.

[49] UN Security Council 2018, Guiding Principle 12.

[50] United Nations 2019.

[51] GCTF 2018b.

[52] Ibid., Good Practices 1–4.

individually tailored interventions;[53] criminal justice responses to enable criminal accountability of returnees;[54] responses regarding returning children;[55] responses regarding returning women;[56] and the role of families and communities.[57]

A key consideration, for instance, when one deals with children, is to ensure that the best interests of the child are the primary consideration when taking action, and that juvenile justice standards are respected in situations that children are entered into a criminal justice procedure.[58] Moreover, it is important to note that reference is also made in the GCTF document to the UN Office on Drugs and Crime (UNODC) Handbook on Children Recruited and Exploited by Terrorist and Violent Extremist Groups: The Role of the Justice System, because the reference strengthens the importance and provides more detailed guidance.[59]

With regard to the responses to women, the GCTF Good Practices underline the importance to be conscious that women and girls have become victims of sexual and gender-based violence and other forms of violence and coercion, which has implications for effective psycho-social responses to deal with traumas, as well as for the criminal justice responses.[60]

5.5 Concluding Remarks

In this chapter, it has been illustrated how the UN and GCTF mutually strengthen their attempts to curb the threat posed by RFTFs. The GCTF contributes to this objective by paving the way for the UN to turn non-binding recommendations and good practices into binding obligations. At the same time, the GCTF often elaborates on the technical 'how to implement' mechanisms that need to be in place to meet the objectives set. These technical details particularly focus on measures to effectively control travel and assist in identification and detection, the criminal justice approach and the need for effective PRR strategies.

Both the UN and GCTF stress the importance of a comprehensive approach. Such an approach, however, should also include active promotion and strengthening of human rights in the implementation of counter-terrorism measures. The central question is whether the policies of the UN and the GCTF sufficiently promote the adherence to human rights obligations to fulfil their own objective to promote a

[53] Ibid., Good Practices 5–7.

[54] Ibid., Good Practices 8–10.

[55] Ibid., Good Practices 11–14.

[56] Ibid., Good Practices 15–17.

[57] Ibid., Good Practices 18–20.

[58] Ibid., Good Practices 11 and 12.

[59] UNODC 2017.

[60] GCTF 2018b, Good Practice 16.

comprehensive approach. Although specific agencies of the UN, such as the OHCHR, in several documents, have offered more specific guidance on how to implement counter-terrorism measures while respecting human rights, these detailed instructions hardly ever translate to operative and binding paragraphs in UN SC resolutions. This is in contrast with the more detailed instruction that often relates to so-called 'hard' security measures, such as border control or criminal justice approaches. An argument oftentimes heard during text negotiations on new policy documents is that the repetitive language with a link to human rights obligations pointing out limitations to the use of specific powers might give the impression that the states are the villains instead of the terrorists whom they are trying to fight. The outcome of such negotiations on the text is to settle for general references to human rights obligations. It is, however, this author's opinion that a more balanced approach is needed, since unclarity on the specific obligations that follow from human rights regarding the way security measures need to be implemented leaves too much room for states to implement measures as they see fit, without respecting human rights while doing it. Criticism in such cases is easily rebutted with a reference to how well they are implementing international counter-terrorism policies, though it is a well-established fact that human rights abuses in counter-terrorism policies can function as a root cause for radicalisation to violent extremism.

Although it is important to note the specific attention attributed to the tailored approach needed to deal with women and children, it seems ironic that the focus on the potential victim status does not translate into a proactive policy to effectively make an end to the continuing situation in which many women and children find themselves in camps in Syria and Iraq, and where they remain vulnerable to further abuse. A genuine comprehensive strategy would, after all, also include a policy to make an end to the inhumane situation in which the people in these camps find themselves. Such a strategy should include a policy regarding the repatriation of nationals. In the words of the US representative, following the veto cast by the US:

> The Indonesian draft resolution before us (S/2020/852), supposedly designed to reinforce international action on counter-terrorism, was worse than no resolution at all. This draft resolution was meant to address the prosecution, rehabilitation and reintegration of terrorists, including foreign terrorist fighters and their accompanying family members. And yet it fails to even include reference to the crucial first step — repatriation to countries of origin or nationality. (…) Terrorist fighters and their families are easily ignored if they are someone else's problem. But I tell the Council now, and I say this with absolute conviction: failing to address head-on the importance of repatriation will inevitably perpetuate the problem of terrorism.[61]

[61] See US Statement in UN Security Council 2020.

References

Articles, Books and Other Documents

Abbott K, Snidal D (2000) Hard and Soft Law in International Governance, International Organization 54:421–456

Bakker E, Paulussen C, Entenmann E (2014) Dealing with European Foreign Fighters in Syria: Governance Challenges and Legal Implications. ICCT Research Paper. https://icct.nl/wp-content/uploads/2013/12/ICCT-Bakker-Paulussen-Entenmann-Dealing-With-European-Foreign-Fighters-in-Syria.pdf Accessed 6 April 2020

Barrett R (2017) Beyond the Caliphate: Foreign Fighters and the Threat of Returnees. The Soufan Center. https://thesoufancenter.org/wp-content/uploads/2017/11/Beyond-the-Caliphate-Foreign-Fighters-and-the-Threat-of-Returnees-TSC-Report-October-2017-v3.pdf Accessed 6 April 2020

Council of Europe Committee on Counter-Terrorism, Working Group of Experts on Terrorism and Transnational Organised Crime (2020) Guidelines on the Links between Terrorism and Transnational Organised Crime. CDCT-TTOC 01 rev 9. https://search.coe.int/cm/pages/result_details.aspx?objectid=0900001680a19655 Accessed 23 August 2021

Cragin K (2017) Foreign Fighter "Hot Potato". Lawfare. https://www.lawfareblog.com/foreign-fighter-hot-potato Accessed 21 February 2021

Cuyckens H, Paulussen C (2019) The Prosecution of foreign fighters in Western Europe: The difficult relationship between counter-terrorism and international humanitarian law. ICCT Publications. https://icct.nl/publication/the-prosecution-of-foreign-fighters-under-international-humanitarian-law-misconceptions-and-opportunities/ Accessed 23 August 2021

Eurojust (2020) Eurojust memorandum on Battlefield Evidence. https://www.eurojust.europa.eu/sites/default/files/2020-09/2020-09-14-Eurojust-Memorandum-on-Battlefield-Evidence.pdf Accessed 22 February 2021

Europol (2015) European Union Terrorism Situation and Trend Report 2015. https://www.europol.eu/content/european-union-terrorism-situation-and-trend-report-2015 Accessed 21 February 2021

France 24 (2019) Repatriate or reject: What countries are doing with IS group families. https://www.france24.com/en/20190611-repatriation-families-islamic-state-group-jihadists-children. Accessed 19 February 2021

GCTF (2012) Rome Memorandum on Good Practices for Rehabilitation and Reintegration of Violent Extremist Offenders. https://www.thegctf.org/Portals/1/Documents/Framework%20Documents/2016%20and%20before/GCTF-Rome-Memorandum-ENG.pdf?ver=2016-09-01-121309-677 Accessed 19 February 2021

GCTF (2014) The Hague-Marrakech Memorandum on Good Practices for a More Effective Response to the FTF Phenomenon. https://www.thegctf.org/Portals/1/Documents/Framework%20Documents/2016%20and%20before/GCTF-The-Hague-Marrakech-Memorandum-ENG.pdf?ver=2016-09-01-150615-977 Accessed 25 August 2020

GCTF (2016) Addendum to The Hague-Marrakech Memorandum on Good Practices for a More Effective Response to the FTF Phenomenon, with a focus on Returning FTFs. https://www.thegctf.org/Portals/1/Documents/Framework%20Documents/2016%20and%20before/Addendum%20to%20The%20Hague-Marrakech%20Memorandum%20EN.pdf?ver=2020-01-13-163556-773 Accessed 19 February 2021

GCTF (2018a) Abuja Recommendations on the Collection, Use and Sharing of Evidence for Purposes of Criminal Prosecution of Terrorist Suspects. https://www.thegctf.org/Portals/1/Documents/Framework%20Documents/2018/GCTF-Abuja-Recommendations_ENG.pdf?ver=2018-09-21-122246-523&timestamp=1580219129062 Accessed 21 February 2021

GCTF (2018b) Good Practices on Addressing the Challenge of Returning Families of Foreign Terrorist Fighters (FTFs). https://www.thegctf.org/Portals/1/Documents/Framework%20Documents/2018/GCTF-GoodPractices-on-Returning-Families-of-FTFs_ENG.pdf?ver=2018-09-25-101427323 Accessed 21 February 2021

GCTF (2019) New York Memorandum on Good Practices for Interdicting Terrorist Travel. https://www.thegctf.org/Portals/1/Documents/Framework%20Documents/2019/New%20York%20Memorandum%20ENG.pdf?ver=2020-01-13-142911-113 Accessed 22 February 2021

Netherlands General Intelligence and Security Service (2017) Focus on Returnees. https://english.aivd.nl/publications/publications/2017/02/15/publication-focus-on-returnees Accessed 22 February 2021

Ní Aoláin F (2019) Time to Bring Women and Children Home from Iraq and Syria. Just Security. https://www.justsecurity.org/64402/time-to-bring-women-and-children-home-from-iraq-and-syria/ Accessed 19 February 2021

OHCHR (2020) Draft Human Rights Principles Applicable to Watchlisting. United Nations Human Rights Special Procedures. https://www.ohchr.org/EN/Issues/Terrorism/Pages/Research-papers-and-Inputs.aspx Accessed 22 February 2021

The Moscow Times (2020) Russia Repatriates Islamic State-Linked Children from Syria. https://www.themoscowtimes.com/2020/02/07/russia-repatriates-islamic-state-linked-children-from-syria-a69195. Accessed 19 February 2021

UN CTED (2018) The challenge of returning and relocating foreign terrorist fighters: Research perspectives. CTED Trends Report. https://www.un.org/securitycouncil/ctc/content/challenge-returning-and-relocating-foreign-terrorist-fighters-research-perspectives Accessed 21 February 2021

UN CTED (2019) Guidelines to facilitate the use and admissibility as evidence in national criminal courts of information collected, handled, preserved and shared by the military to prosecute terrorist offences. https://www.un.org/securitycouncil/ctc/sites/www.un.org.securitycouncil.ctc/files/files/documents/2021/Jan/cted_military_evidence_guidelines.pdf Accessed 22 February 2021

UN General Assembly (2019) Report of the Special Rapporteur on the promotion and protection of human rights and fundamental freedoms while countering terrorism, UN Doc A/74/335

UN Security Council (2001) Resolution 1373 (2001) UN Doc. S/RES/1373

UN Security Council (2004) Resolution 1566 (2004), UN Doc. S/RES/1566

UN Security Council (2014) Resolution 2178 (2014), UN Doc. S/RES/2178

UN Security Council (2017a) Resolution 2396 (2017), UN Doc. S/RES/2396

UN Security Council (2017b) Twentieth Report of the Analytical Support and Sanctions Monitoring Team submitted pursuant to resolution 2253 (2015) concerning ISIL (Da'esh), Al-Qaida and associated individuals and entities, UN Doc. S/2017/573

UN Security Council (2018) Addendum to the guiding principles on foreign terrorist fighters (2018), UN Doc. S/2018/1177

UN Security Council (2020) Letter dated 31 August 2020 from the President of the Security Council addressed to the Secretary-General and the Permanent Representatives of the members of the Security Council, UN Doc. S/2020/870

United Nations (2019) Key Principles for the Protection, Reparation, Prosecution, Rehabilitation and Reintegration of Women and Children associated with Links to United Nations Listed Terrorist Groups. https://www.un.org/counterterrorism/sites/www.un.org.counterterrorism/files/key_principles-april_2019.pdf Accessed 19 February 2021

UNODC (2017) Handbook on Children Recruited and Exploited by Terrorist and Violent Extremist Groups: the Role of the Justice System. https://www.unodc.org/documents/terrorism/Publications/HB%20Children/Handbook_on_Children_Recruited_and_Exploited_by_Terrorist_and_Violent_Extremist_Groups_the_Role_of_the_Justice_System.E.pdf Accessed 21 February 2021

Van Ginkel B (2016) Prosecuting foreign terrorist fighters: what role for the military? ICCT Policy Brief. https://doi.org/10.19165/2016.2.01 Accessed 22 February 2021

Chapter 6
'Foreign Fighters', Syrian Camps and the Jurisdictional Quagmire

Helen Duffy

Contents

Abstract The relevance of international human rights law (IHRL) as a constraining framework, and the ability of victims to challenge rights-infringing measures on human rights grounds, depend on the law applying in the first place. Yet states have increasingly advanced a restrictive approach to the 'extra-territorial' scope of their obligations, purporting to exclude a host of responses to the 'foreign fighter' phenomenon—including targeted killings, citizenship deprivation of persons abroad or decisions regarding repatriation (or not) of nationals—from the purview of IHRL. This chapter surveys the development of jurisprudence on the question of 'jurisdiction,' or extra-territorial scope, across regional and international human rights systems. While recognising divergence of approaches, and outstanding challenges, it also highlights a dominant trend internationally towards a flexible, holistic and fact-specific approach to the jurisdictional nexus. The chapter focuses on the relevance of these standards to decisions regarding the repatriation of persons from abysmal detention camps abroad, and considers the first international decision on

H. Duffy (✉)
University of Leiden, Human Rights in Practice, Leiden/The Hague, The Netherlands
e-mail: helen@rightsinpractice.org

F. Capone et al. (eds.), *Returning Foreign Fighters: Responses, Legal Challenges and Ways Forward*, https://doi.org/10.1007/978-94-6265-571-3_6

the matter, from the UN Committee on the Rights of the Child. This and other recent developments provide grist to the mill of an evolving, multi-factored approach to the jurisdictional nexus. The question of scope explored in this chapter is relevant to an increasing volume of persons caught in the crosshairs of counter-terrorism measures that continue to expand and spread their reach across borders.

Keywords Repatriation · Extra-territoriality · Jurisdiction · Human rights · Human rights litigation · Children's rights

6.1 Introduction

The lawfulness and legitimacy of states' responses to foreign fighters depend on compliance with international human rights law (IHRL). The UN Security Council has reiterated this in multiple binding resolutions.[1] The UN General Assembly, the Council of Europe (CoE), the European Union (EU) in its counter-terrorism directive, the Organization for Security and Co-operation in Europe (OSCE), the African Union and other regional bodies and initiatives all remind us of the imperative that states combat the so-called "foreign terrorist fighter" (FTF) phenomenon *within* the framework of human rights and international law.[2] The reality, of course, is different, with prolific developments in law, policy and practice across the globe since 2014[3] raising myriad human rights concerns, which in turn have prompted an array of national and international legal challenges on human rights grounds.[4]

It goes without saying that the relevance of IHRL as a framework, and the ability of victims to access legal processes and challenge rights-infringing measures on human rights grounds,[5] depend on the law applying in the first place. Yet significant controversy surrounds whether and in what circumstances a state's human rights obligations are applicable at all to those labelled foreign fighters and others associated with them when they are outside the territory of the state in question. Although relatively neglected in analysis to date, in practice, in a range of contexts, states have argued that where alleged violations occur beyond the states' borders, and the

---

[1] See *e.g.* UNSC 2014 Resolution 2178 (2014), UN Doc. S/RES/2178 (2014); UNSC 2017 Resolution 2396 (2017), UN Doc. S/RES/2396 (2017).

[2] See *e.g.* OSCE 2014 ; Directive (EU) 2017/541 of the European Parliament and of the Council of 15 March 2017 on combating terrorism and replacing Council Framework Decision 2002/475/JHA and amending Council Decision 2005/671/JHA, 32017L054, 15 March 2017.

[3] See UNSC 2014 Resolution 2178 (2014), UN Doc. S/RES/2178 (2014).

[4] Duffy 2018, p. 120; see also other general human rights chapters in that volume, *e.g.* Margariti 2018, p. 173.

[5] The competence of most human rights courts and bodies generally depends on the applicability of a specific treaty, from which they derive their authority: see *e.g.* ECHR, ACHR, UNHRC or the Convention on the Rights of the Child discussed in this chapter.

individuals affected were not within the states' physical control, IHRL simply does not apply.

The question of the geographic scope of states' human rights obligations—the "jurisdiction" question[6] or "extra-territorial applicability" of relevant human rights treaties—has long been controversial. The law has developed in a fragmented way, and as this chapter will explore, practice is not always consistent across (and sometimes within) regional and international human rights systems. What is clear and uncontroversial across human rights courts and bodies is that states' obligations do continue to apply beyond their borders in certain circumstances, but consensus does not extend to which sorts of circumstances, nor according to which legal test. Often (but not always) an "effective control test" is cited, but this only gives rise to further questions as to what that means, and the nature of the control in question. Does the state need to have control over a physical space or geographic area, a situation, the people affected by its action, their rights or just the conduct of its own agents that has an impact abroad? As we will see, there are elements of each of these approaches in the rapidly evolving practice of international courts and bodies as they have interpreted the skeletal provisions of human rights treaties that refer, without definition, to the elusive concept of "jurisdiction".[7] An inquiry into this jurisprudence reveals significant divergence of approach between systems and contexts, but also noteworthy trends across most international jurisprudence towards a general broadening of scope, and a recognised need for a holistic, context and issue-specific approach to jurisdiction. Ultimately, the chapter suggests that jurisprudence reveals more similarities than differences of approach emerging in this dynamic, if still troubled, area of IHRL.

The significance of the question in the particular context of "foreign fighter" travel and responses discussed by other authors in this volume are serious and worth recalling at the outset. Undoubtedly, most measures adopted in response to UN Security Council (UNSC) 'FTF' resolutions, from criminal law to administrative measures to expulsion, impact individuals within the state's own borders. But the 'FTF' phenomenon, and responses to it, are an inherently global matter. Many measures target or impact persons who, at the relevant time, are beyond the state's

[6] See *e.g.* European Convention on Human Rights, opened for signature 4 November 1950, 213 UNTS 221 (entered into force 3 September 1953) (ECHR) Article 1; Article 2 of the International Covenant on Civil and Political Rights, opened for signature 16 December 1966, 999 UNTS 171 (entered into force 23 March 1976) (ICCPR) which refer, in slightly different terms, to the treaties' applicability to those within the "jurisdiction" of the state.

[7] The precise language of treaties varies: *e.g.* Article 1 ECHR refers to "secur[ing] to everyone within their jurisdiction" the rights protected therein. Article 1 of the American Convention on Human Rights, opened for signature 22 November 1969, 1144 UNTS 123 (entered into force 19 July 1978) (ACHR) similarly refers to "ensur[ing] to all persons subject to their jurisdiction." The African Charter on Human and Peoples' Rights, opened for signature 27 June 1981, 1520 UNTS 217 (entered into force 21 October 1986) (ACHPR) makes no reference to jurisdiction or territory. Article 2 of the ICCPR refers to the obligation to "respect and ensure to all individuals within its territory *and* subject to its jurisdiction the rights recognised in the present convention [emphasis added]." The ICCPR test is well established as a disjunctive one, however, according to the UNHRC charged with interpreting the provision: see further below.

borders. Ultimately, this includes the lethal use of force, often through drones strikes, where international human rights bodies and experts have sought to reassert the applicability of IHRL in the face of evolving state practice that apparently disregards IHRL.[8] The implications are heightened in a context where states' have shown determination to ensure that individuals *remain* "extra-territorial" and beyond the reach of IHRL—by excluding their return home.[9] Deprivation of citizenship of people while abroad has had profound rights implications, and has often preceded such exclusion or lethal use of force.[10]

Where the extra-territorial scope of human rights obligations has come into perhaps sharpest focus, and is most complex, is in the context of the humanitarian disaster unfolding in camps in North East Syria (NES). As addressed in Sect. 6.2, tens of thousands—the majority of them young children of diverse nationalities—are held in abominable conditions in camps controlled by a non-state actor that has openly called for international support, including with repatriation of nationals.[11] While practice on repatriation varies, and is unfolding, many states are steadfastly resisting ever louder pleas to repatriate their nationals and remove them from imminent danger.

Litigation on the national and international levels has forced states to articulate legal justifications for their refusal to repatriate. In some cases, they have fallen back on the claim that their obligations simply do not apply extra-territorially in the context of the camps. In some cases, as in the well-known Shamima Begum case in the UK, this approach appears to have gone unchallenged by the courts.[12] Attention, therefore, shifts to regional and international courts and human rights bodies before

[8] *E.g.* the UK government's position explicitly excludes the application of the ECHR to drones: "The Secretary of State does not accept, however, that jurisdiction arises on the basis of the exercise of physical power and control over individuals in non-custody cases." In England and Wales High Court (EWHC) (Administrative), *Al-Saadoon and Others (Claimant) v. Secretary of State for Defence (Defendant)*, 17 March 2015, [2015] EWHC 715 (*Al-Sadoon*), para 93. But this has been rejected internally and externally; see *e.g.* Joint Committee on Human Rights (House of Lords, House of Commons) 2016. See also the section on 'Use of armed drones for targeted killings' in UNHRC 2020b, Annex, para 33: "by rejecting its human rights obligations extraterritorially, the US is an outlier, particularly as it relates to the obligation to abide by *jus cogen* [sic] norms, such as the prohibition against arbitrary killings." See also Beinlich 2019.

[9] Peltier E (2020) U.K. Woman Who Joined ISIS in Syria Asks High Court to Let Her Return Home. https://www.nytimes.com/2020/11/24/world/europe/uk-isis-shamima-begum.html. Accessed 29 September 2021.

[10] See *e.g.* Amnesty International 2018, p. 58: "in September 2015, legal action was brought in respect of the killing of the son of a herdsman by a US drone strike in Somalia in February 2012; the strikes had actually been directed at Mohamed Sakr, a British-born Somali who had been stripped of British citizenship on the basis that he was involved in terrorism". Citizenship-stripping cases were dismissed as manifestly unfounded, for lack of a prima facie violation where the individual was a dual national, before jurisdictional issues arose; e.g., ECtHR *K2 v. the United Kingdom,* First Section, 7 February 2017, Application no. 42387/13, para 64.

[11] For the brief facts, see Sect. 6.2 below.

[12] In Supreme Court (United Kingdom), *R (on the application of Begum) (Appellant) v. Special Immigration Appeals Commission (Respondent), R (on the application of Begum) (Respondent) v. Secretary of State for the Home Department (Appellant), Begum (Respondent) v. Secretary of State for the Home Department (Appellant),* 26 February 2021, [2021] UKSC 7 (*Shamima Begum*) the UK Supreme Court implicitly appears to have accepted the policy of treating the UK's obligations

which victims and family members seek to challenge this position, and assert that states have obligations in respect of decisions they make with a direct impact on individuals, including their nationals, in foreign camps. Of particular note are two admissibility decisions by the Committee on the Rights of the Child (CRC) in 2020 and 2021 concerning the French refusal to repatriate child nationals, where the CRC found against the French Government and decided that the children *did* fall within the state's jurisdiction.[13] International litigation against other states for their failure to act has also led to a judgment by the Grand Chamber of the European Court of Human Rights (ECtHR).[14]

The remainder of this chapter explores the question of how 'jurisdiction' has been interpreted to date across international courts and bodies, before considering the potential implications for the situation in the camps in NES. Section 6.2 describes the background facts briefly in relation to the camps. Section 6.3 focuses on how 'jurisdiction' and extra-territorial scope have been interpreted by different human rights courts and bodies, questioning the applicable tests and implications in the FTF context. Section 6.4 focuses on the recent CRC admissibility decisions, which are the first to specifically address the question of applicability of human rights obligations to the camps, and adopted a comparatively expansive approach to find French obligations applicable to decisions concerning repatriation. Section 6.5 concludes with a few reflections on the implications of these decisions and developments for the thorny issue of the extra-territorial scope of human rights protections.

6.2 Background Facts—Individuals Held in Camps in NES

The situation in the camps of NES is deeply troubling and deteriorating. Tens of thousands of individuals who travelled to the ISIS-controlled territory since 2014, and either fled, were displaced or captured, now find themselves in makeshift camps

as *not* engaged extra-territorially in this context. See Shamima Begum, a UK citizen, travelled at the age of 15 to join ISIS in Syria. The UK stripped her of her nationality, and on 26 February 2021, the UK Supreme Court ruled she would not be allowed to return to challenge this decision: BBC (2021) Who is Shamima Begum and how do you lose your UK citizenship?. https://www.bbc.com/news/explainers-53428191. Accessed 29 September 2021; BBC (2021) Shamima Begum cannot return to UK, Supreme Court rules. https://www.bbc.com/news/uk-56209007. Accessed 29 September 2021.

[13] UNCRC 2020: On 30 September 2020, the Committee declared *L.H. et al v. France* admissible, which was promptly followed on 4 February 2021 with a similarly reasoned decision in UNCRC 2021a.

[14] ECtHR, *H.F. and Others. v. France*, Grand Chamber Judgement, 14 September 2022, Application nos. 24384/19 and 44234/20. The cases were communicated on 23 January 2020 and 16 February 2021 and concern French nationals whose daughters travelled to Syria in 2014 and are now detained with their grandchildren in a camp in NES. The ECtHR found that there had been a violation of Article 3 § 2 of Protocol No. 4, and the French Government would, therefore, have to re-examine the requests for repatriation promptly and ensure that safeguards against arbitrariness were afforded in that process.

in NES run by the *de facto* Autonomous Authority for North East Syria (AANES).[15] Information on one such camp, the notorious Al Hol camp, indicates that the majority are children under 12, of diverse nationalities,[16] living in dire conditions of overpopulation, insanitation, with limited healthcare and spiralling child mortality.[17] Organised violent extremism is rampant,[18] with reports referring to "an ISIS resurgence"[19] and Hisbah, the female morality police, having re-grouped within the camp and enforcing ISIS rules[20]—even maintaining a "kill list"[21] and a parallel justice system imposing brutal punishments.[22] Deteriorating security more broadly[23] manifests in sexual violence and exploitation by other detainees and guards[24] and the acknowledged loss of control by the authorities.[25] The UN International Children's Emergency Fund (UNICEF) has reported that 40 adults and two children were killed in Al Hol in the first few months of 2021, 16 of them in March alone.[26] The humanitarian stakes and the urgency of finding solutions was only intensified by the COVID-19 pandemic.[27]

Repatriation of the hundreds of third country nationals held in the camps has remained patchy and intensely controversial despite major efforts by, among others,

[15] International Crisis Group 2019.

[16] OCHA 2020, p. 1. Currently the camp hosts 64,619 women and children, according to the UN Office for the Coordination of Humanitarian Affairs (OCHA), of whom 53% are children under the age of twelve; 48% of its population is Iraqi, 37% Syrian, and 15% are third country nationals held in an international annex.

[17] Human Rights Watch 2020.

[18] Médecins Sans Frontières 2019.

[19] Mironova 2020; Vianna de Azevedo 2020; France 24 (2021) European jihadists' children "at risk of radicalisation". https://www.france24.com/en/live-news/20210328-european-jihadists-children-at-risk-of-radicalisation. Accessed 29 September 2021.

[20] Gardner F (2020) IS prisoners issue a ticking timebomb for the West. https://www.bbc.com/news/world-middle-east-53428928. Accessed 29 September 2021.

[21] Human Rights Watch 2020, pp. 23–24. See also OCHA 2020; on, *inter alia*, honour killings.

[22] Rights and Security International 2020, p. 19; UNHRC 2020a, para 62: the Commission of Inquiry (COI) also reported that two women were stabbed to death in September 2019 following a decision of this makeshift court.

[23] OCHA 2020, para 4.

[24] OCHA 2021; Human Rights Watch 2020: on threats of sexual violence by the guards; Rights and Security International 2020, pp. 20, 23.

[25] Kaijo S (2021) UNICEF Alarmed by Spike in Children's Deaths in Syria's al-Hol Camp. https://www.voanews.com/a/extremism-watch_unicef-alarmed-spike-childrens-deaths-syrias-al-hol-camp/6203748.html. Accessed 29 September 2021. The Authority attributed the recent spike in violence to increased ISIS activity noting that "at night, the camp is virtually under their control…".

[26] UNICEF 2021.

[27] OCHA 2020.

the UN and civil society.[28] States have been robustly criticised for "turning their back on humanity",[29] resisting calls for urgent and essential protection (intensified by the pandemic), especially for children. Growing international concern also points to a short-term and counter-productive approach to security; as the CoE Commissioner for Human Rights stated: "letting the children of suspected ISIS fighters die [in Syria] will not heal the wounded souls of the victims of terrorism. Nor will it bring more security in Europe, or anywhere else".[30]

Alongside the humanitarian and security crisis in the camps is an impunity gap for ISIS crimes that is also fuelled by the refusal to repatriate. AANES announced its desire to ensure accountability for ISIS-related crimes, but international cooperation and support has been limited.[31] Securing justice in this context would depend upon addressing the immediate humanitarian situation and vulnerabilities of victims and alleged perpetrators to make fair trials feasible. AANES has also reportedly expressed its consent to repatriation, as well as calling for international support to address the conditions in camps and the justice deficit, pointedly noting that states that cooperated militarily in the defeat of ISIS should now cooperate in addressing its aftermath.[32]

Multiple legal, moral and political questions arise as to the responsibility of states to resolve this situation. The legal part of that discussion, coming into focus increasingly in the context of litigation, begins with whether and on what basis states' IHRL obligations apply.

6.3 Comparative Approaches to the Scope ('Extra-Territorial Applicability') of IHRL

6.3.1 Introduction

IHRL has wrestled with controversies regarding the scope of application of obligations, and specifically when they extend beyond territorial borders, for decades. A review of practice reveals differences of approach between human rights courts and bodies in their interpretations of the 'jurisdictional' question, as well as noteworthy trends.

---

[28] OHCHR (2021) Syria: UN experts urge 57 States to repatriate women and children from squalid camps. https://www.ohchr.org/EN/NewsEvents/Pages/DisplayNews.aspx?NewsID=26730. Accessed 29 September 2021.

[29] Jeannerod 2020.

[30] Council of Europe Commissioner for Human Rights, Dunja Mijatović 2020.

[31] In February 2020, the AANES announced it would commence trials of foreign nationals, but the Covid-19 pandemic delayed plans, UNHRC 2020a.

[32] On the potential for trials by the Autonomous Authority and the requirements of fair trial, upon which the legitimacy of such proceedings and international cooperation should depend, see legal advice by author at Duffy 2021a.

The starting point is, of course, the treaty provisions themselves, which are slightly differently worded. The European Convention on Human Rights (ECHR) and American Convention on Human Rights (ACHR) provide that states must secure the rights to "everyone within their jurisdiction", while the International Covenant on Civil and Political Rights (ICCPR) refers to "all individuals within its territory *and* subject to its jurisdiction [emphasis added]" (though this has been interpreted as disjunctive rather than cumulative).[33] Both formulations raise the question of what 'jurisdiction' means in this context. The African Charter on Human and Peoples' Rights (ACHPR) and the International Covenant on Economic, Social and Cultural Rights (ICESCR) make no reference to jurisdiction or to territory at all. One thing the treaties have in common then is the failure to provide clear answers to the question of scope from a straightforward textual analysis, and the corresponding importance of their interpretation by the relevant human rights courts and bodies.

In response, some human rights adjudication mechanisms (*e.g.* the ECtHR) have determined the question of scope on a case by case basis in the context of contentious cases. Some others (*e.g.* the UN Human Rights Committee (UNHRC) or the Inter-American Court of Human Rights (IACtHR)) have also done so through advisory opinions and general comments, enabling greater distance from the facts and providing a valuable perspective on the state of the law up to that point on extra-territorial scope, albeit generally focused on particular rights or issues. The result is a patchwork and dynamic legal framework.

It is now clear and legally uncontroversial across courts and bodies that obligations do extend beyond states' borders, and it is often suggested that this arises where the state is deemed to have exercised sufficient 'effective control'. The knock-on question, on which there is a greater divergence of approach, is control of what? Territory? Situations? Activities of their own agents or actions? Persons affected by their conduct, or simply their human rights? As we will see, there is now a vast array of jurisprudence affirming extra-territorial scope, and growing, but not universal, momentum towards a broad, flexible and holistic approach to the jurisdiction question, of direct relevance in this context.

6.3.2 ICCPR: The UN Human Rights Committee

The UNHRC was the first international human rights body to enter into the fray on the extra-territorial applicability issue, when it found Uruguayan officials responsible for kidnapping and mistreatment by Uruguayan security forces on Argentinian soil.[34] It asserted strong words of principle back in 1981, which have resonated across other

[33] UNHRC 2004a. See below for GC 36 and the Inter-American Court's Advisory Opinion on *The Environment and Human Rights*.

[34] See *e.g.* UNHRC 1981b; UNHRC 1981a.

systems since,[35] when it described it as "unconscionable" to "interpret the responsibility under the ... Covenant as to permit a state party to perpetrate violations of the Covenant on the territory of another state, which violations it could not perpetrate on its own territory."[36] The UNHRC's "consistent approach" has been endorsed by the International Court of Justice (ICJ), which has noted that it is "natural" that the ICCPR "is applicable in respect of acts done by a State in the exercise of its jurisdiction outside its own territory".[37]

Assessing the nature of states' obligations generally in General Comment No. 31, the UNHRC stated that "a State party must respect and ensure the rights laid down in the Covenant to *anyone within the power or effective control of that State Party,* even if not situated within the territory of the State Party... [emphasis added]".[38] However, what this "power" or "effective control" entailed remained open to question.

More recently, a General Comment and an individual case, among others,[39] have begun to answer this question in a manner of particular relevance to the situation in the camps of NES. Although General Comment No. 36[40] focuses specifically on the right to life, it provides an important reframing of how to think about the jurisdictional connection between the individual and the state. It interpreted 'jurisdiction' as covering persons "over whose *enjoyment of the right to life* [the state] exercises power or effective control ...[which] includes persons located outside any territory effectively controlled by the State, whose right to life is nonetheless *affected by its military or other activities in a direct and reasonably foreseeable manner* [emphasis added]".[41] It thereby clarifies that the effective power or control it referred to previously extends to control over the enjoyment of the *rights* of individuals, through *impact* on those rights, rather than necessarily control over the individuals themselves.

A recent decision on an individual communication, *A.S. et al. v. Italy* of 27 January 2021, testifies to the importance and complexity of the issue.[42] In a majority decision, the UNHRC found that Italy had the obligation to protect the life of migrants shipwrecked just outside Italian territorial waters who had sent SOS messages that had been received but not adequately responded to, and who ultimately drowned in the

---

[35] See *e.g.* ECtHR, *Tatar v. Romania*, Chamber Judgement, 27 January 2009, Application no. 67021/01; ECtHR, *Issa and Others v. Turkey*, Second Section, 16 November 2004, Application no. 31821/96 (*Issa*).

[36] UNHRC 1981b, para 12.

[37] ICJ, *Legal Consequences of the Construction of a Wall in the Occupied Palestinian Territory*, Advisory Opinion, 9 July 2004, [2004] ICJ Rep 136, paras 109, 111.

[38] UNHRC 2004a, para 10. See also *e.g.* UNHRC 2004b, para 6.

[39] These included the UNHRC observations encouraging states to take measures to avoid violations by companies registered on their territories, but active abroad, which also support a loser approach to jurisdiction than simply state 'control of persons': OHCHR 2012, para 16.

[40] UNHRC 2019, para 63. See also UNHRC 2004a. See below for GC 36 and the Inter-American Court's Advisory Opinion on *The Environment and Human Rights*, para 10.

[41] Ibid.

[42] UNHRC 2021.

Mediterranean Sea. The UNHRC asked whether "the risk of an extra-territorial violation [was] a *necessary and foreseeable consequence* [of the state's conduct] judged on the knowledge the State party had at the time [emphasis added]".[43] The majority concluded that jurisdiction was established as "*in the particular circumstances of the case, a special relationship of dependency* had been established between the individuals on the vessel in distress and Italy [emphasis added]".[44] Of potential relevance also is the UNHRC's explicit reference to broader international law obligations—in that case arising from the law of the sea—as relevant to the interpretation of human rights obligations.

6.3.3 UN Committee on Economic, Social and Cultural Rights and Other UN Entities

Given the relevance (and frequent neglect) of Economic, Social and Cultural Rights (ESCRs) to 'FTF' responses, the approach of the UN Committee on Economic, Social and Cultural Rights (CESCR) is also worthy of note. The ICESCR itself stands apart from most other international human rights treaties considered as it does not refer explicitly to 'jurisdiction',[45] but the Committee has still seen fit to spell out, in concluding observations[46] and General Comments,[47] that the Covenant applies to harm beyond state parties' own borders.[48] It has called for states to prevent their own citizens and companies from violating ESCRs in other countries,[49] recognising that both obligations to "respect" and to "fulfil" rights can be applicable abroad.[50] This approach is supported by detailed soft law principles, notably the Maastricht Principles on Extraterritorial Obligations of States in the Area of Economic, Social and Cultural Rights.[51] A number of years before the UNHRC's General Comment No. 36 drew attention for its focus on a foreseeable impact test, ESCRs have been considered to apply in contexts where rights were impacted as a foreseeable result of a state's conduct.[52]

---

[43] Ibid., para 7.5, reflecting UNHRC (2019) General Comment No. 36: Article 6: right to life, UN Doc. CCPR/C/GC/35, para 10.

[44] UNHRC 2021, para 7.8, see Shany, Heyns and Pazartzis' Opinion (attached to the decision) para 2: the decision "fails to distinguish between situations in which states *have the potential* to place [individuals] under their effective control ..., and situations involving the *actual placement* of individuals under effective state control" [emphasis added].

[45] Vandenhole 2011, p. 430.

[46] See *e.g.* OHCHR 2003, para 15 and OHCHR 2001, paras 11–12.

[47] See *e.g.* UNCESCR 2017, para 25–37.

[48] Langford 2013, p. 7.

[49] UNCESCR (2003) General Comment No. 15: The Right to Water, UN Doc. E/C.12/2002/11 (2003), para 33.

[50] Vandenhole 2020, p. 233.

[51] Extra-territorial Obligations Consortium 2013, Principle 13.

[52] Ibid.

Other UN authorities, such as the then UN High Commissioner on Human Rights' report on Privacy in a Digital Age, also supported a flexible approach to jurisdiction arising through "control of rights" (as opposed to persons). Jurisdiction extended to "*those whose privacy is being interfered with* [emphasis added]", whether at home or abroad.[53]

6.3.4 The European Court of Human Rights: Effective Control of What?

The issue has perhaps been uniquely controversial before the ECtHR, where the "essentially territorial" scope of human rights obligations[54] as a starting point has largely gone unchallenged, and exceptions have been carved out on a case by case basis.[55] The handling of extra-territorial applicability has been erratic before the ECtHR, leading to the (under-)statement that the Court has "not spoken with one voice" on the issue,[56] and the more emphatic rejection of "[t]he morally and legally untenable position of the Court on the jurisdictional threshold" in particular cases.[57]

The Court has set down standards that appear inherently linked to the facts of the particular case. This may explain why such tests have often proved inadequate in light of very different facts in subsequent cases. As such, the Court recently acknowledged that the jurisprudence has "evolved" (or, as one judge put it earlier, decisions have been "effectively overturned"), and the exceptions expanded in line with the issues before the Court.[58]

For example, early cases where extra-territorial jurisdiction was established did concern factual situations where the state exercised control of an area beyond its borders, either directly through occupation, for example, or indirectly through the state's "decisive influence" over a subordinate administration.[59] In the *Banković et al. v. Belgium et al.* case,[60] this "effective control of the relevant territory"[61] was treated as a prerequisite to ECHR applicability. Thus, as the NATO states involved in the

---

53 UNHRC 2014, para 34.

54 ECtHR, *Ilascu and Others v. Moldova and Russia*, Grand Chamber Judgement, 8 July 2004, Application no. 48787/99 (*Ilascu*), para 318; ECtHR, *Banković and Others v. Belgium*, Grand Chamber Judgement, 12 December 2001, Application no. 52207/99 (*Banković*), para 890; ECtHR, *Catan and Others v. Moldova and Russia*, Grand Chamber Judgement, 19 October 2012, Applications no. 43370/04 (*Catan*), 18454/06 and 8252/05.

55 See, among others, *Banković*, above n 54, para 59.

56 ECtHR, *Al-Skeini and Others v. the United Kingdom*, Grand Chamber Judgement, 7 July 2011, Application no. 55721/07 (*Al-Skeini*) J. Bonello's Concurring Opinion, para 6.

57 ECtHR, *Georgia v. Russia* (II), Grand Chamber Judgement, Application no. 38263/08, J. Albuquerque's Dissenting Opinion, paras 22, 30; Duffy 2021b.

58 Ibid., para 114.

59 See *e.g. Banković*, above n 54; *Ilascu*, above n 54; *Catan*, above n 54.

60 *Banković*, above n 54.

61 Ibid., para 71.

1999 bombing of Radio Television Serbia in Belgrade did not control Belgrade or exercise public powers there, it was held that they lacked 'jurisdiction' over the individuals killed in the attack, and the case was inadmissible. The judgement was uniquely controversial for its restrictive territorial approach to extra-territoriality, out of step (even then) with other international bodies' approaches. However, in subsequent cases, the Court changed its approach, and also found states' obligations to arise where state agents exercised other forms of control abroad.[62] Notably, where state agents operating abroad exercised "physical power and control over the person in question", jurisdiction was established. This language also reflected the particular facts of the cases before the Court, where individuals were under the control of the state agents by being taken into custody or subject to lethal force, for example.[63]

While the Court's approach has gradually expanded over time to respond to particular facts before it, it has also taken a few steps back. For example, in *Georgia v. Russia*,[64] it found that during hostilities, in "the chaos of conflict", states lack sufficient control for their human rights obligations to apply. The judgement is intensely controversial (as evidenced by dissenting opinions and critique)[65] but also limited. It purports to exclude only to right to life allegations during the so-called "armed hostilities phase" of an international conflict. In the 'FTF' context this may be relevant to, for example, bombardments of ISIS areas during periods of active hostilities in international conflict.[66] But even other forms of lethal force, such as targeted killings, would most likely not be covered, as the judgment recognised that force involving "isolated and specific acts involving an element of proximity..." would fall within the state's jurisdiction.[67] This is consistent with the range of human rights bodies and experts that have found IHRL applicable to drone strikes[68]—as "the ultimate exercise of physical power and control over the individual who was shot and killed".[69] The Court was also clear that the exclusion of jurisdiction did not apply to detention situations, even in an international armed conflict.[70]

---

[62] *Al-Skeini,* above n 56, para 136. See also *Al-Skeini* case cited in ECtHR, *Jaloud v. Netherlands,* Grand Chamber Judgement, 20 November 2014, Application no. 47708/08, para 139; ECtHR, *Hassan v. the United Kingdom,* Grand Chamber Judgement, 16 September 2014, Application no. 229750/09 (*Hassan*); and *Öcalan v. Turkey*, Grand Chamber Judgement, 12 May 2005, Application no. 46221/99 (*Öcalan*). See *e.g. Issa*, above n 35; ECtHR, *Pad and Others v. Turkey*, Third Section, 28 June 2007, Application no. 60267/00 (*Pad and Others*).

[63] *Al-Skeini*, above n 56; *Hassan*, above n 62; *Öcalan*, above n 62; *Issa*, above n 35; *Pad and Others*, above n 62.

[64] *Georgia v. Russia* (II), above n 57, ECtHR; see also Duffy 2021b.

[65] The number of dissents are discussed in Duffy 2021b.

[66] The exclusion applies in international armed conflict according to the ECtHR in *Georgia v. Russia* (II), above n 57; on the nature of conflicts against ISIS see *e.g.* Bohrer et al. 2020, pp. 22 *et seq.*

[67] *Georgia v. Russia* (II), above n 57, para 132.

[68] UNGA 2013, paras 24, 32–51. See also Callamard 2020.

[69] UNHRC 2020b, Annex, para 43 citing *Al-Saadoon*, above n 8, para 117.

[70] *Georgia v. Russia (II)*, above n 57, paras 83, 223–256.

The judgment does endorse the "two main criteria" for determining extra-territorial scope under the ECHR,[71] raising doubt as to what this means for individuals held in camps in NES under the direct control of the *de facto* Autonomous Authority, who were on the face of it not under the "physical control" of foreign states,[72] or in an area controlled by them.[73] However, a couple of further points on ECtHR jurisprudence are worthy of note before rushing to conclusions as to the two-part test or its (non-)application in the context of the Syrian camps.

First, while much attention is focused on what the ECtHR has said about the "extra-territorial" question, less attention is paid to the many cases where the Court has found violations to arise from domestic state action which produced *effects* abroad,[74] where the Court did not question the applicability of the Convention or treat the issue as an "extra-territorial" one at all. Thus, legislative amendments in Slovenia preventing nationals abroad from withdrawing currency,[75] judicial decisions in Belgium preventing a woman in Canada from being reunited with her child,[76] or sanctions affecting persons who were at all material times outside of the state, were all covered.[77] In each of these scenarios and others,[78] there was sufficient nexus between the state's own decisions at home and those affected by them for jurisdiction to arise, despite the individuals being located abroad and not in any sense under the state's physical control.

In the same vein, in several recent cases, for instance, *Hanan v. Germany*[79] and *Georgia v. Russia*,[80] the institution of an investigation or legal proceedings in a state was recognised as sufficient to establish a jurisdictional link (irrespective of whether or not the underlying allegations, or the individuals being investigated, were within the states' jurisdiction or control). Notably, the Court ruled in support

[71] Ibid., para 115: "The two main criteria established by the Court in this regard are that of "effective control" by the State over an area (spatial concept of jurisdiction) and that of "State agent authority and control" over individuals (personal concept of jurisdiction) (see *Al-Skeini and Others*, cited above, §§ 133-40)."

[72] *Al-Skeini*, above n 56.

[73] *Banković*, above n 54.

[74] *Georgia v. Russia* (II), above n 57, J. Albuquerque's Dissenting Opinion, para 5. Duffy and Maxwell 2020.

[75] ECtHR, *Kovačić and Others v. Slovenia*, Grand Chamber Judgement, 9 October 2003, Applications nos. 44574/98, 45133/98 and 48316/99, para 51.

[76] ECtHR, *Mubilanzila Mayeka and Kaniki Mitunga v. Belgium*, First Section, 12 October 2006, Application no. 13178/03, para 62.

[77] ECtHR, *Nada v. Switzerland*, Grand Chamber Judgement, 12 September 2012, Application no. 10593/08, paras 121–122; see Altwicker 2018, p. 592. *See* likewise, ECtHR, *X and Y v. Switzerland*, Third Section, 14 July 1977, Applications nos. 7289/75 and 7349/76, para 73.

[78] ECtHR, *Soering v. United Kingdom*, Application no. 13038/88, 7 July 1989, para 91.

[79] ECtHR, *Hanan v. Germany*, Grand Chamber Judgement, 16 February 2021, Application no. 4871/16 (*Hanan*).

[80] *Georgia v. Russia* (II), above n 57.

that international obligations of investigation could be borne in mind in interpreting jurisdiction.[81]

The Court has made clear that its jurisprudence on jurisdiction is not static, that it has evolved, and will continue to do so.[82] Its approach is deeply fact-specific; as the Grand Chamber recognised in *Al-Skeini v. UK:* "in each case, the question whether exceptional circumstances exist which require and justify a finding by the Court that the State was exercising jurisdiction extra-territorially must be determined with the reference to the particular facts".[83] A non-exhaustive array of factors have been relevant to those fact-specific determinations case by case.[84] Moreover, in diverse contexts, the Court has taken a contextual and purposive analysis, including considering the implications of its interpretation, and whether it results in a "vacuum of protection" or precludes it from fulfilling its "essential protective purpose".[85] This dynamism is evident in the fact that *Banković* was ultimately "effectively overrul[ed]"[86] in favour of a more flexible standard.

In 2022, in *H.F. and Others v. France*, the Court had to consider extra-territoriality in a challenge to France's refusal to repatriate French women and children from the Syrian camps.[87] Serious doubts arose as to whether the relatively restrictive two-part test, developed in quite different contexts, could apply; would the Court change the test or reject the case? However, the Court decided there was a jurisdictional link with France, but limited to Article 3(2) Protocol No. 4 (the right to enter the territory of the state of nationality), reasoning that the right would be deprived of meaning if it did not apply to nationals beyond a state's borders.[88] This approach enabled the Court to address the key facts, namely decision-making in France, without appearing to change its approach. The judgment is therefore limited, and does little to clarify standards of general application. But a few aspects of its approach are noteworthy, not least for being closer to that of other courts and bodies considered in this chapter than might first meet the eye. This includes the "special features" that justified a finding of jurisdiction under Article 3, Protocol 4 – including nationality, the official requests for help, immediate threats to lives and dignity, vulnerability especially of children, and the material impossibility to reach the border safely without French assistance – as well as the need to ensuring the effectiveness of the Convention in the context of the "contemporary phenomena" of Syrian camps, which reflect factors and approaches cited by other bodies to justify a flexible, contextual approach to

---

[81] Ibid., para 331. See also concerning investigation: Milanovic 2021.

[82] *Georgia v. Russia* (II), above n 57, para 114.

[83] *Al-Skeini*, above n 56, para 132.

[84] The Court saw no reason to extend it in *Georgia v. Russia (II)*, above n 57; for a host of (I have suggested dubious) reasons, implying that it could and may in other situations, see Duffy 2021b.

[85] Duffy 2020, pp. 78 *et seq.*

[86] *Al-Saadoon*, above n 8, para 112; *Banković* above n 54.

[87] *H.F. and Others v. France*, above n 14, paras 204, 214. The Court found a violation of Article 3 § 2 of Protocol No. 4 providing "no one shall be deprived of the right to enter the territory of the State of which he is a national."

[88] Ibid., paras 197–203. Ill-treatment in camps beyond France's territorial or personal control were not within the Court's jurisdiction.

jurisdiction.[89] The ECHR case law on extra-territoriality will need to continue to "evolve" to remain relevant to current challenges in a host of pending cases that do not fit readily into territorial or personal control; these include issues that are inherently transboundary and vital human rights priorities of our time, from climate change to cross border digital surveillance.[90] Whether additional exceptions will be added to that two-part test, or the Court will move towards a more coherent approach capable of addressing other contemporary challenges remains uncertain. For now, it has added a narrow but significant exception, recognising the importance of the influence of European states over the fate of those in the camps of NES, in the context of one specific right and one particularly compelling set of circumstances.

When the Court returns to the issue, it has growing international comparative material on the jurisdiction question from which to draw.

6.3.5 Inter-American System

The Inter-American Commission on Human Rights (IACHR), in its case law, has long acknowledged that the human rights obligations continued to apply when the United States was active abroad—during the United States invasion of Grenada[91] or detentions at Guantánamo Bay.[92] One important and underrated contribution was the *Armando Alejandre 'Brothers to the Rescue'* case, where Cuba shot down two civilian light airplanes,[93] and the Commission considered whether there was a "direct" link between the death of individuals and the state; it found the jurisdictional test to be satisfied when individuals died as a result of "direct actions taken by agents of the Cuban state in international airspace".

A significant development for our purposes is the Advisory Opinion on *The Environment and Human Rights* of 15 November 2017 of the IACtHR.[94] Considering whether greenhouse gas emissions could create an extra-territorial jurisdictional link, albeit based on domestic activities with extra-territorial effect,[95] the Court affirmed that:

---

[89] Ibid., paras 211, 213–214.

[90] On privacy, see ECtHR, *Big Brother Watch and Others v. United Kingdom*, Grand Chamber Judgement, 13 September 2018, Applications nos. 58170/13, 62322/14 and 24960/15; see also UNHRC 2014.

[91] See IACtHR, *Coard et al. v. the United States*, Report N. 109/99—Case 10.951, 29 September 1999.

[92] IACommHR, *Decision on Request for Precautionary Measures* (Detainees at Guantanamo Bay, Cuba), 13 March 2002.

[93] See *e.g.*, IACommHR, *Armando Alejandre, Jr. et al. v. Cuba*, Report N.86/99—Case 11.589, 29 September 1999, para 25.

[94] IACtHR, *The Environment and Human Rights*, Advisory Opinion OC-23/17, 15 November 2017 (*The Environment and Human Rights*).

[95] Ibid.; Berkes 2018.

> a person is under the jurisdiction of the State of origin if there is *a causal link between the action that occurred within its territory and the negative impact on the human rights* of persons outside its territory. The exercise of jurisdiction arises when the State of origin exercises *effective control over the activities that* caused the damage and the consequent human rights violation [emphasis added].[96]

By asserting that what is key is the state's control over its own 'activities' (act or omission), and its impact on rights, the Court makes an important contribution to reframing the discussion on scope in this area.[97] This Advisory Opinion joins an emerging chorus in firmly rejecting the idea that human rights obligations are inapplicable based on formalistic notions of territorial or personal control.

6.3.6 The African Human Rights System

An enquiry into the African system's approach, which has been subject to less international attention, is also revealing. The African Charter on Human and Peoples' rights itself does not deal with jurisdiction or scope, but back in 2003, the Commission appeared not to hesitate to find Burundi, Rwanda and Uganda responsible for human rights violations extra-territorially, albeit without addressing the issue directly.[98] Since then, as with the UNHRC and UNCESCR, it has been through General Comments and Guidelines that the African Commission became more explicit in its approach.

It has adopted a broad approach, suggesting various bases for a jurisdictional link to arise in particular situations. For example, in the Guidelines on Terrorism and Human Rights, the Commission states simply, "Extra-territoriality: States are bound by their human rights obligations while conducting counterterrorism operations abroad".[99] Greater elaboration is found in its General Comment on the right to life, which preceded that of the UNHRC and asserts a range of possible bases for the jurisdictional nexus:

> A State shall *respect* the right to life of individuals outside its territory. A State also has certain obligations to *protect* the right to life of such individuals. The nature of these obligations depends for instance on the extent that the State has jurisdiction or otherwise exercises *effective authority, power, or control* over either the perpetrator or the victim (or the victim's rights), or exercises effective control over the territory on which the victim's rights are affected, or whether the *State engages in conduct which could reasonably be foreseen to result* in an unlawful deprivation of life. [emphasis added][100]

---

96 *The Environment and Human Rights*, above n 94, para 104(h).

97 Banda 2018.

98 ACommHPR, *Democratic Republic of Congo v. Burundi, Rwanda and Uganda,* Communication 227/99, 29 May 2003, paras 79–80.

99 ACommHPR 2015a, para 15.

100 ACommHPR 2015b, para 14. See also para 18 on positive obligations to prevent violations by corporations and third parties on its territory.

6.4 UNCRC: Children in Syrian Camps and the Cases Against France

6.4.1 *Introduction*

It is in light of this ample international jurisprudence that the question of the applicability of states' international obligations to those in the camps in NES fall to be considered.[101] While the standards vary, with ECtHR predominantly focusing on control of territory or persons, albeit on occasion going beyond to cover effects abroad, the vast majority of international bodies reflect a broader approach wherein jurisdiction may arise where the conduct of states has a direct and foreseeable impact on rights. What this means for those in the camps in NES has been considered first by UN Special Rapporteurs, and more recently by the UNHRC.

The UN Special Rapporteurs clearly foresaw emerging jurisdictional controversies in litigation and issued a joint statement on the "*Extra-territorial jurisdiction of States over children and their guardians in camps, prisons, or elsewhere in the northern Syrian Arab Republic*".[102] They suggested that what matters for the applicability of a state's obligations is the "*extent of its control over the applicant or over some of their rights* [emphasis added]". This opinion reflected many of the standards set out above, and foreshadowed the UNCRC decisions the following year.

The CRC decisions of 30 September 2020[103] and 4 February 2021[104] (the Decisions) were the first time the CRC had reached a contentious decision dealing with the jurisdiction question under the Convention on the Rights of the Child, and the first international decision anywhere to deal specifically with the applicability of human rights obligations of foreign states to people in the camps in NES.[105] While the Decisions are brief and regrettably limited in their reasoning, the positions of the parties and the CRC's approach, considered in turn below, provide food for thought on what approach to extra-territoriality is appropriate in challenging contexts such as those arising in the NES camps.

6.4.2 *Submissions on Jurisdiction*

The individual communications were brought by the relatives of children held in the camps in NES, who the French state refuses to repatriate on the apparent basis of their parents' alleged support for ISIS. The applicants argued that "the continued presence" of the children in the Kurdish-controlled camps in NES had its "unique

[101] *Shamima Begum*, above n 12, para 27.

[102] UN Human Rights Special Procedures 2020, p. 11.

[103] UNCRC 2020.

[104] UNCRC 2021a.

[105] See *e.g.* UNCRC 2015, para 22; UNCRC 2012, para 28.a.

origin" in France's decision.[106] They contended that the required nexus was a "'link of responsibility' for the fate of the nationals of States parties by virtue of the 'decisive influence' they have over the authority detaining or holding them".[107] Given the relatively more restrictive approach of the ECtHR case law, it is surprising how much emphasis the applicants placed on it, compared to drawing to the CRC's attention the approach of its sister UN bodies, for example. Nonetheless, they argued that ECtHR case law supports jurisdiction extra-territorially when acts performed by the state (outside its national territory or within) produce effects beyond its borders.[108] In this case, where there was "no material or legal impossibility" to repatriate,[109] and the state decided not to intervene to prevent serious violations, those affected came within its jurisdiction.[110]

Both Decisions cite third party interventions, which noted that customary international law provides the right (and perhaps the duty) of States to protect their own nationals, and the Convention should then be interpreted (as IHRL often is) in light of those parallel norms.[111] The interveners noted the preparatory work of the Convention revealed a broad interpretation of the jurisdiction in favour of extra-territoriality, consistent with the purpose and spirit of the Convention.[112] It was argued that the extreme vulnerability of the children in this case and humanitarian circumstances required a flexible interpretation. It asserted the need to "tak[e] territoriality out of the question", referring to a concurring opinion of one ECtHR judge that "jurisdiction arises from the mere fact of having assumed [human rights] obligations and from having the capability to fulfil them (or not to fulfil them)".[113] The interveners called for a "flexible and child rights focused approach… that responds to increasingly complex contexts, legal and factual, and… the extreme stakes for children in question".[114]

France countered that it lacked jurisdiction over the children.[115] Unsurprisingly, given its assertion of a restrictive approach, it also relied heavily on ECtHR jurisprudence to affirm lack of "territorial" control[116] or of control by French agents over the children held in the Kurdish-controlled camps.[117] In the second case, France explicitly rejected the approach of the UNHRC in its General Comment No. 36 as "overly broad" and inconsistent with the ICCPR's spirit and letter and ECtHR case

[106] UNCRC 2020, para 2.12, and UNCRC 2021a, para 5.7.

[107] Ibid., para 2.15 citing *e.g. Ilascu and Others* above n 54.

[108] Ibid., para 2.12.

[109] Ibid., para 2.14.

[110] Ibid., para 2.15.

[111] Ibid., para 8.2.

[112] Ibid., para 8.5.

[113] *Al-Skeini*, above n 56, para 13.

[114] UNCRC 2020, para 8.8.

[115] Ibid., para 4.1; UNCRC 2021a, at 4.3. Many similar arguments were made in the ECtHR case *H.F. and Others v. France*, above n 14.

[116] UNCRC 2020, para 4.4; UNCRC 2021a, para 4.4.

[117] UNCRC 2020, para 4.5; UNCRC 2021a, para 4.5.

law.[118] While noting that French membership in the international coalition involved military operations, the capture of some detainees, and its relations with the Kurdish group, France posited that these were insufficient links. It also rejected the idea that a "national decision" would suffice to bring the individuals within the jurisdiction of the state.[119] Furthermore, France argued that jurisdiction on the basis that "a state party had not acted" would be "tantamount to … accepting universal jurisdiction".[120] With regard to the nationality of the children, France affirmed that the personal jurisdiction of a State ("i.e., the well-established powers that the State exercises over its nationals abroad") differs from its extra-territorial jurisdiction ("i.e., the legal conditions under which a State may be held responsible for acts performed or producing effects outside its borders").[121] Finally, on a crucial point of controversy, it suggested jurisdiction based on "nationality" would be discriminatory, as the Convention obligations apply regardless of nationality.[122]

6.4.3 Findings and Jurisdictional Factors

The Committee responds to these complex questions of jurisdiction in just a few paragraphs in each decision.[123] It found that in the extreme circumstances involving vulnerable children facing an imminent risk of irreparable harm, where the state had the "capability and the power to protect the rights of the children in question", the children fell within French jurisdiction.[124] The communications were admissible and could proceed to a merits determination of whether rights were violated.[125]

The CRC acknowledged the state's concern that it could not be held accountable for "situations it did not create, over which it has no effective control", solely on the basis of nationality. It does less to clarify exactly on what basis the state *does* have jurisdiction, and what sort of "effective control", if any, the state must have. The Committee does not purport to set down a standard for jurisdiction as such, or to clarify according to which legal test its decisions are reached, leading to uncertainty and understandable criticism of the decision.[126] Given the novelty and significance of the issue, it is perhaps regrettable that the Committee was not more articulate in clarifying the standards it was applying, which may have broader application in other cases and contexts. It therefore limited the contribution of this important decision to the body of jurisprudence outlined above.

118 UNCRC 2021a, para 7.5.
119 UNCRC 2020, para 4.6.
120 Ibid., para 4.7.
121 Ibid.; UNCRC 2021a, para 7.4.
122 UNCRC 2020, para 4.8.
123 Ibid., paras 9.5–9.7; UNCRC 2021a, paras 8.5–8.8.
124 UNCRC 2020, paras 9.7, 10.
125 Ibid., para 11; UNCRC 2021a, para 10.
126 Milanovic 2020.

The Committee does, however, hint at a relevant framework for assessment and alludes to noteworthy factors that are likely to be taken into account in assessing jurisdiction in future cases. It also makes passing references to states' "conduct or effects abroad" and to their "effective control of… a situation", which may provide the framework for its approach.[127] Notably, once again reflecting a surprising emphasis on the ECHR standards, the CRC refers to ECtHR jurisprudence that "[a] State may also have jurisdiction in respect of *acts that are performed, or that produce effects*, outside its national borders [original footnote omitted, emphasis added]".[128]

What is particularly clear in its approach, however, is the promotion of a *flexible, fact-specific and contextual approach* that enables decision-makers to take into account a whole range of *legal and factual* considerations in determining whether the necessary jurisdictional nexus between individuals and the state is established in all the circumstances. As such, the decisions also clearly indicate the need for a *holistic, rather than a formalistic, approach* to jurisdiction.

The range of factors highlighted by the CRC—like the UNHRC *A.S. et al. v. Italy* decision that followed hot on its heels as well as to some extent the ECtHR *H.F. and Others v. France* case the following year[129]—may be one of its most interesting contributions. While deeply fact-specific, and not required or exhaustive, some of these factors are likely to prove relevant to assessing jurisdiction in other cases and contexts, and to resonate beyond the work of the Committee.

Nationality was clearly an important factor in the relationship between the children and the state in these cases. Referring to its own jurisprudence in the migration context,[130] the CRC noted that states "should take extraterritorial responsibility for the protection of *children who are their nationals* outside their territory… through child sensitive, rights based consular protection [emphasis added]".[131] The relevance of *nationality* to human rights protection under human rights treaties is, however, controversial.[132] States obligations under IHRL do not depend on nationality, and indeed they apply "without distinction" on the grounds of nationality, such that distinguishing between individuals on this basis risks amounting to unlawful discrimination.[133] Hence, if the Decisions are read to extend jurisdiction solely on the basis of nationality, they may, as the state suggested, fall foul of the discrimination clause.

The better reading of the cases may be that nationality is *one of a range of factors* relevant to determining whether, in all the circumstances, the relationship between individual and state was such that the jurisdictional link arose. Nationality should

---

[127] UNCRC 2020, para 9.6.

[128] Ibid., para 9.6.

[129] In UNHRC 2021, the UNHRC relies on a combination of factual (*e.g.* contacts between the vessel and the Italian rescue teams) and legal (*e.g.* duty to respond to calls of distress provided by the international law of the sea) factors. *H.F. and Others v. France*, above n 14, while more narrowly framed, includes similar factors as relevant to its determination.

[130] See *e.g.* UNCRC 2018.

[131] UNCRC 2020, para 9.6.

[132] Milanovic 2020, p. 124.

[133] Convention on the Rights of the Child, opened for signature 20 November 1989, 1577 UNTS 3 (entered into force 2 September 1990) Article 2(1).

neither be sufficient nor required: the decisions do not suggest obligations are owed to all nationals (which may be unduly onerous in some contexts) but to identifiable children in the context of the camps. Nor do they suggest that jurisdiction depends on nationality, raising unanswered questions about whether and when non-nationals may also be covered in certain situations. Nationality was, however, undoubtedly an important factor in the state's particular nexus with the individual, and its "capability to protect", in this case and context, albeit one factor among others.

Another crucial factor is clearly the *imminence, urgency and vulnerability of the victims.* Multiple references to the fact that the victims were children, in situations of "extreme *vulnerability* [emphasis added]" that pose "an *imminent risk* of irreparable harm to the children's lives, their physical and mental integrity and their development [emphasis added]" appear in the Committee's short Decisions.[134] This speaks to the UNHRC case which followed, where the question of whether obligations arose in an urgent situation was answered in part by reference to the "special relationship of dependency" that arose on the facts. In the CRC case, this relationship of dependency surfaced in part from the children's nationality, whereas in the UNHRC, it was derived from geographic proximity of the vessel in distress. Nonetheless, both relate to factual realities wherein the individuals appeal to the states closest to them, and in the strongest position to prevent serious harm.[135]

States' *obligations under broader international law* also feature as potentially relevant factors, in this case as well in others before the UNHRC, ECtHR and IACtHR.[136] This is in line with the trend towards a holistic interpretation of IHRL in light of other areas of applicable law—long accepted in relation to the interplay of IHRL and IHL, the law of the UN Charter, environmental law and others,[137] and hereby extended to extra-territorial jurisdiction. A related interpretative trend evident here is the cross-judicial reference between systems.

In conclusion, the situation addressed by *L.H. et al v. France* and *F.B. et al v. France* was an urgent one in which political solutions had proved alarmingly elusive. The CRC added its voice and authority to the chorus of international concern[138] on the failure of states to engage with it in a principled way. It has the potential to help reframe a toxic political discussion through the prism of law, rights and responsibility. It remains to be seen whether the decisions will catalyse France, and other similarly

---

134 UNCRC 2020, para 10; UNCRC 2021a, para 9.

135 UNHRC 2021, para 7.8.

136 UNCRC 2020, para 9.6, the UNHRC decision is more explicit than the CRC in terms of the relevance of broader international law, where additional obligations arising from the law of the sea can be taken into account in a holistic interpretation of human rights treaties. See also *Hanan*, above n 79, in Sect. 6.3.4 above, and the arguments advanced by the third party intervener in the CRC cases.

137 See *e.g.* Duffy 2020, on Interpretative Approaches to IHRL in light of international law on sanctions, immunities, international humanitarian and criminal law.

138 See *e.g.* UN Human Rights Special Procedures 2020; UN News (2021) 'Unknown number' of foreign nationals have died in squalid Syrian camps, say rights experts. https://news.un.org/en/story/2021/02/1084172. Accessed 29 September 2021.

situated states—at least 50 of whom have nationals in the camps[139]—to engage more constructively with the moral and security imperatives behind the case.

Legally, the CRC's approach to jurisdiction is opaque. Like many other formulations, it raises more questions than it answers. However, despite this, by making clear that the effective control was not over territory or persons as such, but over the children's situation, it lends further support to an emerging approach that considers the states' control over its own decisions and "control of rights" of those affected by them.[140] The flexible context-specific approach was underscored by a subsequent decision of the CRC on trans-boundary environmental harm, which adopted the IACtHR approach to question whether states' acts or omissions had a foreseeable cross border impact.[141] Understood within the broader body of jurisprudential trends, it provides grist for the mill of trends towards a more flexible, legally and factually holistic, approach to the jurisdictional nexus.

6.5 Conclusion

Of the many human rights implications of 'FTF'-related responses, the decision to "abandon" young children in dire need on the purported basis of their parents' presumed engagement with ISIS is perhaps uniquely political and morally jarring.[142] It is also strategically dubious, as even a one-dimensional security lens reveals the short term disadvantages of raising thousands of children in environments the AANES themselves describe as "an extremist powder keg".[143] Legally, the extent to which individuals trapped in NES fall into other states' jurisdiction is not, however, straightforward: it is challenging and controversial, rendered more so by the state of disarray of jurisprudence on the 'jurisdiction' question.

While that jurisprudence has taken winding roads, there are, however, trends and commonalities. It is unanimously accepted across all systems that artificial limits on jurisdiction cannot be drawn at a state's territorial borders, and a wave of developments—from the UNHRC General Comment No. 36 and the *A.S. et al. v. Italy* decision, to the IACtHR's Advisory Opinion on *The Environment and Human Rights*, to the African Commission's General Comment No. 3 and the CRC and ECHR decisions against France—all suggest that it is similarly inadequate, if IHRL is to be

139 US Lead Inspector General 2019, p. 23.

140 See courts and bodies above; see also Çali 2020; Duffy and Maxwell 2020.

141 Addressing environmental cross border harm, the CRC found "children are under the jurisdiction of the State on whose territory the emissions originated [...] if there is a causal link between the acts or omissions of the State in question and the negative impact on the rights of children located outside of its territory, when the State of origin exercises effective control over the sources of the emissions in question". UNCRC 2021b, para 9.7.

142 Council of Europe Parliamentary Assembly 2020, para 2.

143 France 24 (2021) Syria Kurds launch security sweep, arrests in camp for IS families. https://www.france24.com/en/live-news/20210328-syria-kurds-launch-security-sweep-arrests-in-camp-for-is-families. Accessed 29 September 2021.

given effect in the modern world, to draw the line at persons under the "physical control" of the state. Uncertainty remains as to whether the ECtHR will continue to consolidate the apparently more restrictive approach of a "two-part test", or expand it in line with evolving cross border challenges, as it has in practice in a range of cases where states' conduct had foreseeable effects abroad, absent control over persons or places. Its approach in *H.F. and Others v. France*, while creating a very narrow exception around a particular right, shows a purposive and contextual approach, to safeguard the effectiveness of the ECHR.[144] In any event, its approach to date must be seen as the outlier on the extra-territorial question, and not a global reference point, despite the disproportionate emphasis placed on it, even in litigation before bodies that themselves adopt more flexible approaches.

Both the CRC and UNHRC cases, like the vast majority of developments set out in this chapter, reflect the shift from a formalistic to a functional approach, focused on the undoubted control State parties have over their own conduct (acts and omissions) and how the exercise of authority and power has a foreseeable impact on human rights. The approach of these bodies, and to an extent the ECtHR in *H.F. and Others v. France*, speak to the need for a deeply fact-specific and contextual approach that takes closely into account dire humanitarian needs, exceptional circumstances of vulnerability and the capacity of particular states to respond to urgent pleas, consistent with the need for a purposive approach to human rights treaties that avoids vacuums of protection, while safeguarding the principle of effectiveness.[145] The growing cross-reference to other obligations under international law, and between systems, is in turn, consistent with a holistic interpretation of IHRL.

A precise articulation of legal standards on extra-territoriality remains elusive, and the threat to legal certainty is real. But so too is the need for the law to be sufficiently flexible to take into account the reality of the diverse ways in which power is exercised, and relationships of control, rights dependency and impact arise between an individual and the state, in the world today. Clarifying the normative framework within which that analysis takes place, while safeguarding that flexibility, is an ongoing challenge.

The questions of scope explored in this chapter are of acute relevance to many caught in the cross hairs of counter-terrorism measures that continue to expand and spread their reach across borders and into all aspects of human rights. Twenty years on from the war on terror whose most notorious wrongs involved the creation of extra-territorial black holes, from CIA black detention sites to Guantánamo Bay,[146] it is striking the extent to which jurisdiction continues to be relied upon to avoid the applicability of IHRL and judicial oversight, detracting from the questions of substance as to the real nature of states' obligations and how to give them effect.

---

[144] Most recently, contrast *Georgia v. Russia* (II), above n 57, which reasserted the control of area or of persons tests, and *Hanan*, above n 79, which extended jurisdiction to investigations, and see other cases involving effects abroad discussed above.

[145] Duffy 2020.

[146] Rights and Security International 2020.

Acknowledgements Thanks to Eva Daniel and Brenda Rodriguez for their assistance; some aspects of this chapter were drawn from a case note *'Communications No. 79/2019 and 109/2019 L.H. et al v. France and 77/2019 F.B. et al v. France: French Children in Syrian Camps: the Committee on the Rights of the Child and the Jurisdictional Quagmire'* on the Leiden Children's Rights Observatory.

References

Articles, Books and Other Documents

ACommHPR (2015a) Principles and Guidelines on Human and Peoples' Rights while Countering Terrorism in Africa. https://www.achpr.org/legalinstruments/detail?id=9. Accessed 2 December 2021

ACommHPR (2015b) General Comment No. 3: The Right To Life (Article 4) https://www.achpr.org/legalinstruments/detail?id=10. Accessed 2 December 2021

Altwicker T (2018) Transnationalizing Rights: International Human Rights Law in Cross-Border Contexts. European Journal of International Law 29(2):581–606

Amnesty International (2018) Deadly Assistance: The Role of European States in US Drone Strikes. https://www.amnesty.org/en/documents/act30/8151/2018/en/. Accessed 29 September 2021

Banda M L (2018) Inter-American Court of Human Rights' Advisory Opinion on the Environment and Human Rights. American Society of International Law 22(6)

Beinlich L (2019) Germany and its Involvement in the US Drone Programme before German Administrative Courts. https://www.ejiltalk.org/germany-and-its-involvement-in-the-us-drone-programme-before-german-administrative-courts/. Accessed 29 September 2021

Berkes A (2018) A New Extraterritorial Jurisdictional Link Recognised by the IACtHR. https://www.ejiltalk.org/a-new-extraterritorial-jurisdictional-link-recognised-by-the-iacthr/. Accessed 29 September 2021

Bohrer J et al (2020) Law Applicable to Armed Conflict. Cambridge University Press, Cambridge, United Kingdom/New York, NY

Çali B (2020) Has "Control over rights doctrine" for extra-territorial jurisdiction come of age? Karlsruhe, too, has spoken, now it's Strasbourg's turn. https://www.ejiltalk.org/has-control-over-rights-doctrine-for-extra-territorial-jurisdiction-come-of-age-karlsruhe-too-has-spoken-now-its-strasbourgs-turn/. Accessed 29 September 2021

Callamard A (2020) The Targeted Killing of General Soleimani: Its Lawfulness and Why It Matters https://www.justsecurity.org/67949/the-targeted-killing-of-general-soleimani-its-lawfulness-and-why-it-matters/. Accessed 8 January 2020

Council of Europe Commissioner for Human Rights, Dunja Mijatović (2020) PACE urgent debate on International obligations concerning the repatriation of children from war and conflict zones. CommDH/Speech/(2020)2. https://rm.coe.int/16809a4481. Accessed 2 December 2021

Council of Europe Parliamentary Assembly, Stefan Schennach (2020) International obligations concerning the repatriation of children from war and conflict zones. Doc. 15055. https://pace.coe.int/pdf/5c1f5b1a78235e597194eb7bc64dab3c4e549d9df0b2874d99e496466bc71650/doc.%2015055.pdf. Accessed 29 January 2020

Duffy H (2018) "Foreign Terrorist Fighters": A Human Rights Approach? Security and Human Rights 29:120–172

Duffy H (2020) Trials and Tribulations: co-applicability of IHL and human rights in an age of adjudication. In: Bohrer J et al. (eds) Law Applicable to Armed Conflict. Cambridge University Press, Cambridge, United Kingdom/New York, NY

Duffy H (2021a) International Legal Advice on the Potential Prosecution of Adult Females in Al Hol by Courts Established by the Autonomous Administration of North East

Syria 2. https://static1.squarespace.com/static/5b82ab175b409b90d4c99071/t/61e548784781ee0cea5bc5ac/1642416250292/Legal+Opinion+NES2+Final.pdf
Duffy H (2021b) Georgia v. Russia: Jurisdiction, Chaos and Conflict at the European Court of Human Rights. https://www.justsecurity.org/74465/georgia-v-russia-jurisdiction-chaos-and-conflict-at-the-european-court-of-human-rights/. Accessed 29 September 2021
Duffy J, Maxwell L (2020) People v Arctic Oil before Supreme Court of Norway - What's at stake for human rights protection in the climate crisis? https://www.ejiltalk.org/people-v-arctic-oil-before-supreme-court-of-norway-whats-at-stake-for-human-rights-protection-in-the-climate-crisis/. Accessed 29 September 2021
Extra-territorial Obligations Consortium (2013) Maastricht Principles on Extraterritorial Obligations of States in the Area of Economic, Social and Cultural Rights. https://www.etoconsortium.org/nc/en/main-navigation/library/maastricht-principles/?tx_drblob_pi1%5BdownloadUid%5D=23. Accessed 2 December 2021
Human Rights Watch (2020) "Bring Me Back to Canada": Plight of Canadians Held in Northeast Syria for Alleged ISIS Links. https://www.hrw.org/report/2020/06/29/bring-me-back-canada/plight-canadians-held-northeast-syria-alleged-isis-links. Accessed 29 September 2021
International Crisis Group (2019) Women and children first: Repatriating the Westerners affiliated with ISIS. https://www.crisisgroup.org/middle-east-north-africa/eastern-mediterranean/syria/208-women-and-children-first-repatriating-westerners-affiliated-isis. Accessed 29 September 2021
Jeannerod B (2020) France Repatriates More Children from Northeast Syria, Government Should Bring Home All Children and their Mothers from ISIS Camps. https://www.hrw.org/news/2020/06/24/france-repatriates-more-children-northeast-syria. Accessed 29 September 2021
Joint Committee on Human Rights (House of Lords, House of Commons) (2016) The Government's Policy on the Use of Drones for Targeted Killing. Second Report of Session 2015-16, HL Paper 141 HC 574. https://publications.parliament.uk/pa/jt201516/jtselect/jtrights/574/574.pdf. Accessed 3 December 2021
Langford M (2013) Global Justice, State Duties the Extraterritorial Scope of Economic, Social, and Cultural Rights in International Law. Cambridge University Press, Cambridge
Margariti S (2018) Defining International Terrorism to Protect Human Rights in the Context of Counter-terrorism. Security and Human rights 29:173–198
Médecins Sans Frontières (2019) Women treated for gunshot wounds amidst violence and unrest in Al-Hol camp. https://www.msf.org/women-treated-gunshot-wounds-amidst-violence-and-unrest-al-hol-camp-syria. Accessed 29 September 2021.
Milanovic M (2020) Repatriating the Children of Foreign Terrorist Fighters and the Extraterritorial Application of Human Rights. https://www.ejiltalk.org/repatriating-the-children-of-foreign-terrorist-fighters-and-the-extraterritorial-application-of-human-rights/. Accessed 29 September 2021
Milanovic M (2021) Georgia v. Russia No. 2: The European Court's Resurrection of Bankovic in the Contexts of Chaos. https://www.ejiltalk.org/georgia-v-russia-no-2-the-european-courts-resurrection-of-bankovic-in-the-contexts-of-chaos/. Accessed 29 September 2021
Mironova (2020) Life Inside Syria's al-Hol Camp. https://www.mei.edu/publications/life-inside-syrias-al-hol-camp. Accessed 29 September 2021.
OCHA (2020) Syrian Arab Republic, North East Syria: Al Hol camp as of 11 October 2020 ('Al Hol Snapshot'). https://reliefweb.int/report/syrian-arab-republic/syrian-arab-republic-north-east-syria-al-hol-camp-11-october-2020. Accessed 29 September 2021
OCHA (2021) Statement by Under-Secretary-General for Humanitarian Affairs and Emergency Relief Coordinator, Mark Lowcock, on Syria. https://reliefweb.int/report/syrian-arab-republic/under-secretary-general-humanitarian-affairs-and-emergency-relief-115. Accessed 29 September 2021
OHCHR (2001) Concluding Observations of the Committee on Economic, Social and Cultural Rights: Israel, UN Doc. E/C.12/1/Add.69

OHCHR (2003) Concluding Observations of the Committee on Economic, Social and Cultural Rights: Israel, UN Doc. E/C.12/1/Add.90
OHCHR (2012) Concluding observations of the Human Rights Committee: Germany, UN Doc. CCPR/C/DEU/CO/6
OSCE (2014) Declaration on the OSCE Role in Countering the Phenomenon of Foreign Terrorist Fighters in the Context of the Implementation of UN Security Council Resolutions 2170 (2014), 2178 (2014). MC.DOC/5/14. https://www.osce.org/files/f/documents/e/a/130546.pdf. Accessed 16 December 2021
Rights and Security International (2020) Europe's Guantanamo: The indefinite detention of European women and children in North East Syria https://www.rightsandsecurity.org/impact/entry/europes-guantanamo-report. Accessed 29 September 2021
UNCESCR (2017) General comment No. 24 (2017) on State obligations under the International Covenant on Economic, Social and Cultural Rights in the context of business activities, UN Doc. E/C.12/GC/24
UNCRC (2012) Concluding Observations of the Committee on the Rights of the Child: Australia, UN Doc. CRC/C/AUS/CO/4
UNCRC (2015) Concluding Observations of the Committee on the Rights of the Child: Switzerland, UN Doc. CRC/C/CHE/CO/2-4
UNCRC (2018) Views adopted by the Committee under the Optional Protocol to the Convention on the Rights of the Child on a communications procedure, re. No. 12/2017, UN Doc. CRC/C/79/D/12/2017
UNCRC (2020) Decision adopted by the Committee under the Optional Protocol to the Convention on the Rights of the Child on a communications procedure, concerning communications No. 79/2019 and No. 109/2019, 4 December 2020, UN Doc. CRC/C/85/D/79/2019-CRC/C/85/D/109/2019 (2020)
UNCRC (2021a) Décision sur la recevabilité du Comité des droits de l'enfant en vertu du Protocole facultative à la Convention relative aux droits de l'enfant établissant une procédure de présentation de communications concernant la communication n° 77/2019, 4 February 2021, UN Doc. CRC/C/86/D/R.77/2019 (2021) (*F.B. et al v. France*)
UNCRC (2021b) Decision adopted on a communications procedure in respect of Communication No. 107/2019, CRC/C/88/D/107/2019 (2021)
UNGA (2013) Extrajudicial, summary or arbitrary executions. Note by the Secretary-General, UN Doc. A/68/382
UNHRC (1981a) *Celiberti de Casariego v. Uruguay*, Communication No. 56/1979, UN Doc. CCPR/C/13/D/56/1979 (1981)
UNHRC (1981b) *Lopez Burgos v. Uruguay*, Communication No. 52/1979, 29 July 1981, UN Doc. CCPR/C/13/D/52/1979 (1981)
UNHRC (2004a) General Comment No. 31: The Nature of the General Legal Obligation Imposed on States Parties to the Covenant, UN Doc. CCPR/C/21/Rev.1/Add.1326
UNHRC (2004b) Concluding Observations of the Human Rights Committee: Belgium, UN Doc. CPR/CO/81/BEL
UNHRC (2014) The right to privacy in the digital age. Report of the Office of the United Nations High Commissioner for Human Rights, UN Doc. A/HRC/27/37
UNHRC (2019) General Comment No. 36: Article 6: right to life, UN Doc. CCPR/C/GC/35
UNHRC (2020a) Report of the Independent International Commission of Inquiry on the Syrian Arab Republic, UN Doc. A/HRC/43/57
UNHRC (2020b) Report of the Special Rapporteur on extrajudicial, summary or arbitrary executions, UN Doc. A/HRC/44/38
UNHRC (2021) Views adopted by the Committee under article 5(4) of the Optional Protocol, concerning Communication No. 3042/2017, UN Doc. CCPR/C/130/D/3042/2017
UN Human Rights Special Procedures (2020) Extra-territorial jurisdiction of States over children and their guardians in camps, prisons, or elsewhere in the northern Syrian Arab

Republic—Legal Analysis. https://www.ohchr.org/Documents/Issues/Executions/UNSRsPublicJurisdictionAnalysis2020.pdf. Accessed 17 December 2021
UNICEF (2021) Two children killed in Al-Hol Camp in Syria. https://www.unicef.org/press-releases/two-children-killed-al-hol-camp-syria. Accessed 29 September 2021
UNSC (2014) Resolution 2178 (2014), UN Doc. S/RES/2178 (2014)
UNSC (2017) Resolution 2396 (2017), UN Doc. S/RES/2396 (2017)
US Lead Inspector General (2019) Operation Inherent Resolve, Lead Inspector General Report to the United States Congress, 1 April 2019-30 June 2019. https://www.dodig.mil/Reports/Lead-Inspector-General-Reports/Article/1926689/lead-inspector-general-for-operation-inherent-resolve-quarterly-report-to-the-u/. Accessed 16 December 2021
Vandenhole W (2011) Beyond Territoriality: The Maastricht Principles on Extraterritorial Obligations in the Area of Economic, Social and Cultural Rights. Netherlands Quarterly on Human Rights 29(4):429–433
Vandenhole W (2020) Towards a Division of Labour for Sustainable Development: Extraterritorial Human Rights Obligations. In: Kaltenborn M et al (eds) Sustainable Development Goals and Human Rights. Interdisciplinary Studies in Human Rights, pp. 221 *et seq*
Vianna de Azevedo C (2020) ISIS resurgence in Al Hawl camp and human smuggling enterprises in Syria: Crime and terror convergence? Perspectives on Terrorism 14 (4):43–63

Case Law

ACommHPR, *Democratic Republic of Congo v. Burundi, Rwanda and Uganda,* Communication 227/99, 29 May 2003
ECtHR, *Banković and Others v. Belgium*, Grand Chamber Judgement, 12 December 2001, Application no. 52207/99
ECtHR, *H.F. and M.F. v. France*, Application nos. 24384/19 and 44234/20. Relinquishment in favour of the Grand Chamber of 22 March 2021. Press Release. https://hudoc.echr.coe.int/app/conversion/pdf/?library=ECHR&id=003-6972761-9386990&filename=Relinquishment%20to%20Grand%20Chamber%20of%20two%20cases%20H.F.%20and%20M.F.%20v.%20France%20and%20J.D.%20and%20A.D.%20v.%20France.pdf. Accessed 20 November 2021
ECtHR, *Kovačić and Others v. Slovenia*, Grand Chamber Judgement, 9 October 2003, Applications nos. 44574/98, 45133/98 and 48316/99
ECtHR, *Ilascu and Others v. Moldova and Russia*, Grand Chamber Judgement, 8 July 2004, Application no. 48787/99
ECtHR, *Mubilanzila Mayeka and Kaniki Mitunga v. Belgium*, First Section, 12 October 2006, Application no. 13178/03
ECtHR, *Al-Skeini and Others v. the United Kingdom*, Grand Chamber Judgement, 7 July 2011, Application no. 55721/07
ECtHR, *Catan and Others v. Moldova and Russia*, Grand Chamber Judgement, 19 October 2012, Applications no. 43370/04, 18454/06 and 8252/05
ECtHR, *Hassan v. the United Kingdom,* Grand Chamber Judgement, 16 September 2014, Application no. 229750/09
ECtHR, *Jaloud v. Netherlands*, Grand Chamber Judgement, 20 November 2014, Application no. 47708/08
ECtHR, *Big Brother Watch and Others v. United Kingdom*, Grand Chamber Judgement, 13 September 2018, Applications nos. 58170/13, 62322/14 and 24960/15
ECtHR, *Georgia v. Russia* (II), Grand Chamber Judgement, Application no. 38263/08
ECtHR, *Hanan v. Germany*, Grand Chamber Judgement, 16 February 2021, Application no. 4871/16
ECtHR, *X and Y v. Switzerland*, Third Section, 14 July 1977, Applications nos. 7289/75 and 7349/76
ECtHR, *Öcalan v. Turkey*, Grand Chamber Judgement, 12 May 2005, Application no. 46221/99
ECtHR, *Pad and Others v. Turkey*, Third Section, 28 June 2007, Application no. 60267/00

ECtHR, *Tatar v. Romania*, Chamber Judgement, 27 January 2009, Application no. 67021/01
ECtHR, *K2 v. the United Kingdom*, First Section, 7 February 2017, Application no. 42387/13
ECtHR, *Issa and Others v. Turkey*, Second Section, 16 November 2004, Application no. 31821/96
ECtHR, *Soering v. United Kingdom*, Application no. 13038/88, 7 July 1989
ECtHR, *Nada v. Switzerland*, Grand Chamber Judgement, 12 September 2012, Application no. 10593/08
England and Wales High Court (EWHC) (Administrative), *Al-Saadoon and Others (Claimant) v. Secretary of State for Defence (Defendant)*, 17 March 2015, [2015] EWHC 715
IACtHR, *Coard et al. v. the United States*, Report N. 109/99 - Case 10.951, 29 September 1999
IACtHR, *The Environment and Human Rights*, Advisory Opinion OC-23/17, 15 November 2017
IACommHR, *Armando Alejandre, Jr. et al. v. Cuba*, Report N.86/99—Case 11.589, 29 September 1999
IACommHR, *Decision on Request for Precautionary Measures* (Detainees at Guantanamo Bay, Cuba), 13 March 2002
Supreme Court (United Kingdom), *R (on the application of Begum) (Appellant) v. Special Immigration Appeals Commission (Respondent), R (on the application of Begum) (Respondent) v. Secretary of State for the Home Department (Appellant), Begum (Respondent) v. Secretary of State for the Home Department (Appellant)*, 26 February 2021, [2021] UKSC 7
ICJ, *Legal Consequences of the Construction of a Wall in the Occupied Palestinian Territory*, Advisory Opinion, 9 July 2004, [2004] ICJ Rep 136

Treaties

African Charter on Human and Peoples' Rights, opened for signature 27 June 1981, 1520 UNTS 217 (entered into force 21 October 1986)
American Convention on Human Rights, opened for signature 22 November 1969, 1144 UNTS 123 (entered into force 19 July 1978)
Convention on the Rights of the Child, opened for signature 20 November 1989, 1577 UNTS 3 (entered into force 2 September 1990)
European Convention on Human Rights, opened for signature 4 November 1950, 213 UNTS 221 (entered into force 3 September 1953)
International Covenant on Civil and Political Rights, opened for signature 16 December 1966, 999 UNTS 171 (entered into force 23 March 1976)

Part III
Responses to the (Returning) Foreign Fighters Phenomenon: The National Dimension

Chapter 7
Evidentiary and Charging Matters in the Context of Prosecuting Returning Foreign Fighters Before National Courts

Christophe Paulussen and Tanya Mehra

Contents

Abstract States have been reluctant to repatriate their foreign fighters and families for a variety of reasons. One of these is of a legal nature, namely that prosecution at home would be too difficult because of a lack of evidence. After a brief overview of possible other options, this chapter will focus on the prosecution of returning foreign fighters before national courts. While acknowledging that securing evidence is and will remain difficult, this chapter points to a number of evidentiary and charging opportunities that show potential in somewhat overcoming this challenge. These could assist prosecutors in focusing on what should have their priority, namely the actual acts committed, such as war crimes and other international crimes. This chapter will also demonstrate that, in addition to membership of a terrorist organisation, there are other charges out there that do not require establishing what the returning foreign fighter has actually done while being abroad. The aim of presenting these in this chapter should not be seen as an endorsement—their critical examination will make

This chapter was finalised on 17 August 2021. Developments after that date have not been incorporated.

C. Paulussen (✉)
T.M.C. Asser Instituut, The Hague, The Netherlands
e-mail: c.paulussen@asser.nl

T. Mehra
International Centre for Counter-Terrorism—The Hague (ICCT), The Hague, The Netherlands
e-mail: t.mehra@icct.nl

F. Capone et al. (eds.), *Returning Foreign Fighters: Responses, Legal Challenges and Ways Forward*, https://doi.org/10.1007/978-94-6265-571-3_7

this quite clear—but as a demonstration of the fact that the refusal to repatriate and prosecute can only be explained by a lack of political will, and not because of a lack of prosecutorial options.

Keywords Repatriation · Prosecution · International crimes · Information collected from conflict zones · Information collected from open sources and social media · Pre-crime space

7.1 Introduction

Many, and especially Western, countries have been reluctant to actively repatriate their foreign fighters and families currently detained in camps in North-East Syria.[1] So far, only a handful of countries, such as Kazakhstan,[2] Uzbekistan,[3] Kosovo[4] and the United States,[5] have taken the politically brave step of actively repatriating not only children and women but also male fighters.

The refusal to repatriate is often based on emotional and symbolic arguments—"these people have forfeited their bond with our societies, and we are definitely not going to use taxpayer's money to bring them back"—and an exaggeration of the security risk. Although the presence of a security risk in the repatriation of the adults—as regards the children, the security risk of non-repatriation has, in fact, been assessed to be higher—[6] cannot be denied, it is very small indeed.[7] But even the tiny chance that a returnee is involved in a terrorist attack back home is too much of a risk for many politicians.

---

[1] See e.g. Mai 2019.

[2] Wolfe and Orozobekova 2021.

[3] Imamova and Kashgarian 2021.

[4] Avdimetaj and Coleman 2020.

[5] 'The United States Has Repatriated 27 Americans from Syria and Iraq Including Ten Charged with Terrorism-Related Offenses for Their Support to ISIS. The International Community Is Urged To Follow Suit and Repatriate Its Citizens from Syria', The United States Department of Justice (Office of Public Affairs) 2020.

[6] See the internal memo of the Dutch National Coordinator for Security and Counterterrorism (NCTV) 2019, p. 393 and further.

[7] See Malet 2019: "Governments are aware of their international obligations to their citizens, and that is why they are getting creative in inventing technicalities to claim that the ISIS immigrants born in their countries weren't citizens at all. These policies violate the spirit of international agreements on foreign fighters. But governments justify them on security grounds by citing research showing that an "average" of approximately ten percent of returnees will become domestic terrorists. This statistic was misinterpreted from a widely-cited 2013 study. Two years later the same researcher found the rate in the ISIS era to be just 0.002 percent, but this update has not had the same impact on policymakers".

Some states have decided to remove citizenship to rescind responsibility. For example, the United Kingdom,[8] Australia[9] and the Netherlands[10] have chosen to deprive foreign fighters of their nationality and, in that way, make these people the problem of other states. As argued before, this is an inefficient and even counterproductive counter-terrorism measure undermining the fight against impunity.[11] Moreover, even if persons have been deprived of their nationality, they can, upon arrest in a third country like Turkey, be deported to their country of origin, as happened with Fatima H. from the Netherlands.[12] Furthermore, stripping of citizenship could also lead to diplomatic tensions with countries that may be relevant partners in combatting terrorism.[13] Finally, states more sensitive to the impunity argument have stated that prosecution is indeed needed, but that this should be done not in the country of origin but by local courts in the region or by an international(ised) tribunal.[14]

As regards local courts in the region: it indeed makes sense to prosecute where the crimes have been committed, for example, because of easier access to witnesses and victims. And, in fact, prosecution in local, national courts is already happening, and in massive numbers, although the focus has been on alleged ISIS members of Iraqi and Syrian nationality. These trials, however, have also received considerable criticism.[15] As explained by Impunity Watch, PAX and SCM (the Syrian Center for Media and Freedom of Expression) in October 2019:

> Domestically, Iraq has sentenced thousands of alleged ISIS members to death or lengthy prison sentences in trials that frequently fail to meet basic standards of fairness. Cases are mainly brought under anti-terror legislation, meaning defendants are frequently convicted on the basis of ISIS membership rather than actual deeds, and victims have little opportunity to participate in or be properly informed of proceedings. The rapid trials in Iraq also leave little opportunity to obtain supplementary information of vital importance to victims' family members, such as the whereabouts of remains. In Syria, the SDF has conducted trial proceedings for Syrian nationals accused of fighting with ISIS, commendable for not imposing the death penalty, but the trials have lacked legal standing due to the territory's lack of sovereignty, limited resources and expertise to hold fair trials, and the challenges of attempting to administer justice in a conflict zone [original footnotes omitted].[16]

---

[8] The most well-known examples are probably the citizenship stripping of Shamima Begum and of El Shafee Elsheikh and Alexanda Amon Kotey, members of the so-called Beatles cell, see Coleman and Cook 2020; and Mehra 2020.

[9] See e.g. Dutton 2018.

[10] See College voor de Rechten van de Mens 2017.

[11] See Paulussen 2018. See more extensively also Chap. 10 by van Waas and Brekoo in this volume.

[12] Cluskey 2019. In April 2021, Fatima H. was convicted to four years' imprisonment for membership of a terrorist organisation, see NOS 2021.

[13] Bolhuis and van Wijk 2020, p. 365.

[14] Although this is not the focus of our chapter, we will still address the issue of international(ised) prosecution briefly, as it sets out the context in which the issue of prosecution before courts of the countries of origin should be seen.

[15] See also Mehra 2017.

[16] Impunity Watch, PAX and SCM 2019.

Zooming in on the foreign fighters detained in Syrian camps in North-East Syria, the Kurdish authorities have begged countries several times to take their responsibility, through repatriation and prosecution, in particular of female foreign fighters. As explained, with the exception of a few cases carrying minimal political risk, such as the repatriation of orphans, or unless forced by courts, Western governments have largely ignored these calls, which reportedly have led to the decision of the Kurdish authorities to prosecute these foreign fighters themselves.[17] However, as also explained above, so far, the Rojava courts have only prosecuted Syrians and Iraqis suspected of belonging to ISIS and other armed groups.[18] Given the urgency of the situation—people are escaping,[19] smuggled out (sometimes with the financial help of relatives back home)[20] or simply released from the camps—it is important that use is made of already-existing courts that can guarantee a fair trial. Not in a few years, but now.

This is also one of the reasons why the idea of an international tribunal—to also touch on that topic—is not viable. There are several political, legal and operational obstacles in the process of establishing a tribunal,[21] such as securing enough support from the UN Security Council (assuming, for now, this tribunal would be established not via a treaty procedure), jurisdictional issues (often it has been said this should become an ISIS anti-terrorism court, without realising no internationally recognised definition of terrorism exists,[22] and without realising that focusing on ISIS will lead to 'victor's justice' critique),[23] the fact that such a tribunal would only be able to prosecute those bearing the greatest responsibility and thus not the vast number of fighters that have committed crimes, not to speak of more practical considerations such as the financial burden. Although the idea of an internationalised or hybrid tribunal (half national, half international) is a bit more appealing than a truly international tribunal, as the former would entail a more sustainable investment in the domestic legal system, several of the obstacles mentioned earlier remain, the most important one being that there is no time to waste, as more and more people disappear

---

[17] Sabbagh 2020.

[18] Mehra and Wentworth 2021.

[19] Also, Turkey's invasion in October 2019 contributed to this, see e.g. BBC News 2019.

[20] Former terrorist Samir A. will soon stand trial for helping 12 Dutch female foreign fighters escape from the camps in Syria. See Kouwenhoven 2021.

[21] For more information, see Impunity Watch, PAX and SCM 2019.

[22] See the Asser Nexus on Conflict and Crime, 'Terrorism', available at: https://www.asser.nl/nexus/international-criminal-law/international-crimes-introduction/terrorism/.

[23] Focusing on prosecution of just one party to the conflict will not lead to true reconciliation in society, especially not if the party responsible, by far, for most of the violence—the Assad regime—is not in the dock. (On 15 March 2020, the Syrian Observatory for Human Rights noted that it had documented "the death of 384,000 persons across Syria since the start of the Syrian Revolution on the 15th of March 2011 to the 14st [*sic*] of March 2020". This number includes 116,086 Syrian civilians. If one breaks down this number by 'perpetrator', one will see, among other things: ISIS (6204), torture: regime prisons (16,163), regime aircraft (26,407) and regime forces (45, 382)). See Syrian Observatory for Human Rights 2020.

off the radar, and hence that already-existing courts that can guarantee fair trials must be resorted to now.

Indeed, all of these options—deprivation of nationality, the suggestion to establish an international(ised) tribunal, or simply hoping that local authorities will be less perseverant—do not mask the dodging of responsibility towards one own's citizens[24] and doing what is right from an international legal, moral and long-term security perspective,[25] which is to repatriate, prosecute, rehabilitate and reintegrate at the national level.[26]

In this context, a more legitimate and legal concern has been raised, namely that authorities may want to repatriate and prosecute at the national level but fear that, because of a lack of evidence stemming from the conflict zone, they can only prosecute foreign fighters, not for the full extent of the crimes they have committed, but merely for the 'safety-net' charge of membership of a terrorist organisation,[27] usually leading to a relatively low sentence. And indeed, so far, the vast majority has been prosecuted for membership of a terrorist organisation, such as ISIS.[28] Moreover, it's true that current charges usually lead to a few years of imprisonment only.[29] In addition, overly broad and vague definitions of membership offences do not sufficiently distinguish between active and passive membership and may not adequately reflect the acts an alleged foreign fighter has been involved in in Syria or Iraq. Distinctions need to be drawn, for example, between someone who is cooking for a terrorist group or supplying weapons to a terrorist group.[30]

While acknowledging that securing evidence from conflict and post-conflict zones was, is, and will remain difficult, this chapter, which draws from a number of the

---

[24] See also Ali et al. 2019: "ISIS may have been defeated on the battlefield; but thousands of Western fighters and their families remain in detention in Syria and Iraq. [...] Western governments, for the most part, have refused to take their nationals back. Some have revoked their citizenship. Others have called for an international tribunal based in Iraq, which amounts to another means of avoiding the tough, but necessary, responsibility of dealing with their own citizens".

[25] It was just explained that there are strong reasons to repatriate, from a security and accountability perspective. But there are more reasons, related to international (human rights) law and morality. See e.g. Mehra and Paulussen 2019; and Paulussen 2020.

[26] See more extensively Mehra and Paulussen 2019.

[27] It is quite remarkable that Sweden until recently could not prosecute suspected terrorists for membership of a terrorist organisation, which is probably why they suggested the establishment of a tribunal, see also The Local 2019. However, that loophole has been repaired since 22 January 2020, see Flyger 2020, pp. 38–39. Other offences with which people who have travelled to Syria and Iraq have been charged include incitement to terrorism, see for instance suspect Hatim R. in the Dutch *Context* case; District Court of The Hague 2015.

[28] See also Council of Europe (Parliamentary Assembly, Committee on Legal Affairs and Human Rights) 2020, para 32.

[29] Dworkin 2019, p. 8. In Belgium, for example, "returnees are typically sentenced to 5 years in jail." (Renard and Coolsaet 2018, p. 33. A recent study of 20 judgements in the Netherlands showed that "suspects who successfully travelled to Syria and who have been convicted for that, received an unconditional prison sentence of between two and 7.5 years, with the majority receiving a punishment of five years or longer [own translation]." See Van Gestel 2020, p. 1012.

[30] International Commission of Jurists 2020, p. 22.

authors' earlier publications, will discuss several evidentiary and charging opportunities that show potential in somewhat overcoming this challenge. These could assist in holding foreign fighters accountable to the full extent of the crimes committed, rather than a prosecution only based on generally formulated charges such as membership of a terrorist organisation. This is important, as it will lead to more tailored prosecutions and not to a 'one size fits all' solution, as well as provide more justice and dignity to the victims. Finally, prosecution for the full extent of the crimes will also lead to higher sentences, which, in turn, may convince politicians that repatriation is, in fact, a viable option.

In the following section (Sect. 7.2), attention will be paid to these evidentiary and charging issues on and around the (digital) battlefield, which will include a renewed focus on international crimes, information collected from the conflict zone by the military, international mechanisms or other actors, and information obtained from open sources and social media. We should stress that it is merely a brief selection and does not constitute an exhaustive overview of the potential of certain evidentiary forms.[31] In Sect. 7.3, we will discuss two other prosecutorial charges (in addition to the well-known charge of membership of a terrorist organisation that will not be further addressed) that could, in theory, be used by prosecutors as a safety-net in case prosecution for the full extent of the crimes committed, in the end, is not feasible: travelling abroad for the purpose of terrorism and staying in an area controlled by a terrorist organisation. As will become clear from their critical examination: we do not present these to inspire prosecutors to take that route but to further strengthen our normative claim that the argument that authorities should not repatriate and prosecute because they would not have enough charging options at their disposal to ensure that foreign fighters are put behind bars upon return is feeble. In Sect. 7.4, we will briefly summarise our findings and offer a few concluding remarks.

Before we start, we should stress that even though it is our conviction that foreign fighters and their families should be repatriated and tried before courts of the country of origin, that does not mean that the evidentiary issues that will be discussed in this chapter may not be relevant as well, in principle, for possible future international(ised) courts and mechanisms. For example, information secured on the battlefield may not only end up being used in the context of court proceedings in Germany but also, perhaps, before an international(ised) court several years from now. Nonetheless, our argument is that given the urgency, we cannot wait for those international(ised) courts to be established first, and hence that we have to start in any case, and without delay, with what is already available, and that is: courts of the country of origin.

[31] Much can for example be said as well about forensic evidence and intelligence information, see generally GCTF 2018.

7.2 Evidentiary and Charging Opportunities On and Around the (Digital) Battlefield

7.2.1 A Renewed Focus on International Crimes

So far, the foreign fighters phenomenon has been mainly discussed in the context of counter-terrorism, which explains the often-used reference, not to foreign fighters as such but the more limited group of foreign *terrorist* fighters.[32] However, investigators, prosecutors and judges have to understand that foreign fighters can commit not only terrorist crimes but also international crimes[33] such as war crimes (but also crimes against humanity and genocide).[34] In fact, the Independent International Commission of Inquiry on the Syrian Arab Republic has indicated that ISIS has committed multiple crimes against humanity and war crimes, as well as the crime of genocide against the Yazidis.[35]

Luckily, there is an increased interest to focus more on international crimes. Several countries, notably Hungary, Sweden, France, the Netherlands, Finland and in particular Germany, have now prosecuted their foreign fighters, but also Syrians who have obtained refugee status in their respective countries, for core international crimes. And not only male but also female foreign fighters.[36] For example, in June 2021, German and Algerian national Sarah O. was convicted by the Higher Regional Court of Düsseldorf for membership of a terrorist organisation and crimes against humanity. Sarah O. travelled to Syria in 2013 and, together with her husband, held five Yazidi women and two Yazidi girls as slaves. Sarah O. was specifically convicted for death as a result of enslavement and persecution, both as crimes against humanity and for aiding and abetting additional crimes. Sarah. O. was a minor at the time of the offences and was convicted to six and a half years in prison under juvenile law.[37] According to one of the German attorneys, Sonka Mehner, it was thanks to the testimonies of the victims participating in the trial that the Chamber extended

---

[32] See, e.g. UN Security Council 2014.

[33] See also UN General Assembly 2020 Report of the Special Rapporteur on the promotion and protection of human rights and fundamental freedoms while countering terrorism, Fionnuala Ní Aoláin, UN Doc. A/75/337, para 21: "The Special Rapporteur discerns a distinct and unfortunate failure to properly address certain violent acts as "war crimes" or other international crimes, such as crimes against humanity, with State preferences to use the nomenclature of terrorism to hazily characterize such harms [original footnotes omitted]".

[34] Prosecution for common offences (such as murder, arson or document fraud) is of course also possible. This is more interesting than the charge of membership of a terrorist organisation, as it focuses more on the actual crimes committed, but not as interesting as international crimes charges, as the latter take the context of the criminality into account better. On the topics of common offences and the interlinkage between terrorism and international humanitarian law (IHL), see Chap. 8 by Van Poecke and Cuyckens in this volume. See also Cuyckens and Paulussen 2019, pp. 537–565.

[35] HRC 2016.

[36] See Eurojust 2020c, pp. 16–24.

[37] See Doughty Street Chambers 2021.

the charges and that "the full extent of the defendant's criminal conduct could be established".[38]

This is an important point that needs emphasising. A valid question to ask is how a renewed focus on international crimes can somewhat assist investigators and prosecutors in overcoming the challenges of securing evidence in a (digital) conflict zone. But this case shows that victims who want to know what happened to their loved ones may not be satisfied with the mere charge of membership of a terrorist organisation, and thus could assist investigators and prosecutors, through their testimonies, to prosecute for the full extent of the crimes committed. This may entail that through the victims' assistance, accountability for international crimes can be established by the prosecuting authorities. This, in turn, will lead to a more accurate judicial record and recognition for the victims' suffering, as well as a higher sentence. This higher sentence will also please the security community, which will want to make sure that returning foreign fighters are removed from society for a longer time. However, it must be admitted that assistance by victims obviously requires that victims know about the case in the first place, which may mean this could only be relevant for victims already located in the prosecuting country, and that they can actually step forward and play an active role in the proceedings.

It should be noted, however, that investigators and prosecutors are not dependent on cooperative victims alone: there is also a willingness by the international community to focus more on international crimes and to assist in securing information that can later be used in the accountability process. Clear examples in the context of Syria and Iraq are the International, Impartial and Independent Mechanism to Assist in the Investigation and Prosecution of Persons Responsible for the *Most Serious Crimes under International Law* Committed in the Syrian Arab Republic since March 2011' [emphasis added] (IIIM)[39] and the United Nations Investigative Team to Promote Accountability for Crimes Committed by Da'esh/ISIL (UNITAD),[40] which was established

> to support domestic efforts to hold ISIL (Da'esh) accountable by collecting, preserving, and storing evidence in Iraq of *acts that may amount to war crimes, crimes against humanity and genocide* committed by the terrorist group ISIL (Da'esh) in Iraq, to the highest possible standards, [...]to ensure the broadest possible use before national courts, and complementing investigations being carried out by the Iraqi authorities, or investigations carried out by authorities in third countries at their request[.] [emphasis added][41]

And a renewed focus on international crimes does not necessarily mean *more* evidence is required, for instance, through the provision of a witness statement. It is sometimes also about making better use of *existing* evidence. As explained earlier:

> whereas in the past a picture showing a fighter posing with a dead body would be used to prove that that person had joined a terrorist organisation, one can use that same picture to

[38] Ibid.

[39] More information available at: https://iiim.un.org/.

[40] More information available at: https://www.unitad.un.org/.

[41] UN Security Council 2017, para 2.

> prove that someone treated a person who is protected under IHL [international humanitarian law] in a gravely humiliating and degrading manner, which is a war crime[.][42]

This happened in the case of Dutch returnee Oussama A., who did not receive the regular five to six years' imprisonment for membership of a terrorist organisation, but was sentenced to seven and a half years instead.[43] His case is a good example of the so-called 'selfie', or 'posing' cases,[44] which have led to cumulative charging for both membership of a terrorist organisation and international crimes such as war crimes.[45] It is admitted that the difference between five to six years, on the one hand, and seven and a half years, on the other hand, is not that big, but the fact that Oussama has now been prosecuted and convicted for the act of posing next to a dead body, involving an actual victim,[46] is to be applauded.

A challenge related to a renewed focus on international crimes such as war crimes is that this obviously requires expertise in the applicable legal fields, such as IHL, a rather technical field of law that many criminal justice professionals may not even have heard of. It requires knowledge of the Geneva Conventions, the Additional Protocols, customary IHL, terms such as (non-)international armed conflicts, establishing a nexus etc. IHL training of criminal justice professionals working in the counter-terrorism field is, therefore, to be advised. If this turns out to be difficult, then it is recommended to at least increase the cooperation and coordination of departments focusing on counter-terrorism and those on IHL and international criminal law. Regular consultations between such departments may lead to new insights and prosecutorial opportunities in specific cases.

7.2.2 Information Collected from the Conflict Zone

Much information and material can be gathered from conflict and post-conflict situations, which could be useful to prosecute foreign fighters. One could think of unexploded Improvised Explosive Devices (IEDs) and components of exploded IEDs, USB sticks with digital information or old-fashioned folders with paper documents, such as registration forms. Not only military personnel could collect and obtain information from the conflict zone, but also other actors present in this conflict zone,[47] especially after active hostilities, such as NGOs and CSOs working in the field[48] or representatives of international bodies and tribunals monitoring violations of IHL

[42] Paulussen et al. 2019.

[43] The Hague District Court 2019.

[44] See Eurojust 2020b.

[45] For more information, see Eurojust 2020c.

[46] The deceased person, presumably Neser Khalef Zowid, was killed "by or on behalf of IS for being an alleged opponent". See The Hague District Court 2019, paras 5.3.2 and 5.3.5.2. See also Lingsma 2019.

[47] See Mehra 2018.

[48] See McIntosh 2019.

and human rights law by the parties involved in the conflict. Pertinent examples are, as already mentioned in the previous subsection, the IIIM, whose information can also be used by national war crimes units,[49] and UNITAD, which noted in May 2021 that "a total of 14 States have requested the Team's assistance with respect to ongoing national proceedings."[50] Central to the success of UNITAD was "the ability of the Team to exploit internal ISIL documentation extracted from digital devices".[51] Moreover, information from UNITAD, such as case briefs, can contribute to efforts of national authorities adopting a structural approach, which will allow national authorities "to collect evidence across a broad crime base and establish the constituent elements of international crimes, in turn allowing prosecutors to act swiftly when individual suspects are identified."[52]

Although the International Centre for Counter-Terrorism—The Hague (ICCT) has published on this topic as early as 2015,[53] the subject of information collected from the conflict zone, sometimes also referred to as battlefield evidence (even though the point should be made it remains to be seen whether such information can actually be used as evidence in court), has recently received increased attention. And the reason for this is the law enforcement potential of such information in the counter-terrorism context. Indeed, it could be used as evidence in court against terrorism suspects, such as foreign fighters returning from Syria and Iraq. In Eurojust's memorandum on this matter from September 2020, one can, for instance, read that "[s]everal respondents confirmed that battlefield evidence had been successfully used in criminal proceedings and provided judgments or case examples."[54] The Eurojust memorandum is just one example illustrating the proliferation of (forthcoming) international, regional and national soft law instruments addressing this evidentiary form[55] engendered by the increased interest in the topic.

At the same time, the topic evokes a number of often very fundamental questions, such as whether the actors mentioned earlier should be involved in such potential evidence gathering in the first place; whether they—if the decision is made that they should indeed—are sufficiently equipped to fulfil such tasks; and what can be learned from earlier experiences where, for example, the military has been involved in law enforcement tasks, such as in the context of countering piracy. Moreover, there are various international law questions that need to be considered. For example, what are the legal frameworks in place for the gathering of possible evidence on the battlefield to begin with? How can human rights violations by, for example, the

---

[49] In the same way as information collected by national authorities could later end up before international bodies, information collected by international bodies can end up in proceedings before national courts. See e.g. UN General Assembly 2021, para 30: "By 31 January 2021, the Mechanism had received 93 requests for assistance from 11 competent jurisdictions".

[50] UN Security Council 2021, para 101.

[51] Ibid.

[52] Ibid., para 137. See also The Soufan Center 2021.

[53] Van Ginkel and Paulussen 2015.

[54] Eurojust 2020a, p. 13.

[55] See UN CTED 2019; GCTF 2018; Eurojust 2020a; NATO 2020; US Department of State et al. 2018; Council of Europe (Committee on Counter-Terrorism) 2020.

military be avoided? What are the implications of such evidence for a suspect's right to a fair trial? Can a suspect, for instance, sufficiently challenge the evidence secured by military personnel?

It goes beyond the scope of this chapter to discuss all these questions, which have been addressed elsewhere,[56] in detail, although a few relevant observations should be mentioned here as well. First of all, if prosecutors seek to link alleged terrorists to the crimes they have committed during a conflict, it is likely that some of the relevant information is located in the conflict zone. Secondly, investigators and prosecutors are often not able to travel to a conflict zone due to the unsafe conditions, nor may international cooperation be possible with the authorities of the countries where the evidence is located. Nonetheless, military personnel or other actors may be on-site and could have access to information that could be relevant as evidence in court. In that sense, 'battlefield evidence' is not a different type of evidence. It can constitute any type of evidence—documents, fingerprints or electronic evidence—but it is collected by actors that are not traditionally mandated to secure evidence for criminal purposes. This means that at the very least, these actors should know how to recognise and secure such information and objects so that these are not destroyed, lost forever, or dismissed later in court because the judge feels the evidence has been tampered with and is no longer reliable. Also, here, this obviously requires training and clear guidelines.[57] At the same time, giving the military additional tasks may backfire, especially in countries where they already have a questionable human rights record in the context of fighting terrorism.[58] And this is also why we feel the rule of thumb presented back in 2015 is still very much valid today: "as civilian as possible, and only as military as needed".[59] It is important to unpack the concept of 'battlefield evidence' and assess concretely how the different types of information can be obtained by the different actors that operate in the conflict zone in a human rights compliant manner as evidence in court. Simply dismissing the potential use of such evidence *tout court* in our view is not useful. Conversely, conducting evidence-based research on how 'battlefield evidence' is being used in bringing alleged terrorists to justice in court would be helpful.

[56] See Van Ginkel and Paulussen 2015 but also Van Ginkel 2016; Mehra 2018; Van Ginkel et al. forthcoming; as well as T.M.C. Asser Instituut and the United Nations Special Rapporteur on the Promotion and Protection of Human Rights and Fundamental Freedoms while Countering Terrorism (2021) Using battlefield evidence in the fight against terrorism: International law dimensions. Webinar. https://youtu.be/siINA1gBEOY. Accessed 21 September 2021.

[57] Cf. also Lubell et al. 2019, paras 78–81 (focusing on investigations into the lawfulness of states' *own actions* in armed conflict).

[58] See e.g. Fröhlich 2020; Amnesty International 2020. See also Van Ginkel et al. forthcoming.

[59] Van Ginkel and Paulussen 2015, p. 16.

7.2.3 *Information Collected from Open Sources and Social Media*

Whereas during the heydays of ISIS, their professional and powerful (social media) presence on the internet was used by the organisation for propaganda and recruitment purposes, that same digital context is now increasingly being used by investigators and prosecutors to make sure foreign fighters' prosecutions are completed successfully. Wil van Gemert, Europol Deputy Director, noted already in January 2017 that "[t]he biggest innovation I've seen in the last year at Europol was our emphasis on social media and open source monitoring."[60] A bit more than a year later, the importance of open source and social media evidence was echoed by Europol's neighbour in The Hague—Eurojust—where during the 24th meeting of the European Network of Contact Points for investigation and prosecution of genocide, crimes against humanity and war crimes in May 2018, "the large number of ongoing cases using open source information as evidence and the increase of judgements for which this type of evidence has been used"[61] was noted. Moreover, looking ahead, "the Network members considered open source information available on social media to be an indispensable and rich source of potential evidence for national authorities in the current and especially the future pursuit of accountability."[62] The same development can be identified before international courts.[63]

In light of this, on 1 December 2020, the *Berkeley Protocol on Digital Open Source Investigations* was launched, marking the further recognition, development and professionalisation in this field, which, due to its digital character, is especially interesting for investigators and prosecutors having no or limited access to the actual crime scene.[64] This Protocol "describes the professional standards that should be applied in the identification, collection, preservation, analysis and presentation of digital open source information and its use in international criminal and human rights investigations".[65]

Despite its high potential, digital open source evidence is not without problems: it is "notoriously susceptible to problems of verifiability, which naturally affects its reliability in any kind of criminal proceeding. It can be hard to concretely establish the time, date, and location of the evidence, and to prove that it hasn't been tampered with."[66] An extreme example of such tampering or manipulation is a deepfake video, but also smaller problems with the authenticity of the information may lead to judges rejecting the evidence in court. In addition, open source evidence is not only easily manipulated, but it can also be readily removed on the basis of algorithms and

60 Cruickshank 2017, p. 15.

61 Eurojust 2018, p. 1, para 4.

62 Ibid.

63 See e.g. Irving 2017.

64 Human Rights Center (UC Berkeley School of Law and Office of the United Nations High Commissioner for Human Rights) 2020, p. 5.

65 Ibid., p. 3.

66 Irving 2017.

machine learning technology from the servers of social media companies like Facebook, YouTube and Twitter, thus possibly removing evidence of war crimes as well.[67] Yet another challenge is that electronic evidence held by service providers is often stored in foreign or multiple locations. In two-thirds of the cases, law enforcement authorities need to obtain such evidence from service providers located abroad.[68] This process can be complicated and slow. That is why in the context of the European Union, the European Commission has drafted a proposal in 2018 for a regulation on so-called European Production and Preservation Orders for electronic evidence in criminal matters,[69] which "allow the judicial authority of a Member State, the issuing State, to directly order a provider offering the service in the EU to hand over or store the electronic evidence."[70] Irrespective of these challenges, digital evidence, which will lead to further cooperation with not only social media companies but also citizen journalists and organisations such as Bellingcat and Witness, will only become more relevant in our increasingly digital world.[71] This underlines the importance of clear guidelines and standards, including on preservation, verification and removal, such as those identified in the *Berkeley Protocol*.[72]

7.3 Residual Charges

The previous section has demonstrated a number of evidentiary and charging opportunities on and around the (digital) battlefield. However, there are also other charges out there which prosecutors—in theory—could use more like a residual charge. There are several examples, including membership and incitement, but two charges have received a lot of attention lately and will be critically examined in this section.

7.3.1 Prosecution for Travelling Abroad for the Purpose of Terrorism

In an effort to curb the flow of people leaving for Syria and Iraq, the UN Security Council adopted UN Security Council Resolution 2178 in September 2014, which obliges all UN Member States under Chapter VII of the UN Charter to criminalise

---

[67] Perrigo 2020. See also Human Rights Watch 2020.

[68] European Commission 2019.

[69] European Commission 2018.

[70] Tinoco-Pastrana 2020, p. 47.

[71] For example, "[m]ore than 500 hours of video are uploaded to YouTube every minute." (Perrigo 2020).

[72] See also GCTF 2018, pp. 9–14 for recommendations on the collection, use and sharing of electronic evidence.

several forms of conduct related to foreign terrorist fighters, including travel and attempted travel for the purpose of terrorism.

Although, as mentioned, such criminalisation may have been designed especially to prevent people from going to Syria and Iraq and be involved in terrorist activity in the first place, it could arguably also be applied to people who *have* successfully travelled.[73] It can be asserted that prosecution for travelling abroad for the purpose of terrorism is not without problems in the context of a case involving someone who *is travelling*, as the prosecutor has to prove that the person's intent of travelling is to be involved in terrorism later on.[74] However, it should be less difficult to prove in the case of someone who *has already travelled* to for example Syria with the aim to join for instance ISIS (even if it is not entirely clear what that person has done exactly in Syria). And indeed, in the earlier-mentioned recent study in which 20 judgements from the Netherlands were examined,[75] it was concluded that "the suspects were almost all convicted for preparatory acts. Travelling to Syria was mainly seen by the judge as a 'preliminary stage' of the commission of terrorist crimes. The judge qualifies the travelling predominantly as (an attempt to) participation in an organisation with terrorist intent."[76] In this context, reference should also be made to Article 9, paragraph 2 of the 2017 EU Directive on Combating Terrorism. In contrast to paragraph 6 of UN Security Council Resolution 2178 and Article 4 of the 2015 Additional Protocol to the Council of Europe Convention on the Prevention of Terrorism, this provision of the EU Directive explicitly criminalises travelling back to EU Member States for the purpose of terrorism.[77] Hence, even if prosecutors cannot prove that someone travelled to Syria, for instance, with the aim to join ISIS, they could rely on this provision for returnees they believe will be involved in terrorist activity in the future.

The problem with these 'travel charges' is that the link to actual criminal conduct and harm is far more removed than in cases where someone is being prosecuted for, for instance, a specific war crime involving an actual victim. This will lead to a greater focus on ('constructing')[78] the intent of suspects, which has its own risks. In the words of the Meijers Committee, a standing committee of experts on international immigration, refugee and criminal law (commenting on the (then) proposal for the new EU Directive on Combating Terrorism):

> Many of the offences in the proposed directive do [...] target acts that would otherwise be considered 'normal' innocent behaviour, such as taking a chemistry course or buying fertilizer [or travelling]. Thus, because the *actus reus* cannot make the difference, a person's alleged intention (*mens rea*) plays an even greater role, and in the field of terrorism there is a greater risk that the authorities may derive such an intention (in part) from ideologies and/or

[73] In Article 9 of the 2017 EU Directive on Combating, travelling (back) to EU Member States has been explicitly criminalised.

[74] For a critical analysis, see Gherbaoui 2020, pp. 241–268.

[75] See n 29.

[76] Van Gestel 2020.

[77] Ibid., p 252.

[78] Paulussen and Pitcher 2018, p. 31.

> religious beliefs. In the current societal context, that means that there is a genuine risk that Muslims will be disproportionately targeted in practice.[79]

Gherbaoui, building on this discussion, has warned that

> [t]his is a consequence of the preventive turn of counter-terrorism law and the "resurgence of dangerousness as a primary concept guiding developments in criminalisation, reflected in the framework of criminal responsibility by a predominance of character and risk responsibility". An approach that attributes criminal responsibility on the basis of character and risk fails to treat suspected foreign fighters as human beings who are ends in themselves. Instead, they are considered a risk to be contained, a danger to be averted. The incapacitation of suspected foreign fighters then becomes a means to achieve a higher end: the prevention of terrorist attacks. Treating suspected foreign fighters as mere means to a higher end, constitutes an assault on the human dignity of suspected foreign fighters qua human beings. They must be held accountable for their actions, not for their thoughts and ideas [original footnote omitted].[80]

Both quotations clearly show that there are serious and deeper societal risks connected to charges that have a stronger focus on a suspect's intent, which is prevalent in the context of the 'travel charges'.

7.3.2 Prosecution for Staying in an Area Controlled by a Terrorist Organisation

Another option is the criminalisation of staying in an area controlled by a terrorist organisation, which is now part of Australian, British and Danish law, and which is currently being discussed in the Netherlands.[81] This charge criminalises the mere presence of a person in an area controlled by a terrorist organisation, and is thus not dependent on any other criminal activity by that person. As such, it is an attractive tool for prosecutors struggling to find enough evidence of what that person was doing exactly in that area. Nonetheless, here also, the measure has received considerable criticism. As argued before, it constitutes "yet another example of the shift of counter-terrorism measures into the pre-crime space"[82] and undermines "other important objectives, including the provision of humanitarian assistance in accordance with humanitarian principles of impartiality, neutrality and independence, and the capacity of journalists and human rights groups to do their vital work independently and without any interference from politics".[83] On 9 March 2021, four UN Special Rapporteurs as well as the UN Working Group on discrimination against women and girls, commenting on the Dutch plans to enact similar legislation, noted that

[79] Meijers Committee 2016, para 8a.

[80] Gherbaoui 2020, p. 261.

[81] This also means, taking into account the legality principle, that the Dutch option is only relevant for future foreign fighters.

[82] Paulussen and Gillard 2021.

[83] Ibid.

> the Bill, as it stands, poses a number of concerns with regard to its potential infringement of international human rights, such as, the rights to freedom of expression, the right to a fair trial, including the principle of legality and the presumption of innocence, the right to freedom of movement, the right to family life, as well as the right to work and the right to enter one's own country.[84]

As a result of this criticism, the Dutch Minister of Justice and Security recently changed his mind,[85] and he will introduce a second bill which will contain a legal exemption for Dutch citizens and Dutch residents who stay in the area with the only purpose to perform activities as an aid worker working for an independent humanitarian organisation. This exemption will also be applicable to Dutch citizens who stay in the area with the only purpose to perform activities as a journalist or publicist in the framework of news gathering/freedom of information. Hence, also these persons can stay, without prior approval, in the designated areas and not be criminally liable. While this is certainly a step in the good direction, the criticism with respect to criminalising non-criminal behaviour remains.

7.4 Conclusion

Prosecutors should seek to prosecute returning foreign fighters for the actual crimes they have committed, utilising the full range of crimes available in domestic law. While it is certainly challenging to secure evidence in conflict zones, this chapter has shown that there are various (overlapping) evidentiary and charging opportunities that can assist in somewhat overcoming this challenge. Focusing more on international crimes (including by making better use of *existing* evidence), information collected from the conflict zone and information collected from open sources and social media are interesting examples in that respect.

Section 7.3 has demonstrated that even if prosecutors are not able to prove the full extent of criminal acts that someone may have committed, there are other charges out there that give prosecutors the theoretical option of making sure that foreign fighters are put behind bars upon return. In addition to, for example, the well-known charge of membership of a terrorist organisation, which was not further discussed in this chapter, one could think of charges related to travelling with a terrorist purpose or—for a smaller group of states—the rather new form of merely staying in an area controlled by a terrorist organisation.

Despite these possibilities, throughout this chapter, several cautious and critical comments were made. Hence, that certain options exist does not necessarily mean that one should also make use of those options. This will also very much depend on the question to what extent international (human rights) law is respected when using these forms and charges.

[84] See Mandates of the Special Rapporteurs and the Working Group on discrimination against women and girls 2021, for the full reference see Other Documents at the end of the chapter.

[85] Eerste Kamer der Staten-Generaal 2021.

This may mean that suspects can only be imprisoned for a few years. However, that should not be the end of the discussion—and in any case, it should never serve as an excuse to not take responsibility for one's own citizens and not to repatriate. This is because judges can still connect many special conditions to the probation, such as a reporting duty, a restraining order, obligatory participation in social and psychological assistance programmes etc., and in that way ensure that the authorities keep an eye on the released person.[86] To again mention the Dutch study earlier alluded to, here it was concluded that "the people who travelled to Syria, both those who were convicted to a relatively brief prison sentence and those who were convicted for a longer time stay under the control of the government for a prolonged time."[87] According to the courts, the reason for a long probation period with special conditions is not only to prevent new criminal facts but also to promote reintegration.[88] Moreover, even after probation is over, criminal as well as administrative law provides plenty of opportunities to ensure that authorities can step in when necessary, for instance, through area bans, measures prohibiting hate speech, and passport revocations, but also criminal charges linked to preparatory acts such as financing of terrorism, recruiting for terrorism, conspiracy to commit terrorist offences and incitement to terrorism.[89]

In our view, this shows that the often-heard complaint that prosecutors do not have enough tools at their disposal to ensure that returning foreign fighters can be prosecuted is incorrect. In fact, the contrary argument can be made, namely that prosecutors have various options at their disposal and that criminal law is even expanding in such a way that one can wonder whether we can still call it an *ultimum remedium*. This is similar to the argument we made a few years ago, in the context of people *leaving* for Syria and Iraq.[90]

It is true that repatriation and, where appropriate,[91] prosecution is in the short term a more costly and complicated option than simply leaving them in the camps in the hope that the Kurdish authorities will act. However, it is also the only correct option taking into account a moral, international legal and long-term security perspective. In the end, the decision to not repatriate, prosecute and take responsibility for one's own citizens can only be explained by a lack of political will and not because of a lack of technical legal possibilities.

---

86 Van Gestel 2020, p. 1009.

87 Ibid., p. 1012 [own translation].

88 Ibid., p. 1011. Cf. Chap. 9 by Mignot-Mahdavi in this volume.

89 See Chap. 12 by van Noorloos in this volume.

90 Paulussen and Pitcher 2018.

91 It should not be forgotten that many of the people we are alluding to in the context of repatriation are (very) young children that ought not to be seen as criminals in the first place but rather as victims.

References

Articles, Books and Other Documents

Ali J et al. (2019) Open Letter from National Security Professionals to Western Governments: Unless We Act Now, the Islamic State Will Rise Again. https://thesoufancenter.org/wp-content/uploads/2019/09/FTF-Open-Letter.pdf. Accessed 20 September 2021

Amnesty International (2020) "They executed some and brought the rest with them" - Human rights violations by security forces in the Sahel'. https://www.amnesty.org/en/documents/afr37/2318/2020/en/. Accessed 21 September 2021

Avdimetaj T, Coleman J (2020) What EU Member States can learn from Kosovo's experience in repatriating former foreign fighters and their families. Clingendael Policy Brief. https://www.clingendael.org/sites/default/files/2020-06/Policy_Brief_Kosovo_experience_repatriating_former_foreign_fighters_May_2020.pdf. Accessed 20 September 2021

BBC News (2019) Turkey-Syria offensive: 'Hundreds' of IS relatives escape camp. https://www.bbc.com/news/world-middle-east-50029540. Accessed 20 September 2021

Bolhuis MP, Van Wijk J (2020) Citizenship Deprivation as a Counterterrorism Measure in Europe; Possible Follow-Up Scenarios, Human Rights Infringements and the Effect on Counterterrorism. European Journal of Migration and Law 22(3):338–365

Cluskey P (2019) Turkey repatriates two women to Netherlands over Isis membership. https://www.irishtimes.com/news/world/europe/turkey-repatriates-two-women-to-netherlands-over-isis-membership-1.4090014. Accessed 20 September 2021

Coleman J, Cook J (2020) Shamima Begum, citizenship revocation and the question of due process. ICCT Perspective. https://icct.nl/publication/shamima-begum-citizenship-revocation-and-the-question-of-due-process/. Accessed 20 September 2021

College voor de Rechten van de Mens (2017) Minister trekt Nederlanderschap in van vier jihadisten. https://mensenrechten.nl/nl/nieuws/minister-trekt-nederlanderschap-van-vier-jihadisten. Accessed 20 September 2021

Council of Europe (Committee on Counter-Terrorism) (2020) Draft Recommendation CM/Rec (202XX)XX of the Committee of Ministers to Member States on the use of information collected in conflict zones as evidence in criminal proceedings related to terrorist offences. https://rm.coe.int/cdct-ge-2020-03-rev-draft-recommendation-on-the-gathering-of-evidence-/1680a032f0. Accessed 21 September 2021

Council of Europe (Parliamentary Assembly, Committee on Legal Affairs and Human Rights) (2020) Addressing the issue of Daesh foreign fighters and their families returning from Syria and other countries to the member States of the Council of Europe. EPP/CD. http://www.assembly.coe.int/LifeRay/JUR/Pdf/DocsAndDecs/2020/AS-JUR-2020-03-EN.pdf. Accessed 23 September 2021

Cruickshank P (2017) A View from the CT Foxhole: Peter Edge, ICE Acting Deputy Director, and Wil van Gemert, Europol Deputy Director. CTC Sentinel 10(1):11–16

Cuyckens H, Paulussen C (2019) The Prosecution of Foreign Fighters in Western Europe: The Difficult Relationship Between Counter-Terrorism and International Humanitarian Law. Journal of Conflict & Security Law 24(3):537–565

Doughty Street Chambers (2021) German court convicts a third ISIS member of crimes against humanity committed against Yazidis. https://www.doughtystreet.co.uk/news/german-court-convicts-third-isis-member-crimes-against-humanity-committed-against-yazidis. Accessed 21 September 2021

Dutch National Coordinator for Security and Counterterrorism (NCTV) (2019) Tweede Deelbesluit Wob verzoek. https://rijksoverheid.sitearchief.nl/#archive. Accessed 21 October 2021

Dutton P (Minister for Home Affairs, Australian Government) (2018) Neil Prakash stripped of Australian citizenship. https://minister.homeaffairs.gov.au/peterdutton/Pages/Neil-Prakash-stripped-of-Australian-citizenshp.aspx. Accessed 20 September 2021

Dworkin A (2019) Beyond Good and Evil: Why Europe Should Bring ISIS Foreign Fighters Home. European Council on Foreign Relations Policy Brief. https://ecfr.eu/archive/page/-/beyond_good_and_evil_why_europe_should_bring_isis_foreign_fighters_home.pdf. Accessed 21 September 2021

Eerste Kamer der Staten-Generaal (2021) Wijziging van het Wetboek van Strafrecht en het Wetboek van Strafvordering tot strafbaarstelling van verblijf in een door een terroristische organisatie gecontroleerd gebied (strafbaarstelling verblijf in een door een terroristische organisatie gecontroleerd gebied). https://www.eerstekamer.nl/behandeling/20210512/verslag_van_een_schriftelijk. Accessed 21 September 2021

Eurojust (2018) Conclusions of the 24th meeting of the European Network of Contact Points for investigation and prosecution of genocide, crimes against humanity and war crimes. https://www.eurojust.europa.eu/sites/default/files/Partners/Genocide/2018-05_Conclusions-24th-Genocide-Network-Meeting_EN.pdf. Accessed 21 September 2021

Eurojust (2020a) Eurojust Memorandum on Battlefield Evidence. https://www.eurojust.europa.eu/sites/default/files/2020-09/2020-09-14-Eurojust-Memorandum-on-Battlefield-Evidence.pdf. Accessed 21 September 2021

Eurojust (2020b) Increase in cumulative charges for terrorism and war crimes. Press Release. https://www.eurojust.europa.eu/increase-cumulative-charges-terrorism-and-war-crimes. Accessed 21 September 2021

Eurojust (2020c) Cumulative prosecution of foreign terrorist fighters for core international crimes and terrorism-related offences. https://www.eurojust.europa.eu/sites/default/files/2020-05/2020-05_Report-on-cumulative-prosecution-of-FTFs_EN.pdf. Accessed 21 September 2021

European Commission (2018) Proposal for a Regulation of the European Parliament and of the Council on European Production and Preservation Orders for electronic evidence in criminal matters. COM/2018/225 final - 2018/0108 (COD). https://eur-lex.europa.eu/legal-content/EN/TXT/?uri=COM%3A2018%3A225%3AFIN. Accessed 21 September 2021

European Commission (2019) Recommendation for a Council Decision authorising the opening of negotiations in view of an agreement between the European Union and the United States of America on cross-border access to electronic evidence for judicial cooperation in criminal matters. Explanatory memorandum. COM(2019) 70 final. https://eur-lex.europa.eu/legal-content/EN/TXT/HTML/?uri=CELEX:52019PC0070&rid=9. Accessed 21 September 2021

Flyger C I (2020) Returning Foreign Fighters to Denmark & Sweden: The Enemies of the State? Master's thesis, Lund University. http://lup.lub.lu.se/student-papers/record/9013797. Accessed 20 September 2021

Fröhlich S (2020) Niger: Fear of terror—and the military. https://www.dw.com/en/niger-fear-of-terror-and-the-military/a-54947989. Accessed 21 September 2021

GCTF (2018) Abuja Recommendations on the Collection, Use and Sharing of Evidence for Purposes of Criminal Prosecution of Terrorist Suspects. https://www.thegctf.org/Portals/1/Documents/Framework%20Documents/2018/GCTF-Abuja-Recommendations_ENG.pdf?ver=2018-09-21-122246-523&timestamp=1580219129062. Accessed 21 September 2021

Gherbaoui T (2020) Criminalising Foreign Fighter Travel in Order to Prevent Terrorism in Europe: An Illegitimate Assault on Human Dignity? In: Paulussen C, Scheinin M (eds) Human Dignity and Human Security in Times of Terrorism. T.M.C. Asser Press, The Hague, pp. 241–268

HRC (2016) "They came to destroy": ISIS Crimes Against the Yazidis. UN Doc. A/HRC/32/CRP.2

Human Rights Center (UC Berkeley School of Law and Office of the United Nations High Commissioner for Human Rights) (2020) Berkeley Protocol on Digital Open Source Investigations. https://humanrights.berkeley.edu/programs-projects/tech-human-rights-program/berkeley-protocol-digital-open-source-investigations. Accessed 21 September 2021

Human Rights Watch (2020) "Video Unavailable": Social Media Platforms Remove Evidence of War Crimes. https://www.hrw.org/sites/default/files/media_2020/09/crisis_conflict0920_web_0.pdf. Accessed 21 September 2021

Imamova N, Kashgarian A (2021) US, UN Officials Hail Uzbekistan's Repatriation of IS Families. https://www.voanews.com/south-central-asia/us-un-officials-hail-uzbekistans-repatriation-families. Accessed 20 September 2021
Impunity Watch, PAX and SCM (2019) ISIS-only tribunal: selective, politicised justice will do more harm than good. Policy Brief. https://www.paxforpeace.nl/media/files/policybrief-iraq-isis-tribunal-2019-eng.pdf. Accessed 20 September 2021
International Commission of Jurists (2020) Counter-Terrorism and Human Rights in the Courts. Guidance for Judges, Prosecutors and Lawyers on Application of EU Directive 2017/541 on Combatting Terrorism. https://www.icj.org/wp-content/uploads/2020/11/Guidance-counter-terrorism-ENG-2020-1.pdf. Accessed 21 September 2021
International Institute for Justice and the Rule of Law (2018) Non-Binding Guiding Principles on Use of Battlefield Evidence in Civilian Criminal Proceedings. https://theiij.org/wp-content/uploads/Non-Binding-Guiding-Principles-on-Use-of-Battlefield-Evidence-EN.pdf. Accessed 21 October 2021
Irving E (2017) And So It Begins... Social Media Evidence In An ICC Arrest Warrant. Opinio Juris. http://opiniojuris.org/2017/08/17/and-so-it-begins-social-media-evidence-in-an-icc-arrest-warrant/. Accessed 21 September 2021
Kouwenhoven A (2021) OM: Samir A. bevrijdde vrouwen namens IS. https://www.nrc.nl/nieuws/2021/07/15/justitie-samir-a-leidde-bevrijdingsoperaties-van-is-a4051109. Accessed 20 September 2021
Lingsma T (2019) First Dutch Islamic State Fighter Convicted for War Crimes. Justice Info. https://www.justiceinfo.net/en/42008-first-dutch-islamic-state-fighter-convicted-for-war-crimes.html. Accessed 21 September 2021
Lubell N, Pejic J, Simmons C (2019) Guidelines on investigating violations of international humanitarian law: law, policy, and good practice. Geneva Academy of International Humanitarian Law and Human Rights and ICRC. https://www.geneva-academy.ch/joomlatools-files/docman-files/Guidelines%20on%20Investigating%20Violations%20of%20IHL.pdf. Accessed 21 September 2021
Malet D (2019) ISIS Foreign Fighters: Keep Your Enemies Closer. Australian Outlook, Australian Institute of International Affairs. https://www.internationalaffairs.org.au/australianoutlook/isis-foreign-fighters-keep-enemies-closer/. Accessed 20 September 2021
Mai HJ (2019) Why European Countries Are Reluctant To Repatriate Citizens Who Are ISIS Fighters. https://www.npr.org/2019/12/10/783369673/europe-remains-reluctant-to-repatriate-its-isis-fighters-here-s-why?t=1628695208764. Accessed 20 September 2021
McIntosh N (2019) The Role of First Responders in Ending Impunity for International Crimes. GRC Blog Post. http://www.globalrightscompliance.com/en/news/the-role-of-first-responders-in-ending-impunity-for-international-crimes-blog-post. Accessed 21 September 2021
Mehra T (2017) Bringing (Foreign) Terrorist Fighters to Justice in a Post-ISIS Landscape Part I: Prosecution by Iraqi and Syrian Courts. ICCT Perspective. https://icct.nl/publication/bringing-foreign-terrorist-fighters-to-justice-in-a-post-isis-landscape-part-i-prosecution-by-iraqi-and-syrian-courts/. Accessed 20 September 2021
Mehra T (2018) Bringing (Foreign) Terrorist Fighters to Justice in a Post-ISIS Landscape Part III: Collecting Evidence from Conflict Situations. ICCT Perspective. https://icct.nl/publication/bringing-foreign-terrorist-fighters-to-justice-in-a-post-isis-landscape-part-iii-collecting-evidence-from-conflict-situations/. Accessed 21 September 2021
Mehra T (2020) The long and winding road to bringing the ISIS 'Beatles' to justice. ICCT Perspective. https://icct.nl/publication/the-long-and-winding-road-to-bringing-the-isis-beatles-to-justice/. Accessed 20 September 2021
Mehra T, Paulussen C (2019) The Repatriation of Foreign Fighters and Their Families: Options, Obligations, Morality and Long-Term Thinking. ICCT Perspective. https://icct.nl/publication/the-repatriation-of-foreign-fighters-and-their-families-options-obligations-morality-and-long-term-thinking/. Accessed 20 September 2021

Mehra T, Wentworth M (2021) New Kid on the Block: Prosecution of ISIS Fighters by the Autonomous Administration of North and East Syria. ICCT Perspective. https://icct.nl/publication/prosecution-of-isis-fighters-by-autonomous-administration-of-north-east-syria/. Accessed 20 September 2021

Meijers Committee (2016) Note on a Proposal for a Directive on combating terrorism. CM1603. https://www.commissie-meijers.nl/sites/all/files/cm1603_note_on_a_proposal_for_a_directive_on_combating_terrorism_.pdf. Accessed 21 September 2021

NATO (2020) NATO Allies agree Policy on Battlefield Evidence from operational theatres to boost efforts against terrorism. https://www.nato.int/cps/en/natohq/news_179194.htm?selectedLocale=en. Accessed 21 September 2021

NOS (2021) Syriëganger Fatima H. veroordeeld tot vier jaar cel. https://nos.nl/artikel/2376469-syrieganger-fatima-h-veroordeeld-tot-vier-jaar-cel. Accessed 20 September 2021

Paulussen C (2018) Countering Terrorism Through the Stripping of Citizenship: Ineffective and Counterproductive. ICCT Perspective. https://icct.nl/publication/countering-terrorism-through-the-stripping-of-citizenship-ineffective-and-counterproductive/. Accessed 20 September 2021

Paulussen C (2020) Towards a Right to Sustainable Security of Person in Times of Terrorism? Assessing Possibilities and Limitations Through a Critical Evaluation of Citizenship Stripping and Non-Repatriation Policies. Journal of Conflict & Security Law 26(1):219–249

Paulussen C, Gillard E-Ch (2021) Staying in an area controlled by a terrorist organisation: crime or operational necessity? ICCT Perspective. https://icct.nl/publication/staying-in-an-area-controlled-by-a-terrorist-organisation-crime-or-operational-necessity/. Accessed 21 September 2021

Paulussen C, Pitcher K (2018) Prosecuting (Potential) Foreign Fighters: Legislative and Practical Challenges. ICCT Research Paper. https://icct.nl/app/uploads/2018/01/ICCT-Paulussen-Pitcher-Prosecuting-Potential-Foreign-Fighters-Legislative-Practical-Challenges-Jan2018-1.pdf. Accessed 21 September 2021

Paulussen C, Cuyckens H, Fortin K (2019) The Prosecution of Foreign Fighters under International Humanitarian Law: Misconceptions and Opportunities. ICCT Perspective. https://icct.nl/publication/the-prosecution-of-foreign-fighters-under-international-humanitarian-law-misconceptions-and-opportunities/. Accessed 21 September 2021

Perrigo B (2020) These Tech Companies Managed to Eradicate ISIS Content. But They're Also Erasing Crucial Evidence of War Crimes. Time. https://time.com/5798001/facebook-youtube-algorithms-extremism/. Accessed 21 September 2021

Renard T, Coolsaet R (2018) From the Kingdom to the Caliphate and Back: Returnees in Belgium. In: Renard T, Coolsaet R (eds) Returnees: Who Are They, Why Are They (Not) Coming Back and How Should We Deal with Them? Assessing Policies on Returning Foreign Terrorist Fighters in Belgium, Germany and the Netherlands. Egmont Paper 101. https://www.egmontinstitute.be/returnees-assessing-policies-on-returning-foreign-terrorist-fighters-in-belgium-germany-and-the-netherlands/. Accessed 24 September 2021

Sabbagh D (2020) Syrian Kurds to put Isis fighters from dozens of countries on trial. https://www.theguardian.com/world/2020/feb/06/syrian-kurds-to-put-isis-fighters-from-dozens-of-countries-on-trial. Accessed 20 September 2021

Syrian Observatory for Human Rights (2020) Syrian Revolution NINE years on: 586,100 persons killed and millions of Syrians displaced and injured. https://www.syriahr.com/en/157193/. Accessed 20 September 2021

The Local (2019) Sweden calls for international tribunal to bring Isis fighters to justice. https://www.thelocal.se/20190307/sweden-calls-for-international-tribunal-to-investigate-returning-isis-fighters/. Accessed 20 September 2021

The Soufan Center (2021) Bringing Terrorists to Justice: Prosecuting ISIL War Crimes and Terrorism. Issue Brief. https://thesoufancenter.org/wp-content/uploads/2021/06/TSC-Issue-Brief_Bringing-Terrorists-to-Justice_June-2021.pdf. Accessed 21 September 2021

The United States Department of Justice (Office of Public Affairs) (2020) The United States Has Repatriated 27 Americans from Syria and Iraq Including Ten Charged with Terrorism-Related Offenses for Their Support to ISIS. The International Community Is Urged To Follow Suit and

Repatriate Its Citizens from Syria. https://www.justice.gov/opa/pr/united-states-has-repatriated-27-americans-syria-and-iraq-including-ten-charged-terrorism. Accessed 20 September 2021

Tinoco-Pastrana Á (2020) The Proposal on Electronic Evidence in the European Union. Eucrim 1/2020. https://eucrim.eu/articles/proposal-electronic-evidence-european-union-spain/. Accessed 21 September 2021

UN CTED (2019) Guidelines to facilitate the use and admissibility as evidence in national criminal courts of information collected, handled, preserved and shared by the military to prosecute terrorist offences. https://www.un.org/sc/ctc/wp-content/uploads/2020/01/Battlefield_Evidence_Final.pdf. Accessed 21 September 2021

UN General Assembly (2020) Report of the Special Rapporteur on the promotion and protection of human rights and fundamental freedoms while countering terrorism, Fionnuala Ní Aoláin, UN Doc. A/75/337

UN General Assembly (2021) Report of the International, Impartial and Independent Mechanism to Assist in the Investigation and Prosecution of Persons Responsible for the Most Serious Crimes under International Law Committed in the Syrian Arab Republic since March 2011, UN Doc. A/75/743

UN Security Council (2014) Resolution 2178 (2014), UN Doc. S/RES/2178

UN Security Council (2017) Resolution 2379 (2017), UN Doc. S/RES/2379

UN Security Council (2021) Letter dated 1 May 2021 from the Special Adviser and Head of the United Nations Investigative Team to Promote Accountability for Crimes Committed by Da'esh/Islamic State in Iraq and the Levant addressed to the President of the Security Council, UN Doc. S/2021/419

US Department of State et al. (2018) Non-Binding Guiding Principles on Use of Battlefield Evidence in Civilian Criminal Proceedings. https://theiij.org/wp-content/uploads/Non-Binding-Guiding-Principles-on-Use-of-Battlefield-Evidence-EN.pdf. Accessed 21 October 2021

Van Gestel B (2020) Bestraffing van Syriëgangers. Ars Aequi, 69:1005–1012

Van Ginkel B (2016) Prosecuting Foreign Terrorist Fighters: What Role for the Military? ICCT Policy Brief. http://icct.nl/app/uploads/2016/05/ICCT-VanGinkel-Prosecuting-Foreign-Terrorist-Fighters-May2016-2.pdf. Accessed 21 September 2021

Van Ginkel B, Paulussen C (2015) The Role of the Military in Securing Suspects and Evidence in the Prosecution of Terrorism Cases before Civilian Courts: Legal and Practical Challenges. ICCT Research Paper. https://www.icct.nl/app/uploads/download/file/ICCT-Van-Ginkel-Paulussen-The-Role-Of-The-Military-In-Securing-Suspects-And-Evidence-In-The-Prosecution-Of-Terrorism-Cases-Before-Civilian-Courts.pdf. Accessed 21 September 2021

Van Ginkel B, Paulussen C, Mehra T (forthcoming) Diversifying the sources of evidence in terrorism cases before criminal courts in (post-)conflict and high-risk situations: the role of the military. In: Finkelstein C, Fuller C (eds) Fighting War as Crime and Crime as War: Alternative Legal Frameworks for Asymmetric Conflict. Oxford University Press, Oxford

Wolfe S, Orozobekova C (2021) Lessons Learned from Kazakhstan's Repatriation and Rehabilitation of "Foreign Fighters". Bulan Institute for Peace Innovations. https://bulaninstitute.org/wp-content/uploads/2021/01/Lessons-Learned-from-Kazakhstans-Experience.pdf Accessed 21 October 2021

Other Documents

Mandates of the Special Rapporteur on the promotion and protection of human rights and fundamental freedoms while countering terrorism; the Special Rapporteur on the promotion and protection of the right to freedom of opinion and expression; the Special Rapporteur on the situation of human rights defenders; the Special Rapporteur on freedom of religion or belief and the Working Group on discrimination against women and girls, OL NLD 2/2021, 9 March 2021, available at: https://spcommreports.ohchr.org/TMResultsBase/DownLoadPublicCommunicationFile?gId=26107. Accessed 21 September 2021

Cases

District Court of The Hague (The Netherlands) *Prosecutor v. Imane B. et al.*. Judgement. 10 December 2015. Case No. 09/842489-14,09/767038-14,09/767313-14,09/767174-13,09/765004-15,09/767146-14, 09/767256-14, 09/767238-14 and 09/827053-15, 09/767237-14, 09/765002-15, 09/767077-14 (*Context* case)

District Court of The Hague (Criminal law section) Case No. 09/748003-18V, ECLI:NL:RBDHA:2019:10647, 23 July 2019, available at: http://deeplink.rechtspraak.nl/uitspraak?id=ECLI:NL:RBDHA:2019:10647

Chapter 8
The Qualification of the Activities of (Returned) Foreign Fighters Under National Criminal Law

Thomas Van Poecke and Hanne Cuyckens

Contents

Abstract National prosecutors and courts usually qualify the activities of foreign fighters (FFs) as terrorist offences. However, the groups FFs join tend to have a "dual nature": they usually qualify as both terrorist groups under counter-terrorism (CT) instruments and non-state armed groups (NSAGs) under international humanitarian law (IHL). Hence, the activities of (returned) FFs are situated at the confines of CT instruments and IHL, which complicates the qualification of their activities under national criminal law. These activities may qualify as serious violations of IHL, namely war crimes, but also as other international crimes, namely crimes against humanity or genocide. Furthermore, some of the activities committed by FFs can also be qualified as "common" offences under domestic criminal law. Ultimately, we conclude that national prosecutors and courts should consider all relevant legal

T. Van Poecke (✉)
Research Foundation Flanders (FWO), KU Leuven, Faculty of Law, Tiensestraat 41, 3000 Leuven, Belgium
e-mail: thomas.vanpoecke@kuleuven.be

H. Cuyckens
Leiden University College The Hague, Anna van Buerenplein 301, 2595 DG The Hague, The Netherlands
e-mail: h.cuyckens@luc.leidenuniv.nl

F. Capone et al. (eds.), *Returning Foreign Fighters: Responses, Legal Challenges and Ways Forward*, https://doi.org/10.1007/978-94-6265-571-3_8

frameworks when qualifying the activities of (returned) FFs. FFs should be prosecuted and punished for international crimes and common offences in addition to, or instead of, terrorist offences if necessary or appropriate.

Keywords (Returned) foreign fighters · Counter-terrorism · Terrorist offences · International humanitarian law · War crimes · Common offences · National criminal law · National courts · National prosecution

8.1 Introduction: Possibilities of Qualification

The foreign fighter (FF) phenomenon has become a prominent issue due to the number of FFs that have travelled to the Levant to participate in the armed conflicts in Syria and Iraq since 2011. It is estimated that as many as 40,000 foreign nationals travelled abroad to join these conflicts.[1] Soon, FFs started to return back home. For example, by 2020, roughly one-third of the about 5,000 European nationals who travelled to the region had returned home.[2] The FFs' home countries were faced with the challenge of managing the return of their nationals who had participated in armed conflict abroad, especially in light of the potential threat the returnees posed at home. An important aspect of the policy measures used by states to manage the return of FFs consists of the "criminal justice response" under a "law enforcement paradigm", including in particular the prosecution of the activities committed by FFs before national courts under domestic criminal law.[3]

This criminal justice response raises the question of how the activities of FFs should be qualified under domestic criminal law. As this qualification trickles down from relevant international legal frameworks, we must take these latter into account. First, a range of international counter-terrorism (CT) instruments require states to criminalise activities typically committed by FFs. Note that it is debated whether there is a proper "international legal regime" or "branch of international law" on terrorism, especially as there is no universally accepted definition of the notion. It is true that terrorism is a phenomenon to which a mixture of international rules applies, like rules of international human rights, humanitarian and refugee law.[4] At the same time, terrorism has led to the adoption of international instruments specifically designed to combat terrorism by requiring states to criminalise conduct associated with it. These CT instruments are the 12 international conventions and their seven protocols

[1] UN Security Council 2017.

[2] Renard and Coolsaet 2019.

[3] CTC/CTED 2015, pp. 2–3; European Commission 2015, p. 14; Paulussen and Entenmann 2016, p. 420; Paulussen and Pitcher 2018, p. 3; Ragazzi and Walmsley 2018, p. 40; cp. Krähenmann 2016, p. 19.

[4] Duffy 2015, p. 6; Krähenmann 2016, pp. 18–19; see e.g. the relevant chapters in Salinas de Frías et al. 2012.

or amendments dealing with terrorism[5] plus the relevant UN Security Council resolutions adopted after 9/11.[6] Notably, UN Security Council Resolution 1373 requires states to ensure that anyone "who participates in the financing, planning, preparation or perpetration of terrorist acts or in supporting terrorist acts is brought to justice" and that such acts "are established as serious criminal offences in domestic laws and regulations".[7] For FFs, the primary international CT instrument is UN Security Council Resolution 2178, which requires states to criminalise the activities of (assistance to) foreign terrorist fighters, like their travel with the purpose of terrorism.[8] The said international conventions and resolutions have been implemented into regional CT instruments[9] and states' national criminal law.[10] As we will show in Sect. 8.2, the result is that the activities of FFs are usually qualified at the domestic level as terrorist offences like participation in the activities of a terrorist group.

Second, FFs are individuals travelling abroad to join a party to an armed conflict, usually a non-state armed group (NSAG).[11] Hence, also the law of armed conflict or international humanitarian law (IHL) plays an important role in the qualification of their activities.[12] We will not assess the status of FFs under IHL in detail. This has been done elsewhere.[13] However, there is a "frequently held misperception that IHL does not apply or applies in a modified manner to groups or persons designated as terrorists".[14] Hence, it is apt to reiterate that even if the NSAG which FFs have joined is widely considered to be a terrorist group (e.g., Islamic State (IS)), this does not change the fact that this group and its members, including FFs, are subject to IHL.[15] This complicates the qualification of the activities of FFs under national criminal law. Should their activities be qualified as terrorist offences, serious violations of IHL—namely, war crimes—or both? Based on an analysis of how national courts have dealt with the relationship between CT instruments and IHL, we will answer this question in Sect. 8.3.

If the activities of FFs constitute serious violations of IHL, like attacking civilians who do not directly participate in hostilities, they constitute war crimes.[16] Numerous

---

[5] UN Office of Counter-Terrorism 2021.

[6] Krähenmann 2016, p. 19. See also Moeckli 2008, p. 157.

[7] UN Security Council (2001) Resolution 1373 (2001), UN Doc. S/RES/1373, para 2.

[8] UN Security Council (2014) Resolution 2178 (2014), UN Doc. S/RES/2178, para 6.

[9] E.g. Directive (EU) 2017/541 of the European Parliament and of the Council of 15 March 2017 on combating terrorism and replacing Council Framework Decision 2002/475/JHA and amending Council Decision 2005/671/JHA [2017] OJ L 88/6.

[10] See generally CTC/CTED 2019.

[11] ICRC 2019, p. 61; de Guttry et al. 2016, p. 1. While the definition of "foreign terrorist fighters" in UN Security Council (2014) Resolution 2178 (2014), UN Doc. S/RES/2178, preamble (para 8) and para 6, does not *require* participation in an armed conflict, it does define the notion "including in connection with armed conflict".

[12] Cuyckens and Paulussen 2019, p. 541.

[13] E.g. Krähenmann 2014; Sommario 2016, pp. 141–160.

[14] ICRC 2019, p. 58.

[15] Ibid., p. 62.

[16] Henckaerts and Doswald-Beck 2005, p. 568, Rule 156.

war crimes have been committed by armed groups commonly joined by FFs,[17] and FFs have been involved in the commission of these crimes.[18] States are obliged to investigate and prosecute war crimes over which they have jurisdiction.[19] In Sect. 8.4, we discuss how a limited number of European states have prosecuted FFs also for war crimes. Furthermore, if the relevant conditions are met, the activities of FFs can qualify as other core crimes of international law, namely crimes against humanity or genocide. These possible qualifications also raise important questions in terms of prosecution at the national level, which have been explored elsewhere.[20] We will not address them specifically in this chapter. Our focus on situations of armed conflict and IHL entails that we will primarily deal with the possible qualification of the activities of FFs as war crimes.[21]

So far, we have addressed the possible qualification of the activities of FFs under CT instruments as terrorist offences and the qualification of their activities as core crimes of international law, essentially delimiting the scope of our chapter to serious violations of IHL, namely war crimes. However, at least as a matter of law, it seems that international CT instruments and IHL do not require states to qualify the relevant conduct respectively *as* terrorist offences or *as* war crimes.[22] Moreover, FFs may engage in activities that qualify more readily as "common" offences rather than terrorist offences or international crimes. Thus, in Sect. 8.5, we discuss a third possibility for the qualification of the activities of FFs related to armed conflict under national criminal law, namely that of common offences like murder, assault or document fraud. In Sect. 8.6, we conclude with our overall view on the qualification of the activities of (returned) FFs, namely that national prosecutors and courts should consider all relevant legal frameworks when qualifying the activities of (returned) FFs.

[17] See e.g. Independent International Commission of Inquiry on the Syrian Arab Republic (2017) Human rights abuses and international humanitarian violations in the Syrian Arab Republic, 21 July 2016–28 February 2017, UN Doc. A/HRC/34/CRP.3.

[18] Eurojust/Genocide Network 2020, pp. 3–5.

[19] Henckaerts and Doswald-Beck 2005, p. 607, Rule 158.

[20] See e.g. Heinsch 2016, pp. 161–185.

[21] As noted in relation to the Syrian conflict by Ip 2019, p. 18, FFs' conduct may render them liable for international crimes, of which "war crimes are the most likely candidate".

[22] For CT instruments, see Husabø and Bruce 2009, p. 367, n 1972; McKeever 2020, pp. 51–52; CTC/CTED 2019. For the EU, Council Framework Decision of 13 June 2002 on combating terrorism (2002/475/JHA) OJ L 164/3 and Directive (EU) 2017/541, above n 9, that replaced it *do* require the qualification or label of "terrorist" offence; Husabø and Bruce 2009, pp. 99–100. For IHL, see ICRC 2015a, pp. 31–32; Gaeta 2015, pp. 621–622. However, see e.g. Dörmann and Geiß 2009, pp. 708–709, arguing that "the very object and purpose of the Geneva Conventions' grave breaches regime" requires specific legislation for its implementation.

8.2 Terrorist Offences

The main international CT instrument regarding FFs, UN Security Council Resolution 2178 (2014), refers to foreign *terrorist* fighters (FTFs) rather than foreign fighters (FFs). Other CT instruments, like the 2017 European Union (EU) Directive on combating terrorism, have copied this terminology. It does not come as a surprise, then, that the domestic criminal justice response to FFs has qualified their activities in the vast majority of cases as terrorist offences.[23] FFs are usually prosecuted for a broad range of "ancillary, preparatory, or inchoate" terrorist offences[24] like providing material support to terrorists or designated foreign terrorist organisations (e.g. United States (US));[25] preparation of terrorist acts [e.g. United Kingdom (UK);[26] training for terrorism (e.g. UK, Netherlands);[27] or membership of or participation in the activities of a terrorist group (e.g. Belgium, Germany, the Netherlands).[28] Relevant case law has been discussed elaborately elsewhere.[29] Hence, we can limit ourselves here to two illustrative cases that we will discuss further in Sect. 8.3, namely the *Context* case (2015)[30] from the Netherlands and the *Sharia4Belgium* case (2015–2016)[31] from Belgium.

The *Context* case was about a recruitment organisation based in The Hague that incited youngsters to join the armed jihad in Syria. There were nine accused, four of whom went to Syria, amongst whom three effectively participated in hostilities, first as members of Islamic State and then of Jabhat al Nusra. All nine accused were convicted. In particular, the three said FFs were convicted of (i) preparing or facilitating murder, manslaughter and causing explosions with terrorist intent;

[23] Eurojust/Genocide Network 2020, p. 5; Ip 2019, p. 119; Mehra 2018; Paulussen and Entenmann 2016, p. 419; Paulussen and Pitcher 2018, pp. 5–6.

[24] Saul 2012, p. 133 ff.

[25] 18 USC §2339A and §2339B; see CTC/CTED 2015, p. 6; Krähenmann 2016, pp. 245–247; Paulussen and Pitcher 2018, pp. 16–17.

[26] Section 5 Terrorism Act 2006 (UK); Ip 2019, pp. 115–117.

[27] Section 8 Terrorism Act 2006 (UK); Article 134a Dutch Criminal Code; Anderson 2013, pp. 237–238; Krähenmann 2016, pp. 242–245.

[28] Article 140 Belgian Criminal Code; Section 129 German Criminal Code; Article 140a Dutch Criminal Code; Paulussen and Entenmann 2016, pp. 393–399 and 405–419; Paulussen and Pitcher 2018, pp. 17–19; Europol 2021, p. 36 ff. Charges of membership in a terrorist group seem to be common also in e.g. Turkey and Tunisia; Hassan 2021.

[29] See e.g. Krähenmann 2016, pp. 242–247; Mehra 2018; Paulussen and Entenmann 2016; Paulussen and Pitcher 2018.

[30] District Court of The Hague (NL), *Context*, 10 December 2015, ECLI:NL:RBDHA:2015:14365 (District Court of The Hague (NL), *Context*).

[31] Court of First Instance of Antwerp (BE), *Sharia4Belgium*, 11 February 2015, File Nos. FD35.98.47-12 – AN35.F1.1809-12, etc. (Court of First Instance of Antwerp (BE), *Sharia4Belgium*); Court of Appeal of Antwerp (BE), *Sharia4Belgium*, 27 January 2016, Judgment No. C/101/2016 (Court of Appeal of Antwerp (BE), *Sharia4Belgium*); Court of Cassation (BE), *Sharia4Belgium*, 24 May 2016, P.16.0244.N. On these cases, see already Cuyckens and Paulussen 2019, pp. 549–559.

(ii) training for terrorist offences; and (iii) participating in a terrorist and (iv) criminal organisation. They received prison sentences of five-six years.[32] Similarly, the *Sharia4Belgium* case was about an organisation based in Antwerp that recruited youngsters to join the armed jihad in Syria. Forty-six individuals were charged with participating in the activities of or directing a terrorist group. Most of the accused were FFs who travelled to Syria and participated in hostilities as members of Jabhat al Nusra or Majlis Shura al Mujahidin. Nearly all accused convicted of participating in the activities of a terrorist group received a sentence of five years; the leaders received sentences of ten-15 years.[33] In a related case, *Hakim E.*, a member of *Sharia4Belgium* who had joined Majlis Shura al Mujahidin, was convicted of participating in the activities of a terrorist group and terrorist murder and received a sentence of 27 years.[34]

Of concern here is the qualification of the activities of FFs as terrorist offences. As noted by Paulussen and Pitcher, more often than not, charges of ancillary, preparatory or inchoate terrorist offences "are being used in the place of principal offences", like actual terrorist crimes (e.g. the terrorist murder in the case of *Hakim E.*) or war crimes (see Sect. 8.4).[35] There are several reasons for this. Of course, if FFs have not (yet) committed an actual, physical crime (e.g. because they are apprehended before being able to travel to a conflict zone), they can only be prosecuted for ancillary offences. Indeed, UN Security Council Resolution 2178 and the EU Directive on combating terrorism focus on such offences, especially in relation to FFs, and have generated "great pressure on the criminal justice sector" to intervene early on in the activities of FFs and prevent them from realizing their travels and further terrorist activities.[36] Even if FFs have committed actual, physical crimes, it is very difficult to prove such crimes if they are committed on a distant and inaccessible battlefield, while also witnesses may be unavailable.[37] Conversely, ancillary terrorist offences are usually broadly defined and much easier to prove.[38] In addition, the application of domestic

---

[32] District Court of The Hague (NL), *Context*, above n 30, paras 21.1–22.59.

[33] See Court of First Instance of Antwerp (BE), *Sharia4Belgium*, above n 31, pp. 87–96. Some accused were also convicted of other terrorist offences (inciting terrorist offences (in Syria), threatening to kill or harm with terrorist intent (in Syria), kidnapping with terrorist intent (in Syria)) and common offences (destruction of property (in Belgium), harassing police officers (in Belgium), forgery (in Belgium/Syria); see also Sect. 8.5).

[34] In this case, six individuals were prosecuted for terrorist hostage-taking and terrorist murder committed against unknown individuals in Syria. Only one of them was convicted. See Court of First Instance of Antwerp (BE), *Hakim E.*, 13 February 2017, Judgment No. 783, File Nos. AN35.F1.1809-12 (FD35.98.47-12) – FD30.97.28-14.

[35] Paulussen and Pitcher 2018, p. 16. See also Mehra 2018.

[36] Paulussen and Pitcher 2018, p. 16. See also Anderson 2013, pp. 237–239; Eurojust/Genocide Network 2020, p. 7; Krähenmann 2016, p. 241.

[37] Eurojust/Genocide Network 2020, pp. 24–25; Paulussen and Pitcher 2018, p. 16; Ruys and Van Severen 2018, pp. 532–533; The Soufan Center 2021, pp. 3–4; Van Steenberghe 2018, pp. 283–284 and 293. On the topic of the securing of evidence, see Chap. 7 by Paulussen and Mehra in this volume.

[38] Cuyckens and Paulussen 2019, p. 538; Paulussen and Entenmann 2016, pp. 419–420. Although the opposite argument has been made, since terrorist offences require proof "of an underlying ideological or political motivation"; see The Soufan Center 2021, p. 7.

criminal law provisions on terrorism usually entails a range of broader investigatory powers for law enforcement authorities.[39]

These reasons are understandable and, in many cases, warrant the qualification of the activities of FFs as terrorist offences. Nevertheless, the (near) exclusive or automatic reliance on CT legislation to prosecute FFs is problematic, especially in light of IHL.

8.3 Relationship Between CT Instruments and IHL

8.3.1 Why the Relationship Is Problematic

IHL and CT instruments are designed to deal with the regulation of violent conduct in different contexts. CT instruments focus on violent conduct in times of peace. However, increasingly, CT instruments are entering the realm of armed conflict, notably as regards FFs.[40] IHL, in turn, applies exclusively to armed conflicts, in which certain acts of violence are permitted. Hence, the essential difference between CT instruments and IHL lies in the fact that "while any act of violence designated as terrorist is always unlawful", "armed conflict is a situation in which certain acts of violence are allowed (lawful) and others prohibited (unlawful)".[41]

The main issue then is that CT instruments may prohibit conduct that is lawful under IHL, like an attack by an FF who is a member of an NSAG against members of the armed forces of the state with which the NSAG is involved in an armed conflict. This is problematic because it undermines the dichotomous rationale of IHL, which is based on the distinction between lawful acts (e.g. attacking military objectives) and unlawful acts (e.g. attacking civilian objects). Criminalising acts that are lawful under IHL undermines the legal incentive to respect IHL on the part of those, like FFs, who are criminalised irrespective of whether or not they comply with IHL.[42] However, this "tension" between CT instruments and IHL does not usually constitute a hard, legal conflict. The NSAGs commonly joined by FFs are parties to *non-international* armed conflicts (NIACs). In such conflicts, there is no combatant privilege or immunity like in international armed conflicts (IACs). This means that IHL does not prohibit states to criminalise activities committed by members of NSAGs that are lawful under IHL, be it as terrorist offences or common crimes under domestic criminal law. Nevertheless, "at the end of hostilities, the authorities in power must endeavour to grant the broadest possible amnesty" to persons who have participated in a NIAC,

[39] Anderson 2013, pp. 237–239; Coco 2013, pp. 427–428; Greene 2014, p. 786; Husabø and Bruce 2009, pp. 75–95; Ruys and Van Severen 2018, pp. 532–533; Saul 2012, p. 163; Shany 2011, pp. 18–19.

[40] On this point, see e.g. Cuyckens and Paulussen 2019.

[41] ICRC 2011, p. 48; ICRC 2015b, p. 17.

[42] ICRC 2011, pp. 48–50 and ICRC 2015b, pp. 17–18; see also ICRC 2019, p. 58.

except for international crimes.[43] However, the implementation of this rule becomes difficult if acts that are lawful under IHL are labelled "terrorist",[44] especially in light of states' obligation to suppress acts of terrorism.

Furthermore, IHL is based on the principle of equality of rights and obligations of the parties to an armed conflict and hence does not take a position on the legitimacy of the cause they pursue.[45] The criminalisation of terrorism, on the other hand, "symbolically expresses community condemnation, and stigmatizes" and delegitimizes offenders.[46] In doing so, it undermines the equality of belligerents, at least in the typical scenario in which a state "outlaws" the NSAG with which it is involved in an armed conflict as a "terrorist" group. Such rhetoric challenges the legitimacy of IHL and may reduce compliance with it on both sides of the conflict.[47] Moreover, "disqualifying non-state adversaries by branding them 'terrorists' [...] may prove to be an obstacle" to peace negotiations and reconciliation efforts that are necessary "to end an armed conflict and ensure peace".[48]

IHL, for its part, does not leave acts of terrorism committed in situations of armed conflict unpunished. First, IHL "prohibits the great majority of acts that would be designated as 'terrorist' if they were committed in peacetime"[49] through its arsenal of "regular" war crimes, like attacking civilians who do not directly participate in hostilities. Moreover, IHL explicitly prohibits terrorism. War crimes include "acts or threats of violence the primary purpose of which is to spread terror among the civilian population".[50] If serious violations of IHL are not criminalised as war crimes in states' domestic law, they should at least be covered by common criminal law provisions

[43] See Article 6(5) of Protocol Additional to the Geneva Conventions of 12 August 1949, and relating to the Protection of Victims of Non-International Armed Conflicts (Additional Protocol II), opened for signature 8 June 1977, 1125 UNTS 609, (entered into force 7 December 1978); Henckaerts and Doswald-Beck 2005, p. 611, Rule 159.

[44] ICRC 2015a, b, p. 18. See also generally Coco 2013.

[45] ICRC 2015a, b, pp. 17–18. Even if for NIACs, one may argue that while perhaps sound in theory, this principle is a fiction (e.g. Sassòli and Shany 2011, p. 431), the principle of equality of rights and obligations of the parties to an armed conflict is a fundamental IHL principle also in NIACs: Sivakumaran 2012, pp. 242–243.

[46] Saul 2006, p. 7; see also pp. 3 and 11 and Anderson 2013, pp. 234–235.

[47] Sassòli and Shany 2011, pp. 434–436.

[48] ICRC 2011, p. 51; ICRC 2015a, b, p. 18.

[49] ICRC 2011, p. 49.

[50] See Article 51(2) of the Protocol Additional to the Geneva Conventions of 12 August 1949, and relating to the Protection of Victims of International Armed Conflicts (Additional Protocol I), opened for signature 8 June 1977, 1125 UNTS 3 (entered into force 7 December 1978) (for IACs) and Article 13(2) of Additional Protocol II, above n 43 (for NIACs). A violation of this IHL prohibition concerning the "conduct of hostilities" constitutes a war crime under customary international law: ICTY, *Galić*, Appeals Chamber Judgment, 30 November 2006, IT-98-29-A, para 98. IHL also prohibits acts of terrorism against civilians "in the power of a party to the conflict" (see Article 33 of the Geneva Convention relative to the protection of civilian persons in time of war (Geneva Convention IV), opened for signature 12 August 1949, 75 UNTS 287 (entered into force 21 October 1950) (for IACs) and Article 4(2)(d) Additional Protocol II, above n 43 (for NIACs)). This IHL prohibition has not (yet) been recognized as a war crime under customary law.

(e.g., murder). Hence, violations of IHL are better prosecuted as war crimes or, if this option is not available, common offences (see respectively Sects. 8.4 and 8.5).

FFs present a particular illustration of the problematic relationship between CT instruments and IHL. The groups FFs are involved with tend to qualify as terrorist groups under the former as well as NSAGs under the latter and thus have a "dual nature". This begs the question of how to go about the relationship between CT instruments and IHL in the qualification of the conduct of FFs under domestic criminal law.

8.3.2 How National Courts Have Dealt with the Relationship

8.3.2.1 The "Exclusion Clause"

States have mainly regulated the relationship between CT instruments and IHL by inserting "armed conflict exclusion clauses" in the former.[51] In varying ways, such clauses exclude activities committed in the context of armed conflicts from the scope of the relevant CT instruments. The most often used exclusion clause first featured in the 1997 Terrorist Bombing Convention.[52] Article 19(2) of that Convention provides that "the activities of armed forces during an armed conflict, as those terms are understood under international humanitarian law, which are governed by that law, are not governed by this Convention".[53] At the regional level, this exclusion clause is included in the CT instruments of the Council of Europe[54] and the EU.[55]

The clause excludes the activities of armed forces during an armed conflict from the scope of the said CT instruments. Although some argue that the clause prohibits states from including these activities within the scope of their domestic criminal law provisions on terrorism,[56] most courts and commentators consider it does not.[57] Nevertheless, some states have implemented the exclusion clause into national law.

[51] For an in-depth assessment of this issue, see Van Poecke et al. 2021.

[52] International Convention for the Suppression of Terrorist Bombings, opened for signature 15 December 1997, 2149 UNTS 256 (entered into force 23 May 2001).

[53] In total, this clause features in six of the twelve international conventions on terrorism, while the International Convention against the Taking of Hostages, opened for signature 17 December 1979, 1316 UNTS 205 (entered into force 3 June 1983) and International Convention for the Suppression of the Financing of Terrorism, opened for signature 9 December 1999, 2178 UNTS 197 (entered into force 10 April 2002) include a particular provision governing their relationship with IHL; on the latter, see below n 66; see in more detail Van Poecke et al. 2021, pp. 301–306.

[54] Article 26(5) of the Council of Europe Convention on the Prevention of Terrorism, opened for signature 16 May 2005, CETS No. 196 (entered into force 1 June 2007).

[55] Recital 11 EU Framework Decision (2002/475/JHA), above n 22, as replaced by Recital 37 Directive (EU) 2017/541, above n 9.

[56] See e.g. Coco 2013, pp. 431–435 and 439–440; Trapp 2014, pp. 179–181.

[57] See e.g. Supreme Court (UK), *R v Gul*, 23 October 2013, [2013] UKSC 64 (Supreme Court (UK), *R v Gul*) para 53; Court of Appeal of The Hague (NL), *LTTE*, 30 April 2015, ECLI:NL:GHDHA:2015:1082 (Court of Appeal of The Hague (NL), *LTTE*) para 10.5, discussed

Different versions of the clause can be found in the national criminal legislation of Belgium, Canada, Ireland, New Zealand, South Africa, Switzerland and the US.[58] Even if the clause is not mandatory, our discussion of case law on the clause will inform the answer to the question of how states (should) qualify the activities of FFs under domestic criminal law. We will focus on three issues surrounding the exclusion clause: (i) whether the clause covers NSAGs; (ii) the aim of the NSAG; and (iii) the application of the clause to activities that extend beyond armed conflict.

8.3.2.2 Whether the Clause Covers NSAGs

A first issue is whether the notion of "armed forces" in the exclusion clause covers NSAGs that are party to a NIAC, which are typically joined by FFs. One view is that the notion of armed forces is reserved for state armed forces and hence does not extend to NSAGs. This view was followed by the Dutch District Court of The Hague, which had to interpret the clause as included in the EU Framework Decision on combating terrorism in the abovementioned *Context* case. The Court held that "the concept of 'armed forces' usually refers to the armed forces of a state", whereas NSAGs are usually referred to as "organized armed groups".[59] Furthermore, the Court stressed that in NIACs, there is no combatant privilege, following which there was no conflict between CT instruments and IHL.[60] Finally, according to the Court, "an interpretation of the exclusion clause on the basis of which terrorism suspects could not be prosecuted under domestic terrorism legislation for their punishable terrorist acts because they were committed in wartime cannot reasonably be reconciled" with the "instruments adopted by the international community" in response to terrorism, notably UN Security Council Resolution 1373.[61] The Court concluded that "members of organized armed groups cannot invoke the exclusion clause, and that the terrorism provisions in the Framework Decision and the Dutch legislation implementing that Decision are applicable to them in their entirety".[62]

---

below. For commentators, see notably Husabø and Bruce 2009, p. 395; Ruys and Van Severen 2018, p. 531.

[58] For references and a more thorough discussion of these domestic exclusion clauses, see Van Poecke et al. 2021, pp. 306–309.

[59] District Court of The Hague (NL), *Context*, above n 30, paras 7.38–7.40. The Court based itself on Article 1(1) of Additional Protocol II, above n 43, which delimits the Protocol's scope of application to NIACs taking place "in the territory of a High Contracting Party between its armed forces and dissident armed forces or *other organized armed groups*" (emphasis added).

[60] Ibid., para 7.41. This argument was used in a similar vein by the Court of Appeal of The Hague (NL), *LTTE*, above n 57, paras 10.4.3.3.1–10.4.3.3.2 and 11.3.1.2. See also Higher Regional Court of Munich (GE), *Sibel H.*, 29 April 2020, 7 St 9/19 (4) (Higher Regional Court of Munich (GE), *Sibel H.*) para 102.

[61] District Court of The Hague (NL), *Context*, above n 30, para 7.42.

[62] Ibid., para 7.44.

The argument that there is no combatant privilege in NIACs was also relied on by the UK Supreme Court in *R v Gul* (2013).[63] In this case, the accused was prosecuted for the dissemination of terrorist publications because he had posted videos online of attacks by members of al-Qaeda and the Taliban against "coalition forces" in Afghanistan and Iraq as well as of attacks against civilians, including 9/11. The defence argued that "whereas there is no international agreement as to the meaning of terrorism, there is a general understanding that it does not extend to the acts of insurgents or 'freedom fighters' in non-international armed conflicts".[64] The Court rejected this argument, among others because "insurgents in non-international armed conflicts do not enjoy combatant immunity".[65] As opposed to the District Court of The Hague, the UK Supreme Court admitted that the 1997 Terrorist Bombing Convention (see above) as well as the 1999 Terrorist Financing Convention[66] "appear to have been drafted so as to exclude insurgent attacks on military forces in non-international armed conflicts from their respective ambits".[67] Nevertheless, the Court held that as the exclusion clause is not mandatory (see above), it does not inhibit the UK from criminalising acts covered by the conventions as terrorist offences.[68]

In Belgium and Canada, which have implemented an exclusion clause into their domestic law,[69] courts have accepted that the clause also covers NSAGs. Two other issues have emerged: (i) the relationship between the aim of the relevant NSAG and the application of the exclusion clause (in Belgium); and (ii) the extent to which the clause applies to activities allegedly constituting terrorist offences that *relate* to a situation of armed conflict, but that have not been committed *in* a situation of armed conflict (in Belgium and Canada).[70]

---

[63] Supreme Court (UK), *R v Gul*, above n 57; on appeal from England and Wales Court of Appeal (UK), *R v Gul*, 22 February 2012, [2012] EWCA Crim 280.

[64] Supreme Court (UK), *R v Gul*, above n 57, para 45.

[65] Ibid., para 50.

[66] Article 2(b) of the 1999 Terrorist Financing Convention, above n 53, defines offences within the scope of the Convention as acts "intended to cause death or serious bodily injury *to a civilian, or to any other person not taking an active part in the hostilities in a situation of armed conflict*, when the purpose of such act, by its nature or context, is to intimidate a population, or to compel a government or an international organization to do or to abstain from doing any act" (emphasis added).

[67] Supreme Court (UK), *R v Gul*, above n 57, para 52.

[68] Ibid., para 53. On *R v Gul*, see also Coco 2013; Greene 2014; Trapp 2014, pp. 175–180. The argument on the non-mandatory nature of the exclusion clause, this time as included in EU law, was also relied upon by the Court of Appeal of The Hague (NL), *LTTE*, above n 57, para 10.5.

[69] In Belgium, Article 141bis of the Criminal Code (Law of 8 June 1867, as amended) provides that Title Iter of the Code on "terrorist offences" *«ne s'applique pas aux activités des forces armées en période de conflit armé, tels que définis et régis par le droit international humanitaire»*. In Canada, Section 83.01(1) of the Criminal Code (RSC 1985, c C-46) provides that "terrorist activity" "does not include an act or omission that is committed during an armed conflict and that, at the time and in the place of its commission, is in accordance with customary international law or conventional international law applicable to the conflict".

[70] The ensuing discussion of this case law is drawn from Cuyckens and Paulussen 2019, pp. 553–559 and Van Poecke et al. 2021, pp. 309–315.

8.3.2.3 The Aim of the NSAG

In Belgium, the exclusion clause has mostly been invoked by individuals who joined jihadist groups like Islamic State or Jabhat al Nusra. The courts have consistently rejected that these groups qualify as "armed forces" under IHL. Therefore, the exclusion clause did not apply to them. This jurisprudence did not always correctly interpret and apply IHL. We use the abovementioned *Sharia4Belgium* case as an illustration.

First, we must recall that under IHL, the existence of a NIAC "is based solely on two criteria: the intensity of the conflict and organisation of the parties".[71] Hence, "the purpose of the armed forces to engage in acts of violence or also achieve some further objective" is irrelevant.[72] In *Sharia4Belgium*, the courts recognized the existence of a NIAC in Syria, but found that Jabhat al Nusra and Majlis Shura al-Mujahideen did not constitute "armed forces" in the sense of IHL.[73] The courts applied a restrictive definition of armed forces. In brief, they set the organisation threshold too high and relied on elements that are irrelevant under IHL to dismiss that the groups constitute armed forces. They stressed the groups' unwillingness rather than their capacity to implement IHL and erroneously took into account their ideology to determine whether they constitute armed forces. The courts emphasised that both groups are engaged in "a violent armed struggle against all infidels, democracy, human rights and humanitarian law".[74] As a consequence, the decisions in the *Sharia4Belgium* case conflicted with the widely held view that at least Jabhat al-Nusra was sufficiently organised to be a party to an armed conflict in Syria.[75]

In the first phase of the *PKK* case (2016–2017),[76] the Belgian courts committed a similar error. Forty individuals and two media companies were charged with participating in the activities of or directing a terrorist group; notably, they were alleged to have helped finance the organisation or spread its propaganda in Belgium. The courts determined the existence of a NIAC between Turkey and the PKK and found that the PKK constituted an armed force. However, once more, they took into account the group's ideology for its qualification as an armed force. They stressed "the place the Kurdish separatist movement takes today in the Syria conflict and the fight against

---

[71] ICTY, *Limaj et al.*, Trial Chamber Judgment, 30 November 2005, IT-03-66-T, para 170.

[72] Ibid.

[73] Court of First Instance of Antwerp (BE), *Sharia4Belgium*, above n 31, pp. 31–36; Court of Appeal of Antwerp (BE), *Sharia4Belgium*, above n 31, pp. 51–54.

[74] Court of First Instance of Antwerp (BE), *Sharia4Belgium*, above n 31, p. 36; Court of Appeal of Antwerp (BE), *Sharia4Belgium*, above n 31, p. 54.

[75] See e.g. Gill 2016, p. 374. Similar criticisms have been voiced elsewhere; see notably: Koutroulis 2015, p. 87; Bartels 2016, p. 65; Wouters and Van Poecke 2018, pp. 1617–1618; Ruys and Van Severen 2018, pp. 533–536; Van Steenberghe 2018, pp. 273–287; Wéry 2019, pp. 108–137; Tropini 2019, pp. 169–179.

[76] Court of First Instance of Brussels, Dutch-speaking (BE), Correctional Pre-Trial Chamber, *PKK*, 3 November 2016, File Nos. FD.35.98.54/09 – FD.35.98.634/06 – FD.35.98.502/07 (Court of First Instance of Brussels, *PKK*); Court of Appeal of Brussels (BE), Chamber of Indictment, *PKK*, 14 September 2017, Judgment No. 2017/2911 – KI 1658/17 (Court of Appeal of Brussels (BE), *PKK* (2017)).

IS"[77] and the fact that the aim of the PKK is "the establishment of an independent state, but not the terrorizing of civilians".[78] However, as mentioned, the aim of a group is irrelevant for its status under IHL and must not affect its qualification as an armed force under the exclusion clause.

As the Court of Appeal's decision in the PKK case was essentially annulled by the Court of Cassation (2018) for lack of motivation in respect of a different matter,[79] the Court of Appeal had to revisit the case. In the second phase of the *PKK* case (2019–2020),[80] the Court of Appeal did not commit the error of taking into account the PKK's aim for its qualification under IHL. The case now revolved around a different issue: the extent to which the exclusion clause may apply to activities allegedly constituting terrorist activities that may *relate* to an armed conflict but have not been committed *in* a situation of armed conflict themselves. This issue was also central to the earlier Canadian *Khawaja* case (2008–2012),[81] which we will briefly discuss first.

8.3.2.4 The Scope of the Activities Affected by IHL

Khawaja is a Canadian national who was prosecuted for a range of terrorist offences that he committed as a member of a small terrorist group (the "Khyam group") based in the UK that was loosely affiliated with al-Qaeda. Notably, he created a device for the remote detonation of explosives. While Khawaja travelled to Pakistan to receive training to fight in Afghanistan, he never participated in the hostilities.[82] In his defence, Khawaja invoked the exclusion clause included in the Canadian Criminal Code.[83] He argued that as his activities related to a situation of armed conflict, he could not be prosecuted for terrorist offences.[84] His argument was dismissed by the Canadian courts.

First, the courts held that Khawaja supported the indiscriminate killing of civilians and did not act "in accordance with" IHL,[85] as required by the Canadian exclusion

---

[77] Court of First Instance of Brussels (BE), *PKK*, above n 76, p 11.

[78] Court of Appeal of Brussels (BE), *PKK* (2017), above n 76, p 17.

[79] Court of Cassation (BE), *PKK*, 13 February 2018, P.17.1023.N.8.

[80] Court of Appeal of Brussels (BE), Chamber of Indictment, *PKK*, 8 March 2019, Judgment No. 2019/939 – KI 555 (Court of Appeal of Brussels (BE), *PKK* (2019)); appeal against which was rejected by Court of Cassation (BE), *PKK*, 28 January 2020, P.19.0310.N/1 (Court of Cassation (BE), *PKK* (2020)).

[81] Ontario Superior Court of Justice (CA), *Khawaja*, 29 October 2008, [2008] OJ No 4244 (QL) (Ontario Superior Court of Justice (CA), *Khawaja*); Court of Appeal for Ontario (CA), *Khawaja*, 17 December 2010, 2010 ONCA 862 (Court of Appeal for Ontario (CA), *Khawaja*); Supreme Court (CA), *Khawaja*, 14 December 2012, 2012 SCC 69 (Supreme Court (CA), *Khawaja*).

[82] Ontario Superior Court of Justice (CA), above n 81, *Khawaja*, paras 1–72.

[83] See above n 69.

[84] Ontario Superior Court of Justice (CA), above n 81, *Khawaja*, para 109.

[85] Ibid., para 130; Court of Appeal for Ontario (CA), *Khawaja*, above n 81, paras 167–168; Supreme Court (CA), *Khawaja*, above n 81, paras 100–102.

clause.[86] Second, they held that the Khyam group and Khawaja's activities extended beyond a situation of armed conflict. Notably, Khawaja "knew of and supported the Khyam group's terrorist objectives, which extended beyond Jihad-related activities in Afghanistan" and included "a broad vision of economic terror throughout the western world" and "an appetite for suicide bombing in countries including Israel".[87] Thus, even if Khawaja's activities with respect to Afghanistan were part of an armed conflict, not all his activities were.[88]

Similarly, in the *PKK* case, the prosecution argued that the accused's activities were not committed in the context of an armed conflict, and hence, the exclusion clause did not apply.[89] However, the Court of Appeal and Cassation held that it is not required that the actual activities for which the accused are prosecuted are governed by IHL. Rather, as the PKK was an armed force, the acts it commits with a terrorist aim in the context of the armed conflict with Turkey benefit from the application of the exclusion clause. The Criminal Code's definition of a terrorist group, in turn, depends on the (intended) commission of such acts. If there are no such acts (or, at least, if such acts benefit from the application of the exclusion clause), the PKK is not a terrorist group in the sense of the Criminal Code. And if the PKK is no such terrorist group, participation in its activities is not a terrorist offence.[90] The Court of Appeal agreed that if the PKK had also committed terrorist acts *outside* the area of the armed conflict (e.g. in Europe), such acts would not be governed by IHL, and the exclusion clause would not apply to them.[91] However, it was not established that any such acts presented by the prosecution (e.g. kidnappings) were attributable to the PKK.[92] Hence, the case against the alleged members of the PKK was dismissed.[93]

With its reasoning, the Court of Appeal has apparently attempted to shape an objective difference between jihadist groups and the PKK. Much like the Canadian courts in *Khawaja*, the Court did recognize that if an NSAG commits terrorist acts also outside the context of armed conflict, these acts do not benefit from the application of the exclusion clause. Thus, the Court left the door open for the qualification of

[86] See above n 69.

[87] Court of Appeal for Ontario (CA), *Khawaja*, above n 81, para 168.

[88] Supreme Court (CA), *Khawaja*, above n 81, para 101.

[89] Court of Appeal of Brussels (BE), *PKK* (2019), above n 80, p. 33.

[90] Ibid., pp. 33–34; Court of Cassation (BE), *PKK* (2020), above n 80, pp. 9–12.

[91] Court of Appeal of Brussels (BE), *PKK* (2019), above n 80, pp. 34–36.

[92] Ibid., pp. 36–44.

[93] In a similar vein, the District Court of The Hague (NL), *LTTE*, 21 October 2011, ECLI:NL:RBSGR:2011:BT8829, acquitted members of the LTTE who had helped financing the organisation from the Netherlands for terrorist offences. However, this decision was overturned on appeal by the Court of Appeal of the Hague (NL), *LTTE*, above n 57, whose judgment was in turn confirmed by the Supreme Court (NL), *LTTE*, 4 April 2017, ECLI:NL:HR:2017:574. The latter confirmed its earlier position, as adopted in Supreme Court (NL), *Kesbir*, 7 May 2004, ECLI:NL:HR:2004:AF6988, namely that the existence of a non-international armed conflict does not exclude the application of the criminal law on terrorism. On the Dutch *LTTE* cases, see e.g. Ferdinandusse and Rademakers 2017, pp. 385–388.

NSAGs that *do* commit terrorist acts outside the context of armed conflicts (e.g. IS) as terrorist groups.[94]

We agree that it makes little sense to criminalise ancillary activities as terrorist offences if the main activity is not a terrorist act (because that act benefits from the application of the exclusion clause). For example, in the EU Directive on combating terrorism, the definition of a terrorist group is intrinsically related to the (intended) commission of terrorist acts.[95] If the relevant acts are not terrorist, the group is not a *terrorist* group, and participation in its activities is not a terrorist offence. Conversely, an armed group *also* committing terrorist acts *outside* the context of an armed conflict (e.g. IS) has a dual nature, following which FFs could be prosecuted for (ancillary) terrorist offences in relation to that group, save if their activities exclusively relate to activities governed by IHL, which fall under the exclusion clause.[96]

Of course, this does not and should not entail impunity. The activities of FFs who joined NSAGs are governed by IHL. If FFs commit serious violations of IHL, they can be prosecuted for war crimes, as illustrated by recent cases from Germany and the Netherlands.

8.4 War Crimes

In Germany and the Netherlands, there have been "cumulative" prosecutions of FFs for both terrorist offences and war crimes.[97] First, we will discuss a set of these cases concerning the war crime of outrages upon personal dignity. Second, we will look at recent cases from Germany in which female IS members were prosecuted for war crimes against property, enlisting a child into an armed group, and killing a person protected by IHL.

We will only deal with cases involving FFs, including women who have travelled abroad to join IS but may not actually have participated in hostilities. We will not discuss similar cases in which Syrian or Iraqi nationals were prosecuted before European national courts for international crimes committed in Syria/Iraq.[98] Nevertheless, the issues raised in such cases are similar to those raised in relation to the cases we will discuss.

---

[94] See further Van Poecke et al. 2021, pp. 315–320.

[95] Article 2(3) Directive (EU) 2017/541, above n 9, defines a terrorist group as "a structured group of more than two persons, established for a period of time and acting in concert *to commit terrorist offences*" (emphasis added). Terrorist offences are, in turn, defined in Article 3 of the Directive.

[96] See further Van Poecke et al. 2021, pp. 320–324.

[97] For an overview of the issue of cumulative prosecutions, see Eurojust/Genocide Network 2020.

[98] For example, in relation to the conflict in Syria/Iraq, there have also been war crime cases in Sweden and Finland, concerning Iraqi and Syrian asylum seekers. On these cases, see e.g. Human Rights Watch 2017 and Trial International, Universal Jurisdiction Database. https://trialinternational.org/resources/universal-jurisdiction-database. Accessed 6 July 2021.

8.4.1 Outrages upon Personal Dignity

The most typical cases in which FFs have been prosecuted for war crimes in EU member states were dubbed "posing cases".[99] In these cases, the accused were generally prosecuted for having themselves photographed or filmed with desecrated bodies of deceased enemy fighters. The relevant charge then constituted the war crime of outrages upon personal dignity,[100] which means that the "perpetrator humiliated, degraded or otherwise violated the dignity of one or more persons".[101]

The relevant cases are based on photographic evidence and are quite similar. In *Aria L.*,[102] the prosecution was based on pictures of a German national posing with the heads of two decapitated Syrian soldiers on sticks. The first *Abdelkarim El B.* case[103] dealt with footage showing a German national kicking the dead body of a Syrian soldier while he was filming and encouraging the mutilation of the body by fellow IS fighters. In a second case, Abdelkarim El B. was additionally convicted of filming fellow IS fighters beating, kicking and threatening to torture with electric shocks an enemy fighter within their control. This case was rather different, as it concerned the mistreatment of a living person. The charge qualified as the war crime of aiding and abetting cruel and inhumane treatment.[104] In the *Oussama A.* case,[105] a Dutch national who had joined IS posed smiling next to a crucified man and subsequently posted this picture on Facebook.

In *Aria L.* and *Oussama A.*, the courts stressed that the victims were persons protected by IHL and that outrages upon personal dignity can also be committed against deceased persons.[106] Furthermore, they found that the relevant acts met the degree of humiliation required for them to constitute the war crime of outrages

[99] Permanent Mission of the Federal Republic of Germany to the United Nations, New York 2019, p. 2.

[100] See Section 8(1)(9) of the German *Völkerstrafgesetzbuch* or Code of Crimes against International Law of 26 June 2002; and Article 6(1)(c) of the Dutch *Wet internationale misdrijven* or Law on International Crimes of 19 June 2003. This war crime reflects a serious violation of Article 3(c) common to the four Geneva Conventions and is, for NIACs, included in Article 8(2)(c)(ii) of the Rome Statute of the International Criminal Court, opened for signature 17 July 1998, 2187 UNTS 3 (entered into force 1 July 2002).

[101] See International Criminal Court (ICC) 2011, p. 27.

[102] Higher Regional Court of Frankfurt am Main (GE), *Aria L.*, 12 July 2016, 5-3 StE 2/16-4-1/16 (Higher Regional Court of Frankfurt am Main (GE), *Aria L*); Federal Court of Justice (GE), *Aria L.*, 27 July 2017, 3 StR 57/17 (Federal Court of Justice (GE), *Aria L.*).

[103] Higher Regional Court of Frankfurt am Main (GE), *Abdelkarim El B.*, 8 November 2016, 5-3 StE 4/16-4-3/16.

[104] Higher Regional Court of Frankfurt am Main (GE), *Abdelkarim El B.*, 24 November 2018, 5-3 StE 4/16-4-3/17. See Section 8(1)(3) of the German Code of Crimes against International Law.

[105] District Court of The Hague (NL), *Oussama A.*, 23 July 2019, ECLI:NL:RBDHA:2019:7430 (District Court of The Hague (NL), *Oussama A.*).

[106] Higher Regional Court of Frankfurt am Main (GE), *Aria L.*, above n 102, paras 150–164; Federal Court of Justice (GE), *Aria L.*, above n 102, paras 13–31; District Court of The Hague (NL), *Oussama A.*, above n 105, para 5.3.4.

upon personal dignity.[107] They were also satisfied that the acts had a *nexus* with the armed conflict because they would not have been possible in its absence, the victims were members of the opposing side,[108] and the acts were designed to demonstrate superiority and mercilessness vis-à-vis the enemy.[109] Aria L. was convicted only of war crimes and not of participation in a terrorist group because it was uncertain which particular group he had joined. Abdelkarim El B. and Oussama A. were both convicted cumulatively of participation in a terrorist group and the war crime of outrages upon personal dignity.[110] The three FFs were respectively sentenced to two years, ten years and seven and a half years of imprisonment.[111]

A fourth case is worth mentioning, although it does not concern someone who was convicted of activities committed as an FF. In addition to other (terrorist) offences, a Dutch woman who participated in the activities of IS was convicted of the war crime of outrages upon personal dignity committed in the Netherlands. While there were strong indications that the accused travelled to Syria in 2015,[112] she was long back in the Netherlands. There, under the name NesmuMutawahiddeen, she shared two videos in a Telegram group of 80 IS supporters. One video showed the burning alive of four persons taken captive by IS, to which she added the comment "like burning chicken"; a second video showed the shooting of a person taken captive by IS and was accompanied by a humiliating text and emoticons of smiling faces and a knife. Even if this was less evident in this case given that the accused did not act from within the ranks of IS in Syria, the Court ruled that there was a nexus with the conflict in Syria as the accused had followed IS' media strategy by acting as a "media mujahedin".[113] It added that the rules of IHL, which aim to protect persons who do not or no longer participate in hostilities, also apply at a (large) distance from the armed conflict.[114] The accused received a prison sentence of six years.[115]

---

[107] Ibid., respectively paras 170–172; paras 47–54; and para 5.3.4.

[108] District Court of The Hague (NL), *Oussama A.*, above n 105, para 5.3.5.

[109] Higher Regional Court of Frankfurt am Main (GE), *Aria L.*, above n 102, paras 173–176; Federal Court of Justice (GE), *Aria L.*, above n 102, paras 55–56.

[110] In addition, Abdelkarim El B. was found guilty of the unlawful possession of weapons ; Oussama A. was also found guilty of preparing and facilitating terrorist offences.

[111] In *Oussama A.* (at para 8.3), the Court took as a "starting point" for participation in a terrorist group a prison sentence of six years; for the war crime of outrages upon personal dignity (of a deceased person) two and a half years; it came to an overall sentence of seven and a half years. In the first *Abdelkarim El B.* case, the Court took as a starting point for participation in a terrorist group as well as for the war crime of outrages upon personal dignity a prison sentence of six years; it came to an overall sentence of eight and a half years (paras 243–269), which was increased to ten years in the second *Abdelkarim El B.* case.

[112] District Court of The Hague (NL), *NesmuMutawahiddeen*, 29 June 2021, ECLI:NL:RBDHA:2021:6620, paras 5.4.5 and 8.3.3.

[113] Ibid., para 6.4.2.

[114] Ibid.

[115] Ibid., "15 De beslissing" (The decision). She was also convicted of participating in the activities of a terrorist group and a criminal group (aiming to commit war crimes); inciting and spreading materials inciting terrorist offences and war crimes; giving and receiving training for terrorist offences; and violations of restrictive measures.

In the cases concerning FFs, the options for the courts were limited. The photographic or video evidence allowed them to convict the accused of limited instances of outrages upon personal dignity or cruel and degrading treatment, but not for any other war crimes these FFs may have committed. At the same time, these cases show that when evidence is available, war crimes *can* be prosecuted. This is illustrated further by more recent cases before German courts concerning war crimes committed by female IS members.

8.4.2 Cases Regarding Female IS Members

The prosecution of the activities of female IS members as war crimes fits in the broader trend that "prosecution practices for returnees appear to have shifted significantly in recent times in light of evolving understandings of the roles of female departees in Iraq and Syria".[116] Initially, women who joined IS were seen as "passive victims of males—consistent with the stereotype of passive 'jihadi brides'".[117] However, as also illustrated by the *NesmuMutawahiddeen* case, the role of women associated with IS must not be oversimplified; "they may be both perpetrators and victims of war crimes".[118]

There are at least eight cases before German courts in which German women who travelled to Syria and joined IS were convicted of war crimes against property due to the unlawful appropriation of houses and apartments in the context of an armed conflict.[119] One case involves the war crime of enlisting a child into an armed group.[120] Lastly, there are a number of cases in which women are prosecuted for or were convicted of international crimes committed against Yazidi girls or women

---

[116] Ragazzi and Walmsley 2018, p. 45.

[117] Ibid.

[118] ICRC 2019, p. 61. See also Cook and Vale 2019; Higher Regional Court of Munich (GE), *Sibel H.*, above n 60, paras 44 and 76–78.

[119] See Section 9 of the German Code of Crimes against International Law. See: Higher Regional Court of Stuttgart (GE), *Sabine Ulrike S.*, 5 July 2019, 5-2 StE 11/18; Higher Regional Court of Düsseldorf (GE), *Mine K.*, 4 December 2019, 2 StE 2/19 (Higher Regional Court of Düsseldorf (GE), *Mine K.*); Higher Regional Court of Düsseldorf (GE), *Derya Ö.*, 17 December 2019, 5 StS 2/19 (Higher Regional Court of Düsseldorf (GE), *Derya Ö.*); Higher Regional Court of Munich (GE), *Sibel H.*, above n 60; Higher Regional Court of Düsseldorf (GE), *Nurten J.*, 21 April 2021, 7 StS 2/20 (Higher Regional Court of Düsseldorf (GE), *Nurten J.*); Higher Regional Court of Frankfurt am Main (GE), *Nasim A.*, 28 May 2021, 5-2 OJs 24/19–4/20 (Higher Regional Court of Frankfurt am Main (GE), *Nasim A.*); Higher Regional Court of Düsseldorf (GE), *Fadia S.*, 1 July 2021; Higher Regional Court Frankfurt am Main (GE), *Kim Teresa A.*, 29 October 2021, 5-2 OJs 29/20–1/21. While war crimes against property were also mentioned in Federal Court of Justice (GE), Ruling on pre-trial detention, *Sarah O.*, 4 April 2019 (Federal Court of Justice (GE), *Sarah O.*), it seems that this charge was eventually not pursued, as it did not form part of the judgment on the merits: Higher Regional Court of Düsseldorf (GE), *Sarah O.*, 16 June 2021, 7 StS 3/19 (Higher Regional Court of Düsseldorf (GE), *Sarah O.*).

[120] See Section 8(1)(5) German Code of Crimes against International Law. See: Higher Regional Court of Düsseldorf (GE), *Carla-Josephine S.*, 29 April 2020, 7 StS 4/19 (Higher Regional Court

whom they kept as slaves. In one case, the relevant conduct was qualified as killing a person protected by IHL and a crime against humanity,[121] in four other cases as crimes against humanity.[122] In all cases, the women were also convicted of participation in a terrorist group. Hence, all cases are examples of cumulative convictions. Moreover, many of the women were also convicted of unlawful possession of weapons[123] and/or other "common" offences, like breaching their parental duty of care (see further Sect. 8.5).[124]

In the cases of war crimes against property, the accused had lived in houses made available to them by IS that had been seized by the organisation after their owners had left them behind because they had to flee for or were killed by IS. It was a systematic practice of IS to expropriate its "enemies" and grant their houses to IS fighters and their families.[125] According to the courts, the act of (illegally) appropriating such houses served to consolidate the ousting of IS' enemies from the territories it conquered and to consolidate the organisation's claims over these territories. As such, it constituted an act of participation as a member in the (terrorist) organisation.[126] At the same time, the act was considered separately as a war crime against property. When analysing the constitutive elements of the war crime, the courts assessed whether the appropriation was of a considerable/significant scope/extent (*erheblichem Umfang*).[127] They found that houses have a high economic value and

of Düsseldorf (GE), *Carla-Josephine S.*); see also Trial International (2021) Carla-Josephine S. https://trialinternational.org/latest-post/carla-josephine-s. Accessed 6 July 2021.

[121] See respectively Section 8(1)(1) and Section 7 of the German Code of Crimes against International Law. See: Higher Regional Court of Munich (GE), *Jennifer W.*, 25 October 2021, 8 St 9/18.

[122] Higher Regional Court of Hamburg, *Omaima A.*, 2 October 2020, 3 St 1/20; Higher Regional Court of Düsseldorf (GE), *Nurten J.*, above n 119, especially paras 144–165; Higher Regional Court of Düsseldorf (GE), *Sarah O.*, above n 119; Higher Regional Court of Hamburg (GE), *Omaima A.*, 22 July 2021, 4 St 1/21. On the cases on crimes against humanity, see e.g. Clooney et al. 2021.

[123] See the cases of *Sabine Ulrike S .*, *Derya Ö.*, *Omaima A.*, *Nurten J .*, *Nasim A .*, *Kim Teresa A .* and *Jennifer W.*

[124] See the cases of *Carla-Josephine S.*, *Omaima A.*, *Nurten J.* and *Fadia S.*

[125] Higher Regional Court of Düsseldorf (GE), *Mine K.*, above n 119, para 229; Higher Regional Court of Munich (GE), *Sibel H.*, above n 60, para 74.

[126] Federal Court of Justice (GE), Ruling on pre-trial detention, *Sarah O.*, above n 119, paras 16, 18 and 30; Federal Court of Justice (GE), *Mine K.*, 15 May 2019, AK 22/19 (Federal Court of Justice (GE), *Mine K.*), paras 15 and 27; Federal Court of Justice (GE), *Nasim A.*, 9 June 2020, AK 12/20 (Federal Court of Justice (GE), *Nasim A.*), para 26; Federal Court of Justice (GE), *Nurten J.*, 9 February 2021, AK 5/21, paras 15 and 25; and Federal Court of Justice (GE), *Kim Teresa A.*, 20 April 2021, AK 30/21, paras 24 and 44–45 and 51; Higher Regional Court of Düsseldorf (GE), *Mine K.*, above n 119, paras 9, 74, 247 and 260; Higher Regional Court of Düsseldorf (GE), *Derya Ö.*, above n 119, para 314; Higher Regional Court of Munich (GE), *Sibel H.*, above n 60, paras 16–17 and 99; Higher Regional Court of Düsseldorf (GE), *Nurten J.*, above n 119, paras 60, 12, 128 and 138.

[127] Section 9 of the German Code of Crimes against International Law; translated as "extensively" by the German Ministry of Justice. www.gesetze-im-internet.de/englisch_vstgb. Accessed 6 July 2021.

are among the existential means of livelihood of their owners.[128] Furthermore, the expulsion of the owners or their flight for IS gave the violation of property as such, as well as the intensification and perpetuation thereof by the accused, a dimension of injustice affecting the international community as a whole.[129]

The courts also held that the appropriation of property had a nexus with the armed conflict. The Federal Court of Justice found that "the accused was only able to take possession of the apartment and its inventory because the legitimate owners had to flee from IS troops or were driven away by them and the association had given the looted property to her and her husband as IS members for use".[130] The prison sentences the accused received ranged from a suspended sentence of two years to a sentence of five years,[131] among others depending on the degree of their involvement in IS and the commission of other offences.

In *Carla-Josephine S.*, the Higher Regional Court of Düsseldorf convicted a German woman for the war crime of enlisting a child into an armed group. The accused travelled to Syria with her three children. There, she was a member of IS, including "Katiba Nusaiba", a female IS unit within which she briefly served as a

---

[128] Federal Court of Justice (GE), *Sarah O.*, above n 119, para 50; Higher Regional Court of Düsseldorf (GE), *Mine K.*, above n 119, para 256; Higher Regional Court of Düsseldorf, *Derya Ö.*, above n 119, paras 342 and 372; Higher Regional Court of Munich (GE), *Sibel H.*, above n 60, para 107.

[129] Federal Court of Justice (GE), *Sarah O.*, above n 119, para 50; Higher Regional Court of Düsseldorf (GE), *Mine K.*, above n 119, para 256.

[130] Federal Court of Justice (GE), *Sarah O.*, above n 119, para 39; see also Federal Court of Justice (GE), *Mine K.*, above n 126, para 29; Federal Court of Justice (GE), *Nasim A.*, above n 126, para 26; Higher Regional Court of Düsseldorf (GE), *Mine K.*, above n 119, para 257; Higher Regional Court of Düsseldorf (GE), *Derya Ö.*, above n 119, paras 347 and 374; Higher Regional Court of Munich (GE), *Sibel H.*, above n 60, para 107; Higher Regional Court of Düsseldorf (GE), *Nurten J.*, above n 119, paras 131–132.

[131] From low to high: two years (suspended): Higher Regional Court of Frankfurt am Main (2021) Nasim A. wegen Mitgliedschaft in der ausländischen terroristischen Vereinigung „Islamischer Staat" sowie wegen weiterer Taten verurteilt. https://ordentliche-gerichtsbarkeit.hessen.de/pressemitteilungen/nasim-a-wegen-mitgliedschaft-in-der-ausl%C3%A4ndischen-terroristischen-vereinigung. Accessed 6 July 2021; two years and nine months: Higher Regional Court of Düsseldorf (GE), *Derya Ö.*, above n 119, para 473; three years: Higher Regional Court of Munich (GE), *Sibel H.*, above n 60, paras 115–123; three years and nine months: Higher Regional Court of Düsseldorf (GE), *Mine K.*, above n 119, para 268; four years: Higher Regional Court of Düsseldorf (2021) Mutter von fünf Kindern wegen mitgliedschaftlicher Beteiligung an der Terrororganisation "IS" verurteilt. www.justiz.nrw/JM/Presse/presse_weitere/PresseOLGs/archiv/2021_01_Archiv/01_07_2021_1/index.php. Accessed 15 February 2022; Higher Regional Court of Frankfurt am Main (2021) Higher Regional Court Frankfurt/Main sentences Kim Teresa A. for membership in a foreign terrorist organisation to a term of imprisonment of four years. https://ordentliche-gerichtsbarkeit.hessen.de/pressemitteilungen/higher-regional-court-frankfurtmain-sentences-kim-teresa-a-for-membership-in-a. Accessed 15 February 2022; four years and three months: Higher Regional Court of Düsseldorf (GE), *Nurten J.*, above n 119, paras 3 and 136; five years: Higher Regional Court of Stuttgart (2019) Urteil in einem Staatsschutzverfahren wegen des Vorwurfs der Mitgliedschaft in der ausländischen terroristischen Vereinigung „Islamischer Staat" u. a. https://oberlandesgericht-stuttgart.justiz-bw.de/pb/,Lde/Startseite/Medien/Urteil+in+einem+Staatsschutzverfahren+wegen+des+Vorwurfs+der+Mitgliedschaft+in+der+auslaendischen+terroristischen+Vereinigung+_Islamischer+Staat_++u_+a_/?LISTPAGE=1178276. Accessed 6 July 2021.

driver. Albeit reluctantly, she agreed that her then six/seven-year-old son be sent to an IS (Ashbal) training camp on three occasions, where "he was physically trained, taught how to handle weapons, introduced to guard duty and shot a gun".[132] The act of enlisting her child was seen as part of the charge of participation as a member of a terrorist group and qualified as a self-standing war crime.[133] The Court emphasized that it is sufficient that the child is enlisted for training in an armed unit; it is not required that the child is enlisted in an active combat unit. Moreover, the enlisting must not presuppose active participation in hostilities, nor be directed towards such participation, nor must such participation be realistic.[134] That is so, among others, "because children must be protected not only from the dangers of deployment to the front, but also from being exposed at a young age and without protection to a culture in which violence and the killing of people are common or advocated and demanded".[135] As the enlisting "took place against the background of the ongoing civil war and served to strengthen the combat power of IS as a party to the conflict", also the nexus requirement was fulfilled.[136] The Court determined a sentence of four and a half years for the war crime of enlisting a child into an armed group; one year for the unlawful possession of a weapon (hand grenade); and two and a half years for participation as a member in a terrorist group (IS). It came to an overall prison sentence of five years and three months.[137]

The case involving the war crime of killing a person protected by IHL is that of *Jennifer W.* before the Higher Regional Court of Munich. Jennifer W. is a German national who joined IS as a member of its "morality police". She was married to Taha A.-J., an Iraqi national who was also a member of IS and who has been prosecuted separately. Taha A.-J. purchased a Yazidi woman and her five-year-old daughter. Together, Jennifer W. and Taha A.-J. kept both Yazidi persons in slavery. To punish the five-year-old girl, Taha A.-J. chained up the girl outside and let her scorch in the burning sun, which resulted in her death. The accused failed to intervene and prevent the girl from dying.[138] In this case, the nexus of the alleged killing with the armed conflict is not as evident as in the cases on outrages upon personal dignity, war crimes against property and enlisting a child into an armed group. The Yazidi girl was no doubt a non-combatant. Moreover, the act of keeping her as a slave and her consequential death took place in the domestic context, away from any hostilities. On the other hand, as part of its morality police, Jennifer W. clearly was a member

132 Higher Regional Court of Düsseldorf (GE), *Carla-Josephine S.*, above n 120, para 55.

133 Ibid., respectively para 102 and paras 109–116.

134 Ibid., para 112.

135 Ibid.

136 Ibid., para 114.

137 Ibid., paras 140–159.

138 Der Generalbundesanwalt beim Bundesgerichtshof (2018) Anklage gegen ein mutmaßliches Mitglied der ausländischen terroristischen Vereinigung „Islamischer Staat (IS)“ wegen Mordes und der Begehung eines Kriegsverbrechens erhoben. www.generalbundesanwalt.de/SharedDocs/Pressemitteilungen/DE/2018/Pressemitteilung-vom-28-12-2018.html?nn=478298. Accessed 6 July 2021; Trial International (2021) Jennifer W. and others. https://trialinternational.org/latest-post/jennifer-w-and-others. Accessed 6 July 2021.

of IS, and the Yazidi girl was a member of a population group IS considered to be its enemy, be it in a non-combatant sense. While we believe that the relevant acts more naturally fit the description of crimes against humanity, if not genocide,[139] it seems that the crimes committed against the girl can fit the definition of the war crime of killing a person protected by IHL and the nexus requirement, if interpreted flexibly. This assessment seems to be confirmed by the fact that recently, the Higher Regional Court of Munich convicted Jennifer W. among others of membership in a foreign terrorist organisation, aiding and abetting attempted murder and a war crime by omission, as well as a crime against humanity resulting in death. She was sentenced to 10 years' imprisonment.[140] The Higher Regional Court of Frankfurt am Main has found Taha A.-J. "guilty of genocide in combination with a crime against humanity resulting in death, a war crime against persons resulting in death, aiding and abetting a war crime against persons in two cases, and bodily harm resulting in death" and sentenced him to life imprisonment.[141] Furthermore, at least three other German women who were a member of IS and kept Yazidi women or girls as slaves were convicted of notably (aiding and abetting) acts like murder, enslavement, rape, unlawful deprivation of liberty and persecution as crimes against humanity.[142]

8.4.3 The Importance of Prosecuting International Crimes

What is important to take away from Sect. 8.4 is that some of the activities of the men and women who joined IS are more appropriately prosecuted and punished as war crimes or other international crimes, namely crimes against humanity or even genocide, than as broadly defined terrorist offences. Offences like membership of a terrorist group may not adequately reflect the full spectrum of criminal acts committed.[143] If a norm sanctioning an international crime is violated, it is important to "express the community's reprobation" of that violation. Thus, the relevant norm "and the social values protected by it" are confirmed, and the confidence in them restored. This may notably help "to prevent future attacks against those norms

---

[139] On the international recognition of the acts committed against the Yazidi people as genocide, see for example UN 2021.

[140] Higher Regional Court of Munich (2021) Strafverfahren gegen Jennifer W. wegen Verdachts der mitgliedschaftlichen Beteiligung an einer terroristischen Vereinigung im Ausland u.a. www.justiz.bayern.de/gerichte-und-behoerden/oberlandesgerichte/muenchen/presse/2021/30.php. Accessed 16 February 2022; Legal Tribune Online (2021) Terrorprozess am OLG München: Zehn Jahre Haft für IS-Rückkehrerin. www.lto.de/recht/nachrichten/n/olg-muenchen-8-st-9-18-is-rueckkehrerin-jennifer-w-haftstrafe-terroristische-vereinigung-beihilfe-mord. Accessed 16 February 2022.

[141] Higher Regional Court of Frankfurt am Main (2021) Higher Regional Court Frankfurt/Main sentences Taha Al-J. to lifelong imprisonment for genocide and other criminal offences. https://ordentliche-gerichtsbarkeit.hessen.de/pressemitteilungen/higher-regional-court-frankfurtmain-sentences-taha-al-j-to-lifelong-imprisonment. Accessed 16 February 2022.

[142] See the references above n 122.

[143] See also Chap. 7 by Paulussen and Mehra in this volume.

and interests".[144] More specifically, to raise awareness about IHL and enhance its implementation, serious violations of IHL should be prosecuted *as* war crimes.[145] Furthermore, by focusing only on ancillary terrorist offences, prosecutors and judges may fail to identify and provide redress to the victims of actual crimes. For example, in the *Jennifer W.* case, the mother of the Yazidi girl who herself was also enslaved by Taha A.-J. and Jennifer W. participated as a witness and co-plaintiff;[146] the same could hardly be achieved in a case merely concerning membership of a terrorist group. Victims of crimes committed by IS have themselves indeed asked for the prosecution of international crimes rather than terrorism.[147] More generally, focusing on broadly defined terrorist offences may insufficiently uncover the atrocities that have happened and fail to contribute to the post-conflict narrative;[148] and result in sentences that hold the perpetrators accountable for only a limited range of their criminal activities.[149]

This is well-illustrated by the case of *Nils D.* Nils D. is a German national who joined IS and was a member of a security unit that tracked down alleged spies and deserters, captured them and brought them to prison. Initially, he was only convicted of membership of a terrorist group and sentenced to four and a half years' imprisonment.[150] However, after a witness came forward and testified that Nils D. not only transported the prisoners and occasionally observed them being tortured but also participated in torturing and killing at least three of them himself, a second case was initiated against him. He is now charged with the war crimes of torturing and killing persons protected by IHL[151] and faces a harsher sentence. Importantly, the

---

[144] Maculan and Gil Gil 2020, p. 147. This refers to the expressionist function of punishment, which draws from the approach of "positive general prevention"; see also Ambos 2013, pp. 71–72.

[145] Pejic 2012, pp. 185 and 198. See also ICRC 2011, p. 51.

[146] Federal Court of Justice (GE), Ruling on pre-trial detention, *Jennifer W.*, 23 January 2020, StB 1/20, paras 18–19. Furthermore, at least three Yazidi women and victims enslaved by Sarah O. acted as witnesses/co-plaintiffs in the cases of *Omaima A.*, *Nurten J.* and/or *Sarah O.* (all relating to crimes against humanity); see Higher Regional Court of Düsseldorf (GE), *Sarah O.*, above n 119 and Clooney et al. 2021, above n 122.

[147] The Soufan Center 2021, pp. 5 and 7; see e.g. in the Belgian context Struys B (2021) Jezidi vragen dat Belgische IS-leden terechtstaan voor genocide. www.demorgen.be/nieuws/jezidi-vragen-dat-belgische-is-leden-terechtstaan-voor-genocide~b0ccc15c. Accessed 16 July 2021, and the resolution of the Federal Chamber of Representatives (2021) Proposition de résolution visant à reconnaître et à poursuivre les crimes de génocide à l'encontre des Yézidis ainsi qu' à leur venir en aide, Doc. 55 1766/001. www.lachambre.be/FLWB/PDF/55/1766/55K1766001.pdf. Accessed 16 July 2021.

[148] However, as noted by Maculan and Gil Gil 2020, the capacity of (national) criminal courts to contribute to victims' rights to justice, reparation, truth and non-repetition—which reflect the four pillars of the "transitional justice" approach—is limited; there may be more appropriate fora to fulfil these rights.

[149] Cuyckens and Paulussen 2019, p. 538; Eurojust/Genocide Network 2020, pp. 3–5 and 26; The Soufan Center 2021, pp. 4–5, 7–8 and 13.

[150] Higher Regional Court of Düsseldorf (2016) Haftstrafe im Verfahren gegen „Nils D." wegen Mitgliedschaft in der ausländischen terroristischen Vereinigung „Islamischer Staat" („IS", vormals „ISIG"). www.olg-duesseldorf.nrw.de/behoerde/presse/archiv/Pressemitteilungen_aus_2016/20160304_PM_Urkteilsverkuendung-Nils-D_/index.php. Accessed 6 July 2021.

[151] See Sections 8(1)(1) and 8(1)(3) German Code of International Crimes.

Federal Court of Justice held that the *ne bis in idem* rule, which provides that one cannot be punished twice for the same crime, did not prevent this second case, as it concerns different facts which were not the subject of the first case.[152] The case of *Nils D.* confirms that, in a procedural sense, convictions of membership of a terrorist group that do not take into account the international crimes committed by the accused do not reflect the latter's full criminal responsibility.

A residual and perhaps sometimes overlooked category of offences that may also help in adequately establishing the full range of criminal responsibility of FFs is that of "common offences".

8.5 Common Offences

It has been suggested that especially at the early stages of the criminal justice response to FFs, prosecutors and judges may have turned to "common", "regular" or "conventional" criminal law provisions with which they are familiar, whilst the legislator was still developing or had only just adopted specific criminal law provisions on terrorism designed to address the FF phenomenon.[153] This "shows that 'regular' criminal law provisions may also be sufficient to secure a conviction" of FFs.[154] However, judges may not always accept innovative interpretations of common criminal law provisions, and this approach may entail issues for international cooperation (e.g. in matters of mutual legal assistance and extradition).[155] Moreover, "[r]elying on non-terrorism offences also runs the risk that the courts will not be able to address the full severity of the case and punishments may be very light, as is often the case when it comes to violations of immigration laws or petty crimes, such as fraud or theft, committed prior to departure for the conflict zone".[156]

In some cases, these concerns may indeed be valid. However, in line with our argumentation above, we want to turn the latter concern on its head. *Merely* prosecuting FFs for broadly defined terrorist offences like membership of a terrorist group may insufficiently reflect the criminal activities committed by FFs. Much like the case for international crimes, common offences may also help in adequately addressing the full range of criminal responsibility of FFs. For example, Eurojust has highlighted that "[i]n some CT investigations and prosecutions, the alleged terrorist activities were committed in combination with other offences, e.g. trafficking (of human beings, drugs), smuggling (of migrants, cigarettes), economic crimes (money laundering or tax offences with possible links to financing of terrorism), computer crimes, explosives-, weapons- and ammunition-related offences, including possession and

[152] Federal Court of Justice, Ruling on ne bis in idem and pre-trial detention, *Nils D.*, 18 December 2018, StB 52/18, para 26.

[153] Paulussen and Pitcher 2018, pp. 12–14.

[154] Ibid., p. 13. See also Greene 2014, p. 791.

[155] On the opportunities offered by existing laws, see e.g. CTC/CTED 2015, pp. 6–7.

[156] Ibid., p. 7.

trafficking, and forgery of official documents".[157] Also Europol noted that in some court proceedings before courts of EU member states concluded in 2020 "alleged terrorist activities were committed in combination with other offences, including core international crimes, firearms or explosives-related offences, document forgery, robbery, theft, and violation of financial legislation".[158]

Prosecuting the enumerated offences can serve at least two goals. First, identifying common offences committed by FFs that may relate to criminal networks and investigating potential links between FFs and organised crime could uncover important leads to other crimes and criminals. This entails that "those who have committed illegal activities related to organized crime and terrorism" should not simply be prosecuted for terrorist offences or only for offences related to organised crime, but for both.[159] Second, much like for norms sanctioning international crimes (see Sect. 8.4.3), it is important to express the (national) community's reprobation of a violation of a norm sanctioning a common offence. An example of common offences deserving to be punished for this reason can be taken from the German cases involving female members of IS. In four cases, a mother who travelled to Syria with her child(ren) was convicted of "child theft" and/or "breach of duty of care or upbringing".[160]

Lastly, and as already mentioned in Sects. 8.3 and 8.4, the qualification of the conduct of FFs as terrorist offences may not always be the best solution. Here, common offences may play a role: in some cases, it may be sufficient and more appropriate to prosecute FFs "merely" for common offences. Thus, in the context of a seminar on the prosecution of FFs under the auspices of the UN Security Council Counter-Terrorism Committee and its Executive Directorate (CTC/CTED), it was noted that consideration must be given to the role of prosecutions in a comprehensive strategy on FFs. As the application of certain legislation, like "harsh" and value-laden CT legislation, may at times be "counterproductive to the larger agenda to prevent terrorist acts […] it might be preferable to charge the offence of illegal border crossing" in cases that warrant a "softer" approach.[161] In a similar vein, Ip has argued that states should target "foreign fighting directly, rather than treating it as a variant of terrorist activity" and hence called for "the reinvigoration of so-called neutrality laws, domestic laws designed to ensure a State's neutrality, and making criminal the act of travelling to and participating in an armed conflict overseas, irrespective of the group joined or acts done in the theatre of armed conflict".[162]

---

[157] Eurojust 2020, p. 7.

[158] Europol 2021, p. 36.

[159] Global Counterterrorism Forum 2018, p. 13.

[160] See respectively Section 235 and 171 German Criminal Code; i.e. the cases of *Carla-Josephine S.*, *Omaima A.*, *Nurten J.* and *Fadia S.*

[161] CTC/CTED 2015, p. 13; cp. Paulussen and Pitcher 2018, pp. 20–21.

[162] Ip 2019, p. 126 and 130.

8.6 Conclusion: All Relevant Legal Frameworks Count

The multidimensional nature of FFs and the diversity of criminal acts they may have committed makes the qualification of their conduct under criminal law a complex issue. We have aimed to answer the question of how the activities of (returned) FFs should be qualified by national prosecutors and courts under domestic criminal law. We have identified three broad possibilities, namely the qualification of their activities as (i) terrorist offences, (ii) international crimes, notably war crimes, and (iii) common offences.

FFs are predominantly prosecuted for broadly defined ancillary, preparatory or inchoate terrorist offences. Nevertheless, this is not the only option for the qualification of their conduct. FFs can and should also be prosecuted for the international crimes they have committed. The FFs this chapter deals with, namely those who travelled to Syria or Iraq, have usually joined groups with a dual nature, i.e. groups qualifying as both terrorist groups and NSAGs, like IS. The activities these FFs committed in the context of an armed conflict are governed by IHL rather than CT instruments, and any serious violations of IHL they committed should be prosecuted as war crimes. As shown in Sect. 8.4, at least in some jurisdictions, the prosecution of war crimes is increasing. This is also the case for the women who joined IS, who were often more than mere "jihadi brides" doing housekeeping: some of their acts can and should be prosecuted as war crimes or other international crimes, namely crimes against humanity or genocide.

Prosecuting FFs not only for broadly defined terrorist offences but also for the international crimes and common offences they have committed is important. FFs should be convicted of the specific acts they have committed. Such an approach delivers more qualitative justice than catching all FFs through a one-size-fits-all approach that does not make a distinction between those who have committed atrocities and those who did not. It increases accountability, is more meaningful for victims and leads to more adequate sentences. Ultimately, national prosecutors and courts should take all relevant legal frameworks into account when prosecuting and trying (returned) FFs, who should be held to account for the full range of their criminal activity.

References

Ambos K (2013) Treatise on International Criminal Law, Volume I: Foundations and General Part. Oxford University Press, Oxford

Anderson D (2013) Shielding the Compass: How to Fight Terrorism Without Defeating the Law. European Human Rights Law Review 3:233–246

Bartels R (2016) Terrorist Groups as Parties to an Armed Conflict. In: Muller K, Kolanowski S (eds) Proceedings of the Bruges Colloquium: Terrorism, Counter-Terrorism and International Humanitarian Law, pp 56–66

Coco A (2013) The Mark of Cain: The Crime of Terrorism in Times of Armed Conflict as Interpreted by the Court of Appeal of England and Wales in *R v. Mohammed Gul*. Journal of International Criminal Justice 11:425–440

Cook J, Vale G (2019) From Daesh to 'Diaspora' II: The Challenges Posed by Women and Minors After the Fall of the Caliphate. ICSR. https://icsr.info/wp-content/uploads/2019/07/ICSR-Feature-From-Daesh-to-'Diaspora'-II-The-Challenges-Posed-by-Women-and-Minors-After-the-Fall-of-the-Caliphate.pdf. Accessed 6 July 2021

Clooney A, von Wistinghausen N, Mehner S (2021) German Court Hands Down a Fourth Conviction for Crimes Against Humanity Committed by IS Against the Yazidis. www.doughtystreet.co.uk/news/german-court-hands-down-fourth-conviction-crimes-against-humanity-committed-isis-against. Accessed 12 August 2021

Cuyckens H, Paulussen C (2019) The Prosecution of Foreign Fighters in Western Europe: The Difficult Relationship Between Counter-Terrorism and International Humanitarian Law. Journal of Conflict and Security Law 24:537–565

de Guttry A, Capone F, Paulussen C (2016) Introduction. In: de Guttry A, Capone F, Paulussen C (eds) Foreign Fighters in International Law and Beyond. T.M.C. Asser Press, The Hague, pp 1–8

Dörmann K, Geiß R (2009) The Implementation of Grave Breaches into Domestic Legal Orders. Journal of International Criminal Justice 7:703–721

Duffy H (2015) The 'War on Terror' and the Framework of International Law. Cambridge University Press, Cambridge

Eurojust (2020) 2019 Eurojust Report on Counter-Terrorism. www.eurojust.europa.eu/sites/default/files/2020a-12/2020-12-Eurojust_Counterterrorism_report_2019.pdf. Accessed 6 July 2021

Eurojust/Genocide Network (2020) Cumulative Prosecution of Foreign Terrorist Fighters for Core International Crimes and Terrorism-Related Offences. www.eurojust.europa.eu/cumulative-prosecution-foreign-terrorist-fighters-core-international-crimes-and-terrorism-related. Accessed 6 July 2021

European Commission (2015) Communication from the Commission to the European Parliament, the Council, the European Economic and Social Committee and the Committee of the Regions: The European Agenda on Security. COM (2015) 185 final. https://eur-lex.europa.eu/legal-content/GA/TXT/?uri=CELEX:52015DC0185. Accessed 29 October 2021

Europol (2021) Terrorism Situation and Trend Report. www.europol.europa.eu/activities-services/main-reports/european-union-terrorism-situation-and-trend-report-2021-tesat. Accessed 6 July 2021

Ferdinandusse W, Rademakers P (2017) The Prosecution of Sanction Busters. In: van den Herik L (ed) Research Handbook on UN Sanctions and International Law. Edward Elgar, Cheltenham, pp 377–399

Gaeta P (2015) Grave Breaches of the Geneva Conventions. In: Clapham A, Gaeta P, Sassòli M (eds) The 1949 Geneva Conventions: A Commentary. Oxford University Press, Oxford, pp 615–646

Gill T (2016) Classifying the Conflict in Syria. International Law Studies 92:353–380

Global Counterterrorism Forum (2018) The Hague Good Practices on the Nexus between Transnational Organized Crime and Terrorism. www.thegctf.org/Portals/1/Documents/Framework%20Documents/2018/GCTF-Good-Practices-on-the-Nexus_ENG.pdf?ver=2018-09-21-122246-363. Accessed 6 July 2021

Greene A (2014) The Quest for a Satisfactory Definition of Terrorism: *R* v *Gul*. Modern Law Review 77:780–793

Hassan L (2021) Repatriating ISIS Foreign Fighters Is Key to Stemming Radicalization, Experts Say, but Many Countries Don't Want Their Citizens Back. www.pbs.org/wgbh/frontline/article/repatriating-isis-foreign-fighters-key-to-stemming-radicalization-experts-say-but-many-countries-dont-want-citizens-back. Accessed 6 July 2021

Heinsch R (2016) Foreign Fighters and International Criminal Law. In: de Guttry A, Capone F, Paulussen C (eds) Foreign Fighters in International Law and Beyond. T.M.C. Asser Press, The Hague, pp 161–186

Henckaerts J-M, Doswald-Beck L (2005) Customary International Humanitarian Law, Volume I: Rules. Cambridge University Press, Cambridge

Human Rights Watch (2017) "These are the Crimes We are Fleeing": Justice for Syria in Swedish and German Courts. www.hrw.org/report/2017/10/04/these-are-crimes-we-are-fleeing/justice-syria-swedish-and-german-courts. Accessed 6 July 2021

Husabø EJ, Bruce I (2009) Fighting Terrorism Through Multilevel Criminal Legislation. Brill Nijhoff, Leiden

ICRC (2011) International Humanitarian Law and the Challenges of Contemporary Armed Conflicts. www.icrc.org/en/doc/assets/files/red-cross-crescent-movement/31st-international-conference/31-int-conference-ihl-challenges-report-11-5-1-2-en.pdf. Accessed 6 July 2021

ICRC (2015a) The Domestic Implementation of International Humanitarian Law: A Manual. www.icrc.org/en/doc/assets/files/publications/icrc-002-4028.pdf. Accessed 6 July 2021

ICRC (2015b) International Humanitarian Law and the Challenges of Contemporary Armed Conflicts. www.icrc.org/en/document/international-humanitarian-law-and-challenges-contemporary-armed-conflicts. Accessed 6 July 2021

ICRC (2019) International Humanitarian Law and the Challenges of Contemporary Armed Conflicts: Recommitting to Protection in Armed Conflict on the 70th Anniversary of the Geneva Conventions. www.icrc.org/en/document/icrc-report-ihl-and-challenges-contemporary-armed-conflicts. Accessed 6 July 2021

International Criminal Court (ICC) (2011) Elements of Crimes. www.icc-cpi.int/NR/rdonlyres/336923D8-A6AD-40EC-AD7B-45BF9DE73D56/0/ElementsOfCrimesEng.pdf. Accessed 6 July 2021

Ip J (2019) Reconceptualising the Legal Response to Foreign Fighters. International and Comparative Law Quarterly 69:103–134

Koutroulis V (2015) Le jugement du Tribunal correctionnel d'Anvers dans l'affaire dite «Sharia4Belgium» et l'article 141bis du Code pénal belge. In: Jacobs A, Flore D (eds) Les Combattants étrangers en Syrie. L'Harmattan, Paris, pp 85–103

Krähenmann S (2014) Foreign Fighters Under International Law. Geneva Academy of International Humanitarian Law and Human Rights, Geneva. www.geneva-academy.ch/joomlatools-files/docman-files/Publications/Academy%20Briefings/Foreign%20Fighters_2015_WEB.pdf. Accessed 6 July 2021

Krähenmann S (2016) Legal Framework Addressing Terrorism and Counter-Terrorism. In: Muller K, Kolanowski S (eds) Proceedings of the Bruges Colloquium: Terrorism, Counter-Terrorism and International Humanitarian Law, pp 17–24

Maculan E, Gil Gil A (2020) The Rationale and Purposes of Criminal Law and Punishment in Transitional Contexts. Oxford Journal of Legal Studies 40:132–157

McKeever D (2020) International Humanitarian Law and Counter-Terrorism: Fundamental Values, Conflicting Obligations. International and Comparative Law Quarterly 69:43–78

Mehra T (2018) Bringing (Foreign) Terrorist Fighters to Justice in a Post-ISIS Landscape, Part II: Prosecution by Foreign National Courts. ICCT Perspective. https://icct.nl/publication/bringing-foreign-terrorist-fighters-to-justice-in-a-post-isis-landscape-part-ii-prosecution-by-foreign-national-courts. Accessed 6 July 2021

Moeckli D (2008) The Emergence of Terrorism as a Distinct Category of International Law. Texas International Law Journal 44:157–183

Paulussen C, Entenmann E (2016) National Responses in Select Western European Countries to the Foreign Fighter Phenomenon. In: de Guttry A, Capone F, Paulussen C (eds) Foreign Fighters in international Law and Beyond. T.M.C. Asser Press, The Hague, pp 391–422

Paulussen C, Pitcher K (2018) Prosecuting (Potential) Foreign Fighters: Legislative and Practical Challenges. ICCT Research Paper. https://icct.nl/app/uploads/2018/01/ICCT-Paulussen-Pitcher-Prosecuting-Potential-Foreign-Fighters-Legislative-Practical-Challenges-Jan2018.pdf. Accessed 6 July 2021

Pejic J (2012) Armed Conflict and Terrorism: There Is a (Big) Difference. In: Salinas de Frías AM, Samuel K, White N (eds) Counter-Terrorism: International Law and Practice. Oxford University Press, Oxford, pp 171–204
Permanent Mission of the Federal Republic of Germany to the United Nations, New York (2019) Note Verbale No. 140/2019
Ragazzi F, Walmsley J (2018) The Return of Foreign Fighters to EU Soil: Ex Post Evaluation, European Parliamentary Research Service Study. www.europarl.europa.eu/RegData/etudes/STUD/2018/621811/EPRS_STU(2018)621811_EN.pdf. Accessed 6 July 2021
Renard T, Coolsaet R (2019) New Figures on European Nationals Detained in Syria and Iraq. Egmont Institute Research Note. www.egmontinstitute.be/content/uploads/2019/10/Renard-Coolsaet-EU-FTF-in-detention_figures.pdf?type=pdf. Accessed 6 July 2021
Ruys T, van Severen S (2018) Art. 141bis Sw. – Vervolging tussen hamer en aambeeld van terreurbestrijding en internationaal humanitair recht. Rechtskundig Weekblad 14:523–541
Salinas de Frías AM, Samuel K, White N (2012) Counter-Terrorism: International Law and Practice. Oxford University Press, Oxford
Sassòli M, Shany Y (2011) Debate: Should the Obligations of States and Armed Groups under International Humanitarian Law Really Be Equal? International Review of the Red Cross 93:425–436
Saul B (2006) Defining Terrorism in International Law. Oxford University Press, Oxford
Saul B (2012) Criminality and Terrorism. In: Salinas de Frías AM, Samuel K, White N (eds) Counter-Terrorism: International Law and Practice. Oxford University Press, Oxford, pp 133–170
Shany Y (2011) Human Rights and Humanitarian Law as Competing Legal Paradigms for Fighting Terror. In: Ben-Naftali O (ed) International Humanitarian Law and International Human Rights Law. Oxford University Press, Oxford, pp 13–33
Sivakumaran S (2012) The Law of Non-International Armed Conflict. Oxford University Press, Oxford
Sommario E (2016) The Status of Foreign Fighters Under International Humanitarian law. In: de Guttry A, Capone F, Paulussen C (eds) Foreign Fighters in International Law and Beyond. T.M.C. Asser Press, The Hague, pp 141–160
The Soufan Center (2021) Bringing Terrorists to Justice: Prosecuting ISIL War Crimes and Terrorism. https://thesoufancenter.org/research/bringing-terrorists-to-justice-prosecuting-isil-war-crimes-and-terrorism. Accessed 15 July 2021
Trapp K (2014) The Interaction of the International Terrorism Suppression Regime and IHL in Domestic Criminal Prosecutions: The UK Experience. In: Jinks D, Maogoto JN, Solomon S (eds) Applying International Humanitarian Law in Judicial and Quasi-Judicial Bodies. T.M.C. Asser Press, The Hague, pp 165–182
Tropini J (2019) La rupture de l'équilibre juridique de l'article 141bis du code pénal belge par la jurisprudence sur les «combattants étrangers» – La remise en cause de la répartition des compétences entre le droit international humanitaire et le droit. Military Law and the Law of War Review 57:144–188
UN (2021) ISIL Crimes Against Yazidis Constitute Genocide, UN Investigation Team Finds. https://news.un.org/en/story/2021/05/1091662. Accessed 6 July 2021
UN Office of Counter-Terrorism (2021) International Legal Instruments. www.un.org/counterterrorism/international-legal-instruments. Accessed 6 July 2021
UN Security Council (2017) Greater Cooperation Needed to Tackle Danger Posed by Returning Foreign Fighters, Head of Counter-Terrorism Office Tells Security Council. www.un.org/press/en/2017/sc13097.doc.htm. Accessed 6 July 2021
UN Security Council Counter-Terrorism Committee and Executive Directorate (CTC/CTED) (2015) Letter dated 18 February 2015 from the Chair of the Security Council Committee established pursuant to resolution 1373 (2001) concerning counter-terrorism addressed to the President of the Security Council, Annex: Bringing terrorists to justice: challenges in prosecutions related to foreign terrorist fighters. UN Doc. S/2015/123

UN Security Council Counter-Terrorism Committee and Executive Directorate (CTC/CTED) (2019) Letter dated 27 December 2019 from the Chair of the Security Council Committee established pursuant to resolution 1373 (2001) concerning counter-terrorism addressed to the President of the Security Council: Technical guide to the implementation of Security Council resolution 1373 (2001) and other relevant resolutions. UN Doc. S/2019/998

Van Poecke T, Verbruggen F, Yperman W (2021) Terrorist Offences and International Humanitarian Law: The Armed Conflict Exclusion Clause. International Review of the Red Cross 103:295–324

Van Steenberghe R (2018) Droit international humanitaire et législation belge antiterroriste : l'article 141bis du Code pénal dans les dossiers syriens et kurdes. Revue belge de droit international 2018/1:269–293

Wéry M (2019) La jurisprudence relative à la clause d'exclusion prévue à l'article 141bis du Code pénal : la difficile application du droit international humanitaire par les cours et tribunaux belges. Military Law and the Law of War Review 57:103–144

Wouters J, Van Poecke T (2018) Van strijdkrachten, terroristen en het Belgisch strafrecht. Rechtskundig Weekblad 41:1616–1621

List of National Cases

Belgium

Hakim E.: Court of First Instance of Antwerp, 13 February 2017, Judgment No. 783, File Nos. AN35.F1.1809-12 (FD35.98.47-12) – FD30.97.28-14

PKK: Court of First Instance of Brussels, Dutch-speaking, Correctional Pre-Trial Chamber, 3 November 2016, File Nos. FD.35.98.54/09 – FD.35.98.634/06 – FD.35.98.502/07; Court of Appeal of Brussels, Chamber of Indictment, 14 September 2017, Judgment No. 2017/2911 – KI 1658/17; Court of Cassation, 13 February 2018, P.17.1023.N.8; Court of Appeal of Brussels, Chamber of Indictment, 8 March 2019, Judgment No. 2019/939 – KI 555; Court of Cassation, 28 January 2020, P.19.0310.N/1

Sharia4Belgium: Court of First Instance of Antwerp, 11 February 2015, File Nos. FD35.98.47-12 – AN35.F1.1809-12, etc.; Court of Appeal of Antwerp, 27 January 2016, Judgment No. C/101/2016; Court of Cassation, 24 May 2016, P.16.0244.N

Canada

Khawaja: Ontario Superior Court of Justice, 29 October 2008, [2008] OJ No 4244 (QL); Court of Appeal for Ontario, 17 December 2010, 2010 ONCA 862; Supreme Court, 14 December 2012, 2012 SCC 69

Germany

Abdelkarim El B.: Higher Regional Court of Frankfurt am Main, 8 November 2016, 5-3 StE 4/16 - 4 - 3/16; second case: Higher Regional Court of Frankfurt am Main, 24 November 2018, 5-3 StE 4/16 - 4 - 3/17

Aria L.: Higher Regional Court of Frankfurt am Main, 12 July 2016, 5-3 StE 2/16 - 4 - 1/16; Federal Court of Justice, 27 July 2017, 3 StR 57/17

Carla-Josephine S.: Federal Court of Justice, Ruling on pre-trial detention, 17 October 2019, AK 56/19; Higher Regional Court of Düsseldorf, 29 April 2020, 7 StS 4/19

Derya Ö.: Higher Regional Court of Düsseldorf, 17 December 2019, 5 StS 2/19

Fadia S.: Federal Court of Justice, Ruling on pre-trial detention, 17 February 2021, AK 7/21; Higher Regional Court of Düsseldorf, 1 July 2021.

Jennifer W.: Federal Court of Justice, Ruling on pre-trial detention, 30 January 2019, AK 61/18; Federal Court of Justice, Ruling on pre-trial detention, 23 January 2020, StB 1/20; Higher Regional Court of Munich, 25 October 2021, 8 St 9/18

Kim Teresa A.: Federal Court of Justice, Ruling on pre-trial detention, 20 April 2021, AK 30/21; Higher Regional Court Frankfurt am Main, 29 October 2021, 5-2 OJs 29/20 - 1/21

Mine K.: Federal Court of Justice, Ruling on pre-trial detention, 15 May 2019, AK 22/19; Higher Regional Court of Düsseldorf, 4 December 2019, 2 StE 2/19

Nasim A.: Federal Court of Justice, Ruling on pre-trial detention, 9 June 2020, AK 12/20; Federal Court of Justice, Ruling on pre-trial detention, 24 September 2020, AK 31/20; Higher Regional Court of Frankfurt am Main, 28 May 2021, 5-2 OJs 24/19 - 4/20

Nils D.: Higher Regional Court of Düsseldorf, 4 March 2016, 6 StS 5/15; second case: Federal Court of Justice, Ruling on *ne bis in idem* and pre-trial detention, 18 December 2018, StB 52/18; pending at Higher Regional Court of Düsseldorf as 6 StS 5/18

Nurten J.: Federal Court of Justice, Ruling on pre-trial detention, 9 February 2021, AK 5/21; Higher Regional Court of Düsseldorf, 21 April 2021, 7 StS 2/20

Omaima A.: Higher Regional Court of Hamburg, 2 October 2020, 3 St 1/20; second case: Higher Regional Court of Hamburg, 22 July 2021, 4 St 1/21

Sabine Ulrike S.: Higher Regional Court of Stuttgart, 5 July 2019, 5 - 2 StE 11/18

Sarah O.: Federal Court of Justice, Ruling on pre-trial detention, 4 April 2019, AK 12/19; Federal Court of Justice, Ruling on pre-trial detention, 25 July 2019, AK 35/19; Higher Regional Court of Düsseldorf, 16 June 2021, 7 StS 3/19

Sibel H.: Federal Court of Justice, Ruling on pre-trial detention, 22 March 2018, StB 32/17; Higher Regional Court of Munich, 29 April 2020, 7 St 9/19 (4)

Taha A.-J.: Federal Court of Justice, Ruling on pre-trial detention, 28 April 2020, AK 10/20; Higher Regional Court of Frankfurt am Main, 30 November 2021, 5-3 StE 1/20 - 4 - 1/20

Netherlands

Context: District Court of The Hague, 10 December 2015, ECLI:NL:RBDHA:2015:14365 (original Dutch version) and ECLI:NL:RBDHA:2015:16102 (English translation)

Kesbir: Supreme Court, 7 May 2004, ECLI:NL:HR:2004:AF6988

LTTE: District Court of The Hague, 21 October 2011, ECLI:NL:RBSGR:2011:BT8829; Court of Appeal of the Hague, 30 April 2015, ECLI:NL:GHDHA:2015:1082; Supreme Court, 4 April 2017, ECLI:NL:HR:2017:574

NesmuMutawahiddeen: District Court of The Hague, 29 June 2021, ECLI:NL:RBDHA:2021:6620

Oussama A.: District Court of The Hague, 23 July 2019, ECLI:NL:RBDHA:2019:7430

United Kingdom

R v Gul: England and Wales Court of Appeal, 22 February 2012, [2012] EWCA Crim 280; Supreme Court, 23 October 2013, [2013] UKSC 64

Chapter 9
The Lack of Individualisation of Sentences and Their Enforcement at the Expense of Reintegration in France

Rebecca Mignot-Mahdavi

Contents

Abstract In 2022, around two hundred and fifty French citizens sentenced to imprisonment for offences of a terrorist character were expected to be released from prison. Many of them were convicted on the basis of their travelling or attempt to travel to areas where terrorist groups are active, like Syria. From 2015 onwards, new offences were created to make sentencing possible for individuals who have travelled or planned to travel to areas where terrorist groups are active. French judges have almost systematically made the choice of prison sentences for individuals planning to travel to Syria or returning from such areas, sometimes based on these mere facts. By definition, these individuals get out of prison after several years as prison sentences are rather short in comparison with sentences that would be pronounced under more demanding thresholds of evidence (they are quite long if we keep in mind that the mere intention to travel is sometimes punished). The question of the reintegration of these individuals into society thus must be asked. These elements of context invite us to analyse the choice of sentences, but also the phase of enforcement of these sentences and detention conditions of French individuals sentenced for offences of a terrorist character. More specifically, the following question arises: does the treatment of this category of offenders by the justice and prison systems

R. Mignot-Mahdavi (✉)
School of Law, Manchester International Law Centre, University of Manchester, Manchester, UK
e-mail: rebecca.mignot-mahdavi@manchester.ac.uk

F. Capone et al. (eds.), *Returning Foreign Fighters: Responses, Legal Challenges and Ways Forward*, https://doi.org/10.1007/978-94-6265-571-3_9

in France facilitate their reintegration into society? The chapter answers this question negatively and explains it by the lack of individualisation of sentences and their enforcement.

Keywords Foreign Fighters · Terrorists · Offenders · Counter-terrorism · Criminal law · Criminal procedure · France · Reintegration · Detention

9.1 Introduction

France is an essential case study when looking at states' responses to the foreign fighter phenomenon, with approximately 1900 French citizens who travelled to Iraq and Syria and a return rate of only 12% in 2018.[1] The French government's reluctance to repatriate its citizens,[2] including children,[3] is accompanied by a repressive response not only towards returnees but also towards individuals who *planned* to travel and join jihadist groups. At the time of finalising this chapter, the trial of individuals suspected of involvement in the 2015 Paris attacks is taking place.[4] The main perpetrators, however, Amedy Coulibaly and the Kouachi brothers, were killed by police forces during the attacks, and the trajectory of their radicalisation appears only in the background of the trial. In 2005, Chérif Kouachi was intercepted at the airport where he was about to travel to Damascus. In 2011, Saïd Kouachi visited Yemen, where he was trained by Al Qaeda. In the coming months, hundreds of French citizens, men, women and children, are expected to seek to return from Kurdish territories in Syria.[5] In 2022, another two hundred and fifty French citizens sentenced to imprisonment for offences of a terrorist character were expected to be released from prison.[6] Many of them were convicted on the basis of their travelling or attempting to travel to areas where terrorist groups train their recruits or plan/conduct attacks, like Syria.[7]

---

[1] Scherrer 2018, p. 32.

[2] Wintour 2021.

[3] Méheut and Hubbard 2020.

[4] Mediapart 2020.

[5] Hubbard and Méheut 2020; Méheut and Hubbard 2020. It should be noted that the new Minister of Justice Dupond-Moretti supports the repatriation of French women and children from Syria: Le Monde 2020.

[6] Arama 2020; Brocard 2020, p. 6.

[7] See below for multiple references to relevant case law. These are a few interesting decisions: Cour de cassation (France), Chambre criminelle, 12 July 2016, 16-82.692; Cour de cassation (France), Chambre criminelle, 7 October 2016, 16-84.579; Cour de cassation (France), Chambre criminelle, 7 February 2017, 16-87.084; Chambre de l'instruction de la cour d'appel de Paris, 15 January 2019, 2019-01-15; Cour de cassation (France), Chambre criminelle, 19 February 2019, 18-81.096; Cour de cassation (France), Chambre criminelle, 20 February 2019, 18-80.777; Cour de cassation (France), Chambre criminelle, 13 March 2019, 18-87.161; Cour de cassation (France), Chambre criminelle, 10 April 2019, 19-80.493; Cour de cassation (France), Chambre criminelle, 4 June 2019, 18-85.042; Cour de cassation, Chambre criminelle, 25 March 2020, 19-83.056.

Several elements must be emphasised in this context: (i) in line with the United Nations Security Council Resolution 2178 (2014),[8] new offences were created to make sentencing possible for individuals who have travelled or planned to travel to areas where terrorist groups are active; (ii) French judges have almost systematically made the choice of prison sentences for individuals planning to travel to Syria or returning from such areas; (ii) these individuals get out of prison after several years. These elements invite us to analyse the choice of sentences, but also the phase of enforcement of these sentences and the detention conditions of French individuals sentenced for offences of a terrorist character. More specifically, considering that these individuals will all exit prison at a certain point in time, the following question arises: does the treatment of terrorists by the justice and prison systems in France facilitate their reintegration into society? The present chapter answers this question negatively and explains this finding by the lack of individualisation of sentences and their enforcement.

Some definitional elements are necessary at this point. Reintegration can be defined as the process through which the criminal justice system supports offenders in their transition from the criminal justice system (including but not limited to incarceration) to their re-entry into society following the execution of their sentence.[9] The objective of reintegration should be at the heart of any criminal justice system.[10] The International Covenant on Civil and Political Rights (ICCPR), which has an infra-constitutional but supra legislative status in France,[11] states that the essential principle of the treatment of prisoners is their reformation and social rehabilitation.[12] The notion of rehabilitation is often used as a synonym of reintegration—but also more specifically used in the context of prisons. In contrast, reintegration is used for any type of sentences.[13] For clarity purposes, awaiting further research clarifying the

---

[8] UN Security Council (2014) Resolution 2178 (2014), UN Doc. S/RES/2178, para 6(a). See also Chap. 5 by van Ginkel in this volume.

[9] United Nations Office on Drugs and Crime (UNODC) 2006. In a similar vein, reintegration has also been defined as as 'a safe transition to the community, by which the individual proceeds to live a law-abiding life following his or her release and acquires attitudes and behaviours that generally lead to productive functioning in society', in Veldhuis 2012. Building upon this definition: Weggemans and de Graaf 2019.

[10] Many scholars and international organisations seem to use reintegration and rehabilitation interchangeably and this epistemological confusion would deserve further research. For the scope and purpose of this chapter, because I am interested in the interactions between the individual and its (local and national) communities and in how detention can help this relationship to move from tense to peaceful, using the concept of social reintegration suffices. I might at times refer to sources using both concepts.

[11] Article 55 of the French Constitution of the Fifth Republic, 1958, https://www.conseil-constitutionnel.fr/le-bloc-de-constitutionnalite/texte-integral-de-la-constitution-du-4-octobre-1958-en-vigueur.

[12] International Covenant on Civil and Political Rights, opened for signature 16 December 1966, 999 UNTS 171 (entered into force 23 March 1976) in accordance with Article 49, Article 10.3.3, the penitentiary system shall comprise treatment of prisoners the essential aim of which shall be their reformation and social rehabilitation. Juvenile offenders shall be segregated from adults and be accorded treatment appropriate to their age and legal status.

[13] UNODC 2006, p. 1.

conceptual distinction between the two concepts, this chapter uses only the broader concept of reintegration as defined above. The UN Standard Minimum Rules for the Treatment of Prisoners state very clearly that even in the case where the primary purpose of a given sentence of imprisonment is to protect society against crime or its perpetrator, this objective is reachable only if the period of imprisonment is used to ensure the harmonious return to society of the offender.[14]

This contribution shows that reintegration cannot take place without the individualisation of punishment and personalisation of how sentences are enforced. The individualisation of punishment and sentence enforcement (hereafter referred to as 'individualisation') can be defined as the choice made by the actors of the justice and penal systems to adapt sentences, conditions of detention and arrangements for early release to the facts of the case, the personality and family as well as professional situations of the offender, but also to his/her behaviour throughout the proceedings and in detention.[15] To reach the objective of reintegration, the principle of individualisation should drive not only the choice of the sanction but also that of the regime of detention and its conditions of application. This requires the justice and penal systems to remain open, flexible and adaptable to the individual.[16] The openness of the penal system is achieved under the condition that legal norms (i) offer a sufficient range of sentences and modalities of enforcement to the judge, but also (ii) allow for procedural channels for interaction and adaptation of the sentence initially pronounced throughout the enforcement period.

I build the idea that there is no such thing as reintegration without individualisation on criminal legal theory drawing from Saleilles,[17] Beccaria,[18] and Marc Ancel[19] and major contemporary criminal legal scholars such as Christine Lazerges[20] or Pierrette

[14] UN Standard Minimum Rules for the Treatment of Prisoners, Adopted by the First United Nations Congress on the Prevention of Crime and the Treatment of Offenders, held at Geneva in 1955, and approved by the Economic and Social Council by its resolutions 663 C (XXIV) of 31 July 1957 and 2076 (LXII) of 13 May 1977, Rule 58.

[15] Beccaria 1764; Saleilles 2018; Cornu 2016.

[16] Makris 2020; the author defines the 'openness' of a legal framework as "the conceptual elasticity of legal norms" as well as "the factual sensitivity of law application".

[17] Saleilles 2018.

[18] Beccaria 1764.

[19] Ancel 1954.

[20] Professor Christine Lazerges was President of the French National Consultative Commission for Human Rights when the legislative proposal for the prevention of recidivism and the individualisation of sentences was debated in Parliament. It is in this quality, but also as former deputy and vice-president of the National Assembly known for being the special rapporteur on a 2000 law reinforcing the presumption of innocence and the rights of victims, that she was heard in Parliament. She emerged as a strong advocate of the principle of individualisation and argued that the law should not only apply it to the sentence but also extend its application to the phase of enforcement of the sentence. See for more details Lazerges 2014 and 2018.

Poncela.[21] All of these prominent thinkers consider individualisation as a cornerstone of sentencing and as the only way to facilitate the offenders' reintegration into society. This explains why most European criminal codes contain such a principle, reinforced in France by a statute of 2014 even if not sufficiently, according to some commentators.[22] Article 130-1 of the French criminal code now explicitly provides that "in order to ensure the protection of society, to prevent that similar offences are committed and in order to re-establish social balance, the objective of a sentence is to (1) punish the offender; (2) facilitate his/her rehabilitation and reintegration".[23] In the same vein, article 132-1 of the criminal code now reads "all sentences should be individualised".[24] Furthermore, I build on empirical insights derived mainly from the most recent report of the General Controller of Places of Deprivation of Liberty, Adeline Hazan,[25] and on a very recently published investigation from within the prison system of "radicalised detainees" and on their conditions of detention.[26]

Although individualisation in sentencing and enforcement of the sanction is key to making the criminal justice system supportive of the objective of reintegration, we see the opposite tendency in how offences of a terrorist character are addressed in France. I exclude from the scope of analysis individuals detected in detention as radicalised and focus only on individuals whose imprisonment sentence responds to offences related to terrorism. In particular, I study the cases of those who had left France to join a terrorist organisation engaged in an armed conflict[27] and cases of

[21] Casadamont and Poncela 2004. Professor Pierrette Poncela was also heard in Parliament on the Draft Law on the prevention of recidivism and the individualisation of sentences, Senate, 14 May 2014, http://www.senat.fr/rap/l13-641-2/l13-641-2.html#toc8. She appeared as even more critical than her colleague: first, she considered that the individualisation of sentences is essential not to prevent recidivism *per se* as the draft law seemed to say, but to facilitate reintegration; second, she regrets the lack of precision on the functions of sentences.

[22] Statute: LOI n° 2014-896, 15 August 2014 relative à l'individualisation des peines et renforçant l'efficacité des sanctions pénales.

[23] Article 130-1 of the French Criminal Code, created by the Statute LOI n°2014-896 of 15 August 2014, Article 1, https://www.legifrance.gouv.fr/codes/id/LEGIARTI000029363621/2014-10-01/.

[24] Article 132-1 of the French Criminal Code, created by the Statute LOI n°2014-896 of 15 August 2014, Article 2, https://www.legifrance.gouv.fr/codes/id/LEGIARTI000029370560/2014-10-01/#:~:text=Article%20132%2D1,-Modifi%C3%A9%20par%20LOI&text=Lorsque%20la%20loi%20ou%20le,la%20juridiction%20doit%20%C3%AAtre%20individualis%C3%A9e.

[25] General Controller of Places of Deprivation of Liberty (in French Contrôleur Général des Lieux de Privation de Liberté, or CGLPL) 2020 (CGLPL Report). The Controller is an independent body whose functions were established by a Law of 30 October 2007. She controls the conditions of management of people who are deprived of liberty, checks the enforcement of their fundamental rights. She does not receive instructions from any authority. See report here: https://www.cglpl.fr/wp-content/uploads/2020/06/CGLPL-Prise-en-charge-p%C3%A9nitentiaire-des-personnes-radicalis%C3%A9es-et-respect-des-droits-fondamentaux.pdf. Adeline Hazan was Controller until 17 July 2020. She has not been replaced yet at the time of finalising this chapter.

[26] Brocard 2020.

[27] de Guttry et al. 2016, p. 2. Their definition built on Geneva Academy of International Humanitarian Law and Human Rights 2014, p. 6: "A foreign fighter is an individual who leaves his or her country of origin or habitual residence to join a non-state armed group in an armed conflict abroad and who is primarily motivated by ideology, religion, and/or kinship."

individuals who were *about* to leave, got arrested at the border or before reaching it based on their online communications, and were sentenced precisely on the basis of their project of departure to conflict zones. I should also mention that when analysing the conditions of detention, I do not include those of accused persons but only the situation of convicted ones.

After observing the lack of individualisation of sentencing for these cases, I show how the enforcement of the sentence also lacks necessary levels of personalisation. This is the case because of systemic and procedural reasons, which negatively constrain the attempts of the different actors who intervene in prison (from carceral staff to psychologists) to individualise the way the sentence is enforced. The first reason for this constraining framework is the choice made by policy makers to use the criminal justice system mainly as a tool to exclude these individuals, and this is reflected in the adoption of new rules incorporated into the criminal code and the criminal procedure code. This criminal policy choice might be understandable when formulated to face security threats, but is also very short-sighted. Indeed, it does not take into consideration that these convicted individuals will inevitably return to society after going through the criminal system. The second major reason for that has to do with the 'law in action': judges tend not to individualise sentencing as much as the law allows them to in terrorism-related cases. As a result, the return to society of these individuals seems even less prepared than for other convicted persons. This phenomenon shows how an exclusive reliance upon the security paradigm is ill-suited to actually make society healthier and safer in the long run.

9.2 "All Dangerous": The Absence of Individualisation of Punishment

> They are all dangerous, all have the potential of planting bombs. The individuals who appear in court in front of me have increasingly concerning profiles. I perceive a dangerousness that I did not perceive before. I adapt. By the end of 2016, there is almost no individualisation of sentencing and punishment.[28]

These are the words of Judge Céline Ballerini, interviewed by Véronique Brocard in her investigation *Les Sortants*. At the time of the facts that she mentions in her testimony, Judge Ballerini was sitting at the 16th chamber of the first instance tribunal of Paris in charge of terrorist affairs. A few months later, she would resign from her functions, feeling that the way she and her colleagues were deciding on cases of terrorism did not correspond anymore to the guiding principles of judicial review and, more generally, of the criminal justice system: the individualisation of punishment. The developments below describe how both law in the text—in particular offences

[28] "Ils sont tous dangereux, tous des poseurs de bombe en puissance. Les personnes qui me sont présentées ont des profils de plus en plus inquiétants. Je perçois cette dangerosité que je ne percevais pas avant. Je m'adapte. À partir de fin 2016, il n'y a quasiment plus d'individualisation de la peine." 16e chambre, Judge Céline Ballerini quoted by Brocard 2020, p. 116.

created in recent years following terrorist attacks in France and law in action, in other words interpretative choices made by judges mainly after the attacks perpetrated on French soil—correspond to systemic sentencing of the accused.

Someone can be found criminally responsible only for his or her own wrongdoing. Criminal judges must identify the individual responsibility of the accused in order to sentence him or her, and this still entails in French criminal law to identify both an *actus reus* (a "guilty act") and a *mens rea* (a "guilty mind"). This section shows that in terrorist cases, both are fading. I find that punishment is not individualised both because the material element, or *actus reus*, is diluted in terrorist cases and because the mental element, or *mens rea*, is less and less a requirement to find the accused guilty.

9.2.1 Intangible: The Actus Reus *in Terrorist Cases*

9.2.1.1 Glorification of Terrorism

A 2016 law "reinforcing the fight against organised crime, terrorism and their financing" criminalised the "apology/glorification of terrorism".[29] Article 421-2-5-1 of the criminal code defines this new offence as the "fact of intentionally and publicly quoting, reproducing or sharing elements that glorify acts of terrorism or encouraging the perpetration of such acts".[30] This new offence has been used to regulate speech not only online but also in the physical world. Case law shows that judges have interpreted the offence in a way that allows them to incorporate a wide range of situations within its material scope. For instance, in a decision of 4 June 2019, the last instance tribunal, the Court of Cassation, annulled a decision of a court of appeal that considered constitutive of apology for terrorism the fact that a hospital patient made mention of his allegiance to ISIS and desire to travel to Syria to the medical staff.[31] The Court of Cassation considered that making a clear and unequivocal "statement of allegiance to a terrorist organisation responsible for several attacks perpetrated on French soil, to intimidate and threaten" the staff of the hospital could only create fear and rejection, and as such, met the material requirements of Article 421-2-5 of the criminal code. The interpretation of the expression of allegiance to a terrorist group as its "glorification" can be defined as an extensive interpretation of the offence's material scope.

---

[29] Statute: LOI n° 2016-731 du 3 juin 2016 renforçant la lutte contre le crime organisé, le terrorisme et leur financement, et améliorant l'efficacité et les garanties de la procédure pénale, https://www.legifrance.gouv.fr/jorf/id/JORFTEXT000032627231/.

[30] Article 421-2-5-1 French Criminal Code, https://www.legifrance.gouv.fr/codes/article_lc/LEGIARTI000032633494.

[31] Cour de cassation (France), Chambre criminelle, 4 June 2019, 18-85.042.

9.2.1.2 Non-Reporting of a Crime

In the same vein, judges have interpreted the material element of the offence of non-reporting of a crime[32] in a loose way in the counter-terrorism context. It should be noted that when an offence indirectly concerns an act committed by someone else, the *actus reus* is composite and includes both the main offence and the personal act (or omission to act). Applied to the non-reporting of a crime, this cornerstone principle should still require identifying (i) the main offence (the non-reported crime) and (ii) the omission to report the main offence. Terrorism-related case law shows, however, that this offence is used to punish non-reporting, not of a crime but of potentially dangerous people.

A defendant was accused of concealing information about the crime committed by a friend of his. He knew, as evidence showed, that this friend had tried to travel to Syria in 2015; she had also mentioned to him her willingness to try again despite the difficulty to cross borders. The investigation established moreover that the accused knew her allegiance to ISIS and her desire to die as a martyr. On the day that she would commit an attack in Paris, she had texted him saying that she had "decided to join the Hereafter rather than to live in this world".[33] From their exchanges that day, she declared that her friend had probably understood that she was about to commit a crime. Among other things, she mentioned the very long messages he had sent her trying to make her change her mind.

On this basis, a first instance tribunal considered that the accused had sufficient knowledge of the radical ideas of his friend and could perceive the imminence of her committing a terrorist act. The first instance judges thus sentenced the accused for not having reported it to the authorities in view of preventing the crime's effects. The Court of Appeal of Paris, in a decision of 15 January 2019, annulled the decision on the basis that the accused did not possess any information about the crime that his friend was about to commit, nor even clear information on whether, where, and how she was going to commit any crime.[34] The Court of Cassation, however, in a decision of 10 April 2019, considered that Article 434-1 does not require that the elements of the main crime are planned, established *or known*.[35] The judges emphasised that the accused was prosecuted for not having reported *a* terrorist act, and not *the* specific terrorist act that his friend had committed. In other words, the court found that the perception that a crime might be committed in the near future is sufficient to be found guilty of this offence.[36]

---

[32] Article 434-1 of the French Criminal Code, https://www.legifrance.gouv.fr/codes/article_lc/LEGIARTI000032207673/.

[33] Cour de cassation (France), Chambre criminelle, 10 April 2019, 19-80.493.

[34] Chambre de l'instruction de la cour d'appel de Paris, 15 January 2019, 2019-01-15.

[35] Cour de cassation (France), Chambre criminelle, 10 April 2019, 19-80.493. Emphasis added.

[36] It is also interesting to note in this case how the *mens rea* is diluted. In theory, this offence requires to have knowledge of the main offence. Not only do we see here that the existence of the main offence had not—as far as we know—started to take shape at the time of the omission to report, but judges also do not expect the knowledge of such a crime to be demonstrated. It shows the cascade effect of depriving an offence of its materiality on its moral prong.

9.2.1.3 Participation in a Terrorist Group

An offence that has played a major role in sending individuals to jail for their (project of) travelling to Syria is Article 421-2-1, which criminalises the participation in a group or alliance established in view of the preparation of acts of terrorism as an act of terrorism itself.[37] Such a 'participation' (we will see how it is defined by case law in a bit), if established, can lead to a sanction of up to ten years imprisonment, or even up to twenty years of imprisonment if the group aims to prepare acts that can cause grave harm to human lives or involve the destruction of explosive substances that can cause human deaths. Leading or organising the activities of such a group can be punished by up to 30 years of imprisonment. Since the 2010s, many individuals who have travelled or planned to travel to Syria have been prosecuted on this basis. Established case law provides that for an individual to be punished on this basis, there is no need for him or her to have participated in the preparation or commission of the group's terrorist acts. It suffices to identify that the accused belongs to the group that commits terrorist acts. Besides, traveling to Syria or planning to travel to Syria are taken as sufficient signs of belonging to the group.

In a decision of 12 July 2016, the Court of Cassation decided upon the case of two French citizens, a couple, who had travelled to Syria in 2013 where, they declared, they were living with ISIS members but had refused to participate in any operation conducted by ISIS.[38] The investigation file contained a picture of one of the defendants holding the head of a beheaded person and several communications of the couple, upon their return in France, with people willing to travel to ISIS camps in Syria. The question was whether, on this basis, the couple could be indicted for participation in a group established in view of the preparation of acts of terrorism. Confirming established case law, the judges answered that Article 421-2-1 does not require evidence that the accused has participated in the preparation of such acts. Rather, evidence of belonging to the group is sufficient. In this case, belonging to the group was, of course, not contested.

The Court of Cassation confirmed this interpretation again in a decision of 13 March 2019 concerning two defendants who had travelled to Syria and respectively joined ISIS and Jabhat al Nusra.[39] There was no evidence of participation in combat or in the preparation of any terrorist acts. Pictures of them carrying weapons were in the file but did not allow them to establish their participation in lethal terrorist operations. The accused alleged that they had only participated in training and surveillance missions. Judges found that in any case, regardless of the exact functions and missions undertaken as members of terrorist organisations, their belonging to the group was sufficient to establish their participation in a group established in view of the preparation of terrorist acts "legitimising and organising assassinations".[40]

[37] Article 421-2-1 of the French Criminal Code, https://www.legifrance.gouv.fr/codes/article_lc/LEGIARTI000006418432/.

[38] Cour de cassation (France), Chambre criminelle, 12 July 2016, 16-82.692.

[39] Cour de cassation (France), Chambre criminelle, 13 March 2019, 18-87.161.

[40] Ibid.

At this point, the evolution of the case law appears quite reasonable even if judges notably adopt a flexible interpretation of 'participation' in a terrorist group. The Court of Cassation went further, however, by sentencing individuals who had planned to travel to Syria to join ISIS on this basis. In a decision of 19 February 2019, the last instance judges confirmed the sentence of six years imprisonment pronounced for participation in a group established in view of the organisation of terrorist acts and assassinations for an individual who had planned to travel to Syria and whose telecommunications showed interest and acceptance of ISIS' ideology (which he did not deny).[41] The Court confirmed the first instance sentencing decision by following this reasoning:

1. The documents and communications found in the phone and computer of the accused show allegiance to ISIS;
2. The United Nations, the Council of Europe and French authorities, have all recognised ISIS as a terrorist organisation;
3. This organisation has claimed multiple acts criminalised by Article 421-1 of the criminal code;
4. Several elements show that in addition to his allegiance to the group, the accused was about to commit some acts in the name of the organisation, such as travelling to Syria and facilitating the departure of other individuals;
5. Article 421-2-1 is constituted regardless of specific information or evidence of involvement in the crimes that the group intends to commit.

On the question of whether the sanction of six years imprisonment without suspension was justified considering that the accused had not even travelled to Syria, the judges considered that he had joined a particularly active and dangerous terrorist organisation. According to them, the identity and actions of the group alone justified the sanction. Going further, the Court of Cassation also considered that first instance and appeal judges did well to consider that the individual whose Facebook profile and online conversations showed allegiance to ISIS and mentioned a potential trip to Syria is a participant in a terrorist organisation under Article 421-2-1 of the criminal code. He was sentenced to four years imprisonment.

Judges follow similar reasoning and pronounce similar sentences even when the accused had a plan to travel somewhere close to areas occupied by terrorist groups but without clear evidence that the accused planned to join that specific area or the terrorist group. This was the situation of a defendant who was, in the last instance, sentenced by the Court of Cassation to nine years of imprisonment.[42] The accused had always denied having travelled to Iraq and Turkey with the objective of joining ISIS in Syria, and no evidence demonstrated with certainty that he had spent time with the group, or even unequivocal evidence that he went there with the hope of joining the group at all. Judges of the Court of Appeal of Paris had found that the accused did not provide any legitimate justification to explain his presence on these foreign territories and for having, beforehand, rejected an offer to extend his working

[41] Cour de cassation (France), Chambre criminelle, 19 February 2019, 18-81.096.

[42] Cour de cassation (France), Chambre criminelle, 20 February 2019, 18-80.777.

contract and put an end to his rental contract in Francewhich he explained by the fact that the apartment was unhealthy.[43] Although he had bought a two-way plane ticket Sofia-Istanbul, judges also considered that travelling by bus from France to Sofia with his child and putting the latter in such extreme travelling conditions revealed a strong desire to get to Turkey that did not correspond to the narrative of the accused that they were merely travelling as tourists. Besides, judges focused on the accused's friendship with a man whose links with ISIS and project to join the group were established. These ties were defined as close and continuous on the basis of 1 356 phone calls between the two men between 12 February 2014 and 29 December 2014. Contacts were also established by the accused and his wife with people in Gaziantep, a city known to be a zone of transfer for people willing to join ISIS. Last instance judges considered well argued the decision establishing that the accused had formed, "together with the persons accompanying him", a group or alliance to organise a trip "in an occult manner" to an area occupied by the terrorist organisation ISIS in order to commit acts of terrorism and sentencing him to nine years imprisonment for such acts. Any other sanction, the court adds, would have been "clearly inappropriate".[44]

9.2.1.4 *Actus Reus*: Concluding Remarks

This section established a few helpful elements. First, the offences that have allowed to place individuals in detention in the counter-terrorism context are offences that do not punish violent acts, but speech or belonging to a group established in view of preparing terrorist acts. Thus, most of these people are detained mainly in order to prevent the harm that they could cause to other members of society. This means that the material element of these offences is already less tangible than that of a criminal offence punishing a directly harmful act. Second, the section has shown that these preventive offences are interpreted in a way that puts the constitutive threshold of the material element quite low. Judges find that the material element of glorification is constituted when someone expresses allegiance to the group. They consider the material element of participation in a terrorist group constituted when a person has plans to join the group, or when a person travels somewhere close to the group's camp and has ties with members of the group. As a result of this case law, what remains of the material element of these preventive offences is reduced, which, in turn, multiplies the instances where people are sentenced.

---

[43] Ibid.

[44] Ibid.

9.2.2 *Vanished: The* Mens Rea *of Participation Dissolved into the Material Elements of the Crime*

The abovementioned Article 421-2-1 of the criminal code punishing the participation in a group established in view of the preparation of acts of terrorism is not a new offence. However, it leads, as we saw, to interesting case law in the counter-terrorism context. This is also true with regard to how judges interpret the mental element of the offence. According to consistent case law, there is no need to demonstrate the willingness of the author to pursue the terrorist objectives of the group for the *mens rea* to be established. Let me unpack this through a first example.

The French wife of a Franco-Turkish ISIS member was prosecuted and sentenced for participation in a terrorist group by a first instance tribunal.[45] Her husband had travelled to Turkey and then to Syria and, upon his return to France, shared stories about his unsuccessful attempt to die as a martyr for the jihadist cause. Investigations showed that his wife had travelled to Turkey and Syria to meet and live with her husband, but also that she is the one who gave him money to travel there. This led the first instance judges to sentence her for participation in a terrorist group. However, the Court of Appeal re-analysed the facts and considered that she had financed his trip to Turkey only because, at first, she thought that he was going to visit his family there. Judges found that she had travelled to meet him in Syria after he threatened to commit suicide if she did not join him; so her reason for traveling was *not* to support his jihadist project, but, on the very contrary, to try and save him from ISIS ideology. They added that she had accepted to marry him in a religious ceremony upon arrival in Syria, not because she embraced ISIS rules but because she needed to go through such a ceremony in order to be authorised to live together with her husband. Finally, judges emphasised that the investigation showed she had acquired a weapon not to combat in ISIS' ranks but to protect herself from them. On this basis, the appeal judges acquitted the defendant as they considered that the intentional element of the offence was not constituted. In the last instance, however, the Court of Cassation while it did not deny any of these established facts on which the Court of Appeal's decision was grounded—decided that Article 421-2-1 does not require to prove any intention to see the terrorist project of the group realised. Judges considered that the *mens rea* is constituted by the mere voluntary participation in their activities, and confirmed the sanction pronounced by the first instance tribunal.

The Court of Cassation went even further when it considered in a decision of 7 October 2016 that Article 421-2-1 is infringed even if the person who materially participates in the group has no precise or concrete knowledge of the group's project of harming lives.[46] The case concerned the brother of an ISIS member who had travelled to Cairo on several occasions to follow language courses, expressed heinous

[45] Facts and procedure recalled by the last instance court's decision, Cour de cassation (France), Chambre criminelle, 7 February 2017, 16-87.084.

[46] Cour de cassation (France), Chambre criminelle, 7 October 2016, 16-84.579.

discourses upon his return—mentioning a necessity to "fight against the Jews, Americans and unbelievers".[47] He had been sentenced in the past for assaulting his brother because he disapproved of his relationship with a Jewish woman. Other elements that played a role in determining his guilt were his declarations on the death of his martyr brother (he said that he was proud of the way he died, as a fighter, by the "enemy, that is France") but also on his religious conversations with his brother before his death. Most of all, the fact that the accused regularly met with his brother before he perpetrated a terrorist offence played an important role in determining his guilt, even if these meetings were not clearly linked to the terrorist offence. Evidence showed that they had met for a football game, for dinner but also, and more suspicious for the court, when his brother stole the scooter that would serve him during the commission of the terrorist offence. The Court of Appeal considered that the radical ideology of the defendant and the fact that he regularly met with his brother was insufficient to consider that he had the knowledge of the acts his brother would commit and even less the intention for him to do so. On the contrary, the Court of Cassation considered that there was no need to identify precise and concrete knowledge of a group's project to voluntarily harm human lives in order to establish the *mens rea* of participation in a terrorist group. Yet, because French criminal law still commands that both the *actus reus* and *mens rea* be identified to find someone guilty of a crime, judges artificially construct the *mens rea*. In a tautological manner, they derive the intention to participate from the participation itself.

In sum, this first part has shown several key elements already. First, offences are interpreted in an extensive manner, and low thresholds are established to define both the intentional and material elements of the crime. Most interestingly, the offence of participation in a group formed with a view to perpetrating terrorist acts is interpreted as requiring no other material element but the belief in ISIS ideology and as requiring no other intentional element but the voluntary participation in activities connected to the group or some of its members. Second, the dilution of the elements of the crime makes sentencing a systemic exercise that consists in pronouncing prison sentences for anybody who shows allegiance to the group, including by planning to travel or travelling to a territory where a terrorist group is known to be established. All in all, these individuals are incarcerated for being dangerous individuals—or rather, potentially dangerous ones.

9.3 From Isolation to "Dry Exit": The Absence of Individualisation of the Enforcement Phase

In order to counterbalance the low thresholds for sentencing, the choice of sanction could be at least partly individualised if judges took into consideration the level of social integration of the offender when choosing the sentence. However, this section shows that policy makers, the legislator and most judges make the choice of excluding

[47] Ibid.

these individuals from the rest of society for as long as possible. A project of social reintegration would require having recourse to alternative measures or early release when it appears meaningful. Because these options are overall excluded, the objective of reintegration is not reflected in the choice of sentences as shown in the first part of this section. Then, as the second part of this section shows, once the offenders start serving their sentence, the objective of reintegration is also absent from the detention process. I study special detention regimes deriving from the detention strategy applied to 'TIS', which is part of the national strategy for the prevention of terrorism on domestic soil. It rests on three pillars: (i) special detention regimes are preferred (either in solitary confinement, or in a "special unit for the evaluation of radicalisation" or in a "special unit for radicalised detainees"); (ii) detection, reporting of radicalised detainees and monitoring of their degree of dangerousness are at the heart of the detention period; (iii) deradicalisation of detainees is supported, including by sharing counter-narratives.[48] Although the detention staff and psychologists intervening in prison may intend to make the detention phase meaningful in that regard, the system forces its actors to focus on security and data collection. Interactions with detainees are not used to facilitate reintegration. Rather, they are meant to track dangerousness and identify who, in detention, needs to be placed in facilities for radicalised persons and who, after the detention phase, will need to be monitored and subjected to close surveillance.

9.3.1 Generalised Isolation from the Outside as Long as Possible

In her 2020 report, the (now former) General Controller of Places of Deprivation of Liberty, Adeline Hazan, explains how the quantum of punishment increased with the adoption of the 2016 Law reinforcing the fight against terrorism.[49] She adds that detention almost always starts before trial, and notices that both men and women are systematically incarcerated for travelling or planning to travel to Syria. She goes on to quote a prosecutor who, she says, is very clear on his objective to exclude as much as possible and for as long as possible from society any foreign fighter or foreign fighter to be:

> The goal is to protect society by putting these individuals as long as possible in prison. Prison is also capable, in principle, of helping their reintegration and rehabilitation. But even though we can lead a horse to water, we cannot make it drink if it is not thirsty. When we have in front of us individuals who are absorbed by deadly desires, keeping them in jail might not be the noblest mission but it has, at least, the imperious virtue of protecting society.[50]

[48] Toutain 2019, pp. 301–304.

[49] CGLPL Report 2020, p. 8. Article 421-3 of the French Penal Code.

[50] Le Monde (2016) Le procureur de Paris François Molins : " Le risque d'attentat est renforcé ". https://www.lemonde.fr/police-justice/article/2016/09/02/francois-molins-l-affaiblissement-de-l-ei-renforce-le-risque-d-attentat_4991439_1653578.html. Accessed 14 November 2020.

This prosecutor does not seem to believe that reintegration can be successfully pursued in detention for this category of offenders. Rather, in his view, prisons should be used to the fullest to exclude these individuals from society as much as possible. This logic practically entails supporting the most severe sanction possible and excluding any adjustment of the sentence throughout its enforcement.

A "dry exit" precisely occurs when the entire imprisonment sentence is spent in detention, and the detainee exits without having benefited from any adjustment of the sentence. This term, common in French criminal law ('sortie sèche'), is not new as it can generally happen that a detainee does not benefit from such adjustments. However, the systematic exclusion of a category of detainees, here the category of individuals sentenced for terrorist offencesofficially referred to as 'TIS'—is new.[51] This exclusion is particularly important to examine for our inquiry because it means that their behaviour and evolution in detention is not followed with favourable measures, although such measures would allow a smoother transition from the inside to the outside.

Since 2015, and even more so since the above mentioned 2016 Law, terrorist offenders do not, *de jure* and *de facto*, benefit from a reduction of the level of their sentence or adjustment of its modalities. First, *de jure*, the Law of 21 July 2016 excludes them from automatic sentence reduction credits that apply to all other detainees to incentivise good behaviour. They can only apply for it. However, and this is why they are *de facto* excluded from such measures, the judge in charge of sentence enforcement generally refuses such requests when they come from terrorist offenders.[52] Of course, there are exceptions to this tendency. In a decision of 25 March 2020, the Court of Cassation annulled the decision of the sentence enforcement tribunal of the Paris Court of Appeal that had refused to place a person who had been convicted to 5 years imprisonment for travelling to Syria under electronic surveillance for the rest of his detention period (20 months).[53] He had completed most of his detention sentence in the pre-trial period. The last instance judges considered that the Paris Court of Appeal should have taken into consideration the signs of social reintegration shown by him in detention.

However, sentence enforcement tribunals very rarely accept requests for sentence adjustment. This is true to such a degree that lawyers speak with the despair of their uselessness in the process of automatic sentencing and in front of judges' reluctance to accept requests to adjust the modalities of enforcement of the sentence. Lawyer

---

[51] For a recent official use of the label "TIS", see Law proposal n° 2554 "establishing security measures (mesures de sûreté) for authors of terrorist offences at the end of the detention period", submitted by the government on 10 March 2020, http://www.assemblee-nationale.fr/dyn/15/textes/l15b2754_proposition-loi. The introduction of the text explicitly uses the term "islamist terrorist" and the label "TIS" as the object and focus of the proposal.

[52] Law proposal "establishing security measures (mesures de sûreté) for authors of terrorist offences at the end of the detention period", submitted by the government on 10 March 2020. In the introduction of their proposal, they refer to this *de jure* and *de facto* exclusion of terrorist offenders from usual sentence reduction or adjustment mechanisms.

[53] Sentence enforcement tribunal of the Court of Appeal of Paris, 26 March 2019, 19-83.056. Annulled by Cour de cassation, Chambre criminelle, 25 March 2020, 19-83.056.

Me Jérémie Boccara recounts his "traumatic" experiences in front of enforcement judges in terrorism cases:

> I will not go back there; it was too traumatic. I was pleading for a client who had been sentenced to three years imprisonment, of which half was to be suspended, for a small case of terrorist funding. He was completely reintegrated and stable, had three kids. He had just started a small business. His offense dated back to quite some time. Anyway, an easy case. I told him: "you will ask the judge in charge of sentences enforcement to adjust eighteen months of imprisonment, you do not need me, you can show up alone in court, just call me if you face any issue". As planned, he got his sentence adjusted. So far, so good. But on the phone, he told me: "I have a problem, though, the prosecutor appeals the decision." When I went to court to discuss the prosecutor's appeal, I do not exaggerate, the prosecutor spoke for three minutes, not more. He opened his statement like this: "I do not want to generalise" and ended with "in any case, for terrorist offenses, no adjustment of penalties is ever acceptable." I pleaded the case for half an hour with all my might, but it did not work. The decision adjusting the sentence was annulled. My client will have to spend the full eighteen months in prison.[54]

The 2016 Law mentioned above also excluded this category of offenders from the scope of sentence enforcement regimes that are specifically designed to allow social reintegration.[55] This is, for instance, the case of day release ('mesures de semi-liberté') where detainees can leave the prison for several hours. Day releases can allow them to engage in professional activity, attend an educational course or a vocational training program, gain work experience or hold a temporary job with a view to their rehabilitation, but also simply to play a role in their family life. The law also deprives the 'TIS' of the possibility to conditionally suspend the enforcement of the sentence, in whole or in part, either at the time of the sentence ('suspended sentence') or subsequently ('early release').

This generalised dry exit is accompanied by surveillance measures outside detention facilities. It is common for the authorities to pronounce post-detention administrative measures, such as residential custody or any other "individual measure of administrative monitoring and surveillance".[56] These types of measures were established in 2017 as a temporary experiment until December 2020 and are used, among other actors, by the French General Directorate for Internal Security to monitor movements and activities of these former detainees as a way to pre-empt risks.

An example of this dry exit followed by strict surveillance measures, similar to a regime of outdoor detention, is the case of Flavien Moreau.[57] Moreau, the first French jihadist sentenced for having travelled to Syria, finished his imprisonment sentence in January 2020. Towards the end of his sentence, judges decided that he should be the object of judicial oversight for exactly eleven months and eighteen days

---

[54] Brocard 2020, p. 149. See for a similar story, ibid., pp. 64–67.

[55] See for a European analysis of criminal sanctions and their functions, reiterating the rehabilitating function of special enforcement regimes: European Commission 2004, p. 87.

[56] Statute: LOI n° 2017-1510 renforçant la sécurité intérieure et la lutte contre le terrorisme (Law strengthening homeland security and the fight against terrorism) 30 October 2017.

[57] Le Monde (2020) Le premier djihadiste français condamné à son retour de Syrie a été libéré. https://www.lemonde.fr/societe/article/2020/01/13/le-premier-djihadiste-francais-condamne-a-son-retour-de-syrie-a-ete-libere_6025744_3224.html. Accessed 14 November 2020.

with the following obligations: visits to the judge in charge of sentence enforcement and to the Prison Rehabilitation and Probation Services. Registered in the FIJAIT, the automated judiciary record of authors of terrorist offences (FIJAIT stands for *fichier judiciaire automatisé des auteurs d'infractions terroristes*), he has to justify his address every three months and declare any foreign travel. Finally, judges decided that he would be under surveillance of intelligence services as long as necessary.

The French Supreme Court ('Conseil Constitutionnel') recently halted an attempt to extend the scope of such surveillance measures.[58] A few words on this recent decision of 7 August 2020 allow us to grasp the criminal justice strategy for this category of offenders that the government, supported by a majority in Parliament, has been pushing for. The law proposal "establishing security measures ('mesures de sûreté') for authors of terrorist offences at the end of the detention period" aimed to facilitate the adoption of surveillance measures for terrorist offenders at the end of their prison sentence: instead of requiring medical expertise, dangerousness could be established otherwise and give rise to a surveillance measure.[59] It was adopted on 27 July 2020 before only one of its Articles was found consistent with the French Constitution.[60] The surveillance measures that the Conseil Constitutionnel, in charge of monitoring the conformity of French laws with the Constitution, found unconstitutional included, among other things, the prohibition against changing residence or job, the obligation to request the authorisation of the judge responsible for enforcing sentences to travel abroad, the obligation to visit enforcement authorities regularly (three times per week, or once if placed under electronic surveillance), and the prohibition to enter in contact with designated persons. This set of measures would be pronounced by the Regional Court of Paris in charge of the post-sentence preventive detention (*juridiction régionale de la rétention de sûreté*), for a year, and be renewable up to ten times.

The Conseil Constitutionnel considered the core provisions of the law unconstitutional. The supreme judges recalled that although taking strict measures to prevent recidivism and ensure public order and safety is accepted, such is only the case if there are no other measures that would allow pursuing this objective in a less harmful way for individual liberties. In this case, they found the measures disproportionate. They disapproved of the fact that the law would allow judges to pronounce such measures without checking that the person has benefitted from the necessary conditions and assistance to allow his or her reintegration while in detention. When conducting the proportionality test, they also found problematic the possibility to renew the measure

---

58 Judgement, Décision n° 2020-805 DC of 7 August 2020.

59 Law Proposal: Proposition de loi n° 2754 instaurant des mesures de sûreté à l'encontre des auteurs d'infractions terroristes à l'issue de leur peine, 10 March 2020, http://www.assemblee-nationale.fr/dyn/15/textes/l15b2754_proposition-loi.

60 Adopted version of the proposed law, after parliamentary debates: Proposition de loi n° 472, adoptée, dans les conditions prévues à l'article 45, alinéa 3, de la Constitution, par l'Assemblée nationale, instaurant des mesures de sûreté à l'encontre des auteurs d'infractions terroristes à l'issue de leur peine, 27 July 2020, http://www.assemblee-nationale.fr/dyn/15/textes/l15t0472_texte-adopte-seance.

based on the exact same criteria as those that were used to pronounce the measure in the first place.

At the end of this constitutional review process, only one article of this new 2020 Law remained valid, and it enacted a meaningful change. From then on, for this category of offenders, the exception of applying a judicial oversight after detention became the rule. This oversight mainly implies for the former detainee to respect several obligations to inform the authorities of any change in his or her situation. These offenders are registered in the FIJAIT and must notify the authorities of any meaningful life change such as an address change or any plan of foreign travel at least 15 days before the planned departure.

In the months and years to come, there will certainly be more political and legislative pressure to enhance post-detention surveillance measures for this category of detainees. In a report of 26 February 2020, the Senate Committee in charge of controlling and evaluating the application of the 2017 Law's experiments mentioned above proposed to further strengthen the surveillance of these former detainees.[61] Their proposition is to apply a ten-year surveillance regime from the outset for those who committed a terrorist misdemeanour and a twenty-year surveillance regime for those who committed a terrorist crime. It will be interesting to see if the Supreme Court keeps on exercising its checks as it recently did, or if it will succumb to the growing climate of fear and political expectation for even stricter measures.

It should be underlined that if the objective of reintegration was instrumental to the sentence enforcement period, post-detention surveillance would probably be less necessary or at least not required on a generalised level. Alain Baches, counsellor in a Penitentiary Integration and Probation Department, emphasised in an interview that in order to prepare a detainee for his or her exit, the penal system and staff must organise with his or her the conditions that should lead the judge to adapt the sentence. This involves, he says, a series of authorisations to exit without which the detainee cannot re-establish ties with his or her family and community or start taking steps to find a job and accommodation. Baches deplores that this trajectory does not exist for the detainees sentenced for terrorist offences because of the quasi-systematic refusal of judges to adapt the modalities of how their sentence is enforced. Éric Ponant, counsellor in charge of 'radicalisation' in a Penitentiary Integration and Probation Department, makes a similar observation:

> We build a file, but even if it is positive, prosecutors and judges in charge of sentence enforcement are the ones who decide in the last instance. It is already complicated in general but in this specific situation, with terrorists, it is even more complicated because we have to manage an even greater frustration. Those that we support for a temporary absence, for instance, have made an even greater and deeper self-development effort in order to reach that stage. So, of course, if judges suddenly slam the door in their faces, it generates anger and disbelief. They feel that if their request is rejected, it is because they have been labelled no matter what they do.[62]

---

[61] Senate Committee 2020.

[62] Brocard 2020, pp. 49–50.

The criminal policy for terrorist offences has clear objectives: first, to exclude as long as possible with a prison sentence that is not adapted, suspended or reduced; second, once outside, to monitor the former detainees for as long as possible.

9.3.2 *Exclusion and Isolation in Detention*

The 'special units for the evaluation of radicalisation' host terrorist offenders for a period of seventeen weeks, during which a multidisciplinary evaluation team assesses their level of radicalisation. We will come back to this risk assessment exercise later on, but we can already mention that during the four months of evaluation, a detention regime close to solitary confinement is applied to detainees who also have to attend a series of interviews with the evaluation team.[63] The 'special units for radicalised detainees' welcome those detainees who have been evaluated and their risk assessed. In practice, the transfer from a special unit of evaluation to a special unit for radicalised detainees is automatic for the detainees who were incarcerated for terrorist offences. Of course, this raises the question of what the special unit for evaluation is useful for. Three possible reasons for this special unit come to mind: first, to give the semblance of individualisation; second, to use all available facilities and expertise to collect data on the detainees; third, to submit the detainees to stricter detention conditions when they start serving their sentence. Once transferred, detainees stay in the special unit for radicalised detainees for six months that can be indefinitely renewed.

Both types of special units are described as prisons inside the prison. Bénédicte Lemieux, Director of Detention Services and Coordinator of the Mission of the Fight against Violent Radicalisation for the region of Lille, declared, for example, that "the rule is to have a reinforced security and absolute sealing. Every building, every wing and every floor is hermetically closed to one another".[64] In a context of hyper-security for this category of detainees, Adeline Hazan deplores the lack of a clear definition of 'radicalised persons', which is used to choose this exceptional detention regime for a very heterogeneous category of persons.[65] It includes detainees sentenced for offences related to terrorism, and those who were sentenced for acts unrelated to terrorism whose radicalisation was detected in detention. Besides, we saw that the persons sentenced for offences related to terrorism have very different profiles from one another. She generally notes a strong confusion between religion, political ideology and radicalisation, including in the criteria used by the actors of the detention system to evaluate detainees' radicalisation. Hazan further laments that the penitentiary administration has a unique policy and one-size-fits-all detention regime based on a "sketchy profiling of detainees".[66]

---

[63] Ibid., p. 119.

[64] Ibid., p. 121.

[65] CGLPL Report, pp. 20–21.

[66] Ibid., p. 21.

Overall, Hazan is not in favour of preventive and generalised security measures that make detention conditions quite strict for one group of detainees. She notes that contrary to commonly applied security measures, the strict regime applies not just exceptionally (for instance, after a violent event occurs in detention), but to prevent bad behaviours from happening, and closely monitor the development of certain detainees in view of their post-detention surveillance. She is concerned that a generalised special regime intensifies feelings of injustice and tensions in detention. Finally, Hazan considers that it is contrary to the objective of detainees' reintegration, which would necessitate the individualisation of conditions of detention.

The criticisms that Hazan formulated were in part successful, as on 31 December 2019, the government published a decree limiting the administration's possibility to detain someone in a special unit for radicalised detainees to a maximum of one year.[67] However, after this one-year period, the special detention regime can be renewed for six months indefinitely by the decision of the Ministry of Justice. The decree, therefore, only superficially answers the concern of the General Controller that maintaining detainees too long in the special units for radicalised detainees can be counterproductive and hinder any social reintegration project.

Isolation in these special units is not only physical; it can also be psychological. Because of the administration's decision to identify as suspicious certain aspects of a person's identity, several detainees have reported to the General Controller of Places of Deprivation of Liberty that books are often confiscated from the 'TIS', in particular religious books, and returned to them only after very long periods. Similarly, the General Controller reports that objects necessary for religious worship are regularly confiscated. Once again, these measures show a lack of individualisation of detention conditions: what triggers suspicion, close monitoring and sometimes extra security measures is not so much how one lives his or her religious belief but signs of religious belief altogether. These isolating measures, both inside special units and common detention facilities, create a feeling of unfairness.

The special measures also follow the reasoning of a regime of exception applied to 'terrorist detainees'. For instance, certain rules of procedure are suspended. First of all, decisions to transfer a detainee to a special unit for radicalised persons are not notified to the detainee as they usually are to the rest of the prison population. In general, it is only in situations of emergency that a Chief Custody Officer can transfer a detainee who poses a threat to the public order with a month's notice only. Originally, when a detainee was transferred to a special unit for radicalised persons, no notification was required at all. However, some improvement was made in 2019 when article 726-2 of the code of criminal procedure was modified to require that the decision of transfer to a special unit be substantiated and be the object of an adversarial procedure. However, General Controller Hazan reports that in practice, despite this positive legal development, actors of the penitentiary administration have not been informed that such a procedure needed to be implemented since the

[67] Decree: Décret n° 2019-1579 du 31 décembre 2019 modifiant le code de procédure pénale (partie réglementaire - décrets en Conseil d'Etat) et relatif aux quartiers de prise en charge de la radicalisation.

modification in 2019.[68] Besides, even if adversarial procedures are finally organised in the near future, the current applicable norms of procedure do not include the usual remedies that would allow the detainees to challenge the decision to detain them in such special units.[69]

Apart from the exclusionary, and sometimes even discriminatory, nature of these detention regimes and measures, the exceptional conditions in which they take place and the involvement of specialised personnel are not used as they could to facilitate social reintegration.

9.3.3 Lost Opportunities of Reintegration Until the "Dry Exit"

An important passage of an interview with Adeline Hazan in *Les Sortants* captures the idea that detention should be about helping detainees prepare their exit:

> The exit is not thought through and the measures of sentence adjustment are inaccessible. Yet, we know that dry exits are dangerous and increase risks of recidivism. If these detainees are considered to be the most dangerous, it is absurd – in the name of a short-term security strategy – not to take into consideration that they will one day exit prison, and that preparing this exit is essential not only for them but for society as a whole.[70]

Instead, because of a very narrow conception of what security means and requires in the short and long term, detention is thought of as a period during which the 'TIS' should be monitored to plan their surveillance post-detention. For this monitoring to take place, specialised personnel, from psychologists to trained probation officers, were hired. They profile detainees and report back on their level of radicalisation and dangerousness. It is a pity to consider that the exact same staff members could have been (and probably wish they were) used to provide psychosocial support rather than to monitor and evaluate. These are lost opportunities for reintegration.

In France, approximately fifty duos, composed of a psychologist and an educator, are hired to evaluate the detainees in the abovementioned special units. The discrepancy between how these duos think of their role and mission and what the administration hired them for is striking. These duos, some of which were interviewed by Véronique Brocard in *Les Sortants*, consider their role as rehumanising the detainees, understanding their trajectory and accompanying them to reflect upon the deep and intimate motives for the offence they committed. During the multidisciplinary commissions in charge of evaluating the detainees, a transcription of which appears in *Les Sortants*, these duos try to explain the detainees' lifepaths and, to borrow the words used by a psychologist, try to go beyond their label "dangerous".[71] Some even

[68] CGLPL Report 2020, p. 26.

[69] Brocard 2020, pp. 181–183.

[70] Brocard 2020, p. 183.

[71] Andréa Citaux, psychologist of the duo of a special unit located in Bourg-en-Bresse. See ibid., p. 101.

try to completely detach themselves from the detainee's file prior to meeting one for the first time in order to avoid bias.[72] This is the case of Julie Martin, an educator who explains that detaching allows her to listen carefully to how the detainees describe the facts, how they live and practice their religious belief, and what meaning they give to the criminal justice decision and the detention sentence.

The special units organise a plethora of activities to ensure that the duos and probation officers meet regularly with the detainees: football, workshops to manufacture soap and essential oils, cooking activities, board games, meditation, cinema-debates, permaculture, and so on.[73] Clarisse Clayes, a psychologist specialising in cognitive and behavioural therapies who has been working for four years in a special unit for radicalised detainees, describes the added value of such activities. They are helpful to work on social relationships, the capacity to lose control, to follow instructions, to care for a project beneficial to the community. However, if the activities must at least help detainees in this way to a certain extent, the administration organises these activities for a different purpose. They are used to identify personality traits and group dynamics: who is impressionable, who is a leading figure in the group, who lacks self-confidence, etc. She concludes that no matter what psychological project they could be helpful for, "for [them], these activities, like all others, are sources of information".[74]

Maëlle Claude, a 35-year-old psychologist, refers to the reality of what they have been hired for: a "hundred percent evaluation".[75] She explains that the prison administration expects them to identify and recommend, not to help the detainee to grow. To make this evaluation as precise as possible, they gather the information that psychologists would generally build on to accompany someone's development: life chronology, important events, family tree and relationships, personality traits. As a result of the institutional framework and strategy, the specialised staff has serious doubts about how meaningfully their deeper work with detainees is used.[76] The specialised duos sometimes try to make recommendations based on their diagnosis, such as a transfer to ordinary detention facilities; however, this is rarely followed. When followed, there have been cases where a detainee ended up being held in solitary confinement. Therefore, they deplore that their fundamental work is not structurally supported, recognised and used appropriately. They regret that what only seems to matter for the institution is collecting data and reporting it back.

This is also what the criminal justice system expects from probation officers, whose job has tremendously evolved in the counter-terrorism context. Far from the old cliché of the guard who merely carries cell keys around, probation officers are now asked not only to organise life in detention and make it safe, but also to evaluate. In 2016, probation officers received a letter asking them to notify the administration

[72] Brocard 2020, p. 140.

[73] It should be noted that these activities are more numerous and frequent in the special units than in common detention facilities.

[74] Interview with Clarisse Clayes in Brocard 2020, pp. 155–156.

[75] Brocard 2020, p. 140.

[76] Brocard 2020, pp. 142–143.

if they were interested in taking care of detainees incarcerated for acts related to terrorism. Their task would be to evaluate detainees, report on their personality and daily habits, and be given a seat at the multidisciplinary commission table. Those who volunteered followed trainings on radicalisation and recruitment processes, on Islam, on terrorist operations and methods such as kidnapping, on geopolitics with an emphasis on the Middle East.[77]

The job of these specialised probation officers is to regularly complete evaluation grids that serve to detect the level of radicalisation of the detainees. These evaluation grids contain about forty questions followed by a 'yes' or 'no' answer, and/or a colour code (for instance, as summed up by Fabienne Maison, Adjunct director of a detention centre in Roanne: yellow for "ostentatious practice of their religion"; orange for "worrying religious signs such as calls to prayer"; red for "hatred discourses against state institutions").[78] These evaluation sheets are also named "grids of data collection" and help "the multidisciplinary identification of the risk of violent radicalisation".[79] The elements that probation officers have to control concern the physical appearance of the detainee, his or her behaviour, routines, anything related to his or her religious practice, discourse, or any event occurring both inside prison and outside, such as correspondence with family and friends, and how relationships evolve. The following are just a few examples of the questions contained in the evaluation grid:[80]

- Does the detainee have religious objects?
- Does the detainee follow a special diet (without pork, vegetarian, does not accept the tray)?
- Does the detainee refuse that his co-detainee exhibits family pictures on the cell walls, including ones representing women?
- Does the detainee refuse television?
- Does the detainee show a particular interest in the news?
- Does the detainee try to impose rules and routines (daily prayers, rules of hygiene and cleanness, physical training, asks other detainees to keep their clothes on in the shower)?

Some probation officers express discomfort about the fact that their reports are used as intelligence, while others are fine with it.[81] Sometimes, the atmosphere in multidisciplinary commissions is awkward because probation officers either have not managed to create enough activities with the detainees (and thus, have not gathered enough data), or have trouble sharing information collected during these encounters.[82] While there is more nuance in how psychologists and educators define their

[77] Brocard 2020, pp. 126–127.

[78] Brocard 2020, p. 52.

[79] This description of the evaluation grid is in the Annex of Brocard 2020, pp. 206–220.

[80] Full evaluation grids are in the Annex of ibid., pp. 206–220.

[81] Brocard 2020, pp. 42–43.

[82] Ibid., p. 167.

roleprobably because they carry the hope and intention to help detainees' reintegration probation officers are unequivocal: "Everything we do is to observe the detainees".[83]

Even the Penitentiary Director for Integration and Probation, Claire Amalfi, who belongs to the penitentiary intelligence services and also participates in these multidisciplinary commissions, wishes she could offer individualised conditions of detention to this category of detainees in a meaningful way.

> The persons we follow have very different profiles from one another. Even if, in the public opinion, they all look alike, their profiles are extremely diverse. The detainee who financed a departure, the one who left for three months, the other who stayed for two years, are different from the one who planted a bomb. The way in which they endure their detention is also very different. [...] I know someone who voted by mail; someone else whose wife goes to McDonalds with their kids; another detainee who asked for an authorisation to go celebrate Christmas with his family. It is important not to treat them in the same way because we run the risk of generating what we fear most: frustration, anger and new violent acts.[84]

The lack of clarity on the role of these various actors is accompanied by a lack of coordination among them. The actors who generally feel less comfortable with a straightforward intelligence-gathering mission are excluded from interactions with intelligence services. This is the case of the duo psychologist/educator, who are often left uninformed (on purpose) when the General Directorate for Internal Security visits the special units. On the contrary, probation officers are often aware of these visits. This difference of treatment leads to internal miscommunications and to further confusing the missions of the various actors in detention.[85]

What if, instead of being labelled 'evaluation centres' and using their resources for that purpose, these special units were focused on (re)integration? More generally, what if, instead of focusing on pre-emptive repressive responses, a psychosocial response was given to those individuals who cannot be pursued and sentenced for anything other than signs of radicalisation?

9.4 Concluding Remarks

In September 2020, UN Special Rapporteur on the promotion and protection of human rights and fundamental freedoms while countering terrorism, Fionnuala Ní Aoláin, urged states "to prosecute their nationals or persons within their effective control for serious violations of human rights and humanitarian law, including war crimes, genocide and crimes against humanity" instead of using offences that might facilitate sentencing (as they do not require much evidence) but do not live up to

---

[83] Interview of Janice Kholer, probation officer in ibid.

[84] Ibid., pp. 101–102.

[85] Brocard 2020, pp. 57–58. The different relationship between the General Directorate for Internal Security (DGIS) and the probation officers, on the one hand, and their relationship with the duo psychologist/educator emerged from a transcribed meeting of the multidisciplinary commission that took place in Roanne on 10 July 2019.

the gravity of the facts.[86] This chapter showed first that it is problematic that imprisonment sentences are the preferred and common choice of judges when confronted with cases of individuals who have travelled to or were planning to travel to Syria and that there is so little room for manoeuvre to adjust the prison sentence to circumstances and positive behaviour. Finally, while detention facilities is a *milieu* that is rarely part of scholarly discussions on risk assessment practices and prevention, this chapter has hopefully shown that it deserves to be studied in the age of prediction. Inside detention facilities, the priority is also to isolate "terrorist detainees" from the rest of the prison population and monitor them in prisons inside the prison until they exit, but also beyond the detention facilities.

Throughout this path in the criminal justice and prison systems, the priority is to prevent the risk of violent offences to be committed. For reasons that need to be further explored, the preferred option in order to prevent such a risk is constant surveillance. Of course, we can already try to understand this security paradigm by looking both outside and inside detention at the multiple attacks perpetrated respectively in the streets and against detention officers in the name of terrorist groups. However, as we touched upon in the final section, it is easy to imagine how existing resources could be used for reintegration purposes, which in itself is a way to prevent terrorist projects from developing. But as a matter of fact, judges prioritise the quantity of prison sentences pronounced to the quality of sentencing for serious and tangible violations of human rights and humanitarian law. Besides, reintegration never seems to be an option or a goal, as if those detainees were already lost causes, reduced to risk assessment objects.

References

Articles, Books and Other Documents

Ancel M (1954) La Défense sociale nouvelle. Editions Cujas, Paris

Arama V (2020) Terrorisme : 43 djihadistes devraient sortir de prison en 2020. LePoint. https://www.lepoint.fr/justice/terrorisme-43-djihadistes-devraient-sortir-de-prison-en-2020--24-02-2020-2364191_2386.php. Accessed 11 February 2022

Beccaria C (1764) An Essay on Crimes and Punishment, Edition with a Commentary by M. de Voltaire. W.C. Little & Co, Albany

Brocard V (2020) Les Sortants. Les Arènes, Paris

Casadamont G, Poncela P (2004) Il n'y a pas de peine juste. Odile Jacob, Paris

Cornu G (2016) Vocabulaire juridique, 11th edn. Presses Universitaires de France

de Guttry A, Capone F, Paulussen C (2016) Foreign Fighters Under International Law and Beyond. T.M.C. Asser Press, The Hague

---

[86] UN Special Rapporteur on the promotion and protection of human rights and fundamental freedoms while countering terrorism, Fionnuala Ní Aoláin (2020) UN Report of the Special Rapporteur on the promotion and protection of human rights and fundamental freedoms while countering terrorism, UN Doc. A/75/337.

European Commission (2004) Green Paper on the approximation, mutual recognition and enforcement of criminal sanctions in the European Union. https://eur-lex.europa.eu/LexUriServ/LexUriServ.do?uri=COM:2004:0334:FIN:EN:PDF. Accessed 15 April 2022

French General Controller of Places of Deprivation of Liberty [Contrôleur Général des Lieux de Privation de Liberté/CGLPL] (2020) Prise en Charge Pénitentiaire des Personnes Radicalisées et Respect des Droits Fondamentaux. https://www.cglpl.fr/wp-content/uploads/2020/06/CGLPL-Prise-en-charge-p%C3%A9nitentiaire-des-personnes-radicalis%C3%A9es-et-respect-des-droits-fondamentaux.pdf. Accessed 15 April 2022

Geneva Academy of International Humanitarian Law and Human Rights (2014) Foreign Fighters under International Law. http://www.geneva-academy.ch/docs/publications/Briefings%20and%20In%20breifs/Foreign%20Fighters%20Under%20International%20Law%20Briefing%20no7.pdf. Accessed 17 June 2015

Hubbard B, Méheut C (2020) Western Countries Leave Children of ISIS in Syrian Camps. The New York Times. https://www.nytimes.com/2020/05/31/world/middleeast/isis-children-syria-camps.html. Accessed 12 November 2020

Lazerges C (2014) Parliamentary hearings concerning the draft law on the prevention of recidivism and the individualisation of sentences, Senate, Professor Christine Lazerges, 13 February 2014. http://www.senat.fr/rap/l13-641-2/l13-641-2.html#toc2

Lazerges C (2018) Introduction. In: Saleilles R (ed) L'individualisation de la peine, étude de criminalité sociale, 3rd edn. Hachette Livre BNF, Paris

Le Monde (2020) Eric Dupond-Moretti dessine sa feuille de route pour ses 600 jours au ministère de la justice. https://www.lemonde.fr/societe/article/2020/07/19/eric-dupond-moretti-dessine-sa-feuille-de-route-pour-ses-600-jours-au-ministere-de-la-justice_6046632_3224.html. Accessed 12 November 2020

Makris S (2020) Openness and Integrity in Antitrust. Journal of Competition Law and Economics 17(1):1–62

Mediapart (2020) Charlie Hebdo: le procès des attentats de janvier 2015 s'est ouvert à Paris. https://www.mediapart.fr/journal/fil-dactualites/020920/charlie-hebdo-le-proces-des-attentats-de-janvier-2015-s-est-ouvert-paris-0?onglet=full. Accessed 11 February 2022

Méheut C, Hubbard B (2020) France Brings 10 Children of French Jihadists Home From Syria. The New York Times. https://www.nytimes.com/2020/06/22/world/europe/france-isis-children-repatriated.html. Accessed 11 February 2022

Saleilles R (2018) L'individualisation de la peine, étude de criminalité sociale, 3rd edn. Hachette Livre BNF

Scherrer A (ed) (2018) The Return of Foreign Fighters to EU soil. European Parliamentary Research Service, PE 621.811. https://www.europarl.europa.eu/RegData/etudes/STUD/2018/621811/EPRS_STU(2018)621811_EN.pdf. Accessed 15 April 2022

Senate Committee (France) (2020) Rapport de la Mission Sénatoriale de contrôle et de suivi de la loi renforçant la sécurité intérieure et la lutte contre le terrorisme. https://www.senat.fr/fileadmin/Fichiers/Images/redaction_multimedia/2020/2020-Documents_pdf/20200226_Rapport_Senat_SILT.pdf. Accessed 15 April 2022

Toutain F (2019) Traitement de la radicalisation en milieu pénitentiaire. Le Genre humain 61 (2):301–304

Veldhuis T (2012) Designing Rehabilitation and Reintegration Programmes for Violent Extremist Offenders: A Realist Approach. ICCT. https://icct.nl/publication/designing-rehabilitation-and-reintegration-programmes-for-violent-extremist-offenders-a-realist-approach/. Accessed 12 November 2020

Weggemans D, de Graaf B (2019) Reintegrating Jihadist Extremist Detainees: Helping Extremist Offenders Back Into Society. Routledge, New York/Abingdon

Wintour P (2021) US pushes France and UK to take Isis fighters back from Iraq and Syria. The Guardian. https://www.theguardian.com/world/2021/jun/28/us-pushes-france-and-uk-to-take-isis-fighters-back-from-iraq-and-syria. Accessed 11 February 2022

UN Documents

UNODC (2006) Custodial and Non-Custodial Measures, Social Reintegration. https://www.un.org/ruleoflaw/files/4_Social_Reintegration.pdf. Accessed 15 April 2022

UN Special Rapporteur on the promotion and protection of human rights and fundamental freedoms while countering terrorism, Fionnuala Ní Aoláin (2020) UN Report of the Special Rapporteur on the promotion and protection of human rights and fundamental freedoms while countering terrorism, UN Doc. A/75/337

Cases

Cour de cassation (France), Chambre criminelle, 12 July 2016, 16-82.692

Cour de cassation (France), Chambre criminelle, 7 October 2016, 16-84.579

Cour de cassation (France), Chambre criminelle, 7 February 2017, 16-87.084

Chambre de l'instruction de la cour d'appel de Paris, 15 January 2019, 2019-01-15

Cour de cassation (France), Chambre criminelle, 19 February 2019, 18-81.096

Cour de cassation (France), Chambre criminelle, 20 February 2019, 18-80.777

Cour de cassation (France), Chambre criminelle, 13 March 2019, 18-87.161

Cour de cassation (France), Chambre criminelle, 10 April 2019, 19-80.493

Cour de cassation (France), Chambre criminelle, 4 June 2019, 18-85.042

Cour de cassation (France), Chambre criminelle, 25 March 2020, 19-83.056

Cour constitutionnelle (Supreme Court), Décision n° 2020-805 DC of 7 August 2020

Chapter 10
Putting the 'Foreign' in 'Foreign Fighter': Nationality Deprivation and the Denial of Readmission

Laura van Waas and Anne Brekoo

Contents

Abstract Although the 'foreign' in 'foreign (terrorist) fighter' typically denotes that the person concerned is 'foreign' in the country where they have gone to 'fight', those who travelled to Syria or Iraq in order to join ISIS are increasingly treated as 'foreign' by their countries of origin. States have deployed two legally distinct but closely related approaches in this regard: deprivation of nationality and denial of readmission. The first is a formal act of foreigner-making; the second is the *de facto* treatment of the individual as a foreigner through the failure to fulfil the international law duty to readmit nationals. This chapter charts the evolution of these two strategies. It looks at the instrumentalisation of nationality policy by states as part of their counter-terrorism response, highlighting the limitations encountered in its use, before turning to discuss how countries of origin moved on to the denial of the rights attached to nationality (even as they left the legal status itself intact). The chapter closes by commenting on some of the wider questions raised by the (re)casting of the 'foreign fighter' issue as 'foreign' to the country of origin—in terms of the impact of this approach on security, inter-State relations, the citizen and the institution of nationality.

L. van Waas (✉)
Tilburg University, Tilburg, The Netherlands
e-mail: Laura.vanWaas@tilburguniversity.edu

A. Brekoo
Erasmus University Rotterdam, Rotterdam, The Netherlands
e-mail: brekoo@law.eur.nl

F. Capone et al. (eds.), *Returning Foreign Fighters: Responses, Legal Challenges and Ways Forward*, https://doi.org/10.1007/978-94-6265-571-3_10

Keywords Denationalisation · Citizenship · Nationality · Readmission · Statelessness · Risk exportation · Counter-terrorism · Administrative measures

10.1 Introduction

United Nations (UN) Security Council Resolution 2178 defines a 'foreign terrorist fighter' as someone who "travel[s] *to a State other than their States of residence or nationality* for the purpose of the perpetration, planning, or preparation of, or participation in, terrorist acts or the providing or receiving of terrorist training, including in connection with armed conflict".[1] The person concerned is 'foreign' in the country where they have gone to 'fight'. It is a term that emerged only relatively recently as the common descriptor for the latest incarnation of the centuries-old phenomenon of 'transnational insurgent'.[2] Simple and alliterative, it has crossed over from the media setting in which it was born[3] to become accepted policy language.[4]

In contemplating the return of contemporary foreign fighters, the word 'foreign' appears to have also acquired a secondary meaning. Those who travelled to Syria or Iraq in order to join ISIS are increasingly treated as 'foreign' by their countries of *origin*. As this chapter exposes, States have deployed two legally distinct but closely related approaches in this regard: deprivation of nationality and denial of readmission.[5] The first is a formal act of foreigner-making; the second is the *de facto* treatment of the individual as a foreigner through the failure to fulfil the international law duty to readmit nationals.

This chapter charts the evolution since 9/11 of these two strategies, developed to externalise the threat of the 'fighter' through the (re)branding of the problem as 'foreign'. It looks first at the instrumentalisation of nationality policy by States as part of their counter-terrorism response, which heralded a renaissance and expansion of denationalisation powers. Thereafter, the chapter discusses the limitations encountered in the use of nationality deprivation and how, especially as the foreign fighter problem came to be felt as more acute following the fall of the Islamic State,[6] countries of origin turned to the denial of the rights attached to nationality (even as they left the legal status itself intact). For each of these approaches, the chapter discusses not just the trends in the responses by States but also the international norms that

[1] Emphasis added. Preamble of UN Security Council (2014) Resolution 2178 (2014), UN Doc. S/RES/2178.

[2] Malet 2010, p. 106.

[3] Ibid., p. 107.

[4] First appearing in UN Security Council Resolution 2170 (2014), before being defined in UN Security Council (2014) Resolution 2178 (2014), UN Doc. S/RES/2178.

[5] Walker discusses how the "export of human subjects" as a counter-terrorism response involves an "ever expanding list of mechanisms" that also include, besides deprivation of nationality and exclusion from the territory, also choice of jurisdiction and rendition. Walker 2020, pp. 36–38. This chapter concerns itself with a discussion only of the former two measures, as those which affect our understanding of the 'foreignness' of the 'foreign fighter'.

[6] Also known as ISIS, ISIL, or Daesh.

are implicated by these responses. It closes by commenting on some of the wider questions raised by the (re)casting of the 'foreign fighter' issue as 'foreign' to the country of origin—in terms of the impact of this approach on security, inter-State relations, the citizen and the institution of nationality.

10.2 Nationality Deprivation

In 1948, prompted by the abhorrent use of denationalisation as a political weapon in the preceding decades, the Universal Declaration of Human Rights affirmed nationality to be a fundamental right and set out the international law prohibition of arbitrary deprivation of nationality. In the same year, the United Kingdom (UK) passed legislation narrowing the circumstances in which a person could be subjected to the withdrawal of nationality.[7] There, as elsewhere, deprivation powers that remained on the books also fell into disuse. In the UK, "by 2002, not a single individual had lost his or her citizenship (other than under fraud provisions) for thirty years".[8] Since then, however, the picture has changed dramatically. In 2017 alone, facilitated by successive amendments that expanded the executive's denationalisation powers,[9] 104 British citizens had their nationality revoked on the grounds that this was "in the public good".[10]

The UK is not the only State to revive its interest in denationalisation. In the past decade, more than a dozen countries have passed laws to make deprivation of nationality (more readily) available to the government.[11] Newly bestowed or long-dormant powers to strip citizenship are also being used in practice (again), now in the counter-terrorism context.[12] In a disconcerting parallel to the interwar period, the justification for denaturalisation once again seeks "legitimacy in a rhetoric of security" while also invoking "appeals to a certain notion of national community".[13] As Bertram observes, politicians today "often make the argument that the excluded person has made a choice to place themselves outside the political community by taking up arms against it on behalf of another State-like organisation, such as Islamic State".[14] On the occasion of legislative reform in Denmark, for instance, the Danish

---

[7] Through the introduction of the British Nationality Act of 1948. See for details Gibney 2014, p. 329.

[8] Ibid., p. 330.

[9] In particular Section 40(4A) of the 1981 British Nationality Act, as introduced by the 2014 Immigration Act.

[10] Dearden 2019.

[11] Besides the UK, other countries include Australia, Austria, Belgium, Bosnia and Herzegovina, Denmark, Egypt, France, Germany, Indonesia, Italy, the Netherlands, Singapore and Turkey.

[12] See further Van Waas 2016; Jaghai and Van Waas 2020.

[13] Discussing the legislative debate surrounding the expansion of nationality deprivation powers in France in 1939: Beauchamps 2017, p. 197.

[14] Bertram 2020, p. 194.

Prime Minister said that the citizens who were to be subject to deprivation of nationality under the new powers had "turned their backs on Denmark and used violence to combat our democracy and freedom" and for this reason "they are not wanted in Denmark".[15]

The predominant and, indeed, in many cases, also explicit target of this measure is the foreign fighter. As the Danish case illustrates, a key purpose of nationality deprivation in policy terms is to stop them from coming home. According to the UK Prime Minister who presided over the most significant reforms to British nationality law, David Cameron, the aim is to "keep out"[16] such individuals, and this requires "a targeted, discretionary power to allow us to exclude British nationals from the UK".[17] Similarly, in the Netherlands—another State in which these powers have been expanded in the past decade—this is how the problem was understood:

> The fact that these people have joined an organisation such as IS and travelled to the conflict area demonstrates, according to the government, that they see the use of violence as a legitimate means to realising their ideals. This is why these people form a threat to the security of the Netherlands if they return [...] The cause of the problem that this group can return to the Netherlands is that the law does not provide any (at least: insufficient) opportunity for return to the Netherlands to be prevented [...] *The only way to prevent a person with Dutch nationality from legally returning to the Kingdom of the Netherlands is to first revoke the Dutch nationality*. Subsequently, the person, *now a foreigner*, is declared undesirable.[18]

For the Netherlands, Denmark, the UK and several of the other States that have adopted this measure with a view to using it against foreign fighters, the aim is to "externalise terrorism risk [through the] exportation of terrorism suspects".[19] Exclusion from the territory of the State is the end, nationality deprivation is the means to that end. In this manner, the 'foreign' in 'foreign fighter' acquired its auxiliary meaning.

10.3 Limits to the Use of Nationality Deprivation

As set out above, nationality deprivation has experienced a renaissance in its instrumentalisation against foreign fighters, with a view to effecting a "two-step exile":

---

[15] Al Jazeera 2019.

[16] Speech in Parliament by then Prime Minister David Cameron in September 2014 in reference to the Immigration Act 2014. As cited in Mantu 2015, p. 16.

[17] Ibid.

[18] Emphasis added. Translated from the original Dutch. Note that the 'declaration of undesirability' (ongewenstverklaring) is an administrative law instrument through which the Netherlands can prohibit a particular foreigner from (re)entering the territory. Bex-Reimert et al. 2020, p. 23.

[19] Walker 2020, p. 38. Note that there are some cases in which the aim pursued is not to extraterritorialise the threat—such as in Finland where new nationality deprivation powers were enacted "to send a 'signal' without interfering with the repatriation of Finns who fought for ISIS". Lepoutre 2020, p. 9.

first, strip citizenship; second, deport the newly minted alien.[20] Legislative reforms to facilitate denationalisation were introduced with much pomp and circumstance, described by Spiro as "security-related theatre, a feel-good move that will be popular with some voters".[21] However, the practical utility of these new or expanded powers has been limited. A combination of foundational principles, such as legal certainty and international law restrictions on States' sovereignty over nationality matters, such as the duty to avoid statelessness, serve to severely constrain the application of this measure.[22]

It is the latter of these examples of limitations that stands out most immediately in the initial analysis of the revival of denationalisation: "there is a broad consensus that deprivation of nationality, even from foreign fighters and (potential) terrorists, should generally not result in the person becoming stateless".[23] The duty to avoid statelessness is a "fundamental principle of international law",[24] existing as a corollary to the right to nationality that is itself enshrined in a multitude of international and regional human rights treaties.[25] In adopting legislation that provides for deprivation of nationality while also guarding against statelessness, States have introduced a measure that can only ever be applied to a limited segment of the 'foreign fighter' population. Dual citizens find themselves exposed, while mono-citizens do not. Data from the Netherlands serves to illustrate the practical implications of this: as of May 2020, a total of 300 Dutch nationals had left the Netherlands to join jihadist groups in Syria and Iraq (*uitreizigers*), of whom approximately 100 are understood to have dual nationality.[26] This means that two-thirds of the country's foreign fighters cannot be touched by denationalisation because statelessness is precluded under the relevant provisions of Dutch law. For States' intent on exporting the terrorist threat, nationality deprivation is not a panacea.

Crucially, the duty to avoid statelessness is just one of the norms that limit the use of nationality deprivation. Even where directed at dual nationals, this measure must comply with other international standards and foundational legal principles,

---

[20] Macklin 2018, p. 164.

[21] Spiro 2018, p. 175. Indeed, in the case of Australia, one survey found that when the question was being debated in 2015, 81% of Australians supported the government's proposal to introduce law reform that would make it easier to strip citizens engaged in terrorism or supporting terrorist groups of their nationality. Crikey 2015.

[22] See for a elaboration of the international law standards that apply to all situations in which States take or consider taking steps to deprive a person of nationality as a national security measure the *Principles on Deprivation of Nationality as a National Security Measure*. https://files.institutesi.org/PRINCIPLES.pdf. Accessed 1 October 2020; to which 60 leading experts in the fields of human rights, nationality and statelessness, counter-terrorism, refugee protection, child rights, migration and other related areas contributed; and the accompanying *Draft Commentary*. https://files.institutesi.org/PRINCIPLES_Draft_Commentary.pdf. Accessed 1 October 2020.

[23] Van Waas 2016, p. 480. Noting the UK as an important exception to this general trend.

[24] UN Human Rights Council (2013) Human rights and arbitrary deprivation of nationality: Report of the Secretary-General. A/HRC/25/28, p. 3.

[25] See further UN Secretary-General 2018.

[26] Data provided by the Dutch General Intelligence and Security Service (AIVD) as cited in Bex-Reimert et al. 2020, p. 56.

one of which is the prohibition of discrimination.[27] Indeed, the very fact of distinguishing between different categories of citizens in determining who can and cannot be targeted for denationalisation raises serious issues from the perspective of ensuring equality before the law. Where the status of some is contingent, while that of others is secure—mono versus dual nationals, but also naturalised citizens versus citizens by birth—this "undermines equality within the class of supposedly equal citizens [...] exposing some, but not others, to additional punishment for the same offences".[28] Moreover, such an approach also leads to indirect discrimination against minorities who are disproportionately represented in the categories of citizens whose nationality has become contingent.[29] This reinforces the stigmatisation of "suspect communities"[30] and echoes the historical experience that "denationalisation's targets have been a tracer for ethnic, religious and national groups who—citizenship notwithstanding—are already considered foreign in the societies in which they live".[31]

Notwithstanding the wider societal implications of nationality deprivation powers that have been enacted in the counter-terrorism context, their unequal application and discriminatory effect raise legal issues, further limiting their use. Commentators have flagged this aspect of the contemporary renaissance of nationality deprivation as problematic in the Belgian and UK contexts, for example.[32] In a case before the Dutch Council of State on this question,[33] the UN Special Rapporteur on contemporary forms of racism, racial discrimination, xenophobia and related intolerance intervened in support of the individual whose citizenship was revoked, with an elaborate brief outlining the international norms that are implicated.[34] Indeed, it is not only discrimination that is at play, but also the prohibition of arbitrary deprivation of nationality, which requires, *inter alia,* that any restriction of a right be the least intrusive means to achieve the purpose that is pursued.[35] Given that "States have

---

[27] Including International Covenant on Civil and Political Rights, opened for signature 16 December 1966, No. 14668 (entered into force 23 March 1976), Article 26; International Convention on the Elimination of All Forms of Racial Discrimination, opened for signature 7 March 1996, 660 UNTS 195 (entered into force 4 January 1969), Articles 1(3) and 5(d)(iii); European Convention on Nationality, opened for signature 1997, ETS 166 (entered into force 1 March 2000) Article 5; Universal Declaration of Human Rights, opened for signature 1948, UNGA Resolution 217, Article 2; European Convention Human Rights, opened for signature 4 November 1950, 213 UNTS 221 (entered into force 3 September 1953) Article 14; American Convention on Human Rights, opened for signature 22 November 1969, No. 17955 (entered into force 18 July 1978) Article 1(1).

[28] Bertram 2020, p. 194. See also Anderson 2013; Burchardt and Gulati 2018; Gibney 2020a.

[29] This aspect of the issue is discussed at length in Van Waas and Jaghai 2018.

[30] Choudhury 2017, p. 227. See also UN Human Rights Council 2018.

[31] Gibney 2020b, p. 208.

[32] Reyntjens 2019; Arnell 2020.

[33] Council of State 30 December 2020, ECLI:NL:RVS:2020:3045.

[34] UN High Commissioner for Human Rights 2018. See also Meijers Committee 2020.

[35] See the discussion of *Principle 7.4: Necessity* and *Principle 7.5: Proportionality* in the *Draft Commentary* to the Principles on Deprivation of Nationality as a National Security Measure. https://files.institutesi.org/PRINCIPLES_Draft_Commentary.pdf. Accessed 1 October 2020, pp. 56–60.

found ways to address security threats posed by mono nationals without denationalising them [then w]hy are these measures not simply applied in the same way to all nationals, without the State reaching for the added and far-reaching instrument of citizenship revocation for some?".[36]

The use of nationality deprivation is further constrained by a number of procedural principles. For instance, the principle of legal certainty requires that any limitation of a right be foreseeable and stands in the way of the retroactive application of newly enacted denationalisation powers.[37] In order to exercise deprivation powers, the State must establish evidence of actions of the foreign fighter or their association with a terrorist organisation *after* the entry into force of requisite legislative reforms that provide for the possibility of denationalisation.[38] The principle of proportionality must also be observed, as well as due process norms, the right to a fair trial, remedy and reparation, and other international legal standards such as the prohibition of *refoulement* and the right to family life.[39] Turning back to the example of the Netherlands for illustration, the aggregate effect of these various limitations comes into view. According to an evaluation published in August 2020, even after politicians who were frustrated by the low number of cases of nationality deprivation ordered the intelligence services to invest additional resources in (re)examining the possibility of revoking the citizenship of more foreign fighters,[40] nationality deprivation was executed in only 21 cases—i.e. against just 20% of Dutch *uitreizigers* who hold dual nationality.[41] Seven of these decisions were subsequently reversed due to failure to meet the requirement of non-retroactivity,[42] leaving 14 deprivation cases intact, for which ten were still in appeal.[43] As such, at the time of the evaluation, just

[36] Van Waas and Jaghai 2018, p. 425.

[37] See the discussion of *Principle 7.3: Legality* in the *Draft Commentary* to the Principles on Deprivation of Nationality as a National Security Measure. https://files.institutesi.org/PRINCIPLES_Draft_Commentary.pdf, Accessed 1 October 2020, pp. 52–54.

[38] Dutch Council of State 17 April 2019, ECLI:NL:RVS:2019:990; Dutch Council of State 17 April 2019, ECLI:NL:RVS:2019:1246. See for an opposing view Parliamentary Joint Committee on Intelligence and Security (2020) Advisory Report on the Australian Citizenship Amendment (Citizenship Cessation) Bill 2019. https://www.aph.gov.au/Parliamentary_Business/Committees/Joint/Intelligence_and_Security/CitizenshipCessation/Report/section?id=committees%2freportjnt%2f024396%2f72479 Accessed 1 October 2020.

[39] See further the *Principles on Deprivation of Nationality as a National Security Measure*. https://files.institutesi.org/PRINCIPLES.pdf. Accessed 1 October 2020.

[40] Dutch Review Committee on the Intelligence and Security Services—CTIVD (2020) *Toezichtsrapport. Over het handelen van de AIVD in het kader van intrekking van het Nederlanderschap in het belang van de nationale veiligheid.* https://www.rijksoverheid.nl/documenten/kamerstukken/2020/06/16/aanbieding-ctivd-rapport-intrekking-nederlanderschap. Accessed 1 October 2020. A special *Taskforce* operated within the AIVD for this purpose from June to September 2019.

[41] This relates to cases in which deprivation of nationality was executed under Article 14(4) of the Netherlands Nationality Act, as introduced by law reform in 2017. Bex-Reimert et al. 2020, p. 35.

[42] Brief van de Staatssecretaris van Veiligheid en Justitie aan de Voorzitter van de Tweede Kamer der Staten-Generaal Den Haag (24 september 2019). https://www.parlementairemonitor.nl/9353000/1/j9vvij5epmj1ey0/vl28lb9mrgtf. Accessed 1 October 2020.

[43] Bex-Reimert et al. 2020, p. 35.

four out of the estimated total of 300 Dutch foreign fighters had definitively lost their nationality (equating to 1.3%), and if further precedents are set by ongoing litigation in other cases, their revocations may also need to be reviewed in future. Moreover, one of the Dutch citizens whose nationality was revoked was nevertheless deported back to the Netherlands, demonstrating that the measure does not necessarily prevent return.[44]

As a means to achieve the exportation of terrorism suspects, nationality deprivation is thus revealed to be a strategy of extremely limited utility. The discussion here only scrapes the surface of the analysis of this measure against international standards, and already the challenges are evident. Indeed, in drafting the *Principles on Deprivation of Nationality as a National Security Measure,* "a holistic and purposive analysis and application of international law standards, led the experts involved [...] to extract the norm that 'States shall not deprive persons of nationality for the purpose of safeguarding national security'".[45] This conclusion, distilled from synthesising the ecosystem of contemporary (international) standards and legal principles, recognises that the cumulative restrictions placed on States make it very hard to identify any circumstances in which nationality deprivation would be legitimate—as also affirmed by the Dutch experience, presented above.

10.4 Denial of Readmission

In light of the constraints on the denationalisation of foreign fighters, States have increasingly resorted to other means to prevent return. Readmission to the country of origin is either actively obstructed or passively through the denial of facilitative instruments that are generally available to nationals. Examples include the withholding of consular protection, the imposition of travel restrictions, and the refusal to renew passports. Albeit falling short of deprivation of nationality, these measures indirectly achieve a comparable effect: exclusion from the country of nationality and thereby externalisation of terrorist risk.

Less than a year after the UK enacted its most far-reaching expansion of nationality deprivation powers with the passing of the *2014 Immigration Act*, a new piece of counter-terrorism legislation was introduced to address the threat that was understood to be posed by those who had travelled abroad to join terrorist groups such as Islamic State.[46] The *2015 Counter-Terrorism and Security Act* provides for a broad range of measures, including bestowing the Secretary of State with the discretionary power to impose 'temporary exclusion orders' on British citizens.[47] This denies the citizen

---

[44] Ibid., p. 57.

[45] *Draft Commentary* to the Principles on Deprivation of Nationality as a National Security Measure. https://files.institutesi.org/PRINCIPLES_Draft_Commentary.pdf Accessed 1 October 2020. p. 29.

[46] Fenwick 2016, p. 174; Blackbourn and Walker 2016, p. 840.

[47] Walker 2020, pp. 54–55.

entry to the UK based on suspicion of involvement in terrorist activities.[48] Although this non-trial-based measure is theoretically temporary in nature—expiring after a two-year duration—an escape clause presents the State Secretary with an opportunity to impose further temporary exclusion orders on the person when a previous one ceases to be in force.[49] In practice, therefore, the citizens concerned could be excluded from the UK indefinitely—skipping the step of nationality deprivation and going directly to exile.

Another measure to emerge is the withdrawal of passports or the refusal to (re)issue one. As recognised by Scott, the employment of such measures relies on the notion that passports serve as conduits for the enjoyment of nationality rights, most prominently the right and ability to travel.[50] It was already common for measures effectuating limitations on the travel movements to be imposed when the citizen is still present in the country.[51] The intended effect, then, is to prevent citizens from travelling *to* areas where they might engage in terrorist activities.[52] France, for instance, legalised the revocation of passports of citizens who are believed to be leaving French territory in order to join a terrorist organisation or participate in terrorist activities.[53] In some cases, States have expanded the use of passport revocation to citizens who are outside of the territory. Rather than preventing travel *to* certain areas, the aim becomes to prevent travel *from* those areas to the State of nationality. In 2015, an amendment to the Canadian *Passport Order* empowered the Minister of Public Safety and Emergency Preparedness to withhold or revoke a passport based on the reasonable belief that it is necessary to prevent a terrorist offence from being committed or to protect Canadian national security.[54] Simultaneously, passport services may be made unavailable to citizens subjected to this measure for a "maximum period of 10 years".[55] Though not expressly stated, nothing in the *Order* precludes the application of its provisions to citizens outside of Canadian territory.

Confronted with the large number of foreign fighters detained in Syria following the defeat of ISIS,[56] States resorted to a measure falling short even of requiring an individual administrative decision: the restriction or denial of consular assistance. In early 2019, as the United States (US) called on European countries to repatriate foreign fighters who had been captured following the defeat of ISIS, statements

48 Counter-Terrorism and Security Act (2015), Sections 2(1) and 2(3).

49 Ibid., Section 4(8).

50 Scott 2020.

51 This accords with UN Security Council (2014) Resolution 2178 (2014), UN Doc. S/RES/2178, which imposes the duty on States to prevent the movement of foreign terrorist fighters. See further Krähenmann 2016; Gherbaoui 2020.

52 Harvey 2015.

53 Law 2014-1353: Strengthening the Provisions Relating the Right Against Terrorism (2014). https://www.legifrance.gouv.fr/jorf/id/JORFTEXT000029754374/. Accessed 1 October 2020.

54 Canadian Passport Order (SI/81-86) (2015). https://laws.justice.gc.ca/eng/regulations/SI-81-86/page-2.html#h-637926. Accessed 1 October 2020, Article 10.1.

55 Ibid., Article 10.2(1).

56 Although estimates widely diverge, some 10,000 to 15,000 foreign nationals have been detained by Kurdish forces (see Francois and Ibrahim 2020, p. 4; Coolsaet and Renard 2020, p. 2).

were issued by, among others, the Netherlands,[57] Norway[58] and Germany[59] that consular assistance would be provided only to those who reported directly to an embassy of their country in the region. There would be no active facilitation of consular assistance. In Denmark, the power to *entirely* withhold consular services was institutionalised in early 2020 with an amendment to the *1983 Foreign Service Act*.[60] The Act now provides that consular assistance to a citizen may be discontinued when there is reason to believe that this person has entered or resides in a conflict area or has participated in activities abroad capable of posing a threat to the security of Denmark or other States. In announcing the proposal for this amendment, which followed on the heels of earlier legislation expanding nationality deprivation powers,[61] the Danish Minister of Foreign Affairs reiterated the view that Denmark "owe[d] absolutely nothing to foreign fighters who went to Syria and Iraq to fight for ISIS".[62] Even as their nationality status is left intact, the path to readmission to their country of citizenship is obstructed through the deliberate denial of consular services, generating a new iteration of what is in effect the same policy. The surrounding rhetoric draws again on the notion that these presumed fighters have already, through their actions, become 'foreign' and are thereby no longer deserving of those rights that are traditionally reserved and afforded to nationals. The same approach has also been applied, by extension, to children of foreign fighters.

10.5 Limits to the Denial of Readmission

Just as the use of nationality deprivation is limited by (international) law, as set out above, so too does the denial of readmission implicate certain legal norms and principles. Central among these is the right of individuals to enter, remain in and return to one's own country, as enshrined in, among others, Article 12(4) of the International Covenant on Civil and Political Rights. Unlike the other paragraphs of this article, this right does not permit limitations on the grounds of national security, and according to the Human Rights Committee, "there are few, if any, circumstances in which deprivation of the right to enter one's own country could be reasonable".[63] Moreover, while requiring States to prevent the movement of foreign terrorist fighters,

---

[57] Tweede Kamer der Staten-Generaal 2019.

[58] Lote et al. 2019.

[59] Roithmaier 2019.

[60] Act No. 150 of 13 April 1983. https://www.retsinformation.dk/eli/lta/1983/150. Accessed 11 August 2020; Act No. 63 of 28 January 2020 amending the Act on Danish Citizenship and the Act on the Foreign Service. https://www.retsinformation.dk/eli/lta/2020/63. Accessed 1 October 2020.

[61] See Al Jazeera 2019.

[62] Kofod 2019.

[63] UN Human Rights Committee (1999) General Comment No. 27: Article 12 (Freedom of Movement), UN Doc. CCPR/C/21/Rev.1/Add.9, para 21.

Security Council Resolution 2178 explicitly notes that it does not oblige any State "to deny entry or require the departure from its territories of its own nationals".[64]

Indeed, the right of a national "to live in his or her own country is commonly considered an essential element of the relationship between a State and its nationals".[65] The duty of a State to (re)admit its own nationals constitutes a "vital means of regulating the coexistence of sovereign entities while also being a necessary corollary thereof"[66]—it is a reciprocal duty which a State "owes to its fellow States".[67] This obligation "is flouted when [the foreign fighter's] State of nationality revokes their citizenship after their departure".[68] However, what if readmission is merely bureaucratically obstructed through the revocation of a passport or the restriction or denial of consular assistance, as set out in the preceding paragraph? This raises the question of what positive obligations are contained within the duty to readmit nationals and the attendant right to (re)enter enjoyed by citizens.

One way to start unpacking this question is to examine the different circumstances in which the denial of readmission can play out. Broadly speaking, there are two scenarios characterised by a different 'distance' between the citizen and their State of nationality. In the first, citizens have direct access to the State of nationality, and there is no question as to the ability of that State to exercise jurisdiction. For example, where a citizen seeks (re)admission *at the border* of his or her State, it is apparent that the State must allow entry to the territory, for otherwise the essence of the right would be impaired. It would seem similarly straightforward in cases where another State seeks to deport a citizen directly to his or her State of nationality: the reciprocal duty that exists between states demands (re)admission be allowed. The right of the State under international law to "expel an alien from its territory"[69] can only be effectively exercised to the extent that the State of nationality readmits its expelled nationals.[70] In the same vein, where a request for repatriation is lodged by a citizen at his or her embassy in a third country, jurisdiction is not in question.[71] As set out above, although States may seek to limit their consular services for foreign fighters, they generally do continue to provide assistance when an individual approaches an embassy or consulate, respecting the commonly accepted practice of States to honour the request for assistance by their nationals when they approach a diplomatic

[64] UN Security Council (2014) Resolution 2178 (2014), UN Doc. S/RES/2178, para 8.

[65] International Law Commission (2007) 'Third report on the expulsion of aliens, by Mr. Maurice Kamto, Special Rapporteur', UN Doc. A/CN.4/581 (19 April 2007), para 48.

[66] Ibid., para 19.

[67] Fisher Williams 1927, as cited in Goodwin-Gill 2014.

[68] Krähenmann 2016, p. 249.

[69] International Law Commission (2014) Draft Articles on the Expulsion of Aliens (2014), UN Doc. A/69/10, Article 3.

[70] Hence, when Turkey announced in 2019 that it was "not a hotel" for detained foreign fighters from other States and that these individuals would be forcibly repatriated to their countries of nationality, those States had no option but to allow readmission of these individuals. See Gall 2019.

[71] UN Special Rapporteur on the promotion and protection of human rights and fundamental freedoms while countering terrorism and UN Special Rapporteur on arbitrary and extra-judicial executions 2020, pp. 18–19.

representation in a third country. In all of the above instances, where nationals are found 'knocking at the doors', States are obliged to allow re-entry.

The second type of scenario is that in which a citizen find themself far-removed from the territory or indeed any consular representation of their country of nationality—such as the large number of foreign fighters held in detention camps in Syria and Iraq. Here, the exact obligations of the State are less clear-cut. Although the right to (re)entry is firmly established in international law, there is little guidance on whether this right is accompanied by a positive duty on behalf of States to actively facilitate readmission. In other words, does the duty to readmit encompass a duty to *repatriate*? At the time of writing, for example, four separate individual communications were pending before the Committee on the Rights of the Child, alleging breaches of the Convention on the part of France and Finland associated with the refusal to repatriate children to foreign fighters,[72] while another application was lodged against France before the European Court of Human Rights.[73] These cases are illustrative of a now acute need to further define the nature of the duty for States to readmit nationals.

Meanwhile, domestic courts have been grappling with this question at the national level. For instance, in 2018, a Belgian Court of First Instance recalled that "the Belgian State cannot deny entry to Belgian nationals, including when they have committed crimes",[74] determining that Belgium should take "all necessary and possible measures" to enable the return of six children and their mothers from Syria.[75] The Court indicated several concrete measures to be taken to give effect to this order, including the provision of travel documents and engaging in diplomatic and consular activities in the area. At the same time, the Court also noted that an order "to take all necessary measures *cannot be worded as an obligation to repatriate*—on the one hand because of the obscure substance of that concept, and on the other hand because there are extraneous and varying circumstances that obstruct the realisation of that commitment".[76] The Court recognised the complexity of exercising jurisdiction on foreign soil and in relation to citizens held by non-state actors, ruling (only) on a positive obligation of conduct (i.e. facilitate readmission) rather than result (i.e. ensure repatriation). Nevertheless, this decision, as well as similar rulings by the Court of First Instance, were later overturned on appeal,[77] which further confirms the uncertainty that exists regarding the duty of readmission. Similarly, while in November 2019, the Dutch State was ordered in summary proceedings to "take all necessary measures […] in so far the State can be *reasonably expected* to do so," to repatriate Dutch children, and where appropriate their mothers, from detention

[72] UN Office of the High Commissioner on Human Rights 2020, pp. 8, 12–13.

[73] See also the individual complaint pending before the European Court of Human Rights, *H.F. and M.F. v. France*, Application No. 24384/19.

[74] Brussels Dutch Court of First Instance 2018, p. 19.

[75] Ibid., p. 22.

[76] Emphasis added. Ibid., p. 20.

[77] E.g., Brussels Court of Appeal 2019; Brussels Court of Appeal 2018.

camps in Syria,[78] within a fortnight this was also reversed by the Court of Appeal, a reversal that was later confirmed by the Supreme Court. The Court of Appeal held that the assessment of the circumstances and the decision (not) to assist in returning these individuals is "up to politicians, and not to the judge" and that it is "politics that [would] have to consider the dire situation of the women and children".[79] This alienation of the judicial from the political reinforces a conception of citizenship rights as a privilege, affording the State large discretionary power to determine which citizens are deserving of them.

As countries of citizenship debate or contest what the right to (re)enter—or the duty of readmission—actually entails, foreign fighters and their families remain in limbo in detention camps where they are exposed to a range of further human rights violations, exacerbated by the effects of the COVID-19 pandemic.[80] The effect of the continued inaction of States thereby implicates other international law standards, including the right to life, the right not to be subjected to torture or cruel, inhuman or degrading treatment, and the right to liberty and security of the person. This direct relationship between the failure to repatriate nationals and their exposure to treatment in serious violations of international human rights law implicates another responsibility of States, namely the "duty to act with due diligence to ensure that the lives of their nationals are protected from irreparable harm".[81] In other words, the legal bond of nationality provides jurisdiction *ratione personae* with respect to the right to enter one's own country, even—or indeed, precisely—while the citizens are outside of the territory of the State, and such jurisdiction must be understood to be engaged when a national can be protected from being "subjected to torture, inhuman and degrading treatment *by providing repatriation*".[82] This has led human rights experts to conclude that:

> the urgent return and repatriation of foreign fighters and their families from conflict zones is *the only international law-compliant response* to the increasingly complex and precarious human rights, humanitarian and security situation faced by those women, men and children who are detained in inhumane conditions.[83]

Just as "the State of nationality's responsibility for the treatment of its citizens in other territories […] becomes all the more compelling when non-derogable jus cogens norms are being unequivocally breached",[84] so too does the special position of

---

[78] District Court of The Hague 2019, para 5.1.

[79] The Hague Court of Appeal 2019, para 7.14.

[80] See Chap. 4 by Capone and Chap. 6 by Duffy in this volume.

[81] UN Special Rapporteur on the promotion and protection of human rights and fundamental freedoms while countering terrorism and UN Special Rapporteur on arbitrary and extra-judicial executions 2020, p. 6.

[82] Emphasis added. Ibid., p. 14.

[83] Emphasis added. Special Rapporteur on the promotion and protection of human rights and fundamental freedoms while countering terrorism 2019, p. 2.

[84] UN Special Rapporteur on the promotion and protection of human rights and fundamental freedoms while countering terrorism and UN Special Rapporteur on arbitrary and extra-judicial executions 2020, p. 19.

children reinforce a purposive interpretation of the duty of readmission to encompass an active role in facilitating repatriation. The Convention on the Rights of the Child, for instance, obliges State Parties to make the best interests of the child a primary consideration in all actions concerning them.[85] In the context of the foreign fighter debate, the UN Counter-Terrorism Centre emphasised that "States should place the child at the centre of considerations and help ensure their rights even when the child is considered a potential security risk".[86] Furthermore, under no circumstances must children be discriminated against or subject to punishment on the basis of, *inter alia*, the activities of the child's parents.[87] In light of these obligations, a number of countries have actively repatriated children of foreign fighters from detention camps, demonstrating a greater willingness to interpret a positive duty on the part of the country of nationality in respect of the exercise by a child of the right to (re)enter one's own country.[88]

A further set of international norms that may be useful to understanding the responsibility held by States towards their citizen foreign fighters are those specifically relating to the provision of consular protection. Consular protection consists, according to Article 5(a) of the 1963 Vienna Convention on Consular Relations, in "protecting in the receiving State the interests of the sending State and of its *nationals*" and encompasses the provision of aid by a State to its citizens in a foreign country.[89] It is generally accepted that the State of nationality has the discretion to determine the scope and nature of the consular protection afforded.[90] A direct right to consular protection, therefore, cannot be identified in international law, nor a positive obligation of the State to actively extend consular services to their nationals. Unless a right to consular protection is codified in domestic legislation, the refusal to protect does not generate legal consequences *per se*. Nevertheless, the action or inaction of consular agents does trigger the jurisdiction of the State of nationality "in relation to the rights affected by [that] State's conduct",[91] as does "the State's exercise of the power to issue a passport".[92] Thus, where the failure to extend consular protection has a direct effect on the fulfilment of the duty to readmit, this can amount to a violation of international law—especially where other human rights violations are causally connected, as set out above.

Moreover, when it comes to cases involving Member States of the European Union (EU), individuals have an opportunity to rely upon EU law to claim consular

---

[85] CRC, Article 3(1).

[86] UN Counter-Terrorism Centre 2019, p. 30.

[87] CRC, Article 2(2).

[88] E.g., Méheut and Hubbard 2020.

[89] Jones-Bos and van Daalen 2008, p. 88.

[90] Denza 2018, p. 467; Guillaume 2019, p. 105; Okano-Heijmans 2011, p. 26.

[91] UN Special Rapporteur on the promotion and protection of human rights and fundamental freedoms while countering terrorism and UN Special Rapporteur on arbitrary and extra-judicial executions 2020, p. 18.

[92] Ibid., p 19. See also UN Human Rights Committee (1999) General Comment No. 27: Article 12 (Freedom of Movement), UN Doc. CCPR/C/21/Rev.1/Add.9, para 9.

assistance. Those in possession of EU citizenship are entitled to receive protection in a third country from the diplomatic and consular authorities of any of the Member States, on equal terms with the protection afforded to the nationals of that State, if the Member State of nationality is "unrepresented".[93] According to Preamble 8 of *Directive 2015/637*, citizens should be considered to be unrepresented not only if their Member State has not established an embassy, consulate or honorary consul in a third country, but also if their representation is "unable for any reason" to provide assistance. Although there are no known cases in practice, the refusal of EU Member States to afford consular protection to foreign fighters could generate an intricate legal and political dilemma. In conceiving of 'absence of representation' as an unwillingness of the State of nationality to provide consular protection, foreign fighters are 'unrepresented citizens' for the purposes of *Directive 2015/637*, and therefore have the right to receive consular protection from another EU Member State on the same conditions as its nationals. Provided that this other Member State has not restricted consular protection for foreign fighters, the individual could be granted such protection and potentially be repatriated to either the country of nationality or another EU Member State—negating efforts to instrumentalise the (non) provision of consular assistance with a view to preventing return.

10.6 The (Legal) Implications of Turning 'Foreign Fighters' into Foreigners

As the preceding sections have shown, the effective transformation of citizen 'foreign fighters' into foreigners is a strategy that confronts numerous international law constraints. The formal act of making foreign—denationalisation—has, to date, drawn the most attention in light of its far-reaching and permanent effect on the status and rights of the individual concerned. Importantly, the analysis in this chapter shows that the *de facto* treatment of the citizen as a foreigner through the denial or obstruction of readmission is no less contentious. It undermines, in much the same way, the status of the individual as well as the function of nationality in the international legal order. The following paragraphs offer some overarching reflections on the questions raised by the (re)casting of the 'foreign fighter' as foreign to the country of origin.

Firstly, there is a genuine question as to the prudence of a policy of externalising terrorism risk through exporting terrorism suspects.[94] This approach assumes that risk can be geographically contained, despite the fact that foreign fighters are "classed as a threat to international peace and security requiring concerted counterterrorism efforts".[95] As Paulussen and Scheinin explain, a measure that seeks to keep foreign fighters outside the territory (and responsibility) of the State of citizenship:

---

[93] EU Council Direction 2015/637, Article 1; TFEU, Article 20(2)(c).

[94] Above, n 19.

[95] Lloyd 2020, p. 220.

> does not bring people to justice, and it fails to rehabilitate and reintegrate them; rather, it shoves the problem temporarily away, into the hands of actors that may have fewer or no capabilities to do something about it. [...] [W]hile politicians state that national security will be strengthened because the person will be removed from the territory or will not be allowed to re-enter it, this constitutes a very narrow perspective of the concept of security – both in terms of time and place – and one that is arguably no longer in sync with the realities of our hyper-connected world.[96]

In terms of the real impact on security, there is a dearth of evidence of the effectiveness of this approach. Researchers tasked with evaluating the power, available in the Netherlands since 2017, to denationalise citizens who have joined ISIS were forced to conclude that "the question as to whether [as a result of these powers] the threat of terrorist activities by members of jihadi organisations on Dutch territory has decreased, and therefore, the degree of national security has increased, cannot be answered".[97] Commentators have meanwhile proffered a whole array of arguments as to why it is likely *not* to be an effective approach.[98] Also, given the roll-over effect on impunity and the failure to demobilise and deradicalise that are associated with such policies, it has been warned that they can actually be counter-effective.[99]

A second and closely related implication of countries of origin adopting a "pass the buck mentality"[100] to foreign fighters is that they are shirking their respective responsibilities in regard to agreed international counter-terrorism efforts.[101] In the context of negotiations around a new Security Council resolution in 2020,[102] intended to promote increased prosecution, rehabilitation and reintegration of foreign terrorist fighters, the US Representative stressed that repatriation constituted a "crucial first step" in addressing the foreign fighter phenomenon, and further provided that:

> It is incomprehensible that other members of this Council were satisfied with a resolution that ignores the security implications of leaving foreign terrorist fighters to plot their escape from limited detention facilities and abandoning their family members to suffer in camps without recourse, opportunities, or hope.[103]

One of the Key Principles that have been articulated by the UN for the Protection, Repatriation, Prosecution, Rehabilitation and Reintegration of Women and Children with links to United Nations Listed Terrorist Groups is that "Member States have

---

[96] Paulussen and Scheinin 2020, p. 225. See also Paulussen 2020.

[97] Bex-Reimert et al. 2020, p. 68. As set out in this report and in the separate evaluation by the CTIVD—as cited above, n 40—both the AIVD and the Dutch Public Prosecution Service (OM) have expressed concerns regarding the use of denationalisation as a counter-terrorism tool.

[98] A summary of relevant literature is set out in Institute on Statelessness and Inclusion 2020.

[99] Malet 2019; Paulussen and Van Waas 2020.

[100] Paulussen and Scheinin 2020, p. 225.

[101] UN Security Council (2014) Resolution 2178 (2014), UN Doc. S/RES/2178, p. 4; PACE Resolution 2263 2019, para 8.

[102] UN Security Council (2020) Indonesia: Draft Resolution (2020), UN Doc. S/2020/852.

[103] US Mission to the United Nations 2020. The resolution was ultimately vetoed by the US for failure to address the issue of repatriation.

primary responsibility for their own nationals".[104] This is how the international legal order operates:

> In a system of equally sovereign States, governments can no longer simply dump their bad apples on other countries. [...] States must assume responsibility for their citizens vis-à-vis other States. This is a core function of nationality in the international system.[105]

In Arendt's analysis, even before the crystallisation of international standards that constrain States' use of denationalisation, "practical consideration and *the silent acknowledgement of common interests* restrained national sovereignty until the rise of totalitarian regimes".[106] As shown in this chapter, contemporary measures intended to ward off a (former) citizen foreign fighter from their country of nationality run counter to the international law duty to readmit one's nationals, which emanates from the sovereign equality of States on the international level. By virtue of customary international law, States are to respect the sovereign equality of other states and the principle of non-interference in the internal and external affairs of other States, which encompasses the right to "sovereignty, political independence, territorial integrity, national unity and security of all States".[107] The denationalisation and/or denial of readmission of foreign fighters violates the territorial integrity of the host State, which is forced to take responsibility for the now stranded (former) citizens of another State and is left to contend with the potential security threat posed by them.

Thirdly, the status of this (former) citizen who has been disowned or banished is precarious in the extreme. UN human rights experts explicitly "emphasise the legal black hole that emerges if the State of nationality is absolved of all meaningful obligations in respect of vindicating the rights of their citizens".[108] A legal vacuum indeed appears to have enveloped the foreign fighters and family members associated with them whose detention is indefinite, and treatment is dire, all without any prospect of oversight, remedy or reparation.[109] Where can these individuals turn to when the State of nationality, which "has the legal capacity to end the systemic violations in question",[110] fails or refuses to act? If this lapse of responsibility has "condemn[ed] children to a life of undulating torture",[111] what kind of future lies in store for them?

---

[104] UN 2019, p. 4.

[105] Bauböck 2020, pp. 390–391.

[106] Emphasis added. Arendt 1968, p. 278.

[107] UN General Assembly (1970) Resolution 2625 (XXV) UN Doc. A/RES/2625; Montevideo Convention of 1933, opened for signature 26 December 1933, (entered into force 26 December 1934) Articles 4 and 11; UN General Assembly (1965) Declaration on the Inadmissibility of Intervention and Interference in the Internal Affairs of States. UN Doc. A/RES/36/103, p. 79.

[108] UN Special Rapporteur on the promotion and protection of human rights and fundamental freedoms while countering terrorism and UN Special Rapporteur on arbitrary and extra-judicial executions 2020, p. 20.

[109] See further Rights and Security International 2020b.

[110] UN Special Rapporteur on the promotion and protection of human rights and fundamental freedoms while countering terrorism and UN Special Rapporteur on arbitrary and extra-judicial executions 2020.

[111] Ibid.

Finally, through stripping foreign fighters of (the core rights and protections attached to) their citizenship, States are tampering with the institution of nationality itself. As has been discussed at length elsewhere, instrumentalising denationalisation in this manner has the effect of making nationality contingent (for some) and undermining its equal(-ising) status.[112] As Bauböck explains, "granting governments powers to revoke [citizenship] status potentially undermines the foundation of their democratic legitimacy".[113] In this light, "the significance of the issue transcends the numbers currently involved",[114] and there is also the risk that States are embarking on a potentially slippery slope when they "pierce even a small—liberal size—hole into citizenship to punish terrorists".[115]

Even where States stop short of—or run up against the limits to the use of—the denationalisation of their foreign fighters and instead resort to denial of readmission, this can also impact the institution of nationality. Given how closely associated nationality is with the unfettered right to (re)enter and remain in that country, the denial of precisely this right raises an issue. Indeed, as discussed above, this right is a corollary of the duty of (re)admission, which is one of the two essential functions of nationality under international law.[116] So integral is this function to the role of nationality in international law that the question has been asked whether it should be understood as (part of) the minimum core content of nationality, without which the legal bond of nationality itself is eviscerated.[117] Does the denial of readmission thereby amount to the deprivation of nationality and, if the foreign fighter who is treated in this manner holds no other citizenship, should he or she be considered stateless for the purposes of the application of international law? If, on the other hand, it is possible for nationality to withstand the hollowing out of one of its core functions, what then is the status of the person affected? Should those foreign fighters who are denied consular assistance or re-entry into their country of nationality be considered *de facto* stateless?[118] Although the term "*de facto* stateless" is not defined in any international instrument, experts have indeed suggested that this concept would apply to persons "outside the country of their nationality who are unable or, for valid reasons, are unwilling to avail themselves of the protection of that country"[119]—protection referring to "diplomatic and consular assistance generally, *including in relation to return to the State of nationality*".[120] Thus, even if the refusal to facilitate or allow readmission does not terminate the formal bond of nationality, the erosion

[112] Including Van Waas 2016; Macklin 2018; Van Waas and Jaghai 2018; Bauböck 2020; Gibney 2020b; Honohan 2020.

[113] Bauböck 2020, p. 393.

[114] Honohan 2020, p. 359.

[115] Gibney 2018, p. 222.

[116] The other being to serve as the basis for the exercise by the State of the right of diplomatic protection. Weis 1979, p. 45.

[117] Edwards 2014, p. 30.

[118] See Macklin 2014, p. 6.

[119] UNHCR 2014, p. 5.

[120] Emphasis added, ibid. The Intergovernmental Committee on Refugees—the predecessor to the UNHCR—on multiple occasions connected statelessness to non-repatriation, which could be caused

of the core content of nationality is such that the use of this measure against foreign fighters raises complex questions about its legal ramifications, whether *de facto* statelessness results and, if so, how this affects the interpretation and application of international law standards.

10.7 Conclusion

By putting the 'foreign' into 'foreign fighter', countries of origin have innovated hitherto unforeseen ways in which to shirk their responsibility towards their citizens and thereby also their duty vis-à-vis other States. The resultant "dumping"[121] of those (suspected to have) engaged in terrorist activities or of being affiliated to a terrorist organisation has stranded thousands in what UN Secretary-General Guterres described as "dire security and humanitarian conditions", subsequently worsened by the global COVID-19 pandemic.[122] As this chapter has shown, the contemporary phenomenon of exporting terrorists implicates a wide array of international norms, while also raising a host of foundational questions about the international legal order that will need to be unpacked further. Ultimately, however, it is the mismatch between the highly symbolic and public disownment of those who (are seen to) have associated themselves with ISIS and any real security gains that is likely to be most persuasive in precipitating a re-think on this policy position.

References

Al Jazeera (2019) Denmark Passes Legislation to Strip ISIL Fighters of Citizenship. https://www.aljazeera.com/news/2019/10/24/denmark-passes-legislation-to-strip-isil-fighters-of-citizenship/. Accessed 1 October 2020

Anderson B (2013) Us and Them: The Dangerous Politics of Immigration Control. Oxford University Press, Oxford

Arendt H (1968) The Origins of Totalitarianism. Houghton Mifflin Harcourt, New York

Arnell P (2020) The Legality of the Citizenship Deprivation of UK Foreign Terrorist Fighters. ERA Forum, Springer

Bauböck R (2020) A Free Movement Paradox: Denationalisation and Deportation in Mobile Societies. Citizenship Studies 24(3):389–403

Beauchamps M (2017) Modelling the Self, Creating the Other: French Denaturalisation Law on the Brink of World War II. In: Leese M, Wittendorp S (eds) Security/Mobility. Politics of Movement. Manchester University Press, Manchester, pp 189–205

Bertram C (2020) Citizenship Deprivation: A Philosopher's Perspective. In: Institute on Statelessness and Inclusion (ed) The World's Stateless: Deprivation of Nationality. Institute on Statelessness and Inclusion (ISI), pp 193–196

---

by either a lack of nationality or a lack of governmental protection. Intergovernmental Committee on Refugees 1944, p. 1. See further Massey 2010.

[121] Mehra and Paulussen 2019.

[122] UN 2020.

Bex-Reimert V et al (2020) Evaluatie wijziging van de Rijkswet op het Nederlanderschap in het belang van de nationale veiligheid. Eindrapport, Rijksuniversiteit Groningen, Groningen
Blackbourn J, Walker C (2016) Interdiction and Indoctrination: The Counter-Terrorism and Security Act 2015. MLR. https://doi.org/10.1111/1468-2230.12217
Brussels Court of Appeal (2018) Case 2018/KR/45. https://www.kennisplein.be/sites/Jeugdrecht/Documents/2018%204%20Arrest%20hof%20van%20beroep%20Brrussel%2012%20september%202018%20(4).pdf. Accessed 22 October 2020
Brussels Court of Appeal (2019) Case 2019/KR/4. https://www.kennisplein.be/sites/Jeugdrecht/Documents/2019%2001%20HvB%20Brussel%2027%2002%202019.pdf. Accessed 22 October 2020
Brussels Dutch Court of First Instance (2018) Case 2018/75/C. https://www.kennisplein.be/sites/Jeugdrecht/Documents/2019%2001%20Rechtbank%20van%20eerste%20aanleg%20Brussel%20Nederlandstalig%20(Kg.)%2026%20december%202018.pdf. Accessed 19 October 2020
Burchardt D, Gulati R (2018) International Counter-Terrorism Regulation and Citizenship-Stripping Laws—Reinforcing Legal Exceptionalism. J Confl Secur Law 23:203–228
Choudhury T (2017) The Radicalisation of Citizenship Deprivation. Critical Social Policy 37:225–244
Coolsaet R, Renard T (2020) From Bad to Worse: The Fate of European Foreign Fighters and Families Detained in Syria, One Year After the Turkish Offensive. https://www.egmontinstitute.be/content/uploads/2020/10/SPB130_final.pdf?type=pdf. Accessed 12 February 2021
Crikey (2015) Essential: Citizenship Stripping—By Courts—Overwhelmingly Popular. https://www.crikey.com.au/2015/06/10/essential-citizenship-stripping-by-courts-overwhelmingly-popular/. Accessed 1 October 2020
Dearden L (2019) Shamima Begum: Number of People Stripped of UK Citizenship Soars by 600% in a Year. https://www.independent.co.uk/news/uk/home-news/shamima-begum-uk-citizenship-stripped-home-office-sajid-javid-a8788301.html. Accessed 1 October 2020
Denza E (2018) Nationality and Diplomatic Protection. NILR 65:463–480
District Court of The Hague (2019) ECLI:NL:RBDHA:2019:11909. https://uitspraken.rechtspraak.nl/inziendocument?id=ECLI:NL:RBDHA:2019:11909. Accessed 25 September 2020
Edwards A (2014) The Meaning of Nationality. In: Edwards A, Van Waas L (eds) Nationality and Statelessness Under International Law. Cambridge University Press, Cambridge, pp 11–43
Fenwick H (2016) Responding to the ISIS Threat: Extending Coercive Non-Trial-Based Measures in the Counter-Terrorism and Security Act 2015. IRLCT. https://doi.org/10.1080/13600869.2016.1145870
Fisher Williams J (1927) Denationalization. Brit Yearb Int Law 8:45
Francois M, Ibrahim A (2020) The Children of ISIS Detainees: Europe's Dilemma. Center for Global Policy. https://newlinesinstitute.org/wp-content/uploads/2020/06/CGP-Children-of-ISIS-June-2020.pdf. Accessed 12 February 2021
Gall C (2019) Turkey Vows to Send ISIS Militants Home. https://www.nytimes.com/2019/11/08/world/middleeast/turkey-syria-isis-prisoners.html. Accessed 1 October 2019
Gherbaoui T (2020) Criminalising Foreign Fighter Travel in Order to Prevent Terrorism in Europe: An Illegitimate Assault on Human Dignity. In: Paulussen C, Scheinin M (eds) Human Dignity and Human Security in Times of Terrorism. T.M.C. Asser Press, The Hague, pp 241–267
Gibney M (2014) The Deprivation of Citizenship in the United Kingdom: A Brief History, Immigration, Nationality and Asylum Law 28(4):326–335
Gibney M (2018) Beware States Piercing Holes into Citizenship. In: Bauböck R (ed) Debating Transformations of National Citizenship. IMISCOE Research Series. Springer, Cham. pp 219–223
Gibney M (2020a) Denationalisation and Discrimination. Journal of Ethical and Migration Studies. 46(12):2551–2568
Gibney M (2020b) Deprivation of Citizenship Through a Political Lens: A Political Scientist's Perspective. In: Institute on Statelessness and Inclusion (ed) The World's Stateless: Deprivation of Nationality, pp 207–209

Goodwin-Gill (2014) Deprivation of Citizenship, Statelessness, and International Law. https://www.kaldorcentre.unsw.edu.au/sites/default/files/gsgg%204-deprivationcitizenship-moreauthority.pdf. Accessed 1 October 2020

Guillaume X (2019) The Duty of Care and Deterritorialized Citizenship: From Governing Citizenship to Acts of Citizenship. In: Graeger N, Leira H (eds) The Duty of Care in International Relations: Protecting Citizens Beyond the Border. Routledge, New York City, pp 105–117

Harvey A (2015) Recent Developments on Deprivation of Nationality on Grounds of National Security and Terrorism Resulting in Statelessness. http://sprc.info/wp-content/uploads/2015/02/Harvey-article.pdf. Accessed 1 October 2020

Honohan I (2020) Just What's Wrong with Losing Citizenship? Examining Revocation of Citizenship from a Non-domination Perspective. Citizenship Studies 24(3):355–370

Institute on Statelessness and Inclusion (2020) Citizenship Stripping as a Security Measure – Policy Issues and the "Effectiveness" Question. In: Institute on Statelessness and Inclusion (ed) The World's Stateless: Deprivation of Nationality, pp 227–238

Intergovernmental Committee on Refugees (1944) Memorandum: The Intergovernmental Committee and Non-Repatriables. https://search.archives.un.org/registration-and-identification-3. Accessed 1 October 2020

Jaghai S, Van Waas L (2020) Stripped of Citizenship, Stripped of Dignity? A Critical Exploration of Nationality Deprivation as a Counter-Terrorism Measure. In: Paulussen C, Scheinin M (eds) Human Dignity and Human Security in Times of Terrorism. T.M.C. Asser Press, The Hague, pp 153–179

Jones-Bos R, van Daalen M (2008) Trends and Developments in Consular Services: The Dutch Experience. HJD. https://doi.org/10.1163/187119008X266173

Kofod J (2019) We Owe Absolutely Nothing to Foreign Fighters. https://twitter.com/JeppeKofod/status/1195671612835745792. Accessed 1 October 2020

Krähenmann S (2016) The Obligations Under International Law of Foreign Fighter's State of Nationality or Habitual Residence, State of Transit and State of Destination. In: de Guttry A, Capone F, Paulussen C (eds) Foreign Fighters Under International Law and Beyond. T.M.C. Asser Press, The Hague, pp 229–258

Lepoutre J (2020) Citizenship Loss and Deprivation in the European Union (27 + 1). EUI Working Paper RSCAS 2020/29, GLOBALCIT

Lloyd M (2020) Framing Foreign Fighting: Exploring the Scope of Prevention and the Categorisation of Fighters in International Law. In: Paulussen C, Scheinin M (eds) Human Dignity and Human Security in Times of Terrorism. T.M.C. Asser Press, The Hague, pp 207–238

Lote P, Krekling D, Carlsen H (2019) Solberg: Norske IS-krigere har rett til å komme hjem. https://www.nrk.no/urix/solberg_-_-norske-is-krigere-har-rett-til-a-komme-hjem-1.14434249. Accessed 1 October 2020

Macklin A (2014) Citizenship Revocation, the Privilege to Have Rights and the Production of the Alien. Queen's LJ 40(1):1–54

Macklin A (2018) The Return of Banishment: Do the New Denationalisation Policies Weaken Citizenship? In: Bauböck R (ed) Debating Transformations of National Citizenship. IMISCOE Research Series. Springer, Cham. pp 163–172

Malet D (2010) Why Foreign Fighters? Historical Perspectives and Solutions, Orbis 54(1):97–114

Malet D (2019) ISIS Foreign Fighters: Keep Your Enemies Closer. Australian Outlook. http://www.internationalaffairs.org.au/australianoutlook/isis-foreign-fighters-keep-enemies-closer/. Accessed 11 October 2021

Mantu (2015) Citizenship in Times of Terror: Citizenship Deprivation in the UK, Conference: ECPR Standing Groups, Warsaw, 29 March–2 April 2015

Massey H (2010) UNHCR and De Facto Statelessness. https://www.unhcr.org/4bc2ddeb9.pdf. Accessed 11 October 2021

Méheut C, Hubbard B (2020) France Brings 10 Children of French Jihadists Home from Syria. https://www.nytimes.com/2020/06/22/world/europe/france-isis-children-repatriated.html. Accessed 8 October 2020

Mehra T, Paulussen C (2019) The Repatriation of Foreign Fighters and Their Families: Options, Obligations, Morality and Long-Term Thinking. ICCT. https://icct.nl/publication/the-repatriation-of-foreign-fighters-and-their-families-options-obligations-morality-and-long-term-thinking/. Accessed 11 October 2021

Meijers Committee (2020) Policy Brief on Differential Treatment of Citizens with Dual or Multiple Nationality and the Prohibition of Discrimination. https://www.commissie-meijers.nl/sites/all/files/cm2016_policy_brief_on_differential_treatment_of_citizens_with_dual_or_multiple_nationality_and_the_prohibition_of_discrimantion.pdf. Accessed 15 February 2021

Okano-Heijmans M (2011) Changes in Consular Assistance and the Emergence of Consular Diplomacy. In: Melissen J, Fernández AM (eds) Consular Affairs and Diplomacy. Martinus Nijhoff Publishers, Leiden, pp 19–41

Paulussen C (2020) Towards a Right to Sustainable Security of Person in Times of Terrorism? Assessing Possibilities and Limitations Through a Critical Evaluation of Citizenship Stripping and Non-repatriation Policies. Journal of Conflict and Security Law 26(1):219–249

Paulussen C, Scheinin M (2020) Deprivation of Nationality as a Counter-Terrorism Measure: A Human Rights and Security Perspective. In: Institute on Statelessness and Inclusion (ed) The World's Stateless: Deprivation of Nationality, pp 223–226

Paulussen C, Van Waas L (2020) The Counter-Productiveness of Deprivation of Nationality as a National Security Measure. Asser Today. https://www.asser.nl/about-the-institute/asser-today/blog-post-the-counter-productiveness-of-deprivation-of-nationality-as-a-national-security-measure/. Accessed 11 October 2021

Reyntjens L (2019) Citizenship Deprivation Under the European Convention-System. A Case Study of Belgium. Statelessness and Citizenship Review 1(2):263–282

Rights and Security International (2020a) Europe's Guantanamo: The Indefinite Detention of European Women and Children in North East Syria. https://www.rightsandsecurity.org/assets/downloads/Europes-guantanamo-THE_REPORT.pdf. Accessed 11 October 2021

Rights and Security International (2020b) Europe's Guantanamo: The Indefinite Detention of European Women and Children in North East Syria. https://www.rightsandsecurity.org/assets/downloads/Europes-guantanamo-THE_REPORT.pdf. Accessed 15 February 2021

Roithmaier K (2019) Germany and Its Returning Foreign Terrorist Fighters: New Loss of Citizenship Law and the Broader German Repatriation Landscape. ICCT. https://icct.nl/publication/germany-and-its-returning-foreign-terrorist-fighters-new-loss-of-citizenship-law-and-the-broader-german-repatriation-landscape/. Accessed 11 October 2021

Scott P (2020) Passports, the Right to Travel, and National Security in the Commonwealth. ICLQ. https://doi.org/10.1017/S0020589320000093

Special Rapporteur on the Promotion and Protection of Human Rights and Fundamental Freedoms while Countering Terrorism (2019) Position of the Special Rapporteur: Return of Foreign Fighters and their Families to the Consultation Meeting with Experts on the Return of "Foreign Fighters" and their Families organised by the Council of Europe Commissioner for Human Rights. https://www.ohchr.org/Documents/Issues/Terrorism/PositionSRreturnsFFsOct2019.docx. Accessed 11 October 2021

Spiro PJ (2018) Terrorist Expatriation: All Show, No Bite, No Future. In: Bauböck R (ed) Debating Transformations of National Citizenship. IMISCOE Research Series. Springer, Cham. pp 173–175

The Hague Court of Appeal (2019) ECLI:NL:GHDHA:2019:3208. https://uitspraken.rechtspraak.nl/inziendocument?id=ECLI:NL:GHDHA:2019:3208. Accessed 25 September 2020

Tweede Kamer der Staten-Generaal (2019) Terrorismebestrijding (Kamerstuk 29754, nr. 492). https://zoek.officielebekendmakingen.nl/kst-29754-492.pdf. Accessed 1 October 2020

UN (2019) Key Principles for the Protection, Repatriation, Prosecution, Rehabilitation and Reintegration of Women and Children. https://www.un.org/counterterrorism/sites/www.un.org.counterterrorism/files/key_principles-april_2019.pdf. Accessed 19 October 2020

UN (2020) Secretary-General Warns Terrorists Are Exploiting COVID-19 Pandemic, Calls for Vigilance, at Virtual Counter-Terrorism Week Opening. https://www.un.org/press/en/2020/sgsm20161.doc.htm. Accessed 19 October 2020

UN Counter-Terrorism Centre (2019) Children Affected by the Foreign-Fighter Phenomenon: Ensuring a Child Rights-Based Approach. https://www.un.org/counterterrorism/ctitf/sites/www.un.org.counterterrorism.ctitf/files/ftf_handbook_web_reduced.pdf. Accessed 19 October 2021

UN High Commissioner for Human Rights (2018) Amicus Brief presented by the UN Special Rapporteur on Contemporary Forms of Racism, Racial Discrimination, Xenophobia and Related Intolerance Before the Dutch Immigration and Naturalisation Service. https://www.ohchr.org/Documents/Issues/Racism/SR/Amicus/DutchImmigration_Amicus.pdf. Accessed 1 October 2020

UN Human Rights Council (2018) Report of the Special Rapporteur on Contemporary Forms of Racism, Racial Discrimination, Xenophobia and Related Intolerance. A/HRC/38/52 https://undocs.org/A/HRC/38/52. Accessed 1 October 2020

UN Office of the High Commissioner on Human Rights (2020) Table of Pending Cases Before the Committee on the Rights of the Child. https://www.ohchr.org/Documents/HRBodies/CRC/TablePendingCases.pdf. Accessed 19 October 2021

UN Secretary-General (2018) Guidance Note of the Secretary General: The United Nations and Statelessness. https://www.refworld.org/pdfid/5c580e507.pdf. Accessed 1 October 2020

UN Special Rapporteur on the Promotion and Protection of Human Rights and Fundamental Freedoms While Countering Terrorism and the UN Special Rapporteur on Arbitrary and Extra-Judicial Executions (2020) Submission in the Case of H.F. and M.F. v. France (Application No. 24383/19) Before the European Court of Human Rights

UNHCR (2014) Handbook on Protection of Stateless Persons. https://www.refworld.org/docid/53b676aa4.html. Accessed 19 October 2021

US Mission to the United Nations (2020) Explanation of Vote on a UN Security Council Draft Resolution on Threats to International Peace and Security Caused by Terrorist Acts. https://usun.usmission.gov/explanation-of-vote-on-a-un-security-council-draft-resolution-on-threats-to-international-peace-and-security-caused-by-terrorist-acts/. Accessed 19 October 2021

Van Waas L (2016) Foreign Fighters and the Deprivation of Nationality: National Practices and International Law Implications. In: de Guttry A, Capone F, Paulussen C (eds) Foreign Fighters Under International Law and Beyond. T.M.C. Asser Press, The Hague, pp 469–487

Van Waas L, Jaghai S (2018) All Citizens are Created Equal, but Some are More Equal Than Others. Netherlands International Law Review 65:413–430

Walker C (2020) Exporting Human Security in the Cause of Counter-Terrorism. In: Paulussen C, Scheinin M (eds) Human Dignity and Human Security in Times of Terrorism. T.M.C. Asser Press, The Hague, pp 35–65

Weis P (1979) Nationality and Statelessness in International Law. Kluwer Academic Publishers Group, Dordrecht

Chapter 11
Family Courts as Part of States' Counter-Terrorism Toolkit: A Welcome Development for the Children of FTFs?

Rumyana van Ark

Contents

Abstract The case for family courts having a bigger or exclusive role in making and monitoring arrangements for the families and, in particular, the children of alleged foreign terrorist fighters (FTFs) is strong. These courts can be a conduit for a whole of government approach in respect of children potentially impacted by radicalisation or extremism and/or children of alleged FTFs. As part of the broader rule of law framework, the family justice system works in cooperation with the criminal justice system to ensure the proper administration of justice in both of these jurisdictions. What makes family law better suited to addressing cases of (potentially) radicalised children or children of alleged FTFs, however, is the best interests of the child principle—a foundational principle of family law regardless of the jurisdiction. What this chapter proposes to do is to put forward the case for family courts and pertinent child support and protection services as a more long-term and sustainable response to the plight of accompanied and orphaned children of alleged FTFs: a response that respects the applicable international legal obligations.

Keywords Foreign fighters · Counter-terrorism · Children's rights · Family courts · Radicalisation

R. van Ark (✉)
T.M.C. Asser Instituut, The Hague, The Netherlands
e-mail: R.Grozdanova@asser.nl

University of Amsterdam, Amsterdam, The Netherlands

F. Capone et al. (eds.), *Returning Foreign Fighters: Responses, Legal Challenges and Ways Forward*, https://doi.org/10.1007/978-94-6265-571-3_11

11.1 Introduction

"They made a huge and terrible mistake … if they return home there are no terrorism issues". These comments were made in March 2015 in respect of Kadiza Sultana (16), Amira Abase (15) and Shamima Begum (15).[1] Kadiza Sultana has since been reported to have died in an airstrike on Raqqa,[2] the whereabouts of Amira Abase are still unknown,[3] and as of 19 February 2019, Shamima Begum is no longer a British citizen.[4] The flight and plight of these three young women have been much rehearsed. It is likely that their infamy has at least in part led to the decision to deprive Shamima Begum of British citizenship. On 14 February 2019, Ben Wallace, the then Minister of State for Security, stated that "As a British citizen [Shamima Begum] has a right to come home here … we are obliged to make sure our citizens have rights, no matter who they are."[5] This is in line with the United Kingdom's Strategy for Countering Terrorism (CONTEST)[6] under which returnees from Syria should be subject to a managed return, a Temporary Exclusion Order,[7] an investigation into alleged criminal behaviour and/or rehabilitation and reintegration into society. Yet, by 20 February 2019, Shamima Begum was no longer a British citizen following an assessment by the then Home Secretary Sajid Javid that her return to the United Kingdom would present a risk to national security.

The furore surrounding their life choices tends to obscure the following particularly important issue—in 2015, all three girls were children in the eyes of international

[1] These comments were made by Sir Bernard Hogan-Howe 2015, the then Metropolitan Police Commissioner in an oral hearing of the House of Commons Home Affairs Select Committee (United Kingdom).

[2] The Guardian 2019b.

[3] Ibid.

[4] Special Immigration Appeals Commission (United Kingdom), *Begum v The Secretary of State for the Home Department*, Open Judgement, 7 February 2020, Appeal No. SC/163/2019. In July 2020, the Court of Appeal found that "fairness and justice must, on the facts of this case, outweigh the national security concerns" thus Shamima Begum must be allowed leave to enter and challenge the deprivation decision in person in England and Wales Court of Appeals (EWCA) (Civil Division), *Begum v The Special Immigration Appeals Commission and Others*, 16 July 2020, [2020] EWCA Civ 918. In February 2021, the Supreme Court *fully reversed* the decision of the Court of Appeal and rather critically noted that the Court of Appeal's approach did not give the "Home Secretary's assessment the respect which it should have received"; further, according to the Supreme Court, "the Court of Appeal ***mistakenly*** [emphasis added] believed that, when an individual's right to have a fair hearing came into conflict with the requirements of national security, her right to a fair hearing must prevail." In The Supreme Court (United Kingdom), *Begum v The Special Immigration Appeals Commission and Others*, 16 February 2021, [2021] UKSC 7.

[5] See The Independent 2019.

[6] See Home Office (United Kingdom) 2018.

[7] A "temporary exclusion order" is an order which requires an individual not to return to the United Kingdom unless they have a permit to return issued by the Home Secretary or the return is the result of the individual's deportation into the United Kingdom. Such an order can be in force for up to two years. See further *Counter-Terrorism and Security Act 2015* (Part 1, Chapter 2), full text available at https://www.legislation.gov.uk/ukpga/2015/6/contents?extent%253Dni. Accessed 5 August 2021.

and domestic law.[8] As such, had one or all three of them sought a managed return to the United Kingdom (UK) before the age of 18, it would have been for a family court to decide on what measure(s) need to be applied in their particular circumstances.[9] So far, approximately 300 cases involving children who may be radicalised, who have attempted to travel to or have returned from Syria, and/or have been born in ISIS-held territories have been adjudicated on in the UK.[10] A broad range of protective measures has been applied to many of these children. Some children have been temporarily made wards of court, i.e. the High Court has become their legal guardian, and as such, its consent is required on decisions such as place of residence.[11] Other children (and their families) have had severe restrictions placed on their travel by obliging them to temporarily surrender their passports to a solicitor.[12] If the family courts' approach is to be summarised relying on the judges' own words, it is that they have followed the principle of "not to risk the incurring of damage to children that it could not repair, but rather to prevent the damage done."[13] In a nutshell, the applicable jurisprudence makes it unlikely that Shamima Begum would have been so swiftly and publicly deprived of citizenship had she sought and secured a managed return to the UK before the age of 18 while she was still legally a child.

---

[8] Under Article 1 of the United Nations Convention on the Rights of the Child, opened for signature 20 November 1989, 1577 UNTS 3 (entered into force 2 September 1990) (CRC) in principle, every human being below the age of eighteen years is considered a child. The Convention has been ratified by 196 states and is considered to be one of the most widely ratified UN treaties. The United Kingdom ratified the CRC in 1991 and follows its definition domestically.

[9] See in particular the Guidance in Munby 2015.

[10] This list is non-exhaustive but sufficiently illustrative. See further Ahdash 2020 and Malik 2019. There are no publicly available statistics to suggest that the relevant courts in countries such as the Netherlands, France and Belgium have dealt with a similar number or diversity of cases.

[11] Illustrative case examples include the cases in respect of 'B', a sixteen-year-old who became radicalised and attempted to travel to Syria through Turkey. She was intercepted by the Metropolitan Police minutes before her flight was due to take off. High Court of Justice (Family Division) (England and Wales), *London Borough of Tower Hamlets v B*, Judgement, 21 August 2015, [2015] EWHC 2491 (Fam) (case 1) and High Court of Justice (Family Division) (England and Wales), *London Borough of Tower Hamlets v B*, Judgement, 13 June 2016, [2016] EWHC 1707 (Fam) (case 2). B was temporarily removed from her family home and placed into foster care due to fears that her home environment facilitated her radicalisation. To prevent further attempts to travel, her passport and those of other immediate family members were given to their family solicitor on the understanding that the alternative would be the harsher measure of removal of the passports by the officers (Tipstaff) of the High Court.

[12] See for example the cases of High Court of Justice (Family Division) (England and Wales), *In the Matter of X (Children) and In the Matter of Y (Children)*, Judgement, 30 July 2015, [2015] EWHC 2265 (Fam)—two individual cases which were heard together due to the similarity of the issues raised in each case. Both cases involved parents and/or other family members who attempted to travel to Syria to allegedly join ISIS with their children. Following representations by the two Local Authorities involved, all children were made wards of court before being placed back in the care and control of their families. The return to the family homes was subject to a range of stringent protective orders.

[13] High Court of Justice (Family Division) (England and Wales), *In the Matter of M (Children)*, Judgement, 20 May 2015, [2015] EWHC 1433 (Fam) and Court of Chancery (England and Wales) *Wellesley v Duke of Beaufort*, Judgement, 1827, (1827) 2 Russ 1.

The case for family courts having a bigger or exclusive role in making and monitoring arrangements for the families and, in particular, the children of alleged foreign terrorist fighters (FTFs) is strong. In jurisdictions other than the UK,[14] the courts tasked with cases involving children are also an intersection at which various actors[15] can interact. In other words, these courts can be a conduit for a whole of government approach in respect of children potentially impacted by radicalisation or extremism and/or children of alleged FTFs. Further, as part of the broader rule of law framework, the family justice system works in cooperation with the criminal justice system to ensure the proper administration of justice in both of these jurisdictions.[16] What makes family law better suited to addressing cases of (potentially) radicalised children or children of alleged FTFs, however, is the best interests of the child principle—a foundational principle of family law regardless of the jurisdiction. This principle is also at the core of the international legal regime governing the rights of the child.[17] In dealing with this challenging range of cases, the UK family courts have emulated another particularly important and relevant aspect of the international legal regime protecting children—namely that children are deserving of special protections by virtue of their age and vulnerability.[18] The UN guidance in respect of children related to or associated with designated terrorist groups expressly advises states to treat such children primarily as victims when devising counter-terrorism responses.[19] Yet, the discourse surrounding the children caught in the FTF phenomenon continues to be dominated by national security risk and threat considerations regardless of the age, vulnerability or personal circumstances of the children involved.[20]

What this chapter proposes to do is to put forward the case for family courts and pertinent child support and protection services as a more long-term and sustainable response to the plight of accompanied and orphaned children of alleged FTFs: a response that respects the applicable international legal obligations. The best interests of the child principle and national security interests can be reconciled as the below examination of the most relevant and striking caselaw of the UK family courts will demonstrate. In general, family court decisions can be difficult to access, if at

[14] In the Netherlands for example, if a minor is involved in a suspected departure, the Child Care and Protection Board will initiate an investigation and based on this investigation the Board may request from the court to (temporarily) place the minor under supervision or within (foster) care or take other fitting measures. For further details, see Ministry of Security and Justice et al. 2016.

[15] For example, local police, social and health services, educational bodies, etc.

[16] Munby 2015.

[17] See in particular CRC, above n 8, Article 3.

[18] On the concept of vulnerability and its various facets, see for example Luthar 2003. The UN Committee on the Rights of the Child has highlighted the vulnerability of young children to "poverty, discrimination, family breakdown and multiple other adversities that violate their rights and undermine their well-being". The Committee has also emphasised what are vulnerable groups of children such as for example children belonging to racial, ethnic, religious or linguistic minorities, indigenous children, displaced children or children with disabilities among other examples. See further the UN Committee on the Rights of the Child 2005 and UN Committee on the Rights of the Child 2007.

[19] United Nations Office of Counter-Terrorism 2020.

[20] For an illustrative example, see The Guardian 2019c. See also The Washington Post 2021.

all, due to the sensitive nature of the issues involved. However, the UK's family courts have published, with anonymisations, redactions and abridgements, a number of decisions involving children affected by the FTF phenomenon. The regularity, range and sophistication of the measures applied by the UK family courts based on the age, family circumstances, living arrangements and exposure to extremism and radicalisation of each child is highly instructive. As such, they deserve more attention and arguably more duplication.

Due to the different structures of domestic legal frameworks, family courts in other jurisdictions may not be able to adopt the same type of measures or impose similar interventions. Nevertheless, as the cases involving the complex harm caused by radicalisation and/or socialisation into violent extremism and terrorism pose new and varied challenges to courts across various jurisdictions, a cross-pollination of judicial practices could be quite valuable. What the fast-growing jurisprudence[21] from the UK family courts does offer is an opportunity to take stock of possible alternatives to the prevailing governmental approach of treating children affected by the FTF phenomenon as a potential security risk. More significantly, perhaps, the jurisprudence arguably demonstrates that counter-radicalisation, -extremism and—terrorism efforts could benefit by adopting a children's rights approach. The protective and preventative role UK family courts can play in respect of children's (in)voluntary involvement in violent extremist and terrorist groups has already been favourably highlighted by at least one UN body.[22]

Regrettably, however, an assessment of the overall regional and international approach to children of alleged FTFs shows that very little attention has been given to (a) states obligations under the UN Convention on the Rights of the Child (UNCRC) and (b) the (in)direct impact on children when security measures are applied to their parents. This is rather problematic as under the provisions of the UNCRC, children are rightsholders in their own capacity, and thus their rights should not be undermined by the alleged activities of their parents. Yet, as the immediately following section will outline, the protections owed to children seem to be treated as a tertiary rather than primary consideration at the international and regional level. Even more problematically, the sporadic references to the children caught in the FTF phenomenon adopt a very monolithic approach that fails to reflect on the individual experiences and vulnerabilities of each child. The stark contrast with the highly individualised and sensitive approach by the UK family courts arguably underlines the need for more cross-pollination of alternative and constructive practices at the domestic, regional and international level in respect of children caught in the FTF phenomenon.

---

[21] While the exact number of cases involving potentially radicalised children is not publicly known or accessible, it has been suggested that it could be up to 300 (during the period between July 2015 and March 2018). See Ahdash 2020, where she notes that obtaining some of the figures required three Freedom of Information requests. As the judgments in a number of cases involving potentially radicalised children (from April 2018 onwards) have been made accessible, it is likely that the number of cases exceeds 300.

[22] UN Office on Drugs and Crime 2017.

11.2 International Legal Obligations and Children Affected by the FTF Phenomenon

The domestic, regional and international responses to the FTF phenomenon have followed a well-established pattern. Even though the relevant legislative and policy security toolkits were already quite extensive,[23] there was a rush to adopt new and amend existing legislative provisions to more effectively respond to yet another manifestation of the 'acute and growing threat' posed by terrorism.[24] The initial international response is aptly illustrated by UN Security Council Resolution 2178. With this Resolution, the Security Council triggered the following two particularly significant developments: (a) the conflation of the foreign fighters and terrorism phenomena,[25] thus facilitating states in applying the full range of applicable counter-terrorism measures to those labelled as FTFs and (b) encouraging states to go even further in intertwining immigration and security measures to prevent the travel of alleged FTFs.[26] Domestically, this has resulted in the adoption or embedding of, what traditionally have been, immigration measures such as citizenship and/or passport cancellation as part of counter-terrorism and security toolkits.[27] In the overall context of the post 9/11 securitisation at the international, regional and domestic level, such developments are as unsurprising as they are undesirable. What is particularly problematic in this iteration of UN Security Council Resolutions addressing various manifestations of terrorism are the (very) limited references to the rights of the children caught in the FTF phenomenon. Even though various other UN documents[28] have expressly highlighted the numerous (in)direct effects that security measures, such as severe restrictions on travel and/or citizenship deprivation, when applied to the parents, have on their children, these have been barely reflected in the texts of the relevant Resolutions.

UN Security Council Resolution 2396, adopted in 2017, is a rare exception that accentuates rather than alleviates the concerns that the rights of the affected children are a tertiary and not a primary concern.[29] In comparison to previous and subsequent

[23] On this point, see for example Roach 2011, Gearty 2013, Blackbourn and Walker 2016 and Lazarus and Goold 2019.

[24] See the language of UN Security Council 2014, which is reflective of previous UNSC Resolutions addressing various aspects of terrorism.

[25] For a critical reflection on this conflation, please see further Capone 2016 and Ip 2020.

[26] In echoing UNSC Resolution 1373, Resolution 2178 reiterated that states should not allow refugee status to be abused by those who have been involved in terrorism activities with the list now including FTFs.

[27] See for example Pillai and Williams 2017 and Scott 2020.

[28] Such documents include United Nations Office of Counter-Terrorism 2020 as well as various reports by the UN Special Rapporteur on the Promotion and Protection of Human Rights and Fundamental Freedoms while Countering Terrorism (for example the Special Rapporteur's Legal Analysis on *Extra-territorial Jurisdiction of States over Children and their Guardians in Camps, Prisons or Elsewhere in the Northern Syrian Arab Republic*. See also the Office of the Special Representative of the Secretary-General on Sexual Violence in Conflict 2019.

[29] UN Security Council 2017.

Resolutions with similar emphasis,[30] Resolution 2396 made several references to the families and children of FTFs. In the relevant paragraphs, the Resolution recognised that children may be especially vulnerable to radicalisation to violence and, as such, in need of particular social support; that these children's rights need to be observed and their dignity respected and that they may also be victims of terrorism. Albeit limited in number,[31] the acknowledgement that children of (alleged) FTFs should be treated as a distinct group requiring special international, regional and domestic policies is welcome. Until this Resolution, very few other international or regional documents had explicitly or implicitly acknowledged that as rights holders in their own capacity, the children caught in the modern FTF phenomenon deserve separate and special attention.

The 2015 Additional Protocol[32] to the 2005 Prevention of Terrorism Convention is another exception within the overall regional and international security response to the FTF phenomenon.[33] Article 8 of the Protocol states that signatories must ensure that implementation of the Protocol, which criminalises a number of activities associated with foreign terrorist fighting, is in accordance with human rights obligations. The Explanatory Report to the Protocol expressly clarifies that the relevant human rights obligations include the UNCRC, which "may be of particular relevance due to the young age of some persons travelling with terrorist purpose".[34] The importance of this clarification is two-fold. While other international human rights documents such as the Universal Declaration of Human Rights and the International Covenant on Civil and Political Rights extend particular care to children, the UNCRC puts forward the most comprehensive and demanding range of obligations states must comply with in respect of children. For example, the UNCRC imposes positive obligations on states to ensure to the maximum extent possible the survival and development of a child.[35] Both of these obligations are particularly relevant to the children affected by the FTF phenomenon, as will be discussed further below. Quite significantly, with this clarification, the Explanatory Report recognises that a child may be a perpetrator as well as a victim of foreign terrorist fighting. The practical implications of this are that any policy of a signatory state to the 2015 Additional Protocol in respect of children caught within the FTF phenomenon needs to be multi-dimensional; it has to be a policy reflective of both children's special status under the UNCRC and of the possibility that they may have engaged in criminal activities.

Placed within the context of the 2015 Additional Protocol on the one hand and the scarcity of explicit and extensive reflection on children's rights in other UNSC

[30] See for example UN Security Council 2014. This Resolution made a single reference to 'youth and families'.

[31] There were nine express references to 'children' and two to 'spouses' in the full text of the Resolution.

[32] Additional Protocol to the Council of Europe Convention on the Prevention of Terrorism, opened for signature 22 October 2015, CETS No. 217 (entered into force 1 July 2017).

[33] Council of Europe Convention on the Prevention of Terrorism, opened for signature 16 May 2005 CETS No. 196 (entered into force 1 June 2007).

[34] Council of Europe 2015.

[35] CRC, above n 8, Article 6 (2).

Resolutions on the other hand, Resolution 2396 (2017) is a significant and positive development. For countries to which the 2015 Additional Protocol is applicable, Resolution 2396 reemphasises the relevance and importance of children's rights; for other countries, it puts them on notice that the protections afforded under the UNCRC need to be respected. While not explicitly cited, the spirit and core goals of the UNCRC are strongly echoed across the references made in respect of the children affected by the FTF phenomenon. The Resolution recommends a whole of government approach as the appropriate means through which to address the complex needs of these children and ensure respect for their rights and dignity. Such an approach should include the involvement of, amongst others, health, social welfare and education sectors within more tailored rehabilitation and reintegration strategies. In other words, it encourages states to take the type of actions that can positively impact the physical and mental well-being of the affected children and help them return to a more normal life in comparison to their experiences, first, within a violent conflict, and subsequently within overcrowded and unsafe camps.[36] These and other recommendations in the Resolution, as well as its express acknowledgement of children as a distinct and vulnerable group impacted in a variety of ways by the FTF phenomenon, are commendable.[37]

Regrettably, however, even though the prospects of successful rehabilitation and reintegration of the children are much higher if they are brought back to their country of citizenship, the Resolution makes no references to repatriation.[38] Active assistance and/or repatriation of children of alleged FTFs or children who grew into adults[39] suspected of FTF activities continues to be a highly charged political issue, and public support is low.[40] The plight of Shamima Begum is a particularly good example of the role public opinion and political posturing can play in this context. A case that has not garnered a similar level of publicity but is nevertheless equally illustrative is that of

[36] In July 2020, the conditions in the al-Hawl camp in Syria had been described as amounting to inhuman and degrading treatment. See the decision of *Begum v The Special Immigration Appeals Commission and Others*, above n 4. Moreover, this report suggests that conditions have since deteriorated. Rights and Security International 2020.

[37] Some other relevant documents include UN 2020.

[38] The recent decision of the Committee on the Rights of the Child is an interesting development in the context of repatriations. The Committee found that France (and thus other relevant states) had jurisdiction over child nationals in Kurdish-controlled camps in Syria; as a corollary, states of nationality have positive obligations to protect the human rights of child nationals. See further, Committee on the Rights of the Child, *L.H. et al v. France*, Communications, 2 November 2020, Communications No. 79/2019 and No. 109/2019, CRC/C/85/D/79/2019-CRC/C/85/D/109/2019. The full impact of these findings is yet to crystallise.

[39] While a detailed reflection is not within the scope of this book chapter, the accepted approach towards so-called 'child soldiers', the concept of offences 'continuous in nature' and victim status extending beyond childhood could be instructive and potentially replicated in respect of the children who grew up into adults suspected in terrorist activities while in Syria. See further International Criminal Court (ICC), *Prosecutor v Thomas Lubanga Dyilo*, Judgement pursuant to Article 74 of the Statute, 5 April 2021, ICC-01/04-01/06-2842, T.Ch. I, UNICEF 2007 and Nyamutata 2020 amongst other relevant readings.

[40] For examples, see Euractiv 2020; Clingendael 2020; European Council on Foreign Relations 2019.

three-year-old Amirah, an Australian citizen.[41] It was reported in February that she was at risk of losing her fingers to frostbite in the squalid conditions in the al-Hawl camp. Despite the immediacy of this threat to her physical and mental well-being in addition to regular malnutrition, Australia has refused to assist or facilitate Amirah's repatriation. The small-scale and irregular repatriations of some orphaned citizen children by countries such as France, Belgium, Norway, the UK and Australia are the exceptions that reaffirm the general Western states policy not to actively facilitate the return of FTFs or their families.[42] It is important not to equate these *ad hoc* case-by-case repatriations with proactive and regular repatriations while hundreds of children remain detained in the camps in Syria and Iraq without any certainty as to whether or when they might be able to return to their country of nationality.[43]

This different treatment of children, depending on whether they are orphaned, unaccompanied or have living parent(s), is interlinked and highly problematic. The unwillingness to assist children of suspected FTFs has been justified for reasons such as the refusal of the Kurdish Armed Forces to separate children from a parent or parents who are alleged to pose a security threat to the country of citizenship.[44] In other words, states are reluctant to help their citizen children due to the alleged criminal behaviour of the parents and the potential security threat the parents continue to pose. Being thus placed in a pre-criminal space[45] due to their parents' choices, these children are rendered ineligible for support by their country of citizenship unless either both of their parents are dead or their mothers have agreed to separate from them.[46] This approach is contrary to the provisions of Article 2.2 of the UNCRC, which imposes the following obligation on states—children should be protected against all forms of discrimination or punishment on the basis of the activities of their parents. The prioritisation of repatriations of orphaned children, limited as it is, creates categories of victimhood and vulnerability instead of treating all children as equally vulnerable and deserving of return to the country of their citizenship and a life away from conflict and dangerous camp conditions.[47]

The case for repatriating all children regardless of the status of the parents is strengthened by states' obligations under Article 6 of the UNCRC. As noted above, this Article requires states to ensure, to the maximum extent possible, the survival

---

[41] See further The Guardian 2020a.

[42] See further The New York Times 2020b.

[43] Open Society Justice Initiative 2021.

[44] Ibid. See also The Guardian 2019d.

[45] For a more detailed discussion on 'pre-crime' and 'pre-criminal' spaces, see Zedner 2007 and Zedner and Ashworth 2019. She argues that since the events of 9/11, crime has been increasingly conceived as risk or potential loss triggering pre-emptive security practices and responses.

[46] See for example The New York Times 2020a.

[47] In December 2020, Germany repatriated three women and twelve children from camps in Syria. These women were under investigation in Germany for allegedly belonging to ISIS; nevertheless, the German Minister Heiko Maas noted that he was relieved that the operation was successful, resulting in twelve children and three mothers returning to Germany. The reasoning behind the repatriation—"need was deemed particularly necessary and urgent"—does however suggest a categorisation of victimhood. BBC News 2020.

and development of a child. Both the survival and development of children have been and will continue to be severely impacted by life in the camps.[48] In November 2019, the District Court of The Hague described the conditions in the camps as "appalling".[49] Both the Special Immigration Appeals Commission and the Court of Appeal in the UK have described the conditions in the al-Hawl camp as meeting the threshold of inhuman and degrading treatment for the purposes of Article 3 of the European Convention on Human Rights (ECHR).[50] The protections of Article 3 of the ECHR and its international equivalent under the UN Convention against Torture are absolute and non-derogable.

By leaving the children to languish in these "appalling" conditions, states are arguably acting contrary to a number of their core international legal obligations.[51] As states' counter-terrorism toolkits and relevant legislation have expanded exponentially in the last decade to cover a wide range of alleged criminal behaviour within and beyond state borders, the potential security risk a parent or the parents might pose is neither a compelling nor a convincing reason to leave their children in the precarious conditions in these camps. States' counter-terrorism toolkits are equally able to manage the prospective security risks posed by a child that travelled to Syria and has since become an FTF. Yet, the unwillingness of states to facilitate repatriations has taken deep roots for now.

This Gordian knot of applicable international legal obligations, the special status of children, unspecified security concerns,[52] political reluctance, as well as public and media hostility can seem nigh impossible to untie. Yet, as the constantly growing jurisprudence of the UK family courts demonstrates, there may be means with which to undo or, at least, loosen the knot. The publicly available—albeit with redactions—decisions of the UK family courts show an alternative way forward for states, a way forward which both recognises and respects the special status and protections to be afforded to children and acknowledges the demands of national security. The following section will focus on select and illustrative UK family court decisions,

---

[48] This is even more so since cases of coronavirus were confirmed in one of the camps which is home to thousands of displaced individuals. Aljazeera 2020.

[49] See further District Court of The Hague, Judgement, 11 November 2019, C-09-581588-KG ZA 19-999; decision in a joint submission by a number of Dutch national mothers and their Dutch national children who were seeking repatriation back to the Netherlands.

[50] *Begum v The Special Immigration Appeals Commission and Others*, above n 4.

[51] The full scope of the extraterritorial application of human rights obligations is a contested issue by states. See further Milanovic 2011 and Milanovic and Papic 2018 as well as Raible 2016 and Raible 2020 and the recent findings of the UN Committee on the Rights of the Child in *L.H. et al v. France*, above n 38.

[52] For example, the UK government has claimed that 'age and gender' are not 'relevant considerations' when determining whether an individual poses a national security threat however this statement contradicts both the adopted age of criminal responsibility, the reasons why an age of criminal responsibility exists and its own strategy (PREVENT) highlighting the importance of early intervention to safeguard children of various ages under 18 from being drawn in extremism, radicalism and terrorism. The PREVENT programme is both part of the CONTEST Strategy and part of counter-terrorism legislation (Counter-Terrorism and Security Act 2015). See also The Times 2020.

which show how the family courts can be at the core of a more sustainable and productive response to the complex challenges posed by children affected by the FTF phenomenon.

11.3 The Family Courts, Counter-Terrorism and Children Affected by the FTF Phenomenon

Family courts and counter-terrorism may seem like strange and uneasy bedfellows.[53] Yet, when it comes to addressing cases involving children of FTFs, children who may have been radicalised and/or children who are at risk of being radicalised, the family courts are arguably best placed to reach a decision that safeguards the best interests of the children while cooperating with police and other agencies. The reasons why the family courts are the apposite institution to tackle this rather challenging task are as follows. The "[best] interest of the individual child … is paramount. This cannot be eclipsed by wider considerations of counter-terrorism policy or operations."[54] This statement by Justice Hayden is an apt summation of the general approach adopted by the UK family courts in respect of children affected by the FTF phenomenon. While expressed differently, the underlying sentiments are at the core of the recent UN guidelines in respect of such affected children. Both are reflective of the special status of children under the CRC. Further, the family courts can be the focal point for social welfare, police and health services in cases involving children affected by radicalisation and/or the FTF phenomenon. How this can operate in practice is well illustrated by the relevant legislation, mechanisms and practices in the UK.

Under the Children Act 1989[55] and the Counter-Terrorism and Security Act 2015,[56] local authorities in the UK have dual duties. The former imposes a general duty to safeguard and promote the welfare of children in need. The latter requires the local authorities to have "due regard to the need to prevent people from being drawn into terrorism".[57] In other words, local authorities have a statutory role and responsibility in countering terrorism and helping protect vulnerable individuals from the

[53] See, for example, Ahdash 2020, p. 3 who argues the "radicalisation cases represent a novel interaction between otherwise very separate areas of state activity, family law and counter-terrorism, creating hitherto non-existent 'family law versions of counter-terrorism'". She criticises this development as the "familialisation" of the threat of terrorism. These views have been echoed by the UN Special Rapporteur on the Promotion and Protection of Human Rights and Fundamental Freedoms while Countering Terrorism who has noted that "the interaction between family regulation and counter-terrorism is accelerating with profound implications for both … and enabling the legal regulation of family life in the name of national security in ways that hitherto would have been inconceivable". Special Rapporteur on Terrorism 2021.

[54] *The London Borough of Tower Hamlets v M and ors* [2015] EWHC 869 (Fam).

[55] https://www.legislation.gov.uk/ukpga/1989/41/contents. Accessed 5 August 2021.

[56] https://www.legislation.gov.uk/ukpga/2015/6/contents/enacted. Accessed 5 August 2021.

[57] The full text of Section 26 is available at https://www.legislation.gov.uk/ukpga/2015/6/contents/enacted. Accessed 5 August 2021.

risk of radicalisation. What this has meant in practice is that the relevant local authorities have started proceedings to request that a child be made a ward of court and/or removed from the care of their parents when there have been concerns that there is a risk of radicalisation at home,[58] that the child is already radicalised[59] or after the parents have been stopped from trying to travel with the child/children to Syria and Iraq.[60] In addition to these three separate points of intervention, local authorities can and have also intervened when suspected FTFs have returned with their child or children from Syria and Iraq. In essence, what this initial local authority involvement leads to is a close collaboration between local police authorities, local educational bodies and other appropriate local welfare services before and after the family court has put in place a suitable support and care plan for a child affected by either radicalisation or the FTF phenomenon. In short, the measures applied by the UK family courts in such cases reflect the whole of government approach espoused in Resolution 2396. The following cases are apt examples of how these measures operate in practice. These cases also show the lengths to which the UK family courts have gone to support and protect children affected by the FTF phenomenon.

In a trio of cases with rather striking facts, the Brighton and Hove City Council (the local authority) sought the family court's permission to make Y a ward of court.[61] Y was described as a particularly vulnerable young person from an extraordinary family where several male members had all committed to "waging jihad in Syria". Three of his brothers travelled to Syria to fight for an Al-Qaeda affiliate; two of the brothers were teenagers when they first engaged in foreign fighting. Both have since died in battle. The third brother was seriously injured in combat but remained in Syria, determined to return to fighting. A close family friend, again a teenager, who had lived in Y's home, also became a foreign fighter and has since been killed in

---

[58] *London Borough of Tower Hamlets v B*, see above n 11, (case 2) and High Court of Justice (Family Division) (England and Wales), *A Local Authority and HB (mother) and MB (father) and ML and BL (The Children)*, Judgement, 26 May 2017, [2017] EWHC 1437 (Fam) are good examples of cases in which the family court has discussed the 'risk of radicalisation' and what factors create and/or facilitate this risk. What these and other similar cases illustrate is that while a parent or both parents may not have directly or deliberately created this risk, they may have facilitated it thus placing their child or children at risk.

[59] *London Borough of Tower Hamlets v B*, see above n 11, para 28, is a useful example of where a child was deemed to have suffered such "serious emotional harm, and, at the very least, continues to be at risk" that "her psychological, emotional and intellectual integrity" could no longer be protected in the family home. While her parents were not found to be directly or deliberately responsible for her radicalisation, "the farrago of sophisticated dishonesty displayed by her parents" made her continued placement in the family home "entirely unsustainable".

[60] See further this particularly illustrative and well-known case of the efficiency with which local authorities can act—The Guardian 2015.

[61] High Court of Justice (Family Division) (England and Wales), *Brighton and Hove City Council v. Mother, Father and Y (A Minor)/Re Y (Risk of Young Person Travelling to Join IS)* (No. 1), [2015] EWHC 2098 (Fam) and High Court of Justice (Family Division) (England and Wales), *Brighton and Hove City Council v. Mother and Y (A Minor)/Re Y (Risk of Young Person Travelling to Join IS)* (No 2) [2015] EWHC 2099 (Fam) and High Court of Justice (Family Division) (England and Wales) *A Local Authority v Y*, Judgement, 24 April 2017, [2017] EWHC 968 (Fam).

battle. To add even more complexity to these unique family circumstances, Y's uncle was a detainee in Guantánamo Bay.

The local authority brought the case due to serious concerns that Y wishes to follow the same path as his brothers and his close friend. There was a plan for Y to travel to Dubai during Easter in 2015 with the source of the money for the flight ticket unaccounted for. As there were more options for travel to Syria from Dubai, the concerns that he may be planning to engage in foreign fighting were exacerbated. According to the local authority, Y's mother had become "so exhausted by grief" that she was unable to put in place any protective measures or appropriate boundaries to prevent Y from travelling abroad. The following were identified as the central objectives of the local authority case:

- Preserve Y's life;
- Prevent Y from travelling abroad;
- Encourage cooperation between the different agencies and the family;
- Permit a flexible approach that would allow Y to be protected at home with targeted support.

The court found that making Y a ward of court was the most suitable vehicle to achieve these objectives. In general, a child who is made a ward of court cannot be removed from the jurisdiction of the family court and where such permission has not been granted, police assistance is sought to prevent such removal. The application of this principle to Y equated to the removal of Y's passport as the most effective means of protecting Y "from himself" amongst other support measures.[62] However, as the wardship dissolves automatically at 18 years of age and due to the continued concerns for Y, the court felt that the specialised support and protective measures needed to continue.[63] The court made clear that Y has not become "less vulnerable merely by chronological age". As a result, the Director of the Children's Services agreed to authorise a bespoke support and protection service to Y until he is 21. This plan was to be reviewed every six months to ensure that it is still reflective of Y's needs.[64]

Even in comparison to the other cases where the family courts have made highly tailored support and protection arrangements for the child or children affected, this is an unusual and striking outcome. It is also highly instructive. It is clear from the first one of the three cases involving Y that both the court, the local authorities and police services considered Y to be "extremely vulnerable, because of his family's history, to radicalisation". Further still, he was deemed "particularly susceptible" to the type of radicalisation which may lead to causing harm because he had come "to dehumanise those involved in the [Syrian] conflict". In other words, it was a matter of time before he sought to engage in foreign fighting. Albeit redacted, the fact-finding and deliberations in all three cases approach Y as both a likely victim of familial

---

[62] As only part of the judgment has been made public, it is not known what the full range of these support and protective measures is.

[63] *A Local Authority v Y*, Judgement, above n 61.

[64] Again, as only parts of the judgment are made available, no further details are available.

radicalisation and a prospective perpetrator of foreign fighting. The necessity and importance of the whole of government approach advocated by Resolution 2396 are compellingly illustrated by the extraordinary personal circumstances of Y. This is also a case which clearly demonstrates that when early and appropriate steps are taken—utilising effectively all the relevant legal provisions—an escalating, sensitive and highly challenging situation can be defused and brought under control. The synergetic operation of family law and counter-terrorism provisions through the family courts shows the constructive reach a state's preventative security toolkit can have in respect of prospective FTFs.

The same can be observed in cases involving (suspected) FTFs who have managed to return with their children. In *Re Y (A Child)*,[65] the family courts had to decide whether an almost three-year-old boy (Y) should be separated from his mother (T) during and after her imprisonment, following her return from Syria. T had travelled to Syria in 2014 when Y was one year old in order to start a new life after her relationship with M (the father) ended. On return to the UK, she was arrested by the Counter Terrorism Unit and subsequently convicted to six years in prison for encouraging acts of terrorism and being a member of a terrorist organisation. She is further subject to an order under the Counter Terrorism Act 2008[66] to notify the police of personal details, including her address, for fifteen years. Y became the subject of protective measures and an interim care order in February 2015; he was then placed with a foster family. T was eligible for release on licence in 2018 and made it clear that she would like to be reunited with her son upon release from prison. As such, the court had to decide what would be in the best interests of Y. The core issue in the case was what harm Y had suffered when he was taken to Syria by his mother.

In her evidence, T refused to accept that she had completely "lost sight" of Y's basic needs for physical and emotional safety. She did, however, acknowledge that she had exposed him to extreme danger during certain periods; she also described Raqqa—where she took her son—as the most dangerous place in the world. Separately, she allowed her son to be used as part of various propaganda materials shared by ISIS online. Despite her inconsistent testimony, there was clear evidence that she had voluntarily allowed this and was an active participant. The judge in T's criminal trial for terrorism offences observed that T was very well aware that the future she was subjecting her son to was very likely to be one of indoctrination and thereafter life as a terrorist fighter. The court observed that there was some evidence that after his return from Syria, Y had displayed signs of being emotionally disturbed. His language and his ability to speak were noticeably delayed, and he was showing a marked and persistent interest in guns and "shooting people".

In conclusion, the court found that the risk of harm to Y was foreseeable. More damningly, it was clear that, at best, T had chosen to ignore it. Thus, it was more

[65] High Court of Justice (Family Division) (England and Wales), *Re Y (A Child)*, Judgement, 22 June 2018, [2016] EWFC 30 (Fam).

[66] See further Section 47 of the Act. Full text available at https://www.legislation.gov.uk/ukpga/2008/28/section/47. Accessed 5 August 2021.

likely that she had deliberately disregarded it as part of her plans to join ISIS. The court found that the Section 31 Children Act 1989[67] threshold had been met—Y was placed within the care of the local authority with parental responsibility shared between the local authority and the paternal grandmother. As the judgment was heavily redacted—the full anonymised decision was given in private—it is unclear what the most current care arrangements for Y are. As no other open judgment regarding Y is available at present, it has to be assumed that parental responsibility is still shared between the local authority and the paternal grandmother.

In a more recent case involving similar issues, *Re J (A Child)*,[68] the eighteen-month-old J has been subject to an interim care order and has been placed with foster carers since her arrival in the UK from Turkey in 2018. Her father, who had been radicalised, travelled to Syria to fight for ISIS and to engage in terrorism-related activity. He is currently in detention in another jurisdiction where criminal proceedings are ongoing. The mother shared the ideology and travelled to Syria with the father. J was born in Syria and lived there with her parents until she was ten months old. Following a fact-finding hearing, Justice Knowles felt that there was a risk that the mother would radicalise her daughter and inculcate her in extremist ideology. The risk was such that the mother would seek to remove J from the UK to an unsafe jurisdiction in pursuit of extremist ideology. There was an additional risk that the mother would behave in a manner consistent with extremist ideology within the UK. Most importantly, perhaps, the mother did not seem to have any understanding of the risk of significant physical and emotional harm the father posed to J and was thus unable to act protectively. Further, the family court received evidence that the mother had not been engaging meaningfully with the Home Office's Desistance and Disengagement Programme (DDP).[69] In this context, J's young age and vulnerability only heightened the concerns about the risks to which she would be exposed in her mother's care. J's right to a safe and loving home was thus found to prevail over a return to the care of her mother, who continues to pose an ongoing risk to her child. The family court placed J in the care of her paternal grandmother under the auspices of a special guardianship. This guardianship is intended to be permanent. In addition, the family court made a child arrangements order defining the ambit of the mother's interaction with J. The mother is only allowed to see J once a month.

The cases of Y and J have arguably posed one of the most challenging and complex questions for the family courts in the context of the FTF phenomenon—should a young and vulnerable child be permanently taken away from the custody of his or her parents? While it is easy to distinguish these two cases from the extraordinary circumstances of teenager Y discussed above, there is an important common

[67] The full text of the Section is available at https://www.legislation.gov.uk/ukpga/1989/41/section/31. Accessed 5 August 2021.

[68] High Court of Justice (Family Division) (England and Wales), *Re J (A Child)*, Judgement, 22 June 2018, [2018] EWHC 2056 (Fam).

[69] The DDP is a highly specialised and rather clandestine rehabilitation programme, which was developed to assist individuals who are already engaged in terrorism or who are suspected of engaging in terrorism to disengage and reintegrate safely, back into society. See further The Guardian 2019a.

thread—familial socialisation and radicalisation into violence. The three children are illustrative of the stages and impact such socialisation and/or radicalisation can have. As an already radicalised teenager within a family of radicalised individuals, Y is a danger to himself and potentially others without an intervention reflective of his age and needs; Y is also a victim of his family's history and beliefs. Almost three-year-old Y is already exhibiting signs of emotional disturbance as a result of the socialisation into violent radicalism. In J's case, the family court felt it was imperative to remove her from a familial environment which can result in socialisation and radicalisation into violence. In all three cases, the family courts engaged in extensive fact-finding and deliberations before imposing individualised sets of measures to support the children going forward. The best interests of these children were a core consideration in each case, which in the latter two cases led to the removal of Y and J from the custody of their mothers. While the judges in the cases acknowledged that these decisions are "distressing" and the cases "difficult and unusual", what mattered most was the protection of the physical and mental well-being of the children.

Each of these cases represents a distinct point on the spectrum of intervention in respect of children affected by the FTF phenomenon—from very early intervention and removal from the alleged source(s) of radicalisation to extended and highly individualised monitoring and support plans. Aside from the available multi-dimensional care for the children, what these and other interventions in similar cases illustrate is the sheer reach the domestic counter-terrorism toolkit can have. Both Y's and J's mothers were already serving sentences for terrorist-related activities imposed by the criminal courts before the start of the family court proceedings. The family court proceedings made clear references to the criminal cases and, in particular, to whether the mothers were actively and honestly engaging with the DDP. The fact-finding exercises that were undertaken as part of the family court cases involved an assessment of whether the women were still radicalised and how they were behaving following their criminal convictions. The importance of family and criminal courts, local authorities and police services assisting one another in such cases were emphasised. In other words, the FTF phenomenon and its varied implications on children have brought the family courts within the fold of the broader state counter-terrorism toolkit. One important implication is that the available and expanding jurisprudence of the family courts—at least in the UK—significantly weakens the already unconvincing arguments that the children of alleged FTFs might pose difficult-to-manage security risks. It is hard to imagine what individual security risks an infant or a toddler might pose to its state of citizenship.[70] To suggest otherwise is to, in essence, assume and impose automatic culpability for future activities due to their parentage in contravention of UN guidelines or rights instruments.[71] Further, domestic criminal justice and social welfare frameworks have well-established mechanisms to manage those

[70] As detailed in this harrowing report, both the physical and mental development of many of the children currently living in the camps has been significantly impacted by the harsh conditions. Further, a number of small children and infants with (access to) European citizenship have died in the last two years. Rights and Security International 2020.

[71] See for example United Nations Office of Counter-Terrorism 2020.

who are deemed to be culpable of criminal behaviour but are still legally children.[72] This suggests that the stumbling block is more likely to be the low public support for repatriation of FTFs and media sensationalism rather than the lack of means and measures to address any alleged security risks.

Assuming that (significantly) reduced media attention could make active repatriations—of children at least—more palatable to states, there is a way forward. As demonstrated by a highly exceptional family court decision in the UK towards the end of 2019, it is possible for a state to facilitate active repatriation without triggering a media circus. In a heavily redacted and abridged public judgment, Justice Keehan provided skeleton details on a case concerning the repatriation of orphaned British citizens who were in Syria.[73] The judgment does not provide any details on whether one, all or none of the children were born in Syria or when and how they became orphaned. What is made clear, however, is that when the children's relatives in the UK became aware that they were in Syria, they immediately instructed solicitors to write to the Foreign and Commonwealth Office (FCO) and to charities operating in Syria to raise the case of the children. One of the relatives submitted an application to the family court asking for the children to be made wards of court—an application that was approved. Further, Justice Keehan made an order for the return of the children to the jurisdiction and "respectfully requested the assistance" of the FCO in securing their safe return. The children were to be placed in the care and control of their families once in the UK. He also disclosed the order to the local authority in whose area the children were to reside upon return.

The children were repatriated with the assistance of the FCO around 20–21 November 2020.[74] To protect the identities and welfare of the children, a strict reporting restriction order was issued on the grounds that the right to privacy and

[72] To use the specific example of the UK—while persons under the age of 18 are legally children, the age of criminal responsibility in England and Wales is currently 10 years old. Thus, children aged between 10 and 17 can be charged with a crime and subject to prosecution within the youth justice system. According to a recent Ministry of Justice report on the UK youth justice system, "the core focus must continue to be rehabilitation ... the 'child first, offender second' principle" must be at core of decision making processes. The youth justice system in the UK is further described in the report as mature. Ministry of Justice 2019.

[73] High Court of Justice (Family Division), *Re Orphans from Syria*, 22 November 2019, Judgement, [2019] EWHC 3202 (Fam). To protect the identity of the individuals involved, the judgment does not offer any information on the number of children repatriated, their ages, the practical details of the repatriation or any locations (where the children were born, where they used to live or where their relatives live). It should also be stressed that this case does not reflect a shift in governmental policy. Reports suggest that the current Home Secretary, Priti Patel, has intervened to block operations to repatriate British orphans and unaccompanied minors from Syria. The Guardian 2019e. See also The Guardian 2020b. In December 2020, the UK Foreign Office denied medical aid to a seriously ill British woman and her infant daughter despite their conditions being described as 'life-threatening'. The Times 2020.

[74] *Re Orphans from Syria*, see above n 73, paras 9, 14, 15.

family life[75] of the children outweighed the right to freedom of expression[76] of the press and the broadcast media. Justice Keehan explicitly stressed that until there has been an assessment of how vulnerable these children are—emotionally and psychologically—after being orphaned and living in a warzone, a cautious approach towards their welfare and best interests is needed. While very limited facts were made available in the public judgment, from the information disclosed, the following points can be made—the repatriation of the children was at least in part triggered by the family court, the best interests of the children were at the core of the judgment, substantial reporting restrictions can play an important role in protecting the welfare of the children and in affording a government space free of media scrutiny to engage in an active repatriation.[77]

Another equally important point somewhat hidden within the judgment is that the relevant local authorities—and the protection and support services they can provide—were made part of the proceedings and are to continue to be involved in the care of the children.[78] In short, the involvement of the family court (a) resulted in the repatriation of the orphaned children and (b) was part of a whole of government approach encouraged in Resolution 2396. Despite the heavy redactions and abridgements within the published judgment, the whole of government approach can be discerned not only from the references to the role of the local authority and the intervention by the family court but also by the monitored return of the children to their relatives' homes and the continuous assessment of how vulnerable the children are. As illustrated in the cases discussed in this section, in threading a careful path between protecting the affected children and acknowledging national security considerations, the family courts have shown a commitment to cooperating with a range of appropriate actors in order to protect children affected by the FTF phenomenon.

[75] An express reference to Article 8 rights under the European Convention on Human Rights was made in paragraph 2 of the judgment.

[76] An express reference to Article 10 rights under the European Convention on Human Rights was made in paragraph 2 of the judgment.

[77] There was very limited and rather vague reporting on this repatriation within the British media. Any reporting focused on the issue of repatriation in general terms without express or implied references to the actual court case which led to the repatriation. See for example The Guardian 2019f.

[78] Paragraph 13 of the judgment makes a reference to the local authority being part of the wardship proceedings.

11.4 Conclusion

As acknowledged by the UK's High Court Family Division itself, the range of cases involving children affected by the FTF phenomenon arose in circumstances without recent precedent.[79] The type of harm which the family courts were asked to evaluate was "a different facet of vulnerability for children than that which the courts have had to deal with in the past".[80] In many respects, this is not surprising as changes in society often tend to first resonate within the family. As such, family courts are and can be "in the vanguard of change in life and society" and thus need to both anticipate and adapt quickly to new challenges.[81] So far, the UK family courts appear to have adjusted quickly to these challenges. The evolving jurisprudence clearly illustrates that the UK family courts have not shied away from imposing intrusive measures disruptive of the existing family environment, daily patterns of living and, at times, family unity where the courts have felt that this disruption is necessary to protect the physical and mental well-being of a child. These measures, while at times as harsh as removing a child from the custody of its parents, have nevertheless been applied in a manner that seeks to achieve "proportionate objectives of child protections".[82] In short, the best interests of each child have been at the core of these complex decisions. Within the fast-growing caseload of the UK family courts in respect of children affected by the FTF phenomenon, the practical application of this principle has resulted in a sophisticated and individualised approach based on the particular circumstances and the needs of each child. One of these needs, as stressed across the jurisprudence,[83] is providing the necessary support to protect or re-establish the independent and critical thinking of a child. As emphasised in various decisions, addressing this need is at the core of shielding children from the harm of (further) radicalisation.[84]

This approach informs why the affected children have not been discussed through a national security lens only but rather as vulnerable individuals who, due to their age and impressionability, have suffered or are likely to suffer harm due to the processes of radicalisation and/or socialisation into violent extremism and terrorism. The children party to many of these cases were expressly or impliedly referred to as victims of either circumstance, familial radicalisation and/or grooming into extremist

[79] See further *London Borough of Tower Hamlets v B*, see above n 11 (case 1), *London Borough of Tower Hamlets v B*, see above n 11 (case 2) and High Court of Justice (Family Division) (England and Wales), *In the Matter of M (Children)*, Judgement, 20 May 2015, [2015] EWHC 1433 (Fam).

[80] Ibid.

[81] Ibid.

[82] *London Borough of Tower Hamlets v B*, see above n 11.

[83] First noted within the trio of cases involving B (*London Borough of Tower Hamlets*, see above n 11 (case 1) and *London Borough of Tower Hamlets*, see above n 11 (case 2) para 30 in particular) and reaffirmed in subsequent jurisprudence. In these cases, Mr. Justice Hayden made comments such as "...opportunity in which she can ... be afforded the chance for her strong and lively mind to reassert its own independence".

[84] Within these cases, radicalisation has been described as capable of causing harm of similar magnitude and complexity as physical and sexual violations to the body.

and radical behaviour.[85] While direct engagement with de-radicalisation efforts is not within the purview of the family courts, as demonstrated, they can nevertheless facilitate de-radicalisation efforts post judicial proceedings through the type of child care measures recommended based on the facts of the particular case and the specific welfare needs of a child. In short, the family courts can play a very constructive and welcome role in reducing both the risk and harm of radicalisation in respect of children.

As time progresses and more returning or repatriated children make their way back into Europe, the relevant courts in countries other than the UK may find themselves at the forefront of, in essence, countering radicalisation and terrorism. Instead of the current inaction and the reluctant repatriation of orphaned children, other European states could make similar provisions allowing the suitable domestic courts to make the appropriate arrangements for children that manage to return. In anticipation of such returns, rather than relying on other countries or circumstances to offer a solution, states should focus on how best to train and equip their domestic (family) courts, local authorities and social services with the necessary expertise and powers to most effectively support children affected by the FTF phenomenon. Such a whole of government approach is in line with the relevant international legal obligations and offers a much more constructive national security response to any prospective risk these children may pose; it is an approach that affords these children a more palatable and kinder future.

References

Articles, Books and Other Documents

Ahdash F (2020) The Interaction between Family Law and Counter-Terrorism: A Critical Examination of the Radicalisation Cases in the Family Courts. Child and Family Law Quarterly 30:389–419

Aljazeera (2020) First Coronavirus Cases reported in Syria's Al-Hol Camp. https://www.aljazeera.com/news/2020/08/coronavirus-cases-reported-syria-al-hol-camp-200806162159182.html. Accessed 5 August 2021

BBC News (2020) Germany and Finland bring Home Women from Islamic State camps. https://www.bbc.com/news/world-europe-55387991. Accessed 5 August 2021

---

[85] Aside from the exceptional case of Y referenced above, see also the case of Family Court (Leicester), *A City Council v A Mother, A Father and Others*, Judgement, 27 June 2019 [2019] EWHC 3076 (Fam). In this case the mother has been described as being a "strong, if not, fanatical sympathiser of terrorism"; the father has also been described as sympathising with "violent extremism and terror". Further, the mother was found to have behaved in a way "which was likely to encourage her children to sympathise with so-called Islamic State, and violent terrorism." Also, the case of High Court of Justice (Family Division) (England and Wales), *Re (A, B, C, D, E)*, Judgement, 16 July 2018, [2018] EWHC 1841 (Fam), which assessed the risk to the five children arising from the alleged extremist beliefs of their parents. The children's father had been the subject of a Terrorism Prevention and Investigation Measure (TPIM). For more details on grooming to radicalisation, see Radicalisation Awareness Network (RAN) 2019.

Blackbourn J, Walker C (2016) Interdiction and Indoctrination: The Counter-Terrorism and Security Act 2015. Modern Law Review 79:840–870
Capone F (2016) Countering "Foreign Terrorist Fighters": A Critical Appraisal of the Framework established by the UN Security Council Resolutions. The Italian Yearbook of International Law 25:227–250
Clingendael (2020) The Debate around Returning Foreign Fighters in the Netherlands. https://www.clingendael.org/publication/debate-around-returning-foreign-fighters-netherlands. Accessed 5 August 2021
Euractiv (2020) Europe still reluctant to Repatriate its Foreign Fighters and Families. https://www.euractiv.com/section/justice-home-affairs/news/europe-still-reluctant-to-repatriate-its-foreign-fighters-and-families/ Accessed 5 August 2021
European Council on Foreign Relations (2019) Beyond Good and Evil: Why Europe should bring ISIS Foreign Fighters Home. https://www.ecfr.eu/publications/summary/beyond_good_and_evil_why_europe_should_bring_isis_foreign_fighters_home. Accessed 5 August 2021
Gearty C (2013) Liberty and Security. Polity Press, Cambridge
Home Office (United Kingdom) (2018) Counter-Terrorism Strategy (CONTEST). https://assets.publishing.service.gov.uk/government/uploads/system/uploads/attachment_data/file/716907/140618_CCS207_CCS0218929798-1_CONTEST_3.0_WEB.pdf. Accessed 5 August 2021
Ip J (2020) Reconceptualising the Legal Responses to Foreign Fighters. International & Comparative Law Quarterly 69:103–134
Lazarus L, Goold B (2019) Security and Human Rights, 2nd edn. Hart Publishing, Oxford
Luthar S (2003) Resilience and Vulnerability. Cambridge University Press, Cambridge
Malik N (2019) Radicalising our Children: An Analysis of Family Court Cases of British Children at Risk of Radicalisation, 2013–2018. Henry Jackson Society (Centre on Radicalisation & Terrorism) https://henryjacksonsociety.org/wp-content/uploads/2019/05/HJS-Radicalising-Our-Children-Report-NEW-web.pdf. Accessed 5 August 2021
Milanovic M (2011) Extraterritorial Application of Human Rights Treaties. Oxford University Press, Oxford
Milanovic M, Papic T (2018) The Applicability of the ECHR in Contested Territories. International & Comparative Law Quarterly 67:779–800
Ministry of Justice (2019) Standards for Children in the Youth Justice System. https://assets.publishing.service.gov.uk/government/uploads/system/uploads/attachment_data/file/957697/Standards_for_children_in_youth_justice_services_2019.doc.pdf. Accessed 10 September 2021
Ministry of Security and Justice et al. (2016) The Netherlands Comprehensive Action Programme to Combat Jihadism: Overview of Measures and Actions. https://data2.unhcr.org/en/documents/details/44369. Accessed 5 August 2021
Munby J (2015) Radicalisation Cases in the Family Courts: Guidance issued by Sir James Munby, President of the Family Division, on 8 October 2015. https://www.judiciary.uk/wp-content/uploads/2015/10/pfd-guidance-radicalisation-cases.pdf
Nyamutata C (2020) Young Terrorists or Child Soldiers? ISIS Children, International Law and Victimhood. Journal of Conflict and Security Law 25:237–261
Office of the Special Representative of the Secretary-General on Sexual Violence in Conflict (2019) Joint Statement on Human Rights and Humanitarian Concerns related to Conflict Affected Women and Children in Syria and Iraq. https://www.un.org/sexualviolenceinconflict/press-release/joint-statement-on-human-rights-and-humanitarian-concerns-related-to-conflict-affected-women-and-children-in-syria-and-iraq/. Accessed 13 September 2021
Open Society Justice Initiative (2021) European States' Obligations to Repatriate the Children detained in Camps in Northeast Syria. https://www.justiceinitiative.org/uploads/d9762590-424c-4cb6-9112-5fedd0d959d1/european-states%E2%80%99-obligations-to-repatriate-the-children-detained-in-camps-in-northeast-syria-20210722.pdf. Accessed 5 August 2021
Pillai S, Williams G (2017) Twenty-First Century Banishment: Citizenship Stripping in Common Law Nations. International & Comparative Law Quarterly 66:521–555

Radicalisation Awareness Network (RAN) (2019) Grooming for Terror: Manipulation and Control. https://ec.europa.eu/home-affairs/system/files/2019-06/ran_hsc_grooming_for_terror_25042019_en.pdf. Accessed 13 September 2021
Raible L (2016) The Extraterritoriality of the ECHR: Why Jaloud and Pisari Should be Read as Game Changers. European Human Rights Law Review 2:161–168
Raible L (2020) Human Rights Unbound: A Theory of Extraterritoriality. Oxford University Press, Oxford
Rights & Security International (2020) Europe's Guantanamo: The Indefinite Detention of European Women and Children in North East Syria. https://www.rightsandsecurity.org/assets/downloads/Europes-guantanamo-THE_REPORT.pdf. Accessed 5 August 2021
Roach K (2011) The 9/11 Effect: Comparative Counter-Terrorism. Cambridge University Press, New York
Scott P (2020) Passports, The Right to Travel, and National Security in the Commonwealth. International & Comparative Law Quarterly 69:365–395
Special Rapporteur on Terrorism (2021) Human Rights Impact of Counter-Terrorism and Countering (Violent) Extremism Policies and Practices on the Rights of Women, Girls and the Family, UN Doc. A/HRC/46/36
The Guardian (2015) British Couple travelling with Four Children arrested in Turkey. https://www.theguardian.com/world/2015/apr/20/british-couple-asif-malik-sara-kiran-arrested-children-turkey-syria. Accessed 5 August 2021
The Guardian (2019a) Extremists living in UK under Secretive Counter-Terror Programme. https://www.theguardian.com/uk-news/2019/apr/05/extremists-living-in-uk-under-secretive-counter-terror-programme. Accessed 5 August 2021
The Guardian (2019b) London schoolgirl who fled to join Isis wants to return to UK. https://www.theguardian.com/world/2019/feb/14/london-schoolgirl-who-fled-to-join-isis-wants-to-return-to-uk. Accessed 5 August 2021
The Guardian (2019c) No more orphans expected to be returned to UK from Syria. https://www.theguardian.com/world/2019/nov/22/no-more-orphans-expected-to-be-brought-back-to-uk-from-syria-isis. Accessed 20 April 2021
The Guardian (2019d) No More Orphans expected to be Returned to UK from Syria. https://www.theguardian.com/world/2019/nov/22/no-more-orphans-expected-to-be-brought-back-to-uk-from-syria-isis. Accessed 5 August 2021
The Guardian (2019e) Priti Patel blocks Rescue of British ISIS Children. https://www.theguardian.com/politics/2019/nov/16/priti-patel-block-rescue-british-isis-children. Accessed 5 August 2021
The Guardian (2019f) Some Orphaned British Children in Syria to be Repatriated. https://www.theguardian.com/world/2019/nov/21/some-british-citizens-in-syria-to-be-repatriated-within-days. Accessed 5 August 2021
The Guardian (2020a) Three-year-old Australian Girl in Syria's al-Hawl Camp may lose Fingers to Frostbite. https://www.theguardian.com/australia-news/2020/feb/17/three-year-old-australian-girl-in-syrias-al-hawl-camp-may-lose-fingers-to-frostbite. Accessed 5 August 2021
The Guardian (2020b) UK Ministers ignore Pleas to Return 'Innocent Orphans' from Syria. https://www.theguardian.com/politics/2020/jul/18/ministers-ignore-pleas-to-honour-vow-and-bring-innocents-back-from-syria. Accessed 20 April 2021
The Independent (2019) Shamima Begum: British ISIS Member who fled to Syria 'has right to return to UK' security minister says. https://www.independent.co.uk/news/uk/home-news/shamima-begum-isis-british-return-uk-london-bethnal-green-syria-terror-a8778821.html. Accessed 5 August 2021
The New York Times (2020a) France brings 10 Children of French Jihadists Home from Syria. https://www.nytimes.com/2020/06/22/world/europe/france-isis-children-repatriated.html. Accessed 5 August 2021
The New York Times (2020b) Western Countries Leave Children of ISIS in Syrian Camps. https://www.nytimes.com/2020/05/31/world/middleeast/isis-children-syria-camps.html. Accessed 5 August 2021

The Times (2020) Foreign Office denies Medical Aid to British Woman and Baby in ISIS Camp. https://www.thetimes.co.uk/article/foreign-office-denies-medical-aid-to-british-woman-and-baby-in-isis-camp-z8d0lw8rq. Accessed 5 August 2021
The Washington Post (2021) New Zealand to Resettle suspected Islamic State Militant and her Children after Australia revoked Citizenship. The Prime Minister of New Zealand is quoted as saying "great care being taken to minimize the security risks in returning the woman and her young children." https://www.washingtonpost.com/world/2021/07/26/zealand-islamic-state-australia/. Accessed 5 August 2021
UN (2020) Key Principles for the Protection, Repatriation, Prosecution, Rehabilitation and Reintegration of Women and Children with Links to United Nations listed Terrorist Groups. https://www.un.org/counterterrorism/sites/www.un.org.counterterrorism/files/key_principles-april_2019.pdf. Accessed 5 August 2021
UN Committee on the Rights of the Child (2005) General Comment No. 7 (2005): Implementing child rights in early childhood, UN Doc. CRC/C/GC/7
UN Committee on the Rights of the Child (2007) General Comment No. 10 (2007): Children's Rights in Juvenile Justice, UN Doc. CRC/C/GC/10
UN Office on Drugs and Crime (2017) Handbook on Children Recruited and Exploited by Terrorist and Violent Extremist Groups: The Role of the Justice System. Vienna, United Nations. https://www.unodc.org/documents/terrorism/Publications/HB%20Children/Handbook_on_Children_Recruited_and_Exploited_by_Terrorist_and_Violent_Extremist_Groups_the_Role_of_the_Justice_System.E.pdf. Accessed 5 August 2021
UN Security Council (2001) Resolution 1373 (2001), UN Doc. S/RES/1373
UN Security Council (2014) Resolution 2178 (2014), UN Doc. S/Res/2178
UN Security Council (2017) Resolution 2396 (2017), UN Doc. S/Res/2396
UN Special Rapporteur on the Promotion and Protection of Human Rights and Fundamental Freedoms while Countering Terrorism and UN Special Rapporteur on Extrajudicial, Summary or Arbitrary Executions (2020) Legal Analysis on Extra-territorial Jurisdiction of States over Children and their Guardians in Camps, Prisons or Elsewhere in the Northern Syrian Arab Republic. https://www.ohchr.org/Documents/Issues/Executions/UNSRsPublicJurisdictionAnalysis2020.pdf. Accessed 13 September 2021
UNICEF (2007) The Paris Principles. Principles and Guidelines on Children Associated With Armed Forces or Armed Groups. https://www.unicef.org/mali/media/1561/file/ParisPrinciples.pdf. Accessed 9 September 2021
United Nations Office of Counter-Terrorism (2020) Children Affected by the Foreign-Fighter Phenomenon: Ensuring a Child Rights-Based Approach. https://www.un.org/counterterrorism/sites/www.un.org.counterterrorism/files/0918_ftf_handbook_web_reduced.pdf. Accessed 5 August 2021
Zedner L (2007) Pre-crime and Post-Criminology. Theoretical Criminology 11:261–281
Zedner L, Ashworth A (2019) The Rise and Restraint of the Preventative State. Annual Review of Criminology 2:429–450

Cases

Committee on the Rights of the Child, *L.H. et al v. France*, Communications, 2 November 2020, Communications No. 79/2019 and No. 109/2019, CRC/C/85/D/79/2019-CRC/C/85/D/109/2019
Court of Appeal (Civil Division) (England and Wales), *Immigration Appeals Commission and Others*, Judgement on Appeal from the Special Immigration Appeals Commission (T2/2020/0644), 16 July 2020, [2020] EWCA Civ 918
Court of Chancery (England and Wales) *Wellesley v Duke of Beaufort*, Judgement, 1827, (1827) 2 Russ 1
District Court of The Hague, Judgement, 11 November 2019, C-09-581588-KG ZA 19-999

England and Wales Court of Appeals (EWCA) (Civil Division), *Begum v The Special*
Family Court (Leicester), *A City Council v A Mother, A Father and Others*, Judgement, 27 June 2019 [2019] EWHC 3076 (Fam)
High Court of Justice (Family Division) (England and Wales) *A Local Authority v Y*, Judgement, 24 April 2017, [2017] EWHC 968 (Fam)
High Court of Justice (Family Division) (England and Wales), *A Local Authority and HB (mother) and MB (father) and ML and BL (The Children)*, Judgement, 26 May 2017, [2017] EWHC 1437 (Fam)
High Court of Justice (Family Division) (England and Wales), *Brighton & Hove City Council v. Mother, Father and Y (A Minor) / Re Y (Risk of Young Person Travelling to Join IS)* (No 1), [2015] EWHC 2098 (Fam)
High Court of Justice (Family Division) (England and Wales), *Brighton & Hove City Council v. Mother and Y (A Minor) / Re Y (Risk of Young Person Travelling to Join IS)* (No 2) [2015] EWHC 2099 (Fam)
High Court of Justice (Family Division) (England and Wales), *In the Matter of X (Children) and In the Matter of Y (Children)*, 30 July 2015, Judgement, [2015] EWHC 2265 (Fam)
High Court of Justice (Family Division) (England and Wales), *In the Matter of M (Children)*, Judgement, 20 May 2015, [2015] EWHC 1433 (Fam)
High Court of Justice (Family Division) (England and Wales), *London Borough of Tower Hamlets v B*, Judgement, 21 August 2015, [2015] EWHC 2491 (Fam)
High Court of Justice (Family Division) (England and Wales), *London Borough of Tower Hamlets v B*, Judgement, 13 June 2016, [2016] EWHC 1707 (Fam)
High Court of Justice (Family Division) (England and Wales), *Re (A, B, C, D, E)*, Judgement, 16 July 2018, [2018] EWHC 1841 (Fam)
High Court of Justice (Family Division) (England and Wales), *Re J (A Child)*, Judgment, 22 June 2018, [2018] EWHC 2056 (Fam)
High Court of Justice (Family Division) (England and Wales), *Re Orphans from Syria*, Judgement, 22 November 2019, [2019] EWHC 3202 (Fam)
High Court of Justice (Family Division) (England and Wales), *Re Y (A Child)*, Judgement, 22 June 2018, [2016] EWFC 30 (Fam)
International Criminal Court (ICC), *Prosecutor v Thomas Lubanga Dyilo*, Judgement pursuant to Article 74 of the Statute, 5 April 2021, ICC-01/04-01/06-2842, T.Ch. I
Special Immigration Appeals Commission (United Kingdom), *Begum v The Secretary of State for the Home Department*, Open Judgement, 7 February 2020, Appeal No. SC/163/2019
The Supreme Court (United Kingdom), *Begum v The Special Immigration Appeals Commission and Others*, Judgement, 16 February 2021, [2021] UKSC 7

Treaties

Additional Protocol to the Council of Europe Convention on the Prevention of Terrorism, opened for signature 22 October 2015, CETS No. 217 (entered into force 1 July 2017)
Council of Europe Convention on the Prevention of Terrorism, opened for signature 16 May 2005 CETS No. 196 (entered into force 1 June 2007)
European Convention for the Protection of Human Rights and Fundamental Freedoms, as amended by Protocols Nos. 11 and 14, opened for signature 4 November 1950, ETS 5 (entered into force 3 September 1953)
Explanatory Report to the Additional Protocol to the Council of Europe Convention on the Prevention of Terrorism, Council of Europe Treaty Series – No. 217
United Nations Convention on the Rights of the Child, opened for signature 20 November 1989, 1577 UNTS 3 (entered into force 2 September 1990) (CRC)

Chapter 12
Legal Regulation of Subversive Expressions in Relation to Terrorist Travel: The Dutch Situation Against the Backdrop of International Human Rights Law

Marloes van Noorloos

Contents

Abstract The boundaries of freedom of expression in relation to terrorist speech—incitement, glorification, promotion of terrorism and the like—have been a pressing problem for decades. As the world has been experiencing a wave of people travelling abroad to join terrorist groups, new questions are raised about the role of subversive expressions and their legal regulation. Legal regulation of such speech includes criminal prosecutions, but a tendency can also be discerned to resort to administrative measures such as area bans and prohibiting (persons to speak at) gatherings. What are the potential ramifications for the right to freedom of expression of those domestic measures to regulate expressions inciting to, glorifying, supporting, propagating, provoking, encouraging or recruiting of travel for terrorist purposes? This chapter uses the Netherlands as a case study to show the options and pitfalls involved

This chapter was finalised mid-2021. Newer developments have not been taken into account.

M. van Noorloos (✉)
Tilburg Law School, PO Box 90153, 5000 LE Tilburg, The Netherlands
e-mail: L.A.vanNoorloos@tilburguniversity.edu

F. Capone et al. (eds.), *Returning Foreign Fighters: Responses, Legal Challenges and Ways Forward*, https://doi.org/10.1007/978-94-6265-571-3_12

in tackling such expressions, and then proceeds to analyse how such measures are to be judged in light of the right to freedom of expression.

Keywords Terrorist speech · Freedom of expression · Incitement · Foreign terrorist fighters · Glorifying terrorism · Article 10 ECHR

12.1 Introduction

The boundaries of freedom of expression in relation to terrorist speech—incitement, glorification, promotion of terrorism and the like—have been a pressing problem for decades. As the world has been experiencing a wave of people travelling abroad to join terrorist groups, new questions are raised about the role of subversive expressions and their legal regulation. Such questions, first of all, pertain to *potential* travellers: how have state authorities reacted to speech that promotes travelling abroad for the purposes of terrorism? And to those recruiting others to travel abroad for terrorist violence? One could also think of speech by returnees, who may incite others in their home countries to terrorist violence and/or to travel for such purposes. Legal regulation of such speech includes criminal prosecutions, but a tendency can also be discerned to resort to administrative measures such as area bans and prohibiting (persons to speak at) gatherings.[1]

All of these options to deal with expressions in the context of the foreign fighter threat have attracted critical notes in light of fundamental rights; as the OSCE has stated, "[e]fforts to suppress recruitment of FTFs [foreign terrorist fighters] and influence the environment in which recruiters operate, for example through overly broad and imprecisely framed incitement or 'extremism' laws (...), can have a serious impact on freedom of expression, or on freedom of thought, conscience, religion or belief, and thereby also erode the quality of democracy itself."[2]

What are the potential ramifications for the right to freedom of expression of those domestic measures to regulate expressions inciting to, glorifying, supporting, propagating, provoking, encouraging or recruiting of travel for terrorist purposes? This chapter will use the Netherlands as a case study to show the options and pitfalls involved in tackling such expressions, and then proceed to analyse how such measures are to be judged in light of the right to freedom of expression.

The focus will be on speech that is perceived as directly or indirectly contributing to the problem of persons travelling abroad for the purposes of terrorism. This contribution deals with *state* regulation of expressions (as influenced by international actors): the responsibility of social media platforms for terrorist speech would require a separate analysis, although we will occasionally delve into the way states have themselves tried to interfere with expressions on social media.

---

[1] Belavusau et al. 2019.

[2] OSCE 2018.

12.2 The Dutch Way of Dealing with Expressions in the Context of Travel for Terrorist Purposes: Amplifying the Range of Prohibited Speech

12.2.1 Criminal Law: Broad Notions of Indirect Incitement in Relation to Terrorist Travel

The Dutch cabinet has devised a comprehensive approach to dealing with extremist speakers that express radical or anti-democratic ideas,[3] including those who incite to joining the armed struggle (but also expressions such as hate speech). This is regarded as part of a broader approach to dealing with "problematic behaviour from certain salafist individuals and organisations".[4] Criminal law is only one part of that approach. The cabinet stresses that fundamental freedoms shall be respected, whatever measure is taken.

Notably, the comprehensive approach to extremist speakers seems to mainly have jihadism in mind and does not explicitly include other forms, e.g. the increasing threat of right-wing extremism (although attention has been paid to this problem in broader Dutch counter-terrorism policy[5]). Most cases from this chapter also deal with jihadism, as the research focuses on expressions in the context of 'foreign fighting' where this link is often present.

12.2.1.1 The 'Context' Case

A key case on the criminal regulation of expressions related to terrorist travel is the case named *Context*, which dealt with a group that recruited young people in The Hague to participate in the terrorist struggle in Syria from 2012–2014, including by spreading jihadist propaganda via social media and on websites such as *deware religie.nl* (DWR, meaning 'the true religion'[6]). Several group members travelled to Syria to join groups like IS and Jabhat al-Nusra. The District Court initially convicted nine persons[7] for, amongst other things, participating in a criminal and terrorist organisation, incitement to terrorist offences by inciting others to join the terrorist fighting

[3] Minister of Justice and Security 2018; see also *Kamerstukken II* 2017/18, 29 614, nr. 66 and *Kamerstukken II* 2019/20, 29 614, nr. 142. The origin of this approach can be found in the Coalition Agreement of 2017, which states that every effort must be made to prevent offering a platform to 'hate preachers'.

[4] Minister of Justice and Security 2018.

[5] See Minister of Justice and Security 2021.

[6] See also the organisation Die Wahre Religion (DWR), which was banned in Germany.

[7] District Court The Hague, *Context*, Judgement, 10 December 2015, ECLI:NL:RBDHA:2015:14365. English translation: https://deeplink.rechtspraak.nl/uitspraak?id=ECLI:NL:RBDHA:2015:16102. Later, the *Context* investigation led to more prosecutions: in 2016, four other persons were convicted. District Court The Hague, Judgement, 22 July 2016, ECLI:NL:GHDHA:2016:8411; 8412; 8464; 8465.

in Syria and recruitment for the armed struggle. Four cases eventually reached the Supreme Court,[8] where the expressions of the defendants on websites and social media, in relation to freedom of speech, came to the fore.

Under Dutch law, incitement to a criminal offence or violent action against the public authorities is a criminal offence under Article 131 Criminal Code (CC); if terrorist (preparatory) offences are incited, the maximum prison sentence of five years[9] is extended by one year and eight months (Article 131 para 2 CC). A key aspect of the Court of Appeal's argumentation in this case—later affirmed by the Supreme Court—was that inciting others to join the armed jihadi struggle in Syria implies incitement to criminal offences because joining the armed jihadi struggle always entails committing terrorist offences.[10] Furthermore, the Court of Appeal pointed out that in this armed struggle, inspired by the strive for and continuation of the 'caliphate', deadly violence was committed and incited against anyone that did not share the groups' ideas about religion. This line of argumentation is widely used in Dutch case law concerning the preparation of terrorist activities, making it easier to convict travellers whose actual behaviour in Syria or Iraq cannot be proven. Applying this argumentation to a speech offence such as incitement, however, does risk extending the scope of criminalisation rather widely.

The Context case focused, amongst other things, on the question of whether tweets and Facebook messages glorifying the armed jihadi struggle—including by glorifying martyrdom and presenting those deceased as heroes—could be qualified as incitement to terrorist offences. The idea of explicitly criminalising glorification of terrorist acts had already entered the Dutch legal sphere several times, with a legislative initiative by the Christian Democrats pending.[11] So far, the Minister of Justice and Security has renounced this proposal with an appeal to freedom of expression and because the most serious expressions could already be covered by existing law (including the prohibitions of incitement, hate speech and attempted recruitment for terrorism).[12]

According to the Court of Appeal, the decisive factor is whether someone could be brought to participate in the armed terrorist struggle—not whether this actually materialised (after all, Article 131 CC is an endangerment offence). Influencing in an indirect manner by reaping the minds of individuals to commit criminal offences can also be incitement, the Court of Appeal held—if this is done with the intention to

[8] Supreme Court (The Netherlands), *Context*, Judgement, 24 March 2020, ECLI:NL:HR:2020:447; 448; 449; 450. The judgement is available at https://deeplink.rechtspraak.nl/uitspraak?id=ECLI:NL:HR:2020:447. See about the Court of Appeal's judgments in these and two other cases: Court of Appeal The Hague, Judgement, 25 May 2018, ECLI:NL:GHDHA:2018:1248 and 1249; see https://www.rechtspraak.nl/Organisatie-en-contact/Organisatie/Gerechtshoven/Gerechtshof-Den-Haag/Nieuws/Paginas/Celstraffen-opgelegd-aan-verdachten-van-terrorisme.aspx.

[9] Or a fine of a maximum of 21,750 Euros.

[10] This argumentation is also used in cases concerning preparation of terrorism, making it easier to convict persons whose actual behaviour in Syria or Iraq cannot be proven.

[11] Initiatiefvoorstel-Van Toorenburg Strafbaarstelling van de verheerlijking van terrorisme, *Kamerstukken* 34466.

[12] *Handelingen II*, 18 September 2014, nr 105, item 6, p. 5.

rouse the temper of those susceptible to it (e.g. if it is directed at an easily impressionable person or a person who already considers travelling to Syria to join a terrorist group). In such a case, according to the Court of Appeal, expressing one's strong appreciation of the armed struggle and of those who have joined it, and glorifying death by martyrdom implies that others ought to follow in the footsteps of the fighters and replicate their actions. The Supreme Court accepted the Court of Appeal's argumentation that an indirect solicitation to a criminal offence can—depending on the circumstances—also be criminal incitement.

The Court of Appeal did draw some concrete lines, e.g. by judging that a YouTube video acknowledging and congratulating the so-called caliphate—while showing the IS flag—did not incite to criminal offences, as it was a very general expression of support for IS which did not mention the idea of travelling to that area to fight.

The Supreme Court followed the Court of Appeal's rejection of the defendants' appeal to the rights to freedom of expression and religion by invoking Article 17 European Convention on Human Rights (ECHR) on abuse of rights. According to the Supreme Court, invoking Article 17 ECHR, which results in the defendants not being able to materially invoke Articles 9 (freedom of thought, conscience and religion) and 10 ECHR (freedom of expression) anymore, should be reserved for exceptional and extreme cases—yet it judged that such was the case here.[13] The Court of Appeal had pointed out that the defendants had aimed at destroying the rights and freedoms proclaimed in the ECHR by—inspired by religious fundamentalism—inciting to join the armed struggle in Syria, which per definition entailed committing terrorist offences. The Court of Appeal had added that a substantive Article 10 ECHR (and Article 9 ECHR) test did not lead to any other findings than its abovementioned conclusion on the basis of Article 17 ECHR,[14] concluding that the interference with the defendants' right to freedom of expression was necessary in a democratic society, as incitement to join the armed jihadi struggle forms a threat to the democratic rule of law or *rechtsstaat*.

12.2.1.2 The Tamil Tigers Case

In an incitement case regarding the struggle by the LTTE (Liberation Tigers of Tamil Eelam) against the Sri Lankan authorities and the activities of Dutch LTTE coordinators, the Court of Appeal took a rather different approach.[15] In the Netherlands,

---

[13] The Advocate-General advising the Supreme Court pointed to the ECtHR's case law in *Belkacem* and *Roj TV* (see Sect. 12.3) to substantiate this argument.

[14] As well as an Article 9 ECHR-test, however, the Court held that the expressions did not constitute a direct manifestation of religion or belief.

[15] Court of Appeal The Hague, Judgement, 30 April 2015, ECLI:NL:GHDHA:2015:1082. The case reached the Supreme Court, which ruled—without further argumentation—that the Public Prosecution Service's complaint against acquittal could not lead to cassation: Supreme Court of the Netherlands, Judgement, 4 April 2017, ECLI:NL:HR:2017:577 and 578. These two and three other defendants were, however, convicted for participating in a terrorist organisation for their involvement in the LTTE, amongst other things for raising funds.

local LTTE leaders organised—amongst other things—gatherings where victims of their struggle were remembered, and fighters were honoured in order to strengthen the morale and support for the struggle. This included theatre songs and texts positively depicting the violence (e.g. "War is war: we will destroy you", "Stand up to expel the enemy, to gather an army"). Because of the context of remembrance and honouring the deceased, as well as the theatrical aspects, the Court of Appeal did not consider this to be incitement—the expressions did not directly incite to participate in the violence and were expressed during peaceful gatherings.

12.2.1.3 Recruitment for the Armed Struggle

Encouraging participation in armed struggle abroad is sometimes also prosecuted under the offence of *recruitment for the armed struggle (or foreign military service)* in Article 205 CC.[16] Recruitment refers to a process of ideologically 'ripening' a person for taking part in the armed struggle, which can take the form of individual conversations where e.g. videos of terrorist groups are shown,[17] but can also involve more general inciteful expressions, e.g. on social media, that aim to influence people to join terrorist groups abroad.[18] In the abovementioned LTTE case, the Court of Appeal acquitted the defendants in relation to recruitment in the Netherlands for the armed struggle against the government in Sri Lanka. It judged that the 'hero gatherings' where terrorist fighters and violent acts were honoured did not point to an intention on the part of the organisation to enact recruitment acts concrete enough to prepare the ground for others to join the fighting.[19] Glorifying or praising the struggle or the attackers does not necessarily imply moving others to join that struggle, the Court held. In other cases, courts judged that there also needs to be a certain stimulation of a person to join the armed struggle, which will usually involve a process rather than one expression:[20] merely making suggestions in a directive manner is not sufficient, and neither is the mere expression of support of one's partner's plans to travel for the armed struggle or the attempt to remove their doubts about such travels.[21] Recruitment of women to go and live in IS territory and marry a fighter does not amount to recruitment for the armed struggle either—the recruitment

[16] See Druijf and van Noorloos 2019, e.g. Court of Appeal's-Hertogenbosch, Judgement, 17 February 2017, ECLI:NL:GHSHE:2017:555; District Court Rotterdam, Judgement, 14 February 2006, ECLI:NL:RBROT:2006:AV1652; Court of Appeal The Hague, Judgement, 2 October 2008, ECLI:NL:GHSGR:2008:BF3987; Court of Appeal The Hague, Judgement, 7 July 2016, ECLI:NL:GHDHA:2016:1979.

[17] *Kamerstukken II* 2003–2004, 28 463, nr. 10, p. 11.

[18] See Supreme Court (The Netherlands), Judgement, 24 March 2020, ECLI:NL:HR:2020:447, Conclusion Advocate-General Hofstee, ECLI:NL:PHR:2019:1235, paras 81–84.

[19] Court of Appeal The Hague, Judgement, 30 April 2015, ECLI:NL:GHDHA:2015:1082.

[20] District Court The Hague, Judgement, 1 December 2014, ECLI:NL:RBDHA:2014:14648; Court of Appeal The Hague, Judgement, 2 October 2008, ECLI:NL:GHSGR:2008:BF3987; Court of Appeal The Hague, 7 July 2016, ECLI:NL:GHDHA:2016:1979.

[21] Court of Appeal The Hague, Judgement, 7 July 2016, ECLI:NL:GHDHA:2016:1979.

should be aimed at direct deployment in the armed struggle, not just at providing moral, ideological or financial support of that struggle.[22]

12.2.2 Administrative Measures (When Criminal Law Is Thought to Fall Short): Hindering Movement or Hindering Ideas?

So far, there has been one case in which the Dutch authorities have used legislation on administrative measures to combat terrorism—adopted in 2017[23]—to deal with expressions that were thought to contribute to persons radicalising and travelling abroad for terrorist purposes. This legislation enables the Minister of Justice and Security to enact 6-month (albeit renewable) requirements to regularly report to the police, as well as area bans and contact bans. These measures can be taken against persons who—based on their behaviour—can be linked to terrorist activities or the support thereof; the measures need to be necessary to protect national security.[24] The Minister thus devised an area prohibition against Fawaz Jneid,[25] a controversial Muslim preacher who had been banned from his mosque and continued his activities in other places. Jneid was notorious for several expressions, including for having cursed Ayaan Hirsi Ali and Theo van Gogh in a 2004 sermon—Van Gogh was killed by a jihadist in 2004. In more recent years, Jneid has been active in an Islamic bookstore in The Hague that was said to be used mainly as a prayer room. After plans transpired that a foundation to which Jneid was connected intended to buy the property where the bookstore was based—thus giving him a more permanent presence—the authorities became particularly concerned about his role in the area. This, after all, was a part of The Hague where relatively many people radicalised who then travelled to Syria and Iraq to join terrorist groups. The Minister thus prohibited Jneid from entering two adjacent neighbourhoods in The Hague where the property was based because, according to the authorities, he had already been influential in spreading jihadist ideas in these areas. The Minister motivated the area prohibition by stating that Jneid "has a prominent role in the salafist movement, makes frequent use of salafist rhetoric which is also used by jihadists and creates a climate where jihadists can thrive"—by depicting a hostile image of atheists, seculars, shi'ites, jews and the Western world and stressing the victimhood of the Sunni Muslim community, letting his listeners draw the conclusion that they have an obligation to act and to defend

[22] Ibid.; see also Supreme Court (The Netherlands) Judgement, 12 June 2018, ECLI:NL:HR:2018:897.

[23] Temporary Law on Counterterrorism Administrative Measures 2016. The legislation is, as the title indicates, temporary: after 5 years it will automatically expire.

[24] Moreover, a prohibition to leave the Schengen area can be enacted if there is a reasonable suspicion that a person will travel outward with the aim of joining a terrorist organisation.

[25] Council of State (Administrative Jurisdiction Division), Judgement, 30 May 2018, ECLI:NL:RVS:2018:1763.

their faith. The Minister, in this case, found it plausible that many of his listeners had, in part as a result of his influence, become convinced of their obligation to participate in or facilitate the violent struggle.

This measure was condoned by the highest general administrative court in the Netherlands, the Council of State.[26] Whereas experts criticised the use of these administrative measures against the spreading of ideas,[27] according to the Council of State, what matters is that this measure was still primarily based on hindering his physical presence in a certain area (notwithstanding that it was motivated by reference to the ideas he spread).[28] Jneid's appeal to Articles 9 and 10 ECHR also failed, amongst other reasons because it was a limited measure in the sense that only two areas were prohibited for a limited time. However, renewal of the 6-month prohibition is possible after a fresh assessment, and Jneid's area prohibition has been renewed six times since then. According to the Minister, there was still a risk of Jneid spreading jihadist thought to vulnerable youth, especially now that people were returning home to these The Hague neighbourhoods from the fighting in Syria in increasing numbers, thus heightening the risk of radicalisation. The area bans obviously did not obstruct Jneid from continuing to spread his ideas online—his messages and sermons on Twitter and Facebook and their relation to political salafism were indeed part of the authorities' argumentation for prolonging his area bans.

In a court case concerning the second, third and fourth prolongation of Jneid's area ban,[29] the defence criticised the way Jneid's expressions were presented by the Minister—in an allegedly decontextualised manner that left out excerpts that would prove his rejection of violence and that could not substantiate the Minister's bold conclusions.[30] Adding to the complexity, the administrative report (drafted by the police) underlying the Minister's decision contained information that remained secret to Jneid.[31] The District Court of The Hague, which did get an insight into the secret documents, did not accept the decontextualisation argument. The defence argued furthermore that the relationship between Jneid's behaviour and terrorist activities

---

[26] Ibid. The issue has been taken up by the ECtHR, *Jneid v the Netherlands*, Fourth Section, 29 September 2020, Application No. 57264/18 (*Jneid*).

[27] Brouwer and Schilder 2018.

[28] On a different note, the government elsewhere also discussed the idea of *digital* 'area bans'—prohibiting a person from using a certain digital platform to spread their ideas—but concluded (in my view rightly) that these would amount to prior censorship of expressions. Minister of Justice and Security 2018.

[29] District Court The Hague, Judgement, 31 March 2020, ECLI:NL:RBDHA:2020:2919. The first prolongation was also declared unfounded by the same Court: District Court The Hague, Judgement, 10 July 2018, ECLI:NL:RBDHA:2018:8172.

[30] Kouwenhoven A (2020) Hoe de overheid een 'haatimam' de mond probeert te snoeren. NRC. https://www.nrc.nl/nieuws/2020/02/17/hoe-overheid-een-haatimam-de-mond-probeert-te-snoeren-a3990732). Accessed 28 July 2021.

[31] The possibility to withhold certain information is provided for in legislation (Article 8:29 AWB), if necessary for national security. This system has been criticised in light of the right to a fair trial and the principle of equality of arms: see Van Gestel et al. 2020, pp. 31 and 43. Moreover, according to lawyers, it is not transparent how the administrative report has been constructed and to what extent opposing views have been considered and exculpating material has been included.

was too loose, as the Minister spoke about him creating a climate for jihadists to thrive and could not substantiate how he was actually spreading violent jihadist (rather than merely salafist) thought. The Court noted—referring to the reports by the Dutch National Coordinator for Security and Counterterrorism (NCTV)—that currently in the Dutch context, the relationship between salafism and jihadism is ambiguous, whereas Jneid's salafist rhetoric forms a fertile ground for radicalisation and plays an important role within the *jihadist* movement, considering his influence. In the salafist ideology that he preaches, Muslims are being incited to turn their backs on non-Muslims and Muslims disagreeing with them and to only acknowledge theocratic authorities, the Court argued. Moreover, the Court pointed to the risk—as identified by the Dutch General Intelligence and Security Service (AIVD)—of salafists tempering their message to the outside world while preaching in a more extremist manner in inner circles. The Court thus considered Jneid's prolonged area bans to be proportionate restrictions on his freedom of expression and religion.

In December 2020, however, the District Court of The Hague judged that the Minister had insufficiently substantiated the fifth and sixth area bans of Jneid with new facts and circumstances related to the person and area concerned.[32] Merely pointing to his presence on social media, to his salafist ideas and to the fact that the two areas were still vulnerable to radicalisation, without making clear what his own current link was with the two areas, was not enough. This is especially relevant in light of the far-reaching fundamental rights ramifications that could, in theory, lead to all political salafists being prohibited from entering areas that harbour people vulnerable to radicalisation.[33]

The Public Prosecution Service has thus far considered Jneid's speeches to fall just outside the scope of criminal law.[34] Administrative measures then enable the government to act against expressions that do not pass this criminal law threshold.[35] This could lead to a situation where criminal law, with its strong due process guarantees, is circumvented by using measures that have to conform to less strict guarantees, e.g. the use of secret information while also having a far-reaching impact on persons' lives. Also, it is possible to act even further in the 'pre-phase' than is already possible in criminal law, increasing the risk of widening the net too broadly. It is thus particularly important that these administrative measures conform to comparably strict freedom of expression standards as in criminal law. In the Dutch legislation, rather broad language is used—"persons who can be linked to terrorist activities or the support thereof". The Council of State judged that the scope is hard to further specify beforehand and is still in line with the 'prescribed by law' criterion in Articles 9 and 10 ECHR. However, the abovementioned case shows that it is difficult to

[32] District Court The Hague, Judgement, 30 December 2020, ECLI:NL:RBDHA:2020:13885.

[33] District Court The Hague, Judgement, 30 December 2020, ECLI:NL:RBDHA:2020:13885, para 6.4.

[34] See Minister of Justice and Security 2018, pp. 9–10 and *Handelingen II*, 2017–2018, 27 maart 2018, nr. 65, item 2.

[35] Although it must be noted that the *Jneid* case is a bit of an odd one out: the administrative measures have mostly been used *after* the person had already served their criminal sentence, in cases where no criminal law monitoring options were open anymore. Van Gestel et al. 2020.

predict who will be included and what kind of expression of political salafist ideas is still within the bounds of the law.

Occasionally, other administrative measures have been used in the context of jihadist speech. In 2015, the mayor of Eindhoven prohibited the organisers of an Islamic conference in a mosque from letting a number of guest preachers speak there, based on Article 172, para 3 of the Municipalities Act, which enables the mayor to give orders necessary for maintaining public order in case of (serious threats of) disturbances to the public order. The local authorities had received information from the Immigration and Naturalisation Service and the NCTV that the speakers had, in the past, expressed anti-semitic, anti-homosexual and anti-Shia speech that showed hatred for secularists and glorified the violent jihadi struggle and denied terrorism.[36] According to those institutions, one of them had fought in Syria with Islamic (possibly jihadist) armed groups. The authorities feared that those receptive to the speakers' ideas, including youth, could be influenced to embrace jihadism. Five speakers had Schengen Information System alerts, and their Schengen visas were withdrawn because of public order risks. In the end, the conference took place without these speakers. The District Court judged that the mayor's measures to ban these speakers violated the fundamental rights to freedom of association and assembly. According to the Court, the Dutch legislature had explicitly designed a system where no preventive action against public manifestations[37] was possible other than in emergency situations. Only if speakers were to actually express themselves in a manner contravening the law, the government could take action (in particular, by criminal prosecution). This leaves unaffected the migration law conditions under which non-EU nationals who are considered to be a threat to public policy or internal security are not allowed to enter or stay in the Schengen area. From 2015–May 2019, in the Netherlands, fifteen visas have been refused or withdrawn of persons that were known to have incited enmity, hatred, or violence against persons or groups.[38]

12.3 International Human Rights Law

12.3.1 The European Convention on Human Rights and 'Terrorist Speech'

The right to freedom of expression in Article 10 ECHR can be restricted if provided for by clear laws and if the measure is necessary in a democratic society with an eye to a legitimate interest, such as protecting the rights of others, public safety

36 District Court Oost-Brabant, Judgement, 30 January 2017, ECLI:NL:RBOBR:2017:415.

37 Based on the Wet Openbare Manifestaties (WOM) 1998 (Public Manifestations Act). The Municipalities Act was not meant to form an additional basis for preventing such manifestations, according to the District Court.

38 *Handelingen II* (Aanhangsel) 2018/19, 2 May 2019, nr. 2523, https://zoek.officielebekendmakingen.nl/ah-tk-20182019-2523.html.

and national security. The European Court of Human Rights (ECtHR) will look at proportionality, whether the state has adduced relevant and sufficient reasons for the restriction and whether there is a pressing social need for the restriction at issue. In terms of proportionate restrictions, criminal law is viewed as a far-reaching means that should not be lightly used.

In the more extreme cases, the ECtHR will declare a complaint inadmissible referring to Article 17 of the Convention on 'abuse of right'; this is reserved for those engaging in activities aimed at the destruction of any of the rights and freedoms the ECHR provides. Thus, if expressions are incompatible with the values proclaimed by the Convention, they are not protected by Article 10 ECHR, and the Court does not perform an elaborate Article 10-test. In two recent cases concerning criminal convictions for extreme speech in the context of terrorism, the Court has considered that the speaker thus abused their right to freedom of expression as meant in Article 17 ECHR.

The spokesperson and leader of *Sharia4Belgium,* Fouad Belkacem, has been the subject of a range of criminal convictions in Belgium as well as a measure depriving him of his Belgian citizenship. In 2015 he was convicted to twelve years' imprisonment for founding and leading *Sharia4Belgium*, which was classified as a terrorist organisation that recruited many Belgians to join IS. By means of trainings and lectures, in a process of indoctrination and isolation, Belkacem was judged to have recruited them to join the armed struggle. However, it was another case against Belkacem that reached the ECtHR in 2017,[39] a case in which he was convicted for incitement to hatred, discrimination and violence against non-Muslims. He had posted several YouTube videos in which he said, amongst other things, that "we have to fight against nonbelievers", "Today we have to talk about Jihad. Today we have to talk about sharia. How we must dominate" (words that were uttered after a shot was heard in the background of the video), and in which he called on listeners to join the group of salafist jihadists, "whose members believe that Islamic countries should be liberated by an armed jihad and the taking up of arms against nonbelievers, and that non-believers should repent or be eliminated." Taking into account the content, tone, explicit character, décor, presentation and repetitive character of his messages, the Belgian courts found him indisputably inciting discrimination, segregation, hatred and violence against non-Muslims. The Court pointed to the markedly hateful nature of Belkacem's views and concluded that such a general and vehement attack on a group (in this case, of non-Muslims) is in contradiction with the Convention's values. Whereas this is indeed among the more extreme cases, it would still have been valuable to see how a full contextual Article 10 ECHR-test would play out in this case.

A full-fledged assessment in light of the right to freedom of expression would also have been useful in the case of *ROJ TV A/S v Denmark*,[40] where a Danish-based TV channel that broadcast Kurdish programmes throughout Europe and the Middle East

[39] ECtHR, *Belkacem v Belgium*, Second Section, 27 June 2017, Application no. 34367/14.

[40] ECtHR, *ROJ TV A/S v. Denmark*, Second Section, 17 April 2018, Application no. 24683/14 (*ROJ TV A/S*).

was convicted for promoting PKK terrorist violence. The ECtHR judged that the applicant could not rely on the protection of Article 10 ECHR by virtue of Article 17 ECHR, as it followed the domestic courts' findings that the channel's programmes—which were broadcast to a wide audience—contained "one-sided coverage with repetitive incitement to participate in fights and actions, incitement to join the organisation/the guerrilla, and the portrayal of deceased guerrilla members as heroes", thus amounting to propaganda for a terrorist organisation (the applicant company had also been financed to a significant extent by the PKK).

In many cases, however, the Court has dealt with expressions in relation to terrorism under the Article 10 framework, thus elaborately assessing whether prohibition of expressions was necessary in a democratic society.[41] From these cases, a number of considerations can be discerned—which are not directly linked to terrorist travel but can give some guidance on how to deal with incitement in that context. If expressions are part of a debate on a matter of general and public concern—e.g. a debate about state violence or the rights of minority groups—restrictions on freedom of expression are to be strictly construed. Nevertheless, states have a large leeway to prohibit speech that incites violence, hostility or hatred against individuals, groups or officials and calls to violence, armed resistance or uprising.[42] It is not necessary that an expression *directly* incites violence; the provocative wording is one of the factors to be taken into account, and depending on other circumstances, prohibition of indirect calls for violence—including glorification or justification of violence—may or may not lead to a violation of Article 10. The Court looks at several factors, including the position of the applicant, the medium by which the expressions are disseminated, the nature of the articles and their wording, as well as the context in which they were published.[43] If expressions are published in a region that is sensitive to conflict and tension—and/or at a time when tensions are high (e.g. shortly after a terrorist attack), certain restrictions of freedom of expression are more easily allowed, even if the wording of the expressions is not directly inciteful.[44] The criminal conviction of a cartoonist for publishing a cartoon in a Basque newspaper on 13 September 2001, depicting the Twin Towers attacked with the caption—"We've all dreamt of it...Hamas did it", did not overstep the bounds of Article 10. According to the Court, the depiction of the attacks as a dream that finally came true was particularly offensive and shocking for the victims and their family. The timing of the publication two days after the attacks also played a role, as well as the fact that the magazine was published in the Basque region with its own terrorism threat. Notwithstanding these factors, it is questionable whether the link between this cartoon and its potentially harmful consequences was strong enough to justify criminal sanctions.

---

[41] See for a more elaborate overview of case law until 2011: van Noorloos 2011.

[42] ECtHR, *Ali Gürbüz v. Turkey*, Second Section, 12 March 2019, Application no. 52497/08.

[43] ECtHR, *Dmitriyevskiy v. Russia*, 3 October 2017, Application no. 42168/06 (*Dmitriyevskiy*).

[44] ECtHR, *Zana v. Turkey*, Grand Chamber Judgement, 25 November 1997, Application no. 18954/91 (*Zana*).

What effect the speech could potentially achieve also depends on the role and authority of the speaker.[45] Yet, in *Dmitriyevskyi v Russia*, the Court judged that an editor's conviction for publishing articles that were presumably uttered by leaders of a Chechen separatist movement—who were wanted in Russia for serious criminal charges—was not a justified interference with the right to freedom of expression.[46] The Court found no incitement to violence or instigation of hatred or intolerance liable to result in violence. Though one of the articles was strongly worded, suggesting that the Russian authorities imposed a continuing genocide on the Chechen people, the Court noted that it was important to debate allegations of such atrocities and that "the fact that statements contain hard-hitting criticism of official policy and communicate a one-sided view of the origin of and responsibility for the situation addressed by them is insufficient, in itself, to justify an interference with freedom of expression".[47] There is thus much room for strong criticism of the government under Article 10—especially if this is meant to draw attention to real human rights abuses. Such criticism may be very harsh and even immoderate, but it may not amount to promoting, justifying and glorifying terrorism by dehumanising the other party to a conflict or representing it as absolute evil. With regard to terrorist travel, we can assume that if such criticism—even if legitimate in itself—within its context can be interpreted as a call to engage in violence, then interferences with freedom of speech are more readily accepted.

In the case of *Gürbüz and Bayar v Turkey*,[48] a statement by Abdullah Öcalan calling for a gathering of patriots under the banner of the PKK (although his threat of resuming violence was in a conditional form: *if* no Turkish-Kurdish dialogue would be developed) amounted to recruitment for terrorism, according to the ECtHR, considering the nature, purpose and previous violent actions of the organisation. The Court also took account of the position of Öcalan as an imprisoned leader giving instructions through his lawyers, and the sensitive context of a proposed ceasefire, in coming to the conclusion that the criminal conviction of the owner and editor-in-chief of a newspaper publishing these statements did not violate Article 10.[49]

As to the medium by which the expressions are spread, an academic book or biography may be less directly inciting people to violence than a call that is spread

---

[45] Ibid.; EctHR, *Hogefeld v. Germany*, Fourth Section, 20 January 2000, Application no 35402/97 (*Hogefeld*).

[46] *Dmitriyevskiy*, above n 43.

[47] Ibid, para 106. See, rather similarly, in the case of *Stomakhin v Russia*: ECtHR, *Stomakhin v Russia*, 9 May 2018, Application no. 52273/07.

[48] ECtHR, *Gürbüz and Bayar v Turkey*, Second Section, 23 July 2019, Application no. 8860/13 (*Gürbüz and Bayar*).

[49] See also *Hogefeld* above n 45, and ECtHR, *Bidart v. France*, Fifth Section, 12 November 2015, Application no. 52363/11: the role of the speaker in past terrorism was also important in these cases, where the applicants were themselves imprisoned and released on licence respectively.

more widely among the public.[50,51,52] Criminal proceedings against media owners or editors are looked at critically in light of the right to freedom to receive information. For instance, in the abovementioned *Gürbüz and Bayar* case, the court criticised the systematic conviction of media publishing statements by terrorist organisations without an analysis of the content or the context in which the statements are written.[53] However, if statements effectively amount to incitement to violence, criminal measures against media owners or editors can justifiably come into play as the right to impart information cannot be a pretext for spreading statements by terrorist groups.[54]

In a case where the applicants had sent letters ending with the wording "'*sayın*' Abdullah Öcalan", an attribute placed before a person's name meaning 'respected', this mark of respect could not, as such, justify prohibition under Article 10. The letters in question contained neither incitement to violence or terror nor propaganda for a terrorist organisation—the Court held that no clear and imminent danger existed that could justify a conviction.[55] If provocative slogans are expressed during non-violent demonstrations, they cannot too easily be interpreted as a call for violence or an uprising.[56]

Calls for separatism—in the absence of incitement to violence—may also fall within the protection of Article 10. A conviction for publishing an article about the "battle for the liberation of the Kurds" resulted in a violation of Article 10: notwithstanding the reference to a 'battle', the ECtHR held that it did not amount to incitement to violence or armed resistance.[57] A battle can also refer to a struggle to have a minority group's rights recognised.

The ECtHR is critical towards excessively broad legal definitions of 'extremism' as a basis for repressive measures. Since such definitions—broad as they are—may also cover indirect incitement or recruitment in relation to terrorist travel, it is worth delving into this discussion here. The Court has focused in particular on the Suppression of Extremism Act in Russia, under which courts may declare books or other materials extremist. As a result, it is prohibited to publish or distribute such works. 'Extremist activity/extremism' under Russian law can include, amongst other things, "the stirring up of social, racial, ethnic or religious discord", "the public justification of terrorism and other terrorist activity", and "propaganda about the exceptional nature, superiority or deficiency of persons on the basis of their social, racial, ethnic, religious or linguistic affiliation or attitude to religion" (including public appeals to

---

[50] ECrtHR, *Polat v. Turkey*, Grand Chamber, 8 July 1999, Application no. 23500/94.

[51] ECrtHR, *Erdoğdu and İnce v. Turkey*, Grand Chamber, 8 July 1999, Application nos. 25067/94 and 25068/94.

[52] ECrtHR, *Öztürk v. Turkey*, Grand Chamber, 28 September 1999, Application no. 22479/93.

[53] *Gürbüz and Bayar*, above n 48.

[54] Ibid., para 44.

[55] ECtHR, *Yalçınkaya and Others v. Turkey*, Second Section, 1 October 2013, Application nos. 25764/09 et al.

[56] ECtHR, *Gül and others v. Turkey*, Second Section, 8 June 2010, Application no. 11976/03.

[57] ECtHR, *Asli Güneş v. Turkey*, Second Section, 27 September 2005, Application no. 11976/03.

carry out such acts, organising, preparing, inciting to, funding or assisting such activities); 'extremist materials' are "documents intended for publication or information in other media calling for extremist activity to be carried out or substantiating or justifying the necessity of carrying out such activity".[58] In the ECtHR case *Ibragim Ibragimov and others*,[59] the publication of certain editions of a well-known commentary on the Qu'ran by the scholar Said Nursi, which was widely used in mosques and schools, was prohibited by the Russian authorities. According to the domestic court—which based its judgment on experts in linguistics and psychology from the Russian Academy of Sciences—the works contained statements that aimed to incite religious discord between believers and non-believers, depicted non-believers in a negative and humiliating way and propagated superiority over non-believers. According to Islamic studies scholars, however, these works belong to moderate mainstream Islam. The ECtHR interpreted freedom of expression in light of freedom of religion (Article 9 ECHR) and concluded that there was a violation—the domestic courts had merely quoted the 'experts' and had failed to assess the nature and wording of the text, but also the context in which the works were published and their potential to lead to harmful consequences. With regard to the second applicant, the text described non-Muslims as "idle talkers" and "little men" and suggested that not following Islam was an "infinitely big crime" (para 114). According to the ECtHR, however, the domestic court quoted these passages out of their context and without considering that statements in religious books proclaiming the superiority of that religion's worldview were common in monotheistic religions. The ECtHR held that these statements could not be regarded as promoting violence, hatred or intolerance, nor did they insult, hold up to ridicule or slander non-Muslims. Moreover, the authorities had not argued that the book "advocated any activities going beyond promoting religious worship and observance in private life of the requirements of Islam, or sought to reorganise the functioning of society as a whole by imposing on everyone its religious symbols or conception of a society founded on religious precepts."[60] The ECtHR pointed to the Venice Commission's Opinion on the Federal Law on Combating Extremist Activity of the Russian Federation,[61] which warned that definitions were so vague as to risk arbitrary interferences with freedom of expression and freedom of religion or belief, using definitions of extremism that did not contain any element of violence.

[58] Federal Law no. 114-FZ on Combatting Extremist Activity of 25 July 2002, Section 1(1).

[59] ECtHR, *Ibragim Ibragimov e.a. v. Russia*, 28 August 2018, Third Section, Application nos. 1413/08 and 28621/11.

[60] See in this regard also the Court's case law on Article 11 ECHR, including ECtHR, *Hizb Ut-Tahrir v Germany*, Fifth Section, 12 June 2012, Application no. 31098/08. See also ECtHR, *Gündüz v. Turkey*, First Section, 4 December 2003, Application no. 35071/97.

[61] European Commission For Democracy through Law 2012.

12.3.2 Other International Law

Other relevant international bodies have also been critical of legislation targeting extremism: the UN Special Rapporteur on the promotion and protection of human rights and fundamental freedoms while countering terrorism[62] has criticised the worldwide use of extremism as an offence in itself, which has been used against non-violent groups, journalists and political activists. The OSCE has recommended to "[a]void in law, policy and practice the use of vague or imprecise terms that are prone to arbitrary application, such as 'extremism', disconnected from specific violent conduct or incitement to violence".[63] The OSCE has also warned against "overly broad offences in criminal lawsuch as apology, glorification or condoning of terrorismthat frequently fall short of the threshold of incitement to discrimination, hostility or violence and lead to impermissible limitations of freedom of expression" and has stressed that criminal responsibility should not be "based solely on association with terrorist groups, or expression of opinions about their activities".[64] These kinds of laws are used to target political opponents, human rights activists and journalists worldwide.

The Human Rights Committee is critical not only of 'extremism' offences, but a broader range of speech restrictions: it stated that "offences such as 'encouragement of terrorism' and 'extremist activity' as well as offences of 'praising', 'glorifying', or 'justifying' terrorism, should be clearly defined to ensure that they do not lead to unnecessary or disproportionate interference with freedom of expression."[65] The UN Secretary-General has indicated (in relation to terrorism) that "[i]ncitement must be separated from glorification. If the first may be legally prohibited, the second may not... for States to comply with international protections of freedom of expression, laws should only allow for the criminal prosecution of direct incitement to terrorism, that is, speech that directly encourages the commission of a crime, is intended to result in criminal action and is likely to result in criminal action."[66]

Such a critical stance towards offences on glorifying, encouraging and justifying terrorism is in marked contrast with the approach of the ECtHR on this matter and with some international 'positive obligations' requiring states to criminalise expressions such as encouragement or glorification of terrorism that do not pass the threshold of direct incitement. Under Article 5 of the EU Directive on combating

---

[62] Special Rapporteur on the promotion and protection of human rights and fundamental freedoms while countering terrorism (2016).

[63] OSCE 2018.

[64] OSCE 2018.

[65] CCPR 2011.

[66] UN Secretary-General (2008) The protection of human rights and fundamental freedoms while countering terrorism, UN Doc. A/63/337, paras 61–62.

terrorism,[67] Member States shall prohibit public provocation to commit a terrorist offence, meaning

> the distribution, or otherwise making available by any means, whether online or offline, of a message to the public, with the intent to incite the commission of one of the offences listed in points (a) to (i) of Article 3(1), where such conduct, directly or indirectly, such as by the glorification of terrorist acts, advocates the commission of terrorist offences, thereby causing a danger that one or more such offences may be committed (…)

—thus introducing the controversial term of 'glorification' and stressing that indirect advocacy is included as well.[68] The 'public provocation' offence in Article 5 of the Council of Europe (CoE)'s Convention on the Prevention of Terrorism does not mention 'glorification', although it does suggest that *indirect* advocacy should be criminalised too.[69] The UN Special Rapporteur on the promotion and protection of human rights and fundamental freedoms while countering terrorism, in his model offence of incitement to terrorism, has suggested using the words "whether or not expressly advocating terrorist offences" rather than "whether or not directly advocating terrorist offences", to make clear that incitement in coded language can be criminalised but without opening the door for prohibiting a large range of expressions.[70] Furthermore, the Special Rapporteur stressed that vague terms such as 'glorifying' or 'promoting' terrorism should be avoided.

As regards the relationship to 'foreign terrorist fighters', it should be noted that the public provocation offence in both the CoE and EU instruments is limited to actual acts of terrorism and does not include provocation of preparatory offences. However, the EU Directive on combating terrorism—apart from its provision on public provocation also calls upon states to criminalise *incitement* to several terrorist offences (Article 14(2)), including *incitement to travelling* (in- and outward travel) for the purpose of terrorism and *incitement to organising or otherwise facilitating travelling* for the purpose of terrorism (referring to Article 10 of the Directive—an offence which is in itself already broadly formulated). In contrast, the CoE's Additional Protocol to the Convention on the Prevention of Terrorism ('Riga Protocol'),

[67] Directive (EU) 2017/541 of the European Parliament and of the Council of 15 March 2017 on combating terrorism and replacing Council Framework Decision 2002/475/JHA and amending Council Decision 2005/671/JHA (2017) OJ L 88/6.

[68] The term '*thereby* causing a danger' may sound confusing (is this still an independent requirement?) but this is explained further in the Preamble (under 10): 'Such conduct should be punishable when it causes a danger that terrorist acts may be committed. In each concrete case, when considering whether such a danger is caused, the specific circumstances of the case should be taken into account, such as the author and the addressee of the message, as well as the context in which the act is committed. The significance and the credible nature of the danger should be also considered when applying the provision on public provocation in accordance with national law.'

[69] Council of Europe Convention on the Prevention of Terrorism, opened for signature 16 May 2005, CETS no. 196 (entered into force 1 June 2007): "'public provocation to commit a terrorist offence' means the distribution, or otherwise making available, of a message to the public, with the intent to incite the commission of a terrorist offence, where such conduct, whether or not directly advocating terrorist offences, causes a danger that one or more such offences may be committed."

[70] Report of the Special Rapporteur on the promotion and protection of human rights and fundamental freedoms while countering terrorism 2010, para 32.

which calls upon States Parties to criminalise (amongst other actions) travelling abroad for the purpose of terrorism, does not oblige criminalisation of incitement to such travels.

In addition, positive obligations to criminalise *recruitment of terrorism* may also be relevant, as indicated in Sect. 12.2 on the Dutch case law. In the EU Directive, recruitment for (organising or facilitating) such travels is not explicitly included (Article 6), but considering the breadth of offences such as "otherwise facilitating travel" (Article 10) and the possibilities for cumulation of these offences, it will probably be covered anyway. Consider also Security Council Resolution 2178 (2014), which calls for prohibition of "the wilful organization, or other facilitation, including acts of recruitment" of a broad range of actions amounting to (outbound) terrorist travel (para 6(c)).

12.4 Conclusion

The legal regulation of expressions related to terrorist travel raises pressing freedom of expression concerns. In the Netherlands, it is notable that messages that do not directly incite terrorism or terrorist travel, but rather glorify the armed jihadi struggle—including by glorifying martyrdom and presenting those deceased as heroes—were qualified as incitement to terrorist offences (although very general expressions of sympathy are not sufficient). This shows how tying broad notions of indirect incitement (including glorification) to terrorist *travel* is likely to amplify the range of prohibited speech. Nevertheless, the broad interpretation of the Dutch incitement offence in the Context case may be a temporary issue connected to the specific situation as it existed several years ago, of (mainly) youngsters at risk of travelling to the 'caliphate': in the judgment, regard was had to the targeted audience that was considered to be easily impressionable by such messages.[71]

Although Dutch criminal law, through the incitement offence (and less so through the recruitment offence), already allows for prohibiting a wide range of expressions in relation to travelling abroad for terrorism, the authorities have nevertheless found it necessary to use administrative measures where criminal law was thought to fall short. Because the requirements for such area bans (and the like) are relatively vague, this has enabled the authorities basically to act against spreading political-salafist thought (with the argument that this creates a climate for jihadists to thrive). This was specifically tied to the vulnerable situation in particular areas at risk of youth travelling to or coming back from terrorist areas; the question is how long this contextual aspect can continue to play a role. Meanwhile, the vagueness of the criteria for these administrative measures and the secrecy about what such measures are based on makes it difficult to predict who could be targeted.

---

[71] See the very different interpretation of incitement and recruitment in the *Tamil Tigers* case.

Considering some of the ECtHR's recent case law (*Belkacem* and *ROJ TV*), it is perhaps not so surprising that the highest Dutch courts in the criminal and administrative cases mentioned could reject freedom of expression claims—in one case even by invoking 'abuse of rights' (Article 17 ECHR).

The ECtHR has, in many other cases on terrorist expression, made a full assessment based on Article 10 ECHR, and the different factors that the Court takes into account provide a rich framework for assessing such expressions in a nuanced manner; it has also been very critical of 'extremism' offences because of their breadth and vagueness. It is striking, however, that the Court does not employ such criticism against 'glorification/justification of terrorism' offences—in marked contrast to other international bodies that have strongly criticised such laws. Regulation of such expressions is especially problematic because definitions of terrorism themselves are still contested and diverging, and utterly political. Thus, prohibitions containing vague notions of glorification or encouragement with regard to such a political matter risk chilling a wide range of expressions that do not conform to the dominant view.

References

Articles, Books and Documents

Belavusau U, Boutin B, Grozdanova R, van Noorloos M, Paulussen C (2019) A Comparative Research Study on Radical and Extremist (Hate) Speakers in European Member States. ICCT/T.M.C. Asser Institute. https://icct.nl/app/uploads/2019/11/NCTV___Report.pdf. Accessed 13 August 2021

Brouwer J, Schilder J (2018) Het gebiedsverbod als wapen tegen verspreiding van jihadistisch gedachtegoed. Justitiële Verkenningen 2:58–69

CCPR (2011) General Comment 34, Article 19: Freedoms of opinion and expression, UN Doc. CCPR/C/GC/34

Druijf E, Van Noorloos M (2019) De strafrechtelijke problematiek van het ronselen voor de gewapende strijd. Crimmigratie & Recht 3(1):19–37. https://doi.org/https://doi.org/10.5553/CenR/254292482019003001003

European Commission For Democracy through Law (Venice Commission) (2012) Opinion on the Federal Law on Combating Extremist Activity of the Russian Federation (2012). Adopted by the Venice Commission at its 91st Plenary Session, Venice, 15–16 June 2012. https://www.venice.coe.int/webforms/documents/?pdf=CDL-AD(2012)016-e. Accessed on 13 August 2021

Minister of Justice and Security (2018) Integrale aanpak extremistische sprekers, letter to the Second Chamber of Parliament, 28 May 2018. https://www.parlementairemonitor.nl/9353000/1/j9vvij5epmj1ey0/vkorj01muovl. Accessed 29 November 2021

Minister of Justice and Security (2021) Reactie op onderzoek extreemrechts, letter to the Second Chamber of Parliament, 8 July 2021, https://open.overheid.nl/repository/ronl-a077da8b-38ad-4bb0-8069-2b6719d529bf/1/pdf/tk-reactie-op-onderzoek-extreemrechts.pdf. Accessed 17 November 2022

OSCE (2018) Guidelines for Addressing the Threats and Challenges of 'Foreign Terrorist Fighters' within a Human Rights Framework. https://www.osce.org/files/f/documents/4/7/393503_2.pdf. Accessed 13 August 2021

Special Rapporteur on the promotion and protection of human rights and fundamental freedoms while countering terrorism (2010) Report of the Special Rapporteur on the promotion and protection of human rights and fundamental freedoms while countering terrorism, Martin Scheinin—Ten areas of best practices in countering terrorism, UN Doc. A/HRC/16/51
Special Rapporteur on the promotion and protection of human rights and fundamental freedoms while countering terrorism (2016) Report of the Special Rapporteur on the promotion and protection of human rights and fundamental freedoms while countering terrorism, UN Doc. A/HRC/31/65
UN Secretary-General (2008) The protection of human rights and fundamental freedoms while countering terrorism, UN Doc. A/63/337
Van Gestel B, Van Kouwenberg RF, Van Berkel JJ (2020) Evaluation of Temporary Law on Counterterrorism Administrative measures. WODC, The Hague. https://repository.wodc.nl/bitstream/handle/20.500.12832/240/Cahier_2020-02_volledige_tekst_tcm28-438810.pdf?sequence=1&isAllowed=y. Accessed 13 August 2021
Van Noorloos LA (2011) Hate Speech Revisited. A comparative and historical perspective on hate speech law in the Netherlands and England & Wales (dissertation Utrecht)

Cases

Council of State (Administrative Jurisdiction Division), Judgement, 30 May 2018, ECLI:NL:RVS:2018:1763. https://deeplink.rechtspraak.nl/uitspraak?id=ECLI:NL:RVS:2018:1763
Court of Appeal's-Hertogenbosch, Judgement, 17 February 2017, ECLI:NL:GHSHE:2017:555. https://deeplink.rechtspraak.nl/uitspraak?id=ECLI:NL:GHSHE:2017:555
Court of Appeal The Hague, Judgement, 2 October 2008, ECLI:NL:GHSGR:2008:BF3987. https://deeplink.rechtspraak.nl/uitspraak?id=ECLI:NL:GHSGR:2008:BF3987
Court of Appeal The Hague, Judgement, 25 May 2018, ECLI:NL:GHDHA:2018:1248 and 1249. https://deeplink.rechtspraak.nl/uitspraak?id=ECLI:NL:GHDHA:2018:1248, https://deeplink.rechtspraak.nl/uitspraak?id=ECLI:NL:GHDHA:2018:1249
Court of Appeal The Hague, Judgement, 30 April 2015, ECLI:NL:GHDHA:2015:1082. https://deeplink.rechtspraak.nl/uitspraak?id=ECLI:NL:GHDHA:2015:1082
Court of Appeal The Hague, Judgement, 7 July 2016, ECLI:NL:GHDHA:2016:1979. https://deeplink.rechtspraak.nl/uitspraak?id=ECLI:NL:GHDHA:2016:1979
District Court Oost-Brabant, Judgement, 30 January 2017, ECLI:NL:RBOBR:2017:415. https://deeplink.rechtspraak.nl/uitspraak?id=ECLI:NL:RBOBR:2017:415
District Court Rotterdam, Judgement, 14 February 2006, ECLI:NL:RBROT:2006:AV1652. https://deeplink.rechtspraak.nl/uitspraak?id=ECLI:NL:RBROT:2006:AV1652
District Court The Hague, *Context*, Judgement, 10 December 2015, ECLI:NL:RBDHA:2015:14365. https://deeplink.rechtspraak.nl/uitspraak?id=ECLI:NL:RBDHA:2015:16102
District Court The Hague, Judgement, 1 December 2014, ECLI:NL:RBDHA:2014:14648. https://deeplink.rechtspraak.nl/uitspraak?id=ECLI:NL:RBDHA:2014:14648
District Court The Hague, Judgement, 10 July 2018, ECLI:NL:RBDHA:2018:8172. https://deeplink.rechtspraak.nl/uitspraak?id=ECLI:NL:RBDHA:2018:8172
District Court The Hague, Judgement, 22 July 2016, ECLI:NL:GHDHA:2016:8411; 8412; 8464; 8465. https://deeplink.rechtspraak.nl/uitspraak?id=ECLI:NL:RBDHA:2016:8411, https://deeplink.rechtspraak.nl/uitspraak?id=ECLI:NL:RBDHA:2016:8412, https://deeplink.rechtspraak.nl/uitspraak?id=ECLI:NL:RBDHA:2016:8465
District Court The Hague, Judgement, 30 December 2020, ECLI:NL:RBDHA:2020:13885. https://deeplink.rechtspraak.nl/uitspraak?id=ECLI:NL:RBDHA:2020:13885
District Court The Hague, Judgement, 31 March 2020, ECLI:NL:RBDHA:2020:2919. https://deeplink.rechtspraak.nl/uitspraak?id=ECLI:NL:RBDHA:2020:2919

ECrtHR, *Erdoğdu and İnce v. Turkey*, Grand Chamber, 8 July 1999, Application nos. 25067/94 and 25068/94
ECrtHR, *Öztürk v. Turkey*, Grand Chamber, 28 September 1999, Application no. 22479/93
ECrtHR, *Polat v. Turkey*, Grand Chamber, 8 July 1999, Application no. 23500/94
ECtHR, *Belkacem v Belgium*, Second Section, 27 June 2017, Application no. 34367/14
ECtHR, *Ali Gürbüz v. Turkey*, Second Section, 12 March 2019, Application no. 52497/08
ECtHR, *Asli Güneş v. Turkey*, Second Section, 27 September 2005, Application no. 11976/03
ECtHR, *Bidart v. France*, Fifth Section, 12 November 2015, Application no. 52363/11
ECtHR, *Dmitriyevskiy v. Russia*, 3 October 2017, Application no. 42168/06 (*Dmitriyevskiy*).
ECtHR, *Gül and others v. Turkey*, Second Section, 8 June 2010, Application no. 11976/03
ECtHR, *Gündüz v. Turkey*, First Section, 4 December 2003, Application no. 35071/97
ECtHR, *Gürbüz and Bayar v Turkey*, Second Section, 23 July 2019, Application no. 8860/13 (*Gürbüz and Bayar*)
ECtHR, *Hizb Ut-Tahrir v Germany*, Fifth Section, 12 June 2012, Application no. 31098/08
ECtHR, *Hogefeld v. Germany*, Fourth Section, 20 January 2000, Application no 35402/97 (*Hogefeld*)
ECtHR, *Ibragim Ibragimov e.a. v. Russia*, Third Section, 28 August 2018, Application nos. 1413/08 and 28621/11
ECtHR, *Jneid v the Netherlands*, Fourth Section, 29 September 2020, Application No. 57264/18 (*Jneid*)
ECtHR, *ROJ TV A/S v. Denmark*, Second Section, 17 April 2018, Application no. 24683/14 (*ROJ TV A/S*)
ECtHR, *Stomakhin v Russia*, Third Section, 9 May 2018, Application no. 52273/07
ECtHR, *Yalçınkaya and Others v. Turkey*, Second Section, 1 October 2013, Application nos. 25764/09 et al
ECtHR, *Zana v. Turkey*, Grand Chamber Judgement, 25 November 1997, Application no. 18954/91 (*Zana*)
Supreme Court (The Netherlands), *Context*, Judgement, 24 March 2020, ECLI:NL:HR:2020:447; 448; 449; 450. https://deeplink.rechtspraak.nl/uitspraak?id=ECLI:NL:HR:2020:447, https://deeplink.rechtspraak.nl/uitspraak?id=ECLI:NL:HR:2020:448, https://deeplink.rechtspraak.nl/uitspraak?id=ECLI:NL:HR:2020:449, https://deeplink.rechtspraak.nl/uitspraak?id=ECLI:NL:HR:2020:450
Supreme Court (The Netherlands), Judgement, 12 June 2018, ECLI:NL:HR:2018:897. https://deeplink.rechtspraak.nl/uitspraak?id=ECLI:NL:HR:2018:897
Supreme Court (The Netherlands), Judgement, 4 April 2017, ECLI:NL:HR:2017:577 and 578. https://deeplink.rechtspraak.nl/uitspraak?id=ECLI:NL:HR:2017:577, https://deeplink.rechtspraak.nl/uitspraak?id=ECLI:NL:HR:2017:578

Index

F. Capone et al. (eds.), *Returning Foreign Fighters: Responses, Legal Challenges and Ways Forward*, https://doi.org/10.1007/978-94-6265-571-3

G

H

I

M

T

V